China to Me

A PARTIAL AUTOBIOGRAPHY BY

Emily Hahn

THE BLAKISTON COMPANY, PHILADELPHIA

Chapter 1

"SHANGHAI? You're going there, are you?" the hairdresser said, putting another wave over my forehead. It was a small deep wave and would look all wrong nowadays, but this was in 1935. We were wearing short bobs then and our heads looked like corrugated iron. The hairdresser probably called himself a barber, because he was working in Hollywood, which carried on a lot of Middle Western habits like that.

"Shanghai's a lovely place," he said, spraying me with sweet-smelling sticky stuff, so that the wave would bake hard. "You'll meet a good class of people there. The same you would meet in Society here. You know, titled people. Oh, you'll have a very nice time; Shanghai's a lovely place."

It was. I sigh for it now, titles and people and all, of any class. I haven't seen it for four years and it must have changed. It would be all different anyway, even without the Japanese, because Shanghai is always changing. I was startled but not really amazed when a fellow repatriate on the *Gripsholm,* that ship of strange destiny which has carried so many bedraggled crowds of homing Americans, told me about an acquaintance in Shanghai: "She married a rich Russian," he said. It was one of those things which would have been impossible four years ago: a rich Russian man in Shanghai. But nothing remains impossible there. Of all the cities of the world it is the town for me. Always changing, there are some things about it which never change, so that I will forever be able to know it when I come back. There will still be the Chinese. There will still be the old codgers, among whom I will someday take my place, drinking a little too much and telling each other how Shanghai isn't what it used to be. No, they can't take Shanghai away from me. Raise the cost of living, crowd in thirty thousand Jewish refugees from Europe, make rich the Russians, make poor the Americans, it will still be there.

Let the aesthetes sigh for Peking and their dream world. I don't reject Peking. Like Carmel, Santa Fe, Fiesole, it is a reward for the afterlife. Shanghai is for now, for the living me.

They used to have a conscientious society editor on the Shanghai morning paper who filled her column with records of parties and lists of guests until she used so much space that the whole thing had to be thrown out. It began to act on us like a repeated bad dream. Seeing the names, day after day, of certain indefatigable party goers was almost as bad as seeing their faces every evening, and indignant people began to write to the paper and complain. The obvious answer was made to them: "Don't read the society column if you don't like it," but you couldn't help it, any more than you could help going out every night. There was a grim, dogged quality in our Shanghai gaiety. Only Thackeray could have done it justice—on paper, I mean. We all did it ample justice in practice.

I have here a cutting from the journal that appeared the day after I arrived in Shanghai with my sister. Without it I would have forgotten that dinner party and everything about it, but now it all comes back to me. We had sailed from San Francisco in the *Chichibu Maru* with tickets for Shanghai and we had been two weeks at sea before the Japanese captain admitted that the ship did not, as a matter of fact, intend to touch at Shanghai at all. I don't know why the NYK deceived us in this matter. Perhaps it was part of a cunning plan to keep us for a while in Japan, tempting us to make a longer stopover than necessary while waiting for another ship. If so, it worked. We spent more than a fortnight in the island of the cherry blossoms and, although it all seems incredible now as I write it, I came away with the greatest reluctance. I arrived in Shanghai definitely sulky.

"I don't really care for the Far East at all," I was saying to myself. "The whole thing is tiresome and I am only indulging Helen by pausing on my way back to Africa. Now, just as I find a reasonably pleasant place—i.e., Japan—in which to loaf about and read, I am dragged away again to stay for some uncomfortable days in a vulgar, loud city like this. I don't know and I don't care who these Chinese persons may be, but everybody is aware that the Japanese are the only *subtle* Orientals. China is garish. China is red and gold and big, everything I don't like. Pooh."

This may puzzle you. I should explain that Japan was then as now sharply divided in her population between the civilians and the disciplined service people, the Army, Navy, and gendarmes. Of this latter class we tourists saw nothing. We saw a smiling Japan filled with charming figures in costume and eager little men in tourist agencies who told us all about Japanese music and drama and art. The only hint we ever had in those days of the stricter pattern behind the delicate landscape was in the formalities we went through when we landed; the endless questionnaires and the sharp examination of our literature. It meant nothing to us because everybody seemed so glad to see us, and there was so much to admire in the porcelain and the lacquer and the mountains and all that. . . . I must stop writing for a bit, to kick myself. We went all mushy over Japan and, as I was saying, I turned up my nose at Shanghai.

The Japs put one over on us and we scarcely noticed. They sent us on to Shanghai in a dirty little tub of a mail steamer, since the *Chichibu,* unlike ourselves, gave that port a complete go-by. And so we were met at the dock and taken out to dinner. Let me pause to examine the guest list.

There was one Chinese customs official, who was invited to do the ordering of the Chinese food. He's in Chungking now, having been caught in Hong Kong on Pearl Harbor day: he stayed hidden for some weeks and finally got out in disguise. There was a French count with his Italian wife. After being caught in Singapore, I believe, they got out before the surrender and are probably either in Free China or India now, as Fighting French. Or if they decided on Vichy they must have stayed in Singapore, but I don't think that in such a case they would have been there anyway. There was a Pole who had been naturalized as a Frenchman; he was in Chungking, as I was, on the day we heard about Paris under the first German attack. We thought it had been badly bombed, I remember, and he was really white with shock. "Terrible, *hein?*" he kept saying—we met in the hostel corridor, both in bathrobes, clutching soap—"truly terrible, *hein?*" and I still recall a faint feeling of indignation over his concern, because we ourselves had been truly terribly bombed in Chungking for weeks and weeks.

I don't remember the others. We were all having a hectic time, day after day, just because everybody was in a hurry for no particular reason. The first few weeks I must have packed pretty full because I intended to go away to Africa shortly, and when I decided at last not to go it was second nature to rush around. I look back on it now with mild wonder. What on earth did we think we were doing? There were feuds between the cliques and I was soon mixed up in them: the arty group battled for my scalp with the plain moneyed class as long as I was a novelty, and in the end nobody won at all, or cared. There were international parties, and plain British parties, and plain American parties, and there were beginning to be a lot of parties with Chinese people. Though I didn't know it, I had stumbled into a critical period of Shanghai history, the era that marked a difference from the old days when only certain Chinese would consent to mix with foreigners, and only certain foreigners wanted to mix with Chinese. Once upon a time it used to be good business to have dinner with your comprador once a year, or it was pleasantly devilish if you were a man to give a stag party at a Chinese restaurant complete with singsong girls. Besides this there were missionary tea parties for students, and that was all. By the time Helen and I got there it was quite different. The diplomats among the Chinese went to a lot of parties, and so did the rich young businessmen and their beautiful wives. Foreign ladies and Chinese ladies invited each other to luncheon. There was a Chinese Women's Club. . . . A good thing? I don't know. It was certainly nicer for people like me, though sometimes I got a lot of wicked joy out of incidents that were not supposed to be funny.

For example, the Garden Club of America was visiting Shanghai about the time I got there, and at the Women's Club one of their ladies gave a little talk on the subject of civic beauty. Now Shanghai has character and I would be the last to deny it, but as for beauty, have you ever seen a Chinese city street? It is a riot of signboards. Huge gilded characters hang on metal frameworks; neon signs flash in English and Chinese from the second stories; the walls between are painted with huge crude murals depicting devils at work in enlarged stomachs, or happy Chinese mothers using electric fans on their infants. Mrs. D—— could never have seen a Chinese street even in San Francisco, because the burden of her talk was an appeal to the women of China to do away with unsightly signboards. "We have succeeded in persuading the Chamber of Commerce in our town to eliminate them," she said, beaming, "and you have no idea what a difference it makes."

The ladies of China clapped with polite warmth and then dispersed to their mah-jongg games.

I don't think that at that time I had given any thought to the Manchurian Incident because I'm pretty sure I had never heard of it. In Shanghai people sometimes talked about "the trouble in 1932," and it began to be forced on my consciousness that the Japanese had been making nuisances of themselves for some years. It is worth remembering that at this date most mentions of the 1932 events were made by older men, veterans of the first World War, and they declared that the fighting as then seen by them proved conclusively that the Japs were no good.

"Saw 'em myself," was the regulation statement. "Let me tell you, if those fellows had been up against *real* soldiers they wouldn't have gotten anywhere. Why, for that matter, give the Chinese decent arms and ammunition and they'll be able to handle the Japs by themselves. Better fighters, man to man, any time. I did the war and I *know*."

There was also a lot of talk among the brokers about a city called Nanking, where lived the Generalissimo and his wife. I think I must have heard of them before, but I'm not sure where it was. Mme. Chiang, said the brokers—some of them, anyway—had a sister who was married to the Minister of Finance, and the whole family was simply coining money by various illegal means. The brokers were angry about this as they felt that any money which was made thus should be made by foreign brokers. They paused in their work long enough to declare with virtuous horror that the Soong family was sending this money abroad, to be placed in foreign banks where it would be waiting for them when their evil practices had caught up with them and forced them to flee. (None of the brokers bought Chinese dollars to keep, of course. They bought and sold, and when they had made as much money as possible they sent it home.)

Even then, however, I didn't swallow all this whole. It was too awful, I heard it too often in too many versions, and it was also beginning to be obvious that Shanghai gossip was fuller, richer, and less truthful than any I had ever before encountered. I had begun to meet and to chat with Chinese ladies. Now a good Chinese gossip, man or woman, can dream up better stories and bigger lies than anybody in the world except maybe an Arab. Once you catch on and learn that you are not expected to take it without a whole salt mine, it is lots of fun. But the habit had spread to Shanghailanders, to use their own unpleasant name for themselves, and to a newcomer it was a little misleading.

There was one factor of Shanghai life which filled our days as much as we wanted and a little more. Mrs. Fritz—Bernardine—had thought of and set into motion a sort of club known as the International Arts Theatre or, anticipating governmental habits, the IAT. She rounded up all the women in town to help, and some did and some didn't. In her apartment she walked around all day talking into a telephone which had the longest extension cord I have ever seen in my life, and she lavished on this club, her extremely creditable brain child, enough thought and management to win a minor war all by herself. In effect the working committee of the club was predominantly American, because it's the sort of thing American ladies would like better than would their European sisters, but she had corralled a lot of modern Chinese girls too, and an occasional Frenchwoman or a Hollander or one of the more accepted Russians. The IAT did concerts and lectures and debates and now and then a play. What made it good was that the concerts were Russian or German or whatever; the debates took into account such extremely controversial subjects as "Birth Control in China" (three

Catholic priests attended, with skyrocket results), and the plays were damn good, especially *Lady Precious Stream* with an all-Chinese cast. I can't say quite as much for the lectures, which in any city are just lectures, after all. Later, at the genteel Amateur Dramatic Association plays in Hong Kong, which were indescribably awful, I sighed for a touch of Bernardine Fritz. At least I did at first, and then I just stopped going.

It all sounds trivial, doesn't it? It was. I was still thinking of Shanghai as a stopping place between boats, and my first-planned two weeks as a long-drawn-out week end. Then one day I realized that I had taken a job and thus committed myself as a resident, at least for a while. The local morning paper, the *North-China Daily News*, was a British-owned journal. They wanted a woman to do feature stories, interviews, and the like, as their own girl was going away to be married, and I said I was willing. I was pleased about it, too, without reflecting at all. Helen went off to Peking to get a quick look at it before she returned to America; her plane was forced down in a paddy field on the way back and she had adventures. By the time she arrived again in Shanghai I had found a flat downtown in Kiangse Road and had dug in for a season. A little later she sailed away to the States; I waved good-by and went back to Kiangse Road.

It is now the moment to say, "Little did I think," et cetera, et cetera, but I cannot tell a lie. I didn't think a little, I thought a lot. I pondered. The subject of these thoughts was a recently remembered party in New York at which a lot of young leftists had been discussing China and the publicized revolt of her Communists.

"Oh, shut up about China," I had grumbled. "You bore me to death about China. China doesn't interest me."

Pondering like anything, I was almost run down by a ricksha in the Bund.

Chapter 2

THE FLAT in Kiangse Road had nothing in the world to recommend it to anybody but me. It was in a Chinese bank building, down on the ground floor, so that the windows looked out on the crowded, screaming street and were always grimy. The furniture belonged to a special genre, to understand which you must know that "Kiangse Road" in Shanghai is a synonym for "red-light district." Whenever I told people where I lived there was a roar of laughter, and dirty old men would whisper hoarsely, "How are all the girls?"

The biggest room wasn't very big, but it was all that counted: the other apartment was just a dingy hole with a dining table in it and a sort of dark brown china cabinet. The big room was painted in green: green walls and ceiling. Over three of the walls was a metallic sort of grillwork constructed to look like bamboo trees and silvered, if that is the proper participle. I can't say "gilded" because it wasn't gold, except in spots where the silver had tarnished. These metal bamboos were uncomfortable to lean against, so the box couch which I used to sit on in the daytime and to sleep on by night was in an unstrategic position, pushed as it was into a bamboo-beautified corner. To protect hair and back from the jagged edges of the bamboo leaves the former tenant had piled on the bed about sixty cushions, covered in brilliant-dyed satin of all colors.

Along the head of the bed was a bookcase completely filled with books. These volumes had obviously been bought by the pound and were chosen because they were of uniform height and thickness. Each one wore a dust wrapper made of paper that had been bought at Woolworth's or somewhere similar: green or silver or gold or peacock blue. Some of this paper was spotted with stars. I forgot to say that the ceiling, too, was covered with stars and had a crescent moon in one corner. The rest of the furniture, wooden lamp stands, chairs, and small tables, was all painted green and silver, and the color came off in flakes or puffed up in blisters.

My sister Helen saw the place only once and she didn't say much. She just stood and looked around. Then she said, "It's cheap, did you say?" and when I assented, rather defiantly, she said no more and soon sailed for San Francisco, staying on in her hotel until the last. Even before she left, my days had assumed a certain pattern. The first program of luncheons with ladies and race meetings with gentlemen had changed. Not that the job was especially demanding. Work with the English has always been more restful than it would be on the same job with Americans, and my routine soon boiled down to one lone interview almost every day with some old-timer of China. It began to be difficult to make the thing sound fresh, as they all said the same things and remembered the old days in the same way—"There used not to be any tramlines in the city at all," et cetera, et cetera. I love working for the English, chiefly because there is no gnawing worry at the back of my mind that if I don't watch my step, or even if I do, ultimately I will get the sack. The English are like me: they really don't enjoy firing people and they try not to.

If I had left it to the newspaper, however, I would scarcely have known that Chinese existed save for faraway-sounding names in news stories of battles and engagements upriver with bandits. The American Shanghai *Evening Post and Mercury* gave a better actual picture of conditions as they were, simply because the Americans were aware of the Chinese as people and most of the British weren't. Oh, I don't mean the Britons didn't *see* the Chinese. They did. They mentioned them often as peasants, dwellers in the picturesque villages we saw when we went houseboating or shooting. They spoke of them as servants, quaint and lovable. Sometimes, even, they thought of them as descendants of those emperors who had made Peking what it was. They were well aware that Chinese kept the shops in Yates Road and the Thieves' Market. The British community, however, reserved its social life for itself and those of the Caucasian groups who could be considered sufficiently upper-class. In short, it was my Hollywood hairdresser all over again.

There, though, I can't generalize. There were some outstanding exceptions. Besides, there was always a small faction of people from Peking, and Peking dwellers were civilized. The whole situation was changing in 1935 when I arrived; it was already getting much, much better everywhere, save, perhaps, in the stately columns of my newspaper. I don't wish to carp too much at the *North-China*. I liked the whole atmosphere of the paper very much indeed, because it made me feel that I was near the more colorful parts of the British Empire: Hong Kong and Singapore and Ceylon and all that.

My letters home show a sudden change after Helen went away. No longer did I bubble for pages about seeing the races from Sir Victor's (Sir Victor Sassoon was our local millionaire) box at the club. My preoccupation with clothes vanished. Now I seemed to spend more time doing things that sounded austere, although they weren't really. I visited Chinese schools and gave courtesy lectures; I inspected new little factories so that I could write them up; I looked at Russian painters' pictures, which were mostly pretty bad in my opinion. The reason for all of this was Sinmay, my Chinese friend. I have written about him already so many times, in so many guises—for Sinmay is inexhaustible and has a phase for any occasion—that I shan't attempt to describe him here. I saw him almost every day, sooner or later, mostly later. Time meant nothing whatever to him.

Sinmay and his immediate family lived down in Yangtzepoo, across the Soochow Creek and some miles farther along the river near the Japanese shipping wharves. In selecting this district he had gone against custom, as most of the well-to-do Shanghai Chinese preferred the newer houses or smart "modern" apartments out near the city limits of the International Settlement. He said himself that he had moved out there so that he would stay at home and work instead of being tempted to go out too much, but the result was merely that he used more time and gasoline driving his long brown Nash up to the middle of town where the tempting bookshops were. I have often envied him his knowledge of the city. I know it pretty well myself by this time, but every brick in every shop front seemed to have its history for Sinmay. Part of the reason for this was that he had been born in Shanghai and had grown up happily there, running as wild as he liked. The real reason, I think, was that he was overwhelmingly curious. He had a mind like a child's, or a puppy's, or an old-fashioned novelist's, prying into everything and weaving stories around whatever caught his attention.

I never knew what he was going to talk about. He had a wide acquaintance in the town and spent a good deal of time meeting his friends in restaurants and eating with them. In China you can always eat; there is some appropriate sort of food for any time of the day. Besides breakfast and lunch and dinner—the Shanghai Chinese eat those meals as we do, though the Cantonese have only two large ones, at eleven and four—you can have your elevenses at any hour of the morning: boiled or fried noodles with ham or tiny shrimps or shreds of chicken. Or you can eat sweet almond broth. For afternoon snacks there are endless sorts of sweet or salty cakes stuffed with ground beans or minced pork or chopped greens. Sinmay always said that he liked "coolie food" best, plain dishes of bean sprouts and salt fish and ordinary cabbage and that sort of thing, but he loved knowing all there is to know about food. He would tell long stories about this dish or that, talking first in Chinese to his friends, who liked listening as much as I did, and then remembering suddenly that I didn't understand him and doing a quick interpretation.

I was bored, often, during these restaurant parties, until I began later to understand a little of the language. Nothing can be more tiresome than sitting for a long time while other people talk in a strange tongue. When, to add to the boredom of it, you are really uncomfortable, the procedure calls for un-American patience, and those restaurants were painfully uncomfortable. Any Chinese restaurant is, I firmly believe.

Why have the Chinese never learned how to make good chairs to sit in? They can boast all they like about their centuries of civilization, and Dr. Ferguson and his cohorts can tell me as much as they wish of Chinese paintings and bronzes, and I myself grow lyrical over their food, but how, how, how can they have gone all these thousands of years sitting on stiff, slippery, shallow, spindly chairs? When I look at loving drawings of the ancient gardens of Soochow my bottom recalls the cold, inadequate comfort of those keglike porcelain stools where the sages sit while they regale their souls with the deliberate symmetry of tamed nature. Even when the Chinese try to make decent chairs they can't do it. I have been in many a foreign-style Chinese house with knives and forks at dinner, and framed oil paintings, and Axminster carpets. In vain: there is always something wrong with the chairs. The overstuffed ones are imitation and are too short, so that when you lean back there is nowhere for your head and neck.

There were compensations, or I could never have gone on as long as I did. In the end I was used to it and forgot to grumble. Sinmay always had another story, and if I waited long enough he would remember to talk English, and then for a time it was the other guests who were bored because they could not understand. Little by little, because of all the Chinese people I met, and all their histories which I heard, I was able to see through new windows. It was not so much that I found a new world with Sinmay and his family, but I went with them around to the back of the scenes and peered out at the same old world through a glow of strange-colored footlights. It was fresh and wonderful that way.

At first I didn't know how much I was getting. I thought it was amusing and even valuable for my job; my feature stories were more fun to write nowadays, and probably they made better reading too. I was left to make my own choice of subjects and I certainly strayed outside the conventional circle of hitherto approved features in my selection. I also discovered that the Shanghai Europeans and Americans were less dull than I had supposed: scarcely one of them was not discussed by the Chinese sooner or later. For me it was like looking at them all over again, with my previous impressions violently superseded.

Something else was happening, though; something which would have alarmed me if I had known about it. Until I came to China I had always been a determined "artiste." I don't mean by that that I had undue faith in my talents as a writer or something: only that according to my philosophy all people like myself, who lived or attempted to live by some applied practical form of "self-expression," were justified in avoiding the mechanics of government. I don't know now why I was so firm about this prohibition, which seems idiotic when I write it down. I permitted myself the pleasures of abstract philosophy in other directions: I had read Plato and even Butler. Modern society, however, I wished to leave severely alone whenever it entered the Senate chamber. Studied as ethnology, yes: as a trained scientist I was not above doing papers on the governing customs and conventions of African tribes, and I could be lured into discussions of public morality, but I balked at taking an interest in state-craft.

"I've never voted," I used to say proudly. Only low, self-seeking people went into politics, I said. Englishwomen who insisted on talking about elections simply terrified me. The only government I would admit worthy of my notice was that of Soviet Russia—not that I really knew anything about it, but "artistes" everywhere approved of Russia, so I did too.

Now if I had stayed in England or America I would have been shaken out of my snootiness by Herr Hitler in good time. Sinmay and his friends quite unconsciously saved Hitler the trouble of educating at least one American. Sinmay was an individualist and took no practical action about his country's government, but he was also a Chinese, a young one whose whole life had been mixed up in civil wars. He had heard his father's cronies talking palace gossip before he himself could talk plainly. The Revolution was within his memory. His classmates went on strike to show their sympathy for this political party or that as our students go to football games. It happened to be his pose to be an exquisite, to claim indifference to the present government in Nanking, but we all knew that he was only playing. Even the old men in China who pretend to care only for the fighting prowess of their battling crickets—even they keep their shrewd old ears to the ground when trouble is brewing in the government.

So it was a full life I had back in those years of 1935 and 1936. My days were crowded. I would wake up reluctantly in that hideous little flat, eat breakfast in the darkness of the dining room, served by a lack-luster boy I had inherited along with the green and the silver, and hasten to the office. Usually my day's assignment could be polished off in the morning. It might be an interview with some retiring magnate (the local name for a successful businessman was *taipan* and I'll probably use it from now on) or perhaps a swimming pool was being opened by an advertising club. Or I might dream up a piece myself, about a Chinese drugstore that hung cages of real Indo-Chinese sloths around to attract trade. As long as I had a column that wasn't news, so that our readers would not be distressed by having to think, it was all right. I could write it up in the office or at home.

Luncheon might be one of any number of amusements. Maybe Bernardine had invited me out to her red-and-black flat to help entertain a visiting millionairess from the States. Or perhaps she had corralled Mei Lan-fang for a meal, which would be a really ultra affair in that case. Instead I might meet a girl for lunch at the Cathay, with drinks first in the lounge; that meant we would pick up men and make a party of it. Once and only once Sinmay called for me in the *North-China* office: his pale face and long gown caused such excitement among the mild British reporters that he became self-conscious and after that made me meet him out in the Bund.

There were numbers of ways to waste time at the lunch hour. Sometimes I just didn't eat out at all but gobbled something on rice at home and then walked out to look in shopwindows or to go to the tailor. I was in that happy state of the newcomer who is not yet blasé about little pottery horses in groups of eight, or miniature nearly-jade screens. I brought home dozens of little fancy boxes with these things in cotton wool.

Then at night, a dinner party or an evening of talk at Sinmay's house, or a movie, or reading in bed. I was very happy, even though I began to smell war in the air. There were Japanese across the creek, waiting. I began to know it, but I was happy.

Chapter 3

IF YOU WERE told how cheaply we did all the amusing things with which we filled our lives in Shanghai you would either call me a liar or resolve to go there as soon as the war is over. During the last two hungry years I have sometimes remembered and gasped at those monthly bills and what they represented. What I didn't know at that time was that the whole giddy structure rested on *rice*. Rice, in 1935, was so cheap that as far as we Caucasians were concerned it didn't cost anything. The Chinese had a different idea of it, but I'm talking about us ignorants. Cheap rice means cheap labor. Cheap labor in a vast city like Shanghai means cheap production: furniture and housework and clothing and green stuff. In placid ignorance I sat on top of a heap of underfed coolies. I didn't run into debt; on the contrary, I was living easily, just within my means, and at length I decided to take a daring step and give up my job, planning thereafter to live on whatever I made at free-lancing for American publications.

If by any chance I give an impression of being a practical and business-like woman, do not believe it: it is false. That decision is a case in point. I can never let well alone if it involves a regular existence. Once upon a time I had a job in an office. There was nothing the matter with it. It was well paid, considering it was my first; it had a future. I could when I liked swing my weight around a bit, and had the right to dictate letters to a stenographer. There was, however, a great drawback to that job: I had to be at the office at nine o'clock and could not leave in the afternoon until five. It is remarkable that I held out at it for a year. It was as if I had made a resolution to give propriety one good chance; with a year of conventional endeavor behind me I ignored it thereafter with a clear conscience. The *North-China* work should have suited me: there was none of this time-clock nonsense about it and I was certainly not being pushed or exploited. But it was, you see, a regular job with a regular pay check, and evidently I couldn't bear that. We seldom understand our own motives. Perhaps my ego doesn't like having a boss. At any rate my argument in giving up the job was specious, since I didn't do any better for myself as a free lance. To be sure I did no worse, but my letters home show after this a familiar state of mind. I seem to have been slightly worried about money all my life. Over and over I come across this phrase: "If I could afford it, I would . . ." or, "Wait until next month and I'll know if I am in the clear."

I am not happy-go-lucky: I hate feeling queasy like that. Yet I have deliberately chosen the uncertain path whenever I had the choice, although it was not always necessary even for leisure to write what I like. For Shanghai it made a lot of difference, though, to have liberty. I took on two or three classes in Chinese colleges, teaching English literature and grammar; I like teaching when the program is not too full, and my Chinese friends always did that sort of thing. A more important freedom was that which made it possible to travel. The shortest trip you took out of Shanghai was the motor drive to Ming Hong, where the Europeans played with small sailing craft and kept a club as a center for houseboats. China is still a nation of canals, and with boats we used to wander a long way into the country. Some of the English used their boats to go shooting from. A greater number of people were not so ambitious, but stayed at anchor the year round and treated their little yachts like stationary shacks, miniature drinking clubs. They would spend the summer week ends out on the water, playing bridge and visiting from one boat to another for drinks. It was all agreeable if you liked people, and I did. There were different flavors to sample in these groups.

Hungjao Road was another good place for languid visiting. The wealthier people lived out there and kept gardens and horses and gave garden parties. I loved garden parties. I could wear long dresses and wide-brimmed hats for them, and be photographed.

All these gatherings were hotbeds of a certain kind of political conversation. Some of the taipans were not stupid when they discussed China: the more successful the man the more likelihood of his having brains. It was usually the middleman who drove me nuts: the man with a good salary out there, who wouldn't have made so high a grade in America. He was the one who talked a little too loud, ate a little too much, and knew nothing. He was the one whose voice could be heard upraised in familiar plaint against the recalcitrant Chinese who refused to help him make his money: "Don't they *want* to make progress? I tell you, the Japs are much more wide-awake. Let me tell you, it would be a good thing for this country if the Japs would move in on 'em. *They* know their onions. *They* know what it's all about. These damned Chinese——"

By the way, it should here be mentioned that people in the Far East seldom call the Chinese Chinamen, and never, never, never call them Chinks. Not since I left America have I heard them called Chinks. Perhaps once upon a time it was so: it is not unlikely, for the Mandarin word for "Chinese person" is *chung kuo jen*. Spoken quickly, it sounds like "Chinkoren." However the practice began, anyway, it hasn't been continued.

When I wasn't teaching or visiting people I was having visitors to that famous flat. One of them was Anna von Schubert, an Estonian lady whose husband made so much money in business that they lived in Hungjao Road and kept horses and did all those things. Anna was something different from most of the taipans' wives in that she painted— painted with a grim but inspired passion which left room for almost nothing else in her life. She gave me a rush, the aim of which was to capture the beautiful Sinmay as a model. For as long as she could bear it she called on me in Kiangse Road, but the colors of my walls and my cushions made her shudder.

"How can you live here?" she would demand tragically. "You cannot live here; you cannot do good work. No, you cannot. I am so sorry for you. Why do you do it? It is not poverty, for to live in beauty costs nothing in China. Why, why, my dear Mickey?"

I would say patiently, "Because I don't care, Anna. I don't pay attention to my surroundings. I really don't. I don't bother."

"But one cannot ignore the surroundings. These bad colors must sink *in:* they are destructive to your soul; they hurt your work. It must be so. No, I cannot come to see you here any more, my dear Mickey. You must come to my house. When is that Mr. Zau calling on you?"

Then there were the younger men of the different nations' consular and legation staffs. Six or seven of the unmarried ones and I dined together every Monday evening, taking turns as host. The rule was that we were not to go out or make merry; the evening was to be quiet and talky, a rarity in Shanghai, and the guests were always to go home by eleven at the latest. It worked out well until the group unfortunately developed a name: the Monday Night Club. This title attracted public attention. People wondered what we did with ourselves and why we didn't go to the movies or otherwise kill the evening hours. Then somebody made the suggestion that we were having Orgies. After a couple of years the club became more of a nuisance than a pleasure, what with other people trying to get into it, and it fell away into oblivion.

Sinmay liked my flat. He didn't mind its ugliness because he thought most foreign-style houses ugly anyway; perhaps he even considered the metallic bamboo forest "modern" and thus praiseworthy. What he liked about it was that it was in the middle of town and made an excellent stamping ground for himself, a place to meet friends and to talk, and to use the phone. He brought his friends in for everything but meals. I could never understand why he ate there so seldom, though once in a while he and his favorite brother did stay to lunch. This brother, Huan, had been educated in Paris and spoke French; he was handsome and fat and sweet and not very bright. He is a guerrilla general now and a good one. In those days he was just a nice boy without any work, but he was honest, and he liked to laugh, and it was he who confessed that Chinese people never got enough to eat when they lunched with me.

"When I have my meal here," he explained, "I go first to Jimmy's Kitchen and eat something. Or I go over afterwards to Sun Ya and have noodles. Without rice, we Chinese go hungry." After that I always had rice with meals even if it meant a bad selection of food values.

An important thing for me happened in the green-and-silver room. Among all Sinmay's hundreds of friends there were some who became intimate with me because they spoke English well and were fond of America or of England. There was Chuan Tsen-kuo, who had studied at Illinois. There was Wen Yuan-ning, more British than the British themselves, from Cambridge. Yeh Chu-yuan I met in Hangchow, and he later came to live in Shanghai as did a Hangchow friend, Mr. Yu, a novelist with a famously beautiful wife. Yeh is one of my more mirthful memories. He was very conscious of his home town, Hangchow, because it is one of *the* beauty places of China and because there is a famous school of poets there. Yeh tried to live up to the other poets. He modeled himself on the ancient Hangchow style and chanted his poetry in the Hangchow way, nodding his massive head as he recited and paced the room. He was a determined conservative, and my first visit to Hangchow was made memorable by a fierce argument I had with him on feminism, of all things; we shouted and struggled in a room overlooking the lovely lake. Regarding the exquisite hills in the distance, we went on talking like Yankee undergraduates. . . . It was a shame, but it was just like China.

Those were palmy days for writers with a knowledge of both Chinese and English. Lin Yutang could vouch for this statement. He was another friend of Sinmay's, and in those days was thinking of his first English book as he worked at editing a Chinese humorous weekly, the *Analects*. His was a popular name among the Chinese literati and Pearl Buck had to keep after him, at long distance, to persuade him to the English venture.

These people were drawn together in an exciting new project, a magazine to be published in English, devoted to bringing about more mutual understanding between West and East by means of literature. The idea behind it was political but that was concealed. The same statements go for the man behind it—Sun Fo, the son of the founder of the Republic, now in Chungking and at that time spending a period, I believe, in Europe. The name of the magazine, a monthly, was decided upon as *T'ien Hsia*, which means "everything under the sky" and is of course, like any other connection of words in Chinese, a quotation. It means by connotation "the world." A board of editors was formed with the names I have mentioned, plus a few others including Dr. John Wu, on the masthead. They asked Sinmay to write for them and he blithely promised, and sometimes even kept the promise. They asked me and I kept my promise much more lavishly. I loved writing for *T'ien Hsia*. I could be as snobbishly literary as I wanted and they liked it all the better. I reviewed a book for almost every number after they really got started, and now and then I did an article besides. Most of the other articles, I thought, were on the pedantic side, but that was only natural in China. People there like to be pedantic. They revere scholarship, and when they say "scholarship" that is exactly what they mean, in the old sense. Wen Yuan-ning was editor in chief, an ideal choice, for although his Chinese is not fluent —he is a *hua chiao,* an overseas Chinese—his ideals were thoroughly oriental. He loved learning and classical language. This love didn't affect his sincere affection for T. S. Eliot, and led directly to a profound admiration for A. E. Housman. Then there was John Wu, who at that time was just beginning to be convinced that he should join the Roman Catholic Church. John had studied law at Harvard and was a pupil of Justice Holmes, with whom he corresponded for years. Now he was attempting to reconcile his Western past with his Chinese present; he was, like

Sinmay, so Chinese that he refused to wear Western dress, and his house was severely in the old fashion. He went further than Sinmay and spoke English with a deliberate Chinese accent, a *Ningpo* accent, Sinmay told me. John was an odd, charming duck and he knew it.

All of them, Lin and Wu and Yeh and Chuan, all but Wen, were reflecting the government's actions in Nanking half consciously in these attempts to go back to Chinese tradition. Chiang Kai-shek was preaching resistance to aggression from outside, and the more emphatically he spoke the more blandly did Japan put on the screws. A lot of the Chinese journals were talking openly about the inevitable war. Chiang didn't go quite so far. His enemies were in the happy position of being able to attack him from both sides, as being too precipitate in his desire for national independence and too much inclined to like Japan. Sinmay was a fire-eater. He wrote a lot of editorials for different radical papers and he had an editorial sort of mind; at least he did that year.

" 'We will wait until the limit has been reached,' " he quoted Chiang in scornful tones, " 'and then we will rebel.' But the limit *has* been reached, surely. What does he consider the limit?"

The more I remember the way the British carried on in those long-ago days the less I can understand the Japanese attitude of hatred toward them now. England then seemed willing to give away as much Chinese territory as Japan deemed necessary to keep the peace. War would interfere with English trade and endanger her oriental holdings; Japan looked strong and would be the better ally (tacitly) in any case. The British diplomats of the Orient were of the stanch old-fashioned sort and all the Chinese talk of Russia and Communism frightened them even more, evidently, than it did Chiang Kai-shek. With Japan at least they knew where they stood in regard to those Communists. It is a small matter, but Japanese were permitted in the Shanghai Club whereas Chinese were not.

Once during that first year I ran slam-bang into the British on the vexatious question of Russia. A young Englishman whose job was supposed to be decoding cables took me home from a party. I happened to mutter crossly about an Australian policeman who had, I thought, behaved badly in a mob the day before, keeping order. "He knocked an old Chinese man on the head with his truncheon," I said angrily.

The Briton cast a sidelong glance at me. "What do you do with yourself all day?" he asked in a careless tone. "Who do you spend your time with?"

He went on looking at me sideways, and I said to myself, "Aha. Intelligence Service." I was right, of course, and I enlivened the rest of a hitherto dull evening by allowing him to pump me. He elicited from me a lot of interesting facts. Besides having what he called an "anti-police complex," I had Russian friends. Every Wednesday, I confessed tearfully, I met three bearded Russians at midnight, in a cellar on Bubbling Well Road, and we discussed Communist plots. The interview ended with my promise to be a good girl thereafter, and he took his leave excitedly. I went to bed in a cheerful frame of mind and promptly forgot the whole trivial incident.

A few weeks later I ran into our own Intelligence officer at a cocktail party. He grabbed me by the shoulders and gave me a severe shaking. "What's that for?" I demanded, hurt and puzzled.

"That," said McHugh, "is for the trouble you have given me with the British. They have a dossier on you about a mile high. They did a lot of work, too, until somebody with a grain of sense wrote on the top page, 'Disregard Miss Hahn's entire story.' Don't you do that to me again."

I didn't. Of course, considering what has happened to me since, I'm sorry now that I pulled their legs. I tell the story for what it is worth as a curiosity.

Chapter 4

I WENT to Nanking when I was free of the newspaper work. There were other trips, but Sinmay wanted me to see the nation's capital as soon as I could, because in a shamefaced way he was proud of it, still remembering his turbulent youth when he was one of the politically-minded students who tried to take a hand in remodeling the world. All the Chinese were proud of Nanking, the only capital, I suppose, that ever did duty for so many thousands of years in the same capacity.

Once I met Loy Chang there just after I got off the train. Loy is as American a Chinese as you will ever meet: he was educated at Harvard and his children in Shanghai were students at the American School. Yet he said to me, "I love coming here, don't you? It's so exciting and stimulating. And you see so few foreigners!" Then, realizing what he had said, he blushed and laughed. But I understood what he meant. It was honest pride that his country was governing itself at last without being helped too much by us. Even at that late date I was surprised at the long list I heard recited of American and British advisers to Chiang or

Madame. Why, I asked Sinmay, were the Chinese so hungry for advice?

"Perhaps they ask for it only to be polite," he suggested shrewdly.

The excitement Loy spoke of was that which one feels in any new, busy place. Nanking, the ancient city, was now a hopeful, bustling metropolis which existed for the most part in blueprints while the architects waited for material and labor with which to build it. Indeed, the Nanking Sinmay's friends showed me as we bowled along in an ancient car looked itself like a blueprint. The roads were there, nobly and widely marked out on the dusty ground; estates were marked out too, with stakes and chalk lines and even, here and there, a fence. But except for a few costly and beautiful government buildings there was nothing there in the new city, just a modern hotel and miles and miles of horizon, including the Purple Mountain and Sun Yat-sen's elaborate tomb on the mountainside. For life we had to go and see the older houses near the university, and the clubhouse where diplomats disported themselves. Usually Sinmay lived in a Chinese hotel in the old town. I stayed in the Metropolitan, a chromium-plated social center which must be the darling of the Japanese Government's heart nowadays.

"When I took part in the Revolution of 1927," Sinmay said reminiscently, "I had a disagreeable job, helping rebuild Nanking. I was not the only one to work on it, you understand, but I had the cruel part to do. I rode out on a horse and told the workmen what houses to pull down so that we could have all these big wide streets. How the coolie people hated us! But we thought it was splendid, to tear down all of old China."

"Then you're a member of the Kuomintang," I said. You can see that I had been learning about Chinese politics or I would not have known that word.

"I used to be. It was the People's Party and we believed in it, but now I do not. I retired long ago from politics. I am an old man," said Sinmay, who was thirty, "and I didn't know when I was young how dirty politics can be."

Nevertheless he evidently retained some connection with the 1927 circle, for during those week-end visits I met many Kuomintang people who had been his contemporaries at school and university, and they had a lot to talk about. The conversational topic could not have always been just old times, I decided. Students, too, called on Sinmay as a favorite professor whenever word went around Nanking that he was there. A Mr. Tao who had a high position in the government was introduced to me in Nanking but spent most of his time in Shanghai. He became a familiar in my house, walking up and down the living room, waving his arms and ranting. For Mr. Tao was a dramatist and he dearly loved to act out his plays, making long, long speeches. . . . "This play Mr. Tao is going to produce," I said one day after he had gone, leaving Sinmay silent and weary, "it must be rather boring. All that propaganda."

"Oh, it is," said Sinmay. "You will see for yourself because he is sending you tickets for the first performance and it is necessary for politeness that you go to see it. And it will be good for your Chinese. Because of all his propaganda Mr. Tao is liked very much by government people and he has an important duty, which is why he stays in Shanghai."

"Can you tell me what he does, or is it a secret?" I asked eagerly.

"It is very secret but everybody knows. He decides upon the government executions. The Kuomintang are always discovering people who are working against them. Judgment is passed and it is Mr. Tao who sees that they are executed," said Sinmay.

"You mean he is judge at the trials?"

"Oh, there is no trial, in *public*. It is Mr. Tao's responsibility to find out if they are guilty or innocent, a very secret work, of course. He does the execution afterwards. Not himself, but it is upon his responsibility. He hires the people to do the work."

"But, Sinmay, that's assassination!"

"No, it is execution."

Was he kidding the foreigner? I never knew, but I think he was telling the truth this time. Mr. Tao's finely chiseled face frightened me thereafter. It would not faze me at all nowadays; I have seen too much.

Anyway, the play wasn't good. It was at the Carlton Theatre and in being bad was rather an exception for that place. I've seen a lot of good modern plays there. A stock company of eager and intelligent young people had a splendid time those last few years, breaking down tradition. Chinese tradition says that actors are a low-class lot; a number of old-timers were amazed that we in America and Russia made such a fuss about Mei Lan-fang, a mere artiste. Then too Chinese tradition used to have a strangle hold on the stage. Classic Chinese plays were like the classic poetry: they had long histories and were set in their ways—picturesque but dead. Sinmay was one of the reformers of poetry; he followed Hsu Tse-mo, a famous and beloved young poet who brought revolutionary ideas home from France and forced his country to accept new, supple poems in the vernacular. Hsu died in a plane accident, leaving a legend that did as much as he had done himself for his school of literature. As a loyal adherent, Sinmay refused to see any good in the old ways. Secretly he loved his classics, but he wouldn't admit it. "You take the children to the theater," he begged his wife of an evening, when the youngsters clamored to see the Monkey plays. "I hate it. All that noise of the orchestra and the singing; it gives me a headache and I can't sleep afterwards."

A memory has suddenly come to me of my first trip to Nanking. Helen was with me and we were introduced on the train to Chu Min-yee, Wang Ching-wei's brother-in-law, later to become puppet Ambassador to Japan after the war's beginning, in 1937. Chu trained in Paris as a doctor, and used to be famous as an eccentric rather than a traitor's relation by marriage. He began to be famous with his choice of a doctor's thesis at the Paris School of Medicine: "A Study of the Vaginal Vibrations of the Female Rabbit."

When I met him he was dressed oddly in greenish-drab riding trousers and a fascist sort of shirt, and high soft Russian boots. Chu has always gone in for public games: kite flying, lantern making, fancy gymnastics, anything that a crowd can take an interest in and use for competition. Speaking to us, he discovered that we were both fond of riding. "You must ride my horses in Nanking," he said. "I will arrange it all."

"But we have no riding clothes with us, Dr. Chu. We didn't expect——"

"I will arrange everything," he said.

Next day a package was delivered to our room and we unwrapped two suits of Dr. Chu's distinctive clothes, green trousers, boots and all. His chauffeur told us to put them on quickly, as the horses were waiting out at the race track. Very hastily we did so and were driven out to the course, just under the tomb of Sun Yat-sen. It was a beautiful course with the loveliest view, I should think, in all the world. Waiting patiently were two steeds. One was an old, cynical Australian horse; the other was a young, sturdy, but disinterested Mongol pony. The grooms explained the procedure:

"This pony," they said, "has a bad temper, so please do not ride him. He came along so that the horse would not mind leaving the stable. This horse is a real horse. He is very big and Dr. Chu likes him and says please do not hurt him."

We were puzzled to know just what we were to do about our ride, but the groom explained. We took turns. First Helen got up and started at a slow, safe walk around the track. I thought she would gain speed pretty soon, but the groom, holding the bridle and walking rapidly at the horse's head, could not or would not walk faster, nor would he let go. After one turn around the course Helen, quite naturally, was thoroughly satisfied and gave the horse up to me without a murmur.

I had the same experience except that we went slower because the groom was tired. Then we got into the car again and returned to the hotel, and changed our clothes, and sent the boots and everything back to Dr. Chu.

But Nanking is a lovely place for horses. Don't let me discourage you. Without Dr. Chu one used to get plenty of satisfactory riding.

It wasn't for some years that I got fed up with racing. The other evening at a New York party a man told a story about a Chinese. I didn't interrupt him this time, or say that China bores me, because he told it more or less in my honor and I was glad that so many people think about China nowadays. This man hadn't been to China but he was obviously very fond of the place and had collected lots of anecdotes to show that the Chinese are a philosophical, gentle race. "Did you ever hear," he said, "about the Chinaman they took to the races? Along about the third race he got up and started out, and when they said, 'Here, where are you going? It isn't nearly finished yet,' the old boy said, 'In our country it was proved thirty centuries ago that one horse can run faster than another.'"

The man smiled approvingly at his own anecdote and looked at us, a few old China hands, for comment.

"Maybe it was proved thirty centuries ago, but most of the Chinese have forgotten it again," said C. V. Starr. "Or they take a lot of convincing. Mickey, do you remember the Shanghai racecourse on opening day?"

Of course I did. There is nothing like it in the world, except other race days in other parts of China. How they love it! They love any kind of gambling, and this kind more than anything else. Everybody was dressed up: everybody went around and around looking up at the grandstand and showing himself off. The little ponies ran valiantly, and one went faster than the others, and then the winner was led in, his big gangling jockey grinning, and the girl who led him had her picture snapped for the papers, and we went into the boxes for another drink. On big days the people who owned boxes used to give luncheon parties. We had Bagdad people in Shanghai, and Turks and Persians, so the luncheons were never dull. There were highly flavored gadgets and special curries and many other methods of getting away from English cuisine. The shops all closed on the opening day of the racing season; so did the banks. Nobody dreamed of working.

I wonder what happened to racing in Shanghai. I know what happened in Hong Kong. The Japanese always explained in advance that racing is encouraged "to improve the breed of the horses of the Emperor." Just idle enjoyment of good horses or of anything else which is pleasant won't do. The Japs get a lot of money out of racing in Hong Kong. They make the Chinese pay a large per cent of the wagers they make in taxes, win or lose. And still, though the Chinese have to pay out most of the money they bring for the privilege of gambling, though the races are absolutely fixed beforehand and nothing is left to chance, though our friends feel guilty, knowing they should not dabble in anything so pleasant as racing while a Chinese soldier remains alive to fight—still the course is jammed, packed, full and overflowing. Only there is a difference in their appearance. They don't wear their pretty clothes any more. The men need shaves. The girls dress in wadded gowns, not fur coats. They don't laugh; they watch glumly as they win or lose their few cents. But they still keep coming to the races. A habit of thirty centuries is difficult to break. Even the Japanese cannot do that.

It doesn't take long for a newcomer to discover that printing and publishing are ludicrously cheap in the Paris of the East. What makes it cost so much here? Paper? It was made in Japan and China, and the best quality was cheap, but we didn't use the best quality when we started out. Labor? But I was in China, and though labor was troublesome, the trouble was not on account of money. Anyone can publish something in Shanghai and almost everybody does.

Sinmay was a publisher from way back. He had spent a legacy on a large, elaborate printing press that included a rotogravure section. Most of the time the press worked at printing other people's publications, but in bygone days Sinmay had done a lot of publishing to please himself and some of his poet friends. Remnants of this former glory could be found in a small bookshop of his in Soochow Road, where "slim volumes" of forgotten poetry collected dust on the back shelves. The best sales were made by large, popular, cheap pictorial papers; Sinmay printed these too, and the famous humor magazine *Analects*.

"Why should we not have a magazine?" he said suddenly one afternoon in the shop. "A double-language one, English on one side and Chinese on the other. I suggest it because of the format, which will be original. You see, Chinese writing reads from the back of the book, and from right to left. Well, English is just opposite. Well, let the book be printed in such fashion that the English and Chinese meet in the middle! I can get plenty of advertising for the Chinese half; what do you think about the English?"

The story of *Vox,* our first bilingual paper, is a sad and common one. I hired one person after another to get advertisements. Usually it was a Russian who was willing to try it out when we talked, and then tried to sell me something widely disassociated from publishing. I sold two half-page ads myself. We gave away a good deal of space so that it would look all right, and as an afterthought I wrote the reading matter. We had good drawings because I used Chinese artists and Sinmay had plenty of those at his press—good ones, too. Whenever I needed a special drawing in a hurry Sinmay did it. *Vox* ran for three numbers, I believe. It was amateurish but would probably make interesting reading now, considering the date—1936.

I moved at last from the multicolored love nest in the bank. At the end of the year a bigger flat became available upstairs, unfurnished. I forgot my nervous dislike of owning property and bustled about buying things: a wardrobe and bedstead of luan wood, the blond material that is so handy for cheap things in China. I bought yards of burlap from the Ewo Cotton Mills where they made flour sacks, and I dyed it henna color and made curtains out of it, and cushion covers. I bought thin but gay-colored rugs, crockery, secondhand bookshelves, and a studio couch. I found an old man named Chin Lien to cook for me; on New Year's Day he gave me the regulation present, a bowl of goldfish, and there it was all complete—a furnished flat. One could give parties in such a flat, eating off the refectory table and sitting on benches.

In almost no time at all a year had gone by. I have here at my elbow letters that I wrote home from Shanghai in those months, and one of them gives an idea of what must have been happening in our correspondence, Mother's and mine. During those years of travel Mother was always telling me indirectly, I suppose, that I ought to come home. She had no special reason for doing this, of course, except that mothers always want their children at home. According to Mother's expressed philosophy women have as much right to independence as men have, and she brought us up to think that it is a fine thing for women to earn their own livings. Nature will out, though, and there was another state of mind in which Mother really passed her days. These hidden thoughts popped out when she wrote to me. She probably never said it outright, but I felt it when I read her letters; between the lines she said, over and over, "Come on home. Come on home, where I can watch you and make sure you are safe. Come on home. Why haven't you married, so that I could put you out of my mind and off my conscience? Why are you living alone over there so many miles away, where I don't know what you are doing? Come on home."

She never spoke so openly, but at times her control gave way and she went so far as to say that, after all, I could do my writing just as well in Winnetka. This gentle, constant tugging at my sleeve must have bothered me a lot. How much I have just realized, looking at these shabby old papers that she kept all these years put away in a shoe box. I remember now. I remember how that soft, insistent pull brought me out of the Ituri Forest and home from Africa, all the way around the world, back in '32. I remember how often I told myself savagely that she would not be satisfied until I did something desperate, something to cut the silver cord once and for all, something that would show her how I too was grown up, just like all my sisters.

"She won't admit my right to a separate existence," I mused, "until I have had a baby. If I had a baby she wouldn't keep asking me to come home. I can't follow her reasoning, but I know it's true."

This decision didn't help matters. Still in my unguarded, silent moments I heard that plaintive little call, secret and unspoken: "Come home, come home, come home. Come back to Mother."

At least once, then, I seem to have answered at the top of my voice. Here is the letter:

About my coming home and why you want me to. Of course it's because you want to see me. A very proper reason. I want to see you too, very much. But, darling, that isn't the only thing we have to think about, is it? If I could afford it I would go back much oftener to see you, but I can't. . . . I know you would rather, in a way, that I get a job and stay in Chicago or, better still, marry someone and "settle down" somewhere not too far away. But jobs aren't so simple any more; anyway, I am set in my work, which is writing, and as for marriage—well, it just hasn't happened. . . .

I am certainly doing more work than I ever did. Can't you take this sort of seriously? Can't you believe I belong here just as much as if I were married to a man with a job out here? I'm not just wandering about childishly! Dear, I know you can't trust any place but America, and of course we miss each other or I wouldn't worry so—your letters have been bothering me terribly. But what can I do? I can't just drop things and run. What would I do after I got home? Go through all those gestures again of getting settled in? I'm in the middle of a book; I'm in the middle of a magazine; I'm in the middle of China! I'll come back when it's time, and when there's something for me to do there. . . .

Now please, dear, be good, and don't worry any more about my health; you never carried on like that about the marshy airs of Oxford. I think it's the word "Shanghai" that scares you. . . . Now will you stop believing everything you read in the papers? A lot of us, women, were talking the other day at lunch about the things our mothers cut out of the papers and send us, stories about China, and I swear I don't know where they come from. I promise to take care of myself if there is a war; suppose I'd been in Africa?

Well, well; suppose I had? Here I sit typing on a dining-room table in New York, after a busy day. I telephoned twice today to the nursery school where my daughter spends her mornings. They told me both times that she was quite all right, but of course I was uneasy until she came home, and even now . . . Just a minute while I open the door that leads into her bedroom. She might wake up and need something.

Chapter 5

I HAD NOT BEEN long in the upstairs flat before I realized that my life was becoming far more social than before as a result of the move. The big long living room was a temptation to invite guests and so was Chin Lien, whose talent as a cook made me house-proud for the first time. He came from Peking, where people are proud of understanding the science of cookery. He was one of the few remaining cooks in China who could make a certain sweet, a basket composed entirely of glazed fruit and crème de marrons, covered with a cloud of spun sugar. Chin Lien began to enjoy a well-deserved fame, and people asked each other where he came from. Surely, they said, such a genius could not have lived long without being known among the foreigners in the town. It was Grace Brady, an elderly woman who was born in Shanghai and knew everybody, who traced him down.

"He worked for my friend Mrs. Davis," she said, "and he was a wonderful cook, always, but his temper was difficult. In fact Mrs. Davis says that she had to let him go on that account. He was marvelous except for that queer temper of his—clean and honest for a Chinese cook boy, and, of course, just about the best cook in the world. But he had such a rotten temper. Have you noticed, my dear?"

Had I noticed! I spent whole hours cowering in my bedroom because Chin Lien was on a rampage and shouted wildly at his wife in the kitchen. At such times his old parchment-wrinkled face looked like a mask of drama; he seemed ready to weep with rage. These attacks always came on when I hadn't given him enough work to do. Unlike most geniuses of his class, Chin Lien was a happy man on the days we had dinner parties. When he was happy I was happy, and so . . . and so I gave more and more dinners. Fortunately I was beginning to make better money in America at writing, so I kept pace with the grocery bills.

Sinmay now produced a new version of his old darling, the Chinese-English periodical. I can't remember now if he thought of it first or if it was the idea of C. V. Starr, publisher of the *Evening Post*. Starr at any rate was willing to back the notion in a trial flight, while we used our own editors, and the idea was this:

Vox had failed. It was not the first bilingual magazine to come to grief. There was something in the idea that was fallacious to begin with, as Starr pointed out: just because Shanghai was a bilingual city, that didn't mean that people wanted to read their magazines in two languages, did it? A man reads English or he reads Chinese. Very few people read both with equal ease. Therefore, why should he buy a paper when he knows he will use only half of it? If we wanted to publish articles for both Chinese- and English-speaking people we must fall back on an older system, that of double production. Give a man his choice, an entire paper in English or an entire paper in Chinese, but don't thrust both down his throat. Why not publish identical magazines, one in English and one in Chinese, but separate?

This idea made a lot of sense, at least to my amateur ear. Sinmay and I were both full of enthusiasm and went to work immediately planning each our own paper. Mine was to be called *Candid Comment* in English, and the Chinese twin had a name that meant the same, or, more directly in translation, *Free Speech*. My first hopeful plans of exact copies, one with an English title and the other Chinese, but with the heading stamped on the back for Chinese consumption, had to be given up. Chinese can be printed much more cheaply than English because the soft paper that takes printed characters is cheaper and also because you can get thousands of words into comparatively small space. The use of a different kind of paper necessitated using different types of illustrations generally. And then, too, the same illustrations, even the same cover, would not appeal to both publics. No wonder we had not been able to make a go of *Vox!* We had been idiots to try. In the end we struck a compromise: my magazine and Sinmay's used the same chief leader and many of the articles, but in format, illustration, and all other art we went our separate ways. Whenever I received and used an English article that Sinmay liked, he translated it and used it. The same went for his Chinese contributions. I had the better of that bargain. My contributing public was limited; how many Americans and English in the Far East are expert writers? Whereas through Sinmay I had the choice of all China's output, insofar as Chinese writers sent their contributions to him. It wasn't quite as nice as that for me, because Sinmay's time and good will limited me; I was at his mercy. I saw only what he bothered to submit to me in translation. Nevertheless it was a good field.

Whenever we ran short of text we wrote some. Whenever we needed illustrations we called on Sinmay's artists. I found out that almost every educated Chinese is a good draftsman; it is the result of their calligraphy, which gives a manual control that we don't develop in our Western writing. Young men who wanted to specialize in this branch of art, who felt they had more than just technical talent, often drifted into Sinmay's printing factory and adopted desks where they could work among friends. Two of our crowd were the famous Chang boys, caricaturists who had developed an attractive style of burlesquing the classic paintings and drawings of ancient China. They had a host of imitators and followers. I was to meet them often in Hong Kong after the surrender: they were left alone by the gendarmes for months as harmless artists, and they ran a gay little restaurant in the sad, dull city that was an oasis for all of us, refugees from Shanghai days. In time, of course, they had to run for it. They are in Chungking now.

One day Grace Brady, the woman who traced Chin Lien's history, dropped in on me. I was always glad to see Grace. She had a passion for creating things out of material that other people threw away, and she kept an entire village of Chinese workmen employed on her ideas. It is hard to sum up what Grace made, as her conceptions varied. Her whole house was an original creation. Certain rooms of it she never left alone. Her bedroom at the time I left Shanghai was made of shells from the South Sea Islands; walls and ceiling were lined with the shells and the windows were made of the same material polished down until it was translucent. She used many mirrors, too. I can't describe it better than that, but you felt as if you had come into a deep-sea cave when you entered the door. Her dressing-table top was glass, with soft, many-colored lights inside; so was another table she kept near by. She dreamed up handbags out of any and every sort of thing. I still have one that her workman made of the undershell of small turtles, soft and blond in color. There was another bag made completely of ducklings' bills and feet. It had a beautiful cobwebby color, I remember. Grace knew a lot about Chinese things; I mean what I said, *things*. Carved wooden gods, and bird cages, and woven material that I never saw anywhere else. One saw nothing hackneyed in her house, and Sinmay had a lot of respect for her. Of course most people thought she was crazy but they didn't resent her, because her husband had been head of the Stock Exchange at one time, which made her a solid citizen and not suspicious at all. She was, I suppose, an old woman but I never thought of her as anything but a beautiful one.

This morning she came straight to the point. "I have a large family of nephews and nieces," she said, "whom you have never met."

I looked inquiring.

"My brother is a brilliant man in a way," she continued. "He takes after my father, who was editor of the paper here, you know. Desmond speaks about fifty Chinese dialects perfectly, so that you couldn't tell with any one of them that he did not come from the district himself. Well, he married a Chinese woman." She paused for a moment, then with an effort said, "I don't see why he should not have done it. She is a woman from Peking and has been a good wife to him. But Desmond doesn't face reality. They have all these children and he has never been quite able to cope. You have never met them at my house."

"No," I said.

Grace looked worried. "I do what I can for them. I'm particularly fond of Paddy, the eldest boy. That child is so talented, you won't believe it if I tell you, and so I want you to meet him. I would like your friend Mr. Zau to look at his drawings. Paddy is only sixteen, but if Mr. Zau thinks it worth doing, we might give him a little exhibition, and then, perhaps, educate him abroad. . . . I don't know. Everything costs so much nowadays, and Desmond never seems able to help; why, he hasn't bothered to get himself any false teeth and he needs them terribly. May I bring Paddy to lunch? Please ask that nice Mr. Zau to be here too."

She departed soon afterward, and I looked after her smart, slim figure wonderingly. I had the customary American attitude toward the people we call "Eurasians." That is to say, my attitude was customary to those Americans who haven't lived in the East. I didn't think much about them one way or the other; I had toward them none of the definite reaction we are all given by environment toward the Negro race. Probably we Americans, even before China became our ally in this war, thought it romantic to have a touch of oriental blood. Certainly it added to the glamor of a movie actress or a dancer if she could claim a Chinese or East Indian ancestor, not *too* recent. . . . But any United States citizen, save perhaps a Californian, was shocked at his first experience with the China Coaster attitude toward Eurasians. (N.B. I use the term "Eurasian" to denote a person with Asiatic and Caucasian blood.) Why, I realized suddenly, Grace was as ashamed of her brother's family as if he had been in America and married to a Negress! It is probably obvious to any reader who knows what category I fall into that I don't see why white people should not marry Negroes, but my category does not include the majority of the public.

Now I found that a lot of "foreigners" in China and Japan feel about Eurasians as our own Southerners do about mulattoes. I had just begun to realize it. That is why I was sorry for Grace Brady. She was a lovely lady and an intelligent one, and yet she felt that her brother's marriage had been a tragedy. It wasn't her fault; it was just that she was British and brought up in Shanghai. I wasn't young enough or sure enough of myself to be indignant with Grace, but my imagination was stirred, and I waited eagerly for the lunch with Paddy.

He came walking softly, like a lean young leopard, in the footsteps of his aunt. He was of the age when some boys are spotty, but his skin was clear and he looked almost completely Chinese, with high wide cheekbones and thick, straight, black hair. He wore the tight-waisted shoulder-padded coat that high school boys in the Shanghai Chinese schools were using that year, and evidently he was growing very fast because although it was not an old coat the sleeves came down only to the top of his slender, well-shaped wrists. Paddy O'Shea looked like any modern healthy Chinese lad until I saw his eyes. They were Grace's eyes, arrestingly beautiful: huge, mournful, brown Irish eyes with thick lashes.

Grace treated him like a little boy and he acted like one, staring at his shabby shoes except when she asked him direct questions. Sinmay was late, as he always was, and Grace flatly refused a cocktail for Paddy when I offered it. "He is a little boy," she said, just like the kindly but watchful aunt that she was. Then we were both surprised, because Sinmay drifted in on a breeze of chatter with the servant, and he and Paddy nodded carelessly to each other and said in Chinese, "You here?"

"You've met?" demanded Grace.

"Oh, ah, yes." Sinmay looked puzzled. "This is your nephew?"

Paddy murmured something in the Shanghai dialect. "It is really funny," said Sinmay; "I know this boy well, but never did I know that he was English. He is in my press every day, drawing pictures," he explained to Grace. "We consider him a very talented boy. I have always thought he was Chinese. I have never thought about it at all, that is to say. We call him 'Chow.'"

"Well, isn't that nice," said Grace, looking as though she thought it not very nice, really. "Then I needn't have made you come out to lunch today. How *naughty* of Paddy not to let you know he was English. . . . I hope he doesn't get in your way when you are working?"

We were not gay at lunch, and afterward Paddy sat in silence for a long time, tacitly refusing to go away with Grace until she asked him outright, "Paddy, are you coming with me?"

Paddy shook his head with a sweet smile that was fleeting. "No."

Then he and Sinmay went on talking rapidly in Chinese. Defeated, Grace left us alone at last, and as the door closed Paddy relaxed in his chair with an eloquent sigh. He smiled again, straight into my face. "I like your house," he said. "May I have a drink now? My poor aunt worries about such things so I humor her."

We talked all afternoon about *Candid Comment*. I am anticipating a little but it doesn't matter; Paddy ultimately gave me a cover design for the magazine and it was by far the best that I ever published, though I had some good ones. A few months after this he had his exhibit. He also had a full-page spread in the Sunday *North-China* rotogravure section. Grace was proud of him, but when the Sunday-paper feature was arranged she went privately to ask the reporters not to mention Paddy's relationship with her in the write-up. Poor Grace. Paddy died the next winter, suddenly, of a throat infection.

Sinmay and I went to dinner with her some months after his death. She lived alone in her big palace in Ziccawei; she had lived like that ever since her husband died, but until then I always thought she filled the house sufficiently all by herself. After all it was her own creation; she should have been mistress of her strangely conceived rooms. Now she wasn't any longer. We inspected all the new things dutifully, the Ningpo bed she had discovered, a huge room in itself, all of red lacquer, with yards of mattress and a window on each side of the framework, and gilded pictures all over the outside. We went up to the sun porch. There was an exquisite bird cage up there, with a stuffed bird in it. "The Chinese keep dead birds in their cages rather than leave them empty," explained Grace. It looked mournful, and the stone floors were cold all over the house, and the lights, shining through polished sea shells, were too dim. And Grace had shrunk and did not trouble to be beautiful. Her life looked dim that night as the light through the polished shells.

"He would not have died if I had always taken care to see that he had good food," she said suddenly. "That house, it was not properly run. Desmond's wife has too many children. There is still the next boy, Dennis, but I cannot feel the same about Dennis. He can take care of himself. He is studying to be an engineer," she said with a queer snobbish scorn in her voice. "Must you go? I hate this house; it is too big. Come back soon, my dear."

"Oh, it is terrible," said Sinmay as we drove away. "That house is not only full of ghosts, it is a ghost itself. I will never go back. Yes, I must. We should go back every night. I must bring all my children. Oh, poor Mrs. Brady. You foreigners do not know how to manage death: I am sure Paddy's mother does not suffer in this way."

Of course he did not bring all his children, nor did he go back. Grace died after the Japanese took Shanghai; I hope she was allowed to live in her house until it happened.

Paddy's was not a real Eurasian story. The tragedy was not his but his aunt's. Being a Eurasian had nothing to do with Paddy's short life; he considered himself thoroughly Chinese, and because he was young and had his drawing there was no trouble in his mind about what would happen to him in that small, foolishly cruel community. I think he lived very much as did the other artists in Sinmay's big studio. It is not Poor Paddy, not at all. It is Poor Grace.

Candid Comment attracted attention and had a success, especially among the Chinese readers. The Chinese version sold at a low price and gave a lot for the money, and the political opinions that Sinmay published were strong—stronger than mine, although they were along the same lines. After almost a year I had to give up, but we took over Sinmay's side of the publication and carried on with it ourselves for much longer than that. Indeed, I think we are entitled to boast a little, for the Japanese paid us a sincere compliment on the magazine. One day a man named Ken—I think that was it—invited me out to lunch. (This, by the way, was after the Japs had moved into China in 1937 and surrounded our Settlement. You must allow me to anticipate a little, because the story belongs here.)

Ken—I don't know if it was his first or his last name—said he was a newspaper agency man. He brought with him to the luncheon another Japanese, a bald, unlovely man whom he called "Colonel." We three ate at the Metropole, the best restaurant in town, and they asked me right away if I owned *Candid Comment;* I proudly admitted it.

"It's a good paper," said Ken, "a good paper. But you haven't much advertising."

"No, unfortunately that is true," I said.

"We have been told by a little bird," said Ken, "that the *Evening Post* people are helping you out on the financial end. Now everyone on that paper has to make money outside, one way or another. Look at the editor, Randall Gould: how can he run that new car of his on his salary? He can't."

"Randall has other connections, you know," I said. "He writes for papers at home."

Ken shrugged and the colonel snorted. "I don't say he is not honest," he said doubtfully. "But about your paper. Have you tried to get Japanese advertising?"

I said that I had not thought of it. Ken said, "I think I could get you so much advertising that it would amount to a subsidy of—let's see—about five hundred a month. How does that sound?"

"Generous," I said.

"We would want a lot of copies, too, for our troops in China," said Ken. "It is an unusually good paper for a Chinese publication. I wonder if you really know, sometimes, what you are printing. You don't read Chinese, do you?"

"No, not enough for that, anyway."

"Well, sometimes your articles are very strong. . . . You must have a good editor. Who is he?"

"I don't know," I said.

"You don't *know?*"

I shook my head. "I haven't any one editor. These articles come in the mail and if there is a Chinese around my office I ask him to read them, and if he seems to like them, and if it's a Chinese whose judgment I respect, why, I pop it into the paper."

I gave out this nonsense carelessly, but I had a reason. In theory I was not answerable for my paper to the Japanese, not at that time, but in actuality they surrounded us and did fairly well what they liked. Assassinations were becoming common. Naming people would have been asking for trouble.

If Ken was angry with me he gave no sign of it. He was a smoothie. "Then no doubt you are being used as an innocent tool," he said. "Some of your articles, you obviously don't realize, are anti-Japanese. I might even call them violent. Now I'm sure you don't really feel that way. This girl, Colonel, is a real friend to Japan," he added to the bald man. "She may not know it but she has the same aim and ideal that we have—a free Asia. Now, Miss Hahn, we can promise you increased circulation and plenty of advertising: that is settled. If only you can change your policy, I mean your unconscious policy, and be more friendly to Japan——"

"But there is one reason I hesitate to be friendly," I said in my most stupid voice. "I feel that you Japanese are not friendly to us foreigners."

Ken was amazed. "What? Why ever should you feel that?"

"But, Mr. Ken, isn't it true that the Japanese want to kick all foreigners out of Asia?"

Speechless with surprise, he turned again to the colonel with his eyebrows upraised. At last he gasped, "Did you hear what she said, Colonel?"

The colonel had heard. Together they assured me earnestly that I was all, all wrong. I said I was awfully glad to hear it. We had apple pie à la mode for dessert and I never saw Ken or the colonel again. They didn't seem to think I was worth following up.

Chapter 6

THOSE WERE still the days when people who came into money spent it on travel, and the slick magazines were full of stories about flower-scented Hawaiian air and people kissing in it, temples with wind bells in old China and people kissing in front of them, the wide African veldts, the lavender-shadowed Southwest deserts, and beautiful young men and women kissing each other all over the landscape. The literature of barbershop magazines and the blurbs of travel agencies had a strong effect on all of us. I don't suppose it was an inborn Sense of Adventure, as they used to call it, or even the maps I studied in my geology classes that first sent me wandering off. Let's blame it on Conrad primarily, and then on all the cheaper-press influences of an American environment. I have reflected with mild surprise lately on the fact that I used to be wanderer. Because that was way back in my unregenerate days, and you could hardly call me a wanderer now. It would be unfair. I was shocked and resentful a few weeks ago when I looked at an apartment that was to let, and the landlady said, "Oh, I don't think I can sublet to *you*. That's just what I don't want to happen—to sublet to a tenant who will go wandering off again as soon as she's settled in. You're the sort of person who might wake up tomorrow morning in Alaska or somewhere."

I replied in astonishment: "But not at all. I've been in one place for years, in China!"

She was not convinced. Being in China at all, she implied, was a rackety, unbalanced state, and very drifting. Just so do the Chinese think of us in America, as crazy will-of-the-wisps dashing about romantic places like Arkansas and Rhode Island and Iowa, never settling down sensibly like solid Chinese citizens in dull Szechuan and prosy Shantung.

Wanderers from New York and Chicago and St. Louis used to drop in on Shanghai when their ships stopped there en route to Manila or India. Sometimes they came in organized tours and sometimes they just came on their own, tourist class; once in a while they came in the guise of awfully rich people who didn't travel just for the fun of it, but to carry out a carefully laid plan in regard to training race horses for the next Hong Kong meet, or being there when the jewel dealers held the annual jade auctions in Burma. However they came and whoever they were, I used to claim that they always had letters of introduction to me. I exaggerated. Three times as many people brought letters to Bernardine, for example, as came to me. And there were many more Americans in Shanghai who had their work cut out for them when the ships came in. We were gay enough between ships, but during those periods when the tourists were in port Shanghai just about blew the top off. Such crowds at the night clubs! Such cocktail parties given! Such wine consumed, and curios bought, and promises made of future hospitality in other ports! We, the residents, sat there in our Eastern city and watched the world bring us amusing books and news and people, week after week: there are, as I have often said before, much worse existences.

I still feel that Shanghai, as far away as it is, was the best center I have ever found for European and American developments. Back in Chicago when the Abyssinian fever first took hold of Italy, how much did you know about it? Only what you saw in the papers and heard on the radio. Now in America you can listen in to European radio, of course—I mean, when there isn't a world war going on. You aren't exactly isolated, I admit. But out in Shanghai we were better off than that: we were in neutral territory and we had small bits of all the governments in the world right there, where we could talk to them. I dined with Italians while all this was going on. I could talk to them—ships' captains and consuls. I could turn around at the same dinner and talk to British diplomats. It happened often, because Shanghai hostesses couldn't be expected to remember all the strains and stresses of European politics when they planned their dinners. I don't wish to claim that I knew any more about Italy's actions in Africa just because I met some idiotic little Italian officer at a cocktail party, but certainly I knew more about why Italy did what she did.

The same thing was true of the British and their policy in Asia. Shanghai was full of baby diplomats and consuls from England. Because they studied language in Peking they tended to an aesthetic rather than a practical appreciation of China's qualities, and I made fun of them for it. I said that they were lost in a dream of the Ming Dynasty, and used all their expensively acquired proficiency in Mandarin only to chaffer for porcelain in the market place, but I was wrong. England's diplomats were working away like beavers, trying to come out ahead in the struggle between Japan and China. Some of these youngsters learned quickly what was going on, and many of them were intelligent and rebellious and they didn't like it. Close-mouthed as they were trained to be, that much was evident. I doubt if any diplomat now in office in England would deny that his nation played her cards foolishly then. England backed the wrong horse. He kicked his backer in the backside.

These horsey similes must be recurring to me because I am lost in the mists of the 1936 weeks, caught up in the old atmosphere of the stables. It was early in the spring of that year that I went down to Hong Kong to attend a race meeting, along with a girl named Babs Hutchins and Nunky Sassoon, a sweet old man who was Sir Victor's uncle. Nunky was an ardent racer and he chaperoned us on the trip, so it was a merry one, full of champagne and gaiety. It wasn't, however, particularly worth remembering except for Wang Ching-wei.

You know now who he is. In those days, even, you might have heard of him over in America, if you watched what went on in China. Just at that time he was being awfully quiet, following his attempted assassination in Nanking when a man dressed as a newspaper photographer fired at Wang out of his phony camera. Afterward Wang still carried a bullet in his back, and because he is a diabetic this grave condition was the more grave. It was all elaborately explained to the press, because Wang was now sailing for Germany to have a specialist examine the bullet with an eye to removing it. Nobody was to be given a chance to say Wang was going away for any other reason—fear of another attempt, or something like that. He was just a private citizen on leave of absence from his governmental duties. We didn't know he was aboard until we had left port. Then we encountered one Tang Leang-li, a stocky man with a nose so flat that it seemed to consist of two holes directly into his head. He spoke English with a heavily Teutonic accent. Dutch, he explained— he came from Java and spoke only one Chinese dialect, and that haltingly. In spite of the accent he spoke amusingly, and he kept his eye on me. He always kept his eye on women. He interested me. He interested Babs too: she said while Tang was out of the room, "You know who he is, of course? He's Wang Ching-wei's most faithful follower; writes his English books and all that."

I didn't see the rest of the political party until the *Gneisenau* sailed into evening. Then, attended by Tang Leang-li and his five bodyguards, the man with a bullet in his spine came up on deck for an airing. He swung around the deck in a businesslike manner, keeping step with his companions. His eyes were fixed on the deck, but he listened carefully to what Tang was saying. After going around about five times he passed word along the bodyguard and they disappeared into the lower regions. We were five days on the way to Hong Kong and Wang came up every evening, once, after dark. In Hong Kong he hid himself and wouldn't come ashore; it was said that the British asked him not to try, for fear of more phony photographers and their attempts on his life. The bodyguard came out, though, and that is how it happened that my first view of the city which was going to mean so much to me was in the company of Tang Leang-li, future traitor to his country. On second thought I suppose Tang was a traitor already. But he didn't think of himself as one. He was busy and reasonably contented; on his way to his beloved Europe, pleasantly whiling away part of his tour with a lady who listened to him talk.

Tang was what the Cantonese call "wet salt," a slang term for "amorous." He concealed this chronic state pretty well by chattering along about Far Eastern politics, and he did his best to educate me on points in these matters about which I knew nothing. He hired a car to take us for the drive up the Peak and around the island, that drive which you must take as soon as you disembark in Hong Kong. He told me the interesting fact that if we had come along some years earlier he would not have been permitted to go past a certain point on the Peak Road as a tourist. Only Chinese who were servants of white residents were given passes to enter the holy land on the mountaintop in the old days. Even now, he said, no Chinese could live as a resident up in those rare regions; it was not an openly published law but an agreement between landowners and landlords, and everyone was faithful to it. Only one Chinese, an old fellow named Sir Robert Ho-tung, Tang told me, was permitted past these magic if imaginary portals. Sir Robert was too rich to ignore, so the British allowed him to build his house on his own Peak land, and to live there when he wanted to.

It all sounded ridiculous to me. Shanghai had none of that kind of discrimination by the time I came along. There was discrimination in Shanghai, but not in real estate. Our own American country club, the Columbia, wouldn't take Chinese as members or guests. Some businessman created a scandal by bringing Anna May Wong, American citizen, to bowl in the Columbia bowling alley. They wouldn't let her do it. "You have to be careful," the committee would say vaguely when they were asked what it was all about. Shanghai wasn't perfect on that score, not by any means; it was thanks to Tang Leang-li, however, that I learned all about Hong Kong and how stupid a British colonial crowd can be when it tries.

We had tea on the veranda of the Repulse Bay Hotel; the Lido hadn't been built yet. I can smell the flowers now if I close my eyes. I see wisteria all over the front of the hotel, and the red flame-in-the-forest that hung in the trees. There is no scent of flowers now at Repulse Bay Hotel, which is a convalescent hospital for Japs. Friends of Tang Leang-li, they are.

"The British," he told me on the hotel veranda, back in the spring of 1936, "are in for a rude awakening."

And he told me how wonderful was his boss, Wang Ching-wei. He had to hurry back to the ship, as Wang was inclined to be nervous while the *Gneisenau* was still in port. Tang sent me a post card from Singapore with a photo of a baby gorilla. The ape had a nose so flat that all you could see of it was two holes leading directly into his brain. "Does this remind you of anybody?" he had written across the picture. Tang was likable enough. I gave him the address of my family in Chicago, because he said he would come across the States on his way home, and he had a long visit with them a few months later. He had, he told them, a wonderful time in Europe, because he shook hands with Hitler (who had a flabby grip), and enjoyed himself thoroughly in Rome with Mussolini.

There is another reason why I should remember Hong Kong in that spring of 1936, because I spent a lot of the week with Needa, and years later I had occasion to remind him of it. Victor Vander Needa spells his name like that because his mother, who was Japanese, didn't know how else to spell it. His father was Dutch, and probably the name was slightly more complicated than this version, but Victor wouldn't know. He was born in Tsingtao and spent most of his childhood there, but he remembers that his mother took him to Japan for a little while, and he learned to speak Japanese in her home. Later he needed the language just as much in Tsingtao, a popular place with Japanese, but by that time his mother was dead and the little boy had been adopted informally by an American broker.

"He was talking about sending me to the States to be educated, for a doctor or something," said Needa, "but I was eighteen and I wanted to go out on my own. Besides, I had begun riding and was a sort of hero in Tsingtao. I thought I was hot stuff, and I owned that town, honest. So I went in for brokerage."

Although that may sound like a non sequitur to an innocent Westerner, any China hand will know what Needa meant. Racing in the East is based on the illusion that all the riders are amateurs, "gentlemen jockeys." Actually they are just professional jockeys like any riders anywhere in the world, with the few exceptions of some rider-owners. The ordinary boys who can't afford to ride for the fun of it always go in for something light and gentlemenly, usually brokerage, to earn their livings when they aren't following the races, and enthusiasts give them orders to keep them comfortable between meetings. Needa was for years the best jockey they had on the Coast. He was a beautiful rider, but too big to make a go of racing anywhere but in China, where the largest jockeys in the world ride the smallest horses. He had a struggle to get down below a hundred and forty pounds, but the tough little Mongol ponies were used to that. He was a good-looking, big boy, a textbook example of "hybrid vigor."

He was famous for his good nature. Stable owners made a butt of him and never wondered if he didn't sometimes resent it. That meeting he won the Derby, one of the biggest events, so we were wined and dined all over Hong Kong. I had long been a friend of his, and so he confided something to me. "I'm getting out of this if I can," he said. "It's no good for a regular income, fooling round with horses. I may want to be getting married one of these days; it's time these fellows took me serious."

I knew what he was talking about. A few years later he kept the promise he made to himself, and slowed down on his racing, and stepped up in his brokerage, and married his girl. This was the difficulty: she was English. Her father, a wealthy shipping man with a passion for his stable, was furious that his daughter had married a Eurasian, and did not rest until he had separated them. He waited until the young people were having money troubles and then he pounced. By that time there was a baby, a little girl, and the whole thing—his wife did leave him— was a bad shock to Needa. It's my theory that he didn't really become anti-foreign until his marriage was spoiled, but maybe I'm wrong. Perhaps the seeds of hate were sown back at the race meeting in Hong Kong when everyone thought it funny to make a butt of Victor Vander Needa, the best-natured man riding on the Coast. Remember his name, because it will occur again.

The abdication of Edward, King of England, was more to me than just a delightfully exciting piece of gossip, owing to my current romance of that year. I was somewhat infatuated with an English naval officer. It was a strange choice for me: Robert was a saturnine young man who was disliked by his fellow officers because he was sarcastic and fiercely in love with his job. His zeal was unpopular. Most naval officers in the Far East, of any nationality, used to fall under the spell of that easy life and they did no more work than they had to, spending all their leisure playing games or going to parties. Not Robert. He thought all his waking moments of navigation, and I think he divided his dreaming time equally between the girl at home and the ship. I wasn't the girl at home, but I let him talk about her. As a result I spent a good deal of time that year going up the river to whatever outport his little gunboat was honoring with her presence.

I was fascinated by the trips, by the boat herself, and in a somber sort of way by Robert's conversation, which was so technical that I could never understand a word of it. "Dear old thing," he would write, "a rather funny thing happened yesterday. The skipper was——" Then followed six closely written pages about navigation or something else nautical that I didn't understand, and the letter ended with, "I did laugh! Good-by now; be good."

Well, that was the boy friend. In a boat the size of these river craft there were only three officers at most in the wardroom: the commanding officer, the mate (that was Robert's job), and the doctor. Sometimes in small boats there was no doctor and then the other officers hated each other with a deadly poisonous intensity, the result of too much time together in a trying climate. When there were three men, though, it was a little better. Two could get together and hate the third one. Relief came fairly often when they were stationed at bigger outports where they could use the country club, dine out, and otherwise relax. Two or three times I took a rackety little plane up to one of these places and met them, and with the wardroom visited around the city, drinking with the representatives of oil companies and tobacco companies.

Also whenever the boat went to Nanking I went up to see Robert. It was easy to go that far and it was always fun. Sinmay's Nanking was one kind, Robert's was the other. The young foreigners of the town were busy trying to make the place as pleasant to live in as their lamented Peking had been. This could not be done, but there were lots of the same people there, who had been moved with their legations, in spite of all their protests, from the northern capital, so we had the old gossip and the old traditions. They organized riding parties and drag hunts over the lovely low hills that surrounded Purple Mountain.

Two Nanking week ends stand out in my mind. Both of them depend for their memorability on the royal family of Great Britain. I happened to come up for a visit just when the scandal of Mrs. Simpson broke on the world, and I found Robert and his brother officers in a state of collapse. As an American I didn't quite understand the way they felt. To me it was an exciting and humorous incident, intensely interesting but not really near the heart. Of course I was secretly tickled, anyway, that it was an American woman who had so ruffled the dignity of our cousins across the Atlantic: it is the British themselves who have made us feel that way about them. I'm trying to explain my bad manners, not excuse them, for there was really no excuse for what I did. At dinner that night on board the gunboat I held up my glass of wine and said:

"Gentlemen, I give you——"

Expectantly the officers held up their glasses. . . .

"Mrs. Simpson," I finished.

The captain was the first to speak, as they lowered their goblets to the tablecloth untasted. "Please pass the potatoes," he said stiffly.

Later Robert gave me hell. "You don't seem to see it," he said, tears standing in his eyes. "Can't you understand? If this horrible thing is true, all my life becomes meaningless. Everything the Navy *means* has disappeared."

"I'm sorry," I said. "I'm sorry, but I really don't see it."

Well, it was true. My next Nanking week end was in celebration of the Coronation; the Navy seemed to have survived the shock bravely. Host of the Coronation Ball was the Ambassador, Sir Hughe Knatchbull-Hugessen. Soon he was to be wounded by a Jap machine gun. We spent a lot of time that evening lightheartedly wondering what the champagne had cost him.

As I read over this typescript I am overtaken by nostalgia of a strange sort. Oh, yearns my heart, for those happy evenings spent with the British, because we danced so much! Americans beyond a certain age never dance at all, do they? I had forgotten. I am remembering now. Up until ten years ago when I spent an occasional year in the States, usually in New York, our social hours were passed in speakeasies. Night clubs were kept for visiting firemen, and on the rare occasions when we did visit such places they were too crowded for dancing. Englishmen are different; they dance, they dance well, they like to dance. Nor does it matter how old the lady may be: she is still permitted to dance. Women all like it, you know; all they need is a chance.

Sinmay didn't dance. He said, "I do only those things which I do well, and I am too short for dancing." Besides, he had no use for the Chinese dancing crowd, the girls and boys who thronged to their favorite place, the Park Hotel, and aped the foreigners in giving parties out in the open instead of hiring private rooms at long-established restaurants. When cornered by his insistent young cousins he fell back on another reason.

"A day of reckoning is coming," he said severely. "I do not know how much longer that man Chiang Kai-shek will go on making brave speeches and doing nothing. Even he cannot go on like this forever. Japan is owning the country now. Yesterday they came and arrested two of my friends, editors, for printing anti-Japanese sentiments in their paper. These men will go to prison, for what? For saying what the Generalissimo says every day of his life." He frowned at us and we were abashed into silence.

"For you," he added, addressing himself to me, "I have nothing to say, I cannot scold you. It is not your country's problem. But these young

Chinese, these children of compradors! They have money and no brains. At least their fathers have brains enough to make that money out of the foreigners."

It was later than we thought.

Chapter 7

I FIND that I am reluctant to come to grips with the Japanese, even in the harmless paper battles of this book. It was such a short time I had with China, when you count it up, just a little bit more than two years, and after that I was locked up in a Japanese concentration camp on a huge scale, that grew smaller and smaller with time. I cling to the harmless, happy memories of China before the engagement at Marco Polo Bridge.

Among the photographs that I left in Hong Kong are a few that mean a lot to me. They are of outdoor scenes in the Yellow Mountain district of Anhwei, and they depict about twelve Chinese, girls and men, with Miss Hahn standing among them. We all wear walking clothes, even Sinmay having abandoned his long brown robe in the interests of comfort, and we carry stout sticks, and we look cold and damp. It was a famous and much-publicized jaunt, comprising as it did practically all the important Chinese editors and journalists in Shanghai, with the artist-photographer Long Chin-san coming along to immortalize us with his camera and brushes among the mountain peaks.

On this trip I was amazed by my intellectual Chinese friends. I had always thought of them as effete creatures moving softly around their libraries or studies, now and then indulging in an hour of restrained alcoholic gaiety and poem-chanting in company, after the old tradition of the sages. I failed to remember how surprising the physiology of the Chinese can be. Those delicate willow wands of girls can eat a tremendous lot without half trying, and now I was to find out that they can all qualify without training for the Olympic track team. We climbed the mountain all day, every day, investigating different peaks famous for countless legends. We scrambled up and slid down stone steps which had been built by the order of a Ming emperor and had been kept in dubious repair since. At the beginning of our ten-day trip we put up at the China Travel Service Hotel, near a mineral hot spring, but as we wandered further afield we found it necessary and agreeable to stay in temples up on the mountaintops. The country was thickly wooded with pines up to a certain level and above this we walked through an austere world of bare rock and clouds that came down to swirl in the valleys beneath us. The thin cold air was intoxicating and made me strong, but I was always being humiliated by the prowess of the other women, including one old dame of sixty-odd who had bound feet but who left me behind every time. I am supposed to be a fairly good walker, but I discovered then that there is far too much of me. The thin little maidens and slender youths leaped lightly up the ancient stairs as I trudged weightily behind them, leaning on my pilgrim's staff and puffing loudly.

It was good, though, to be among trees again after the bare flat ugliness of Shanghai countryside. Even though I slipped in the mud and fell on my hands and sprained a wrist, I enjoyed all of it. In the evening after our meal of Buddhist vegetables we would sit around on those excruciatingly stiff chairs the Chinese use and tell ghost stories or let the monks tell us about other tourists. One day we ran into a friend, that Chang who was famous for his painted tigers. He was enjoying himself in an innocent way, dressed as a pilgrim in a huge straw hat lined with blue peasant cloth, walking through the aged rocks with a map in his hand. This map was in reality a long scroll painting of the Yellow Mountain. It had been executed three hundred years before, but I have never seen anything that so much resembled a modern geological cross-section drawing, faithful to scale and neatly done. We made a great fuss of Chang and his map. It was possible to trace a few places where erosion had made a difference to the land's surface, but there were not many.

Long made photographs which he touched up with a technique of his own invention. Wherever he thought the composition needed it he put in clouds, or pine trees, or spaces. We wound up our expedition in Hangchow, acting in all propriety as Chinese poets have done for generations before us: we went on the lake in boats and wrote poems.

That was the biggest trip I ever managed to make into the interior until much later, when I went to Chungking. The Zaus and I, however, often dashed off for little journeys. I accompanied a few of them to Wuhu more than once and saw the famous silk mills, idle by the time I came there, and I sat in Wuhu plum gardens. I went to Peking once, and only once: Sinmay and I had to go up in July when all the foreign residents were away in Peitaiho. It was just as I knew it would be. It is heaven and if I am good I shall be able to go there to die. Hangchow is a smaller heaven, so is Soochow, so is Yangchow. They tell me that the Japanese have made a concentration camp in Yangchow and put a lot of prisoners there. I can't picture it. It is a very old, moss-grown city, dank and green and untouched, and cut off from the bustle of Chinkiang by a fiercely flowing river. The day we went across this river to see it a storm blew up and cut us off for three days from the other side, as no boats would cross. In the streets people were unfriendly and called me a Japanese, because I was a foreigner and they thought Japanese were foreign-looking. They know the difference now.

I had frivoled away another year in my superior Kiangse Road apartment, on top of the bank. Things had happened and were happening, but they were all of a level in intensity. One had the feeling that this was the way conditions went in China; they were exciting, and there was always a threat that they would become more so, but I began to assume they would never go too far. There was the kidnaping of the Generalissimo. That had been tense indeed. We acted like ostriches most of the time in the treaty ports, but this development was of such magnitude that even we, the half-wits of the world, paused and looked at each other, and stopped chattering for a little. Then he came back again, safe, and we laughed shrilly, and poured out more cocktails.

I wish I had had the sense to keep an eye, those days, on the few Japanese I knew. Only two really had much to do with my life and they were both newspapermen. One became more familar to me later, in Hong Kong, as Yoshinori Horiguchi: he has a by-line on the dispatches from Lisbon and there was some sage comment under his name almost every day in the Hong Kong *News*. Just before I left, for instance, he was making good use of the phrase "falling back in order to advance" when he described the Germans' new "elastic warfare." It is hardly fair to blame him, though, for what he says: Domei tells him to say it. We used to know Yoshinori as Bob. He's fairly well known to all newspapermen who have ever been East. He is another example of hybrid vigor; a Belgian mother and a Japanese father contributed the genes that account for his height—about six feet, pretty good for a Japanese. Bob had a pretty American wife, Karen, who met him first in the classrooms of the Missouri School of Journalism. I don't know where she is now. We younger people used to whisper to each other, asking, "Do you think she Regrets it?"

I met Bob and his boss through an American friend, Ake Hartman, who spent his holidays in Japan and talked the language and kept up with Japanese people as much as he could. Bob's boss made up for the social deficiencies of Bob, in my opinion (Bob was an undependable drunk and could be nasty). Shigei Matsumoto, the Domei chief in Shang-

hai, had been in China twelve years and had an advantage over his compatriots; he was tall and he looked like a Chinese, by which I mean he
was neither ugly nor toothy. He looked rather like Wang Ching-wei, and
he liked to be told so, because he knew and admired Wang. Ake told
me a lot about Shigei and his wife. They were truly modern, Ake said
sympathetically, and for this reason had a hard role to play whenever
they went back to the island of their ancestors. Mrs. Matsumoto was an
accomplished pianist who had been trained in England. There were
three children and the family lived out near Kiangwan in a thickly populated Japanese community. Shigei sent them home to Japan on some pre-
text early in the spring and was living alone when I asked him one day
to help me in a dilemma. An old Japanese, Shindo, had crossed the
Pacific in the *Chichibu Maru* with Helen and me when we came from
America, and he and I had struck up a warm friendship although we
could not speak one word in common. I suppose he was planning for
the war all the time, but in my innocence I thought he was a pet, and
perhaps he is now saying just the same things about me. At any rate we
used to write a letter to each other every six months or so, with interpreters helping out on both ends.

"To think you have settled in Shanghai, and that your heart is no
longer Japanese," he wrote soon after I took my first job. "Behold me
sunk in deepest desolation!" I thought it perfectly charming. Also I remembered with mixed feelings the speech his secretary had made to me,
the last day on the boat: "Mr. Shindo admires you intensely. Unfortunately he has a wife in Japan, and since this is his third marriage he
feels he should not make any more changes. But he would be delighted
to meet you, any time, in London."

Now he was passing through Shanghai and had invited me to call at
his hotel. I asked Shigei to come with me, to act as interpreter.

Shigei knew the States pretty well so he wasn't shocked at my temerity.
He is related to Prince Konoye and is extremely aristocratic, but he came
along anyway and helped me out. I haven't thought much about Shindo
since the beginning of this war, but now that I muse on that visit of his
I think it was interesting. Shigei sat there smiling a little and doing the
honors well, I think, because Shindo was flattered and happy. I arranged
for the ordeal of taking him out alone to lunch, and then I took Shigei
back to his office and thanked him.

"I didn't know you had friends in Japan," he said. "I am pleased. You
know, I was at Yale for a while and I am fond of America. I hope we
meet again soon." Yes, I thought he was a swell guy: the memory of

my stay in Japan was still silvery and special, in spite of what had happened since in North China. I also felt affectionate toward Shindo when I called at his Japanese hotel later in my car.

As for the car, I had just acquired it, a shiny blue Chevrolet coupé. Sir Victor gave it to me, and let me pick out the kind of car, too. My friends and I had argued for a long time over what sort I should buy: a small Morris, which would cost more, or this Chevvy, which would use more gas? In the end we settled on the Chevvy because you could hold more people in it, and it would be comfortable for long trips in the interior. I never took it into the interior; I didn't have a chance. As for the editorial "we," I use it deliberately. All my belongings belonged to the Zau family too, and in a lesser degree to the outer circle of friends. But I was talking about Shindo.

I was proud of the car but I didn't drive it very well. Sir Victor had had to insist that I learn to drive before he let me buy it. We were making our way toward the Garden Bridge when I nearly ran down a ricksha coolie. It was entirely my fault, but the smaller fellow always looks funny, and this coolie's indignation made Shindo laugh. I can still hear the tone of voice, contemptuously amused, in which he said, "Chinese!"

It was the last time, as it happens, that I saw Shindo. The war began a few weeks later, as we all know, at Marco Polo Bridge.

Chapter 8

ACCORDING TO PEOPLE who had been in Shanghai during the war of 1932, things were moving according to schedule. We were bidden to obey the new curfew laws, and the local Volunteers went to live at their posts, and people who had uniforms started to wear them, and there was a shortage of tin helmets. Although we were not supposed to be involved in this war, strictly speaking, it was no time to split hairs. The Chinese on the outskirts of the city put up a braver and more effective defense than lots of us had expected, and week followed week without much change in the conditions under which we lived. That is, we were awakened early by the noise of bombing, and all day long there were evidences of the war in the distance; clouds of smoke and flame sometimes when a part of Chapei was fired, and loud explosions of guns and shells.

The municipal council was busy defining laws for our protection. The municipal police bore the brunt of the war; those who were on duty down in the dangerous area across the creek lived under shellfire most of the time. We were still so sure of ourselves, so used to thinking of ourselves as the privileged overlords of the East, that the danger was muted; it took on the aspect of a sort of constant threat of accident, like driving a car with faulty brakes. We worried about shells bouncing over the border, or irresponsible Japanese who overstepped their rights, but not many of us went further than that for the time being. It was like being too near the line of fire in a duel between two other people. That the survivor of the duel might then shoot at us was a possibility that did not occur to many. My favorite story was about the man who barely escaped death from that Black Saturday bomb that fell on the Bund. He landed in a pile of rubble, his clothes torn and blackened from the explosion, and he was a little dazed. As they helped him out of the debris he put his hand to his head and said:

"My God, this will set extrality back twenty years!"

What of Sinmay? It took me several days to find him, after the war began. He made no effort at first to report to me his change of address, because we had quarreled. The family had continued stubbornly to stay in the Yangtzepoo house, in spite of all my Cassandra acts, until the first noise of the war itself. The brown family car was out of commission with a flat tire. Sinmay hastily commandeered an ancient Ford belonging to his father, which had two gallons of gasoline in the tank. With whatever Zoa had time to pack, the entire household drove out of the dangerous area into the Settlement and from there to his father's house in Frenchtown. Before I found them again they had moved into a one-room apartment not far from the ancestral house, and they were in an awful mess.

I was still well out of the trouble, living in a Yuyuen Road house I had taken from friends. We were near the city limits at Jessfield Park, but the Japanese hadn't as yet worked their way around that far, although now and then a little shrapnel fell into the garden or on the roof.

Just about now the British decided to evacuate their women and children. It was a confused business. The general public thought that they had been ordered *officially* to evacuate, and few thought of arguing; ships were filled and sent off in a terrific hurry. But one consular official who didn't want his wife to go away pointed out that the order was not watertight. Until he was told in a legal way to separate himself from his family, he said stanchly, he would not do anything of the sort. His wife stayed, and other women followed her example. Not many, though.

Hong Kong filled up with people who had packed and hurried away, and the overflow went on to Manila. In the course of time we heard loud complaints from the evacuated ladies, of how badly they were being treated in the refugee camps. One woman who was the first to listen to the call of duty and rush aboard ship turned around and managed to be the first to come back.

It has been a long time, but I can hear in my memory even now the mixture of complaints and accusations that followed close on the beginning of all that Shanghai trouble. We Americans only grumbled a bit about our diplomats neglecting our interests; it was the usual thing and we didn't take ourselves seriously. Our most severe punishment was that the banks moved away from the middle of town for a while, way out in Frenchtown, and it was a nuisance getting there. When the scare died down they came back.

But the British! They had, as usual, the best quarters in town for their consular staff. The British are that way; they take care of their officials and they are farseeing about such things as buildings and other external appearances in foreign countries. In Shanghai they had held onto the best site they could possibly have owned, a large tract of land fronting the Bund down at Soochow Creek, and running back a whole long block. There were houses there for the staff beside the large buildings that constituted the consulate. On the day the excitement started they all dropped their work on their respective desks, grabbed their families and their belongings, and rushed for safety. It was later alleged that they made no effort to save the government records, to do anything about the flag, even to lock the buildings or to put a guard on the grounds—they just ran. In excuse they said that they had been stampeded by their air attaché, who warned them of horrible happenings if Chinese bombs aimed at the flagship *Idzumo* should fall wide of the mark. In vain did they make excuses, for the Shanghai public enjoyed a chance to poke fun at them and the matter was a highly humorous scandal for some days. All was forgiven and forgotten in time, however, and the officials went back to work on the Bund and behaved as though nothing whatever had happened to disturb their dignity, though there was perhaps a touch of added severity in their deportment for a small while.

Personally, I was glad to give over teasing them. The English took much more of a helpful line with all of us than the Americans did. They tried to deal with the Japanese, to enforce some recognition of our rights south of the creek, whereas the Americans adopted a sort of wait-and-watch policy that was expensive after a time. It was at the British consulate that I found out they were organizing rescue fleets of trucks to go into Yangtzepoo and salvage foreigners' belongings: the Americans did nothing in this line. It was the British who finally arranged permission, through the municipal police, for people to visit their homes, under escort if necessary. I tried twice to get in to look at Sinmay's house, claiming that it was my dwelling place too. This was practically true, anyway. I saw the house and was able to report to Zoa and Sinmay that a lot of their heavy furniture was still there.

Before we could do any important salvaging, though, I had to go through several formalities. Sinmay's printing press would be confiscated by the Japs if he, a Chinese and an enemy, were known as the owner, so we drew up an agreement whereby I became the purchaser of that press as of a year or so in advance of the war. The deputy commissioner of police, Malcolm Smythe, helped me a lot. He sent a policeman down with me once or twice while I carried out loads of Sinmay's household goods; sadly battered and looted they were, too. It was my first view of the after effects of war and I was nauseated at the wicked cruel waste of it—the slashed family photographs, the smashed toys, the bureau drawers chopped to bits in disappointment. All the houses that I saw were the same. The Japs controlled the process of salvage thus: a guard on Garden Bridge inspected my permit and gave me a Japanese marine to come along and keep an eye on me. I was not allowed to bring in any Chinese coolies to help with the loading, but Russian workmen, being whites, were permitted to pass with me. I hired a truck and ten workmen, and all day we loaded furniture and carted it out, past the bridge, and came back for more. The ticklish part of it was that bridge, because the guards there were often nasty and temperamental. The affair went smoothly enough, just the same, until the all-important day when I loaded up with Sinmay's books. These had been saved by not being in his house. They were stacked up in a warehouse near by, and nobody had burst in, by good luck. There was an old Chinese watchman still in control and he made difficulties for us, even standing up to the English policeman who came with me. He wanted a good squeeze, but we beat him down at last and he let us empty the room.

Sinmay had a valuable library. Most of it was Ming, but some was even older. It was the one day that I hadn't been nervous of bringing the trucks out: what ordinary sentry, I had asked myself, would care about old books? By bad luck, though, the sentry that day was not ordinary. He was a man of education, and he liked the library as soon as he saw it. He promptly stopped us and said that he would confiscate the load until he could be sure that it contained no Communist literature.

For three anxious hours I hung about on the wrong side of the bridge waiting for matters to be straightened out. A nasty little fat man with an admiral's hat—at least that's what it looked like—shook my arm and said over and over, "You go back. No cross bridge. Go back Yangtze-poo." I phoned the invaluable Malcolm and he sent the police interpreter, and everybody talked at once, and in the end they gave in to the claim that I was a Chinese scholar, and let me go. It was a bitter cold day but I sweated a lot. I felt very much like a heroine when I came home at last to the anxiously waiting Zaus. They had been sitting in front of my fire, but they ran out into the street as we rolled up triumphantly, and there was a little dance of rejoicing, and afterward Chin Lien brought me a dish of his own famous meringues, of which there were never quite enough. Today I had enough and more. We spent happy hours in the following weeks, sunning the books and looking them over for silver fish, the tropical insect that is the scourge of libraries.

The fighting crept around the edge of the town and now it was getting close, too close, to Yuyuen Road. There came a day when I admitted that it was too close. A plane swept over the house so low that it almost hit the chimney, and soon after it dropped bombs in the area near Jessfield Park and knocked over some neighboring cottages. In a great hurry I went out and found another house in the French Concession a few miles away, on Avenue Joffre. It was an ancient little bungalow which had been evacuated by a family of women now in Hong Kong, according to the landlord. He was a shambling, stuttering young man who did not seem to know or care much about the house, but he said I could live there as long as I liked, and that if I found it too cold, even with fireplaces, he would help me buy a cheap coal stove.

I hurried back to Yuyuen Road, all among the whistles and crashes of small shells, and loaded the car with the books of my erstwhile landlord. The rest of the furniture, they had said, didn't matter; the books did. All afternoon I traveled back and forth doing my duty, saving those damned books.

(A year later I had a tearful letter from the landlord. He said that one of the books had disappeared, and although he and his wife had looked carefully through all their things, they could not find it. How, he asked reproachfully, could I have been so careless?)

By the time all the rest of the neighborhood had moved out I was about ready to start taking care of my own possessions. It lasted the better part of next morning, but by noon I had settled all over again into the bungalow in Avenue Joffre. Soon afterward the Zaus pulled themselves together and resolved to find a bigger place for their family.

After having moved three times they found another empty cottage in the same group of houses that I had moved into, and there they settled, and there, I believe, they still are.

We did a lot of rushing around during those weeks, driven by nervous energy. There was a long time, as it seems now, when we were certain that the war would spread into the foreign town and create another international incident. The Volunteers stayed in their barracks on the racecourse; business did not resume its normal swing; the newspapermen caught up with us. One by one and two by two they came, all the way from America and England and Australia. They moved between Nanking and Shanghai, where they spent their evenings in the Tower, a small night club on top of the Cathay Hotel, and there too we went, as often as we could, to drink and to watch the war. People liked the Tower as well as any place in town for the view it afforded of dogfights and general shooting and excitement.

I saw for the first time during those evenings a lot of people who came back again and again, later, throughout the whole dreary pageant of the China Incident. There were Knickerbocker, and Art Menken, and the English fellow who was killed one day by a stray bullet, during a battle, and Luigi Barzini, the Italian-American who turned out in the end to be Italian rather than American. There were Colin MacDonald and many others who were sunk in the *Panay* up near Nanking—Barzini was one of those. Knickerbocker introduced me to Stinnes, the German general who was advising Chiang's army and who was supposed to be an ancient and inveterate enemy of Hitler's. It was Knickerbocker, too, who phoned me in the new cottage one morning to announce that the last Chinese resistance had broken down.

"They're almost up to Nanking now," he shouted excitedly, "and if they always make as good time as this they'll be in Tibet before Christmas."

"You're all vultures," I said. "This means you'll all be leaving town; that's one good thing."

I hung up so viciously that the receiver almost cracked. Sinmay probably knew already, I reflected. Well, it would mean normality again, more or less. Only there would be no more trips into the country. We were surrounded. It couldn't go on forever like this. Someday the Chinese would drive them out again, surely? Surely!

Chapter 9

ONE OF MY LETTERS sums up the state of affairs pretty well. It is dated August 24:

They say the mail is going out. I can scarcely believe it, and won't until I begin to get letters again, but I can't send air mail too often or I will go broke, and anyway I can just write scrawls in the time we get; nobody knows until the last minute, usually, just when the people who evacuate can get on the boats.

Not nearly so many people are trying to go now. Elaine Coutts and her sister keep canceling their passages just as promptly as their menfolks engage them, and I can't blame them. Why on earth must women be bundled out of town, down to an overcrowded city like Hong Kong, where cholera is raging and one fourth of a room is fifteen dollars a day? . . . I don't know what the papers have been doing; worrying you to death, probably. I am so terribly sorry about that; I can only imagine how worried you were. . . . Americans aren't allowed off at Hong Kong, which is too crowded; they must go on to Manila. The ships . . . are *charging big sums* to evacuate! I never heard of such a thing, did you? The Germans are taking their refugees out free, at least. . . .

I was dining last night with a Chinese who met me at the door—and said, "So sorry the other guests will not be here. They were all badly wounded in Nanking Road. Henry Wei is especially bad. Well, come along and have dinner, it's a good one."

From the Park Hotel I saw the different parts of the native city burning. It was beautiful and horrible, with planes swooping around, adding to it. The streets are always thronged with Chinese carrying their children, gathering in crowds—you can't teach them not to—and peering into the sky. Now that I am in Avenue Joffre I don't have planes overhead any more. It was constant before, and was getting on my nerves. But though I am careful and don't take risks—the curfew makes everyone be home before ten o'clock at night—the most peculiar thing is that I have not been afraid as yet. Dick Smith says it is because I haven't seen a real bombing, and pieces of body all around. I am sometimes nervous, but not very. I am, however, very, very angry all the time, and sick at heart. . . . I cannot be interested much in who is winning. Nobody wins a war. . . . Customs College is full of refugees and my students have most of them gone, but Loy hopes to open sometime soon. Nobody can tell if the war will stay here or what.

We did open Customs College, quite soon. The war had not yet moved off from Soochow Creek and we were near the scene of operations: many times I had to stop lecturing until the reverberations of a bomb had ceased, because the students couldn't hear me. They didn't lead interesting lives for some weeks, poor boys. Because they wore the school uniform it was decided that they had better not go outdoors at all, and they were virtually locked up all that time. A Chinese building is spacious enough, with courtyards for taking the air, so it wasn't unhealthy, but they waited eagerly for teachers from outside such as myself to bring them the daily papers.

Loy Chang took his job of president very seriously, as seriously as he did the rest of his Customs work. Often he dropped in and talked over problems of teaching and curriculum. One day I mentioned idly that I was still in touch with some of the Japanese. "I don't know how to cut off the acquaintanceship," I complained. "I don't dislike Matsumoto. In fact I like him very much. He's lived so long in China that I think he is sincerely against this war. But I've met another one who calls himself 'Tiger' from some Rotary party—Tiger Kanai. He's a nasty piece of work, and he's been asking me to give him English lessons. I know that isn't what he really wants. He's trying to do a little spying on the foreign community. His English is all right."

"But you should do it," said Loy. "Do it, by all means. You might learn something from him, do you see? Yes, give him English lessons, and then tell me what he is saying."

"Oh, in that case . . . It might be fun."

Thereafter for some time I saw Mr. Tiger Kanai three times a week at the hotel where he lived. He never told me anything particularly interesting in itself, but he was my first good specimen of the unofficial ambassador. I listened for minutes on end to his fluent if ungrammatical exposition of Japan's *true* aims. She was waging this war, he assured me, with a breaking heart. And anyway it was all for China's good. And anyway it wasn't really war. Nobody had declared it as war. The Chinese didn't understand Japan, that was the whole trouble; soon they would, and then we would all be happy again.

The Matsumoto friendship was another matter entirely, and was built upon a melodramatic incident. I was at Sinmay's house one night when a few overheated young newspapermen had a meeting there. Sinmay and I often agreed that the Shanghai Chinese were far from perfect, and chief among their imperfections was a taste for indirect battle rather than the open, fair kind. They went in for assassination whenever they could, but very few of them volunteered for the more dangerous life of the Army. We heard countless stories of "guerrilla" activity on the outskirts of town, where small bands of Chinese bullies set themselves up to investigate lone travelers at night. If the man proved himself a "loyal" Chinese he was allowed to proceed; if, however, he was a "traitor" they robbed him.

"It's not good enough," I said. "They're just little cowards using the war as an excuse."

"Yes," said Sinmay, "I hate all that loose talking."

We heard a lot of it that night from the newspaper boys. They drank a little yellow wine and decided to "execute" the traitor Matsumoto. I stayed long enough to hear them make some rather fuzzy plans, and then I went home and phoned Shigei.

"Are you still living out near Kiangwan?" I asked him.

"Yes, though I spend most of my time at the Domei office."

"Well, I oughtn't be doing this, but I don't approve of assassinations. . . . There's probably nothing to it, but if I were you I wouldn't go home alone after dark."

"I see," said Shigei. "It is only natural, I suppose. Though I have lived here twelve years and thought I had no enemies. Thank you, Mickey."

And so, though I was now beginning to hate Japan with all the emotions I usually deplore, generalizing about race and working myself up to a strong desire for vengeance, I continued to see Matsumoto. We had a lot of conversation in those days when Shanghai was surrounded and besieged. I dined with him often, at least once every fortnight. I dined with him unwillingly, though, when the news reached Shanghai about Nanking. It was not because I had forgotten that Matsumoto was Japanese that I had managed to get along with him. I had liked his being Japanese. He was my last chance, I felt, to discover what was going on in the minds of these people before I closed and locked the door against them. I don't like finalities, and I still felt in those long-gone days that there could be a way out of war, if only people would be wise, if only they would try. That night after the sack of Nanking I lost my hopes. I suppose Shigei was the only Japanese in town who wouldn't have lied to me that night.

"It's all true, what they're saying about the soldiers and the way they behave?" I demanded.

Shigei nodded slowly. "It's all true," he said.

"But why? How can you account for it? The Japanese I met weren't like that, surely? What has happened to your country, Shigei?"

"It is the Army," said Shigei. "You can't know what they are like. You didn't meet those poor peasants who have been brutalized after years in the Army. They are permitted to do this. It is worse than that; they are encouraged. It is their reward for taking a town; the officers promise them three days to do as they like, when a town is captured. They always do. . . . It is because Nanking is so important that you Americans hear about it this time, but it has always been true." He walked up and down his living room, much agitated. "It is a universal shame," he said. "I will tell you something. When I was younger, to avoid serving my military term I made myself ill. I starved for a year, so that I would be too ill to be accepted for military service. I succeeded: they put me into the seventh class, which is very poor. But now there is no escape for a pacifist. I cannot fight the nation alone. Nanking is a *fait accompli*. It is our destiny to be here, in China, for some years at least. We will have power. We will have hatred, too, from China and the other nations, but we will have power. Do not doubt that."

"And you are proud of it," I said accusingly. "I can see, you're proud."

"It is possible," admitted Shigei. "I am human."

It was Sinmay who first heard that I was suspected by the government of China, at least by some of the officials. I believe they actually put a "tail" on me, and discovered that the rumors were true, and that I was, indeed, in the habit of calling on a Japanese named Kanai three times a week. Anyway I was fed up with the Tiger, and he never said anything interesting once he had gone through his repertoire; after that it was all repetition. I gave him up without regret, but I did not give up Matsumoto. After about six months of rapidly increasing "power" in his office, during which all the other Japanese residents, too, gained in political weight, Matsumoto fell ill. He phoned one day to say that he was really not feeling well at all, and when I heard of him again he was struggling for his life against a bad case of typhoid. He recovered somewhat; his wife came and took him back to Japan, and he went on long sick leave. I didn't see any more Japanese socially. Ake tried to make a success of one of his mixed parties, during Christmas; he invited Sinmay and me to dinner and among the guests were the Horiguchis. Sinmay talked politely enough with Yoshinori, but before we had finished the first bowl of Swedish punch he decided to go home, and I didn't blame him.

One day I stopped at the Shanghai Pet Store and looked in the window. Mr. Mills, in a large cage with a little tree in it, looked out at me. He didn't get a good view from the branch on which he squatted, so he climbed down to the floor and put his head to one side and looked at me again. His face was black; his fur was beige. He turned a somersault.

I ran into the shop. "What is that in the window?" I demanded.

The shopkeeper, a Filipino, smiled lovingly. "A gibbon from Singapore," he said. "I show you."

Mr. Mills went running around the room, pausing now and then to look at me from odd angles. When I grabbed at him he bit me gently.

"Hold him by the hand, not the body," advised the Filipino.

In the course of the next ten minutes before I bought him I learned something about him. He was quite young, not a baby, but about the same stage as a three-year-old child. He didn't like cold weather. He ate fruit and cake and insects, and especially worms of the kind the Chinese use to feed their birds. I could bathe him if I insisted; he didn't mind very much.

Mr. Mills bit me a couple more times and then I bought him, paying one hundred and seventy Shanghai dollars, which was only about one third the usual market price on gibbons. The war was forcing the Filipino to close out his shop. I bought the cage too, and went home in a state of hysterical happiness. I have always been fond of apes and monkeys, but I had throttled my natural affections since coming to China. The average commonplace monkey in those parts is the Singapore rhesus, not a particularly easy animal to manage in the house. This gibbon was something quite special.

I must have been a pathetic picture of a spinsterish woman at this time. I used to laugh at the picture of those two sisters in *The Old Wives' Tale* and their troubles over the poodle and the other dog, and now, I realized uncomfortably, I was contributing to a picture not unlike that one. I couldn't help it, though; being self-conscious about such things doesn't cure them. My letters home, which I have here at my elbow, were packed with stories of Mr. Mills and his cleverness. I would have groaned at such a letter from any proud mamma among my relatives, but I just couldn't help it.

"It's old age," I said in a worried way to Sinmay. "I've made this sort of life for myself and I shouldn't complain about it, I suppose. I must make up my mind to it. I'll get old and fat out here, with my comfortable little cottage, and people will call on me, I hope, on Sunday afternoons."

"Oh, you are morbid," said Sinmay. "It is not like that at all. You are part of my family and will never be alone. I tell you what we can do: you must marry me and then it will be really all right."

"Marry you?" Nothing Sinmay said had surprised me for more than two years, so I was not surprised. But I was puzzled. "Now how would you work that?" I asked. "You're married already. Zoa wouldn't like it a bit."

"Yes, she would. We have been talking about it. No, do not laugh; we have been quite serious. It is about the press. You are claiming that it is yours, but perhaps the Japanese won't accept our word for that. So Zoa herself has made this suggestion, because you have said the other evening that you will never marry. Of course if you were to want to marry we could not do it. Zoa and I, according to the foreign law, have never married. It is often that way in careless old families like mine. Now suppose you were to declare yourself as my wife; the printing-press matter is settled, and all the work you have done for us, protecting us, becomes more permanent. In return for this help you have a family. You have us already, of course, but in this way it becomes true in the eyes of our friends, which would be nicer, wouldn't it? One of our children, any one you like (except my son as I have only him) will be yours, legally. We give her to you. I suggest Siao Pau, but it is for you to choose. The others will be yours and Zoa's together. Anyway they already call you 'Foreign Mother.' And when you are dead you will be buried in our family graveyard at Yuyao. And when you are old you will come to live in our house, as I am always asking you to do now only you do not like it, I don't know why. I think it a good idea."

Sinmay's ideas were so many and so fantastic that I didn't take it too seriously at first. Later, however, I decided it was not so fantastic. In the end I actually did sign a paper in his lawyer's office, declaring that I considered myself his wife "according to Chinese law," and Zoa presented me with a pair of mutton-fat jade bracelets, in accord with one of the many customs of China. It was half a joke; none of us took it seriously. The paper was put away to be used if the Japanese demanded proof that I really owned the press, and I forgot about it for some years. But in one way Sinmay had been right: the thought of that grave in Yuyao comforted me, for some absurd reason. I ceased to worry about my old age.

Chapter 10

THE FOREIGNERS of Shanghai, after having made sure that the war had indeed moved westward, began to creep out of their fox holes and adjust themselves. Those who had lived long enough in China to remember some of her many civil wars decided at last that it was no more than one of those. We saw the signs of increasing damage every day, in the slow death of all native business enterprise chiefly. Then, too, many of our Chinese friends crept away, but the foreigners didn't notice that so much. The brokers did, but they tried to be hopeful, meantime keeping a sharp eye on the Shanghai dollar, which slipped and slipped and slipped.

The "comprador class," Sinmay's scorned acquaintances, moved down to Hong Kong where they could go on living like bright young things in safety. They didn't like Hong Kong very much; the band at the Hongkong Hotel wasn't really hot and the old-fashioned Cantonese didn't encourage them to enjoy themselves in a European fashion. Young men about town were limited to the older-style dissipations of West Point, and the young Chinese women of Shanghai found that they were expected to act demure and sober in Hong Kong. Nobody English thought of inviting Chinese people to informal parties. Not that they wanted to go, especially, but Shanghai was certainly friendlier.

The T'ien Hsia crowd had happier experiences. They departed from Shanghai in a tremendous hurry and a blue funk, soon after the fireworks started. Wen Yuan-ning was positive that his name was first on the Black List. That Black List needs some mention before I go any further: I was to hear about it all over China and Hong Kong whenever there was trouble in the offing. I still believe it is a figment of the lively Chinese imagination, and by this time I ought to know, but you will never convince the Chinese. They still believe in it. Well then; the Black List is supposedly made up by the Japanese Secret Service of the names of all the people most inimical to the Japanese conquest of Pan-Asia. One would suppose that such enemies of the Rising Sun would be led by generals, admirals, and other warlike experts, but according to literati like Wen, or certain brokers I have met, or even prominent hotelkeepers, the Japanese hate *them* first of all, individually and fiercely. Wen was certain that in the Japanese estimation he himself was Public Enemy Number One. I still doubt it, and as I have said before, I ought to know. . . . But I will never convince Wen. I used to try to, and oddly enough, instead of being reassured he was insulted.

Seriously, absurd as it may seem to an outsider, these claims were not the only preposterous ones I have heard made, and Chinese are not the only proud people who have made them. I've known many Englishmen and Americans to indulge in the same fantasies. One of the worst of this kidney was W. H. Donald. He was always sure that he was being followed, listened in on, set upon by bribed domestics, and otherwise harried. I don't deny for a moment that the Japanse did spy on Mr. Donald and on the hotelkeepers as well, and the brokers and Wen Yuan-ning and everybody else, even me, but I do deny that any one of us was as closely watched as he thought he was . . . or as important an enemy to the Japanese genius. I still think that the Japs would rather capture Chiang Kai-shek, for example, than any of us. I'll have a lot more to say about this. A lot more of it happened. For the time being we are talking about the precipitate flight of *T'ien Hsia* from Shanghai.

Wen would not have been quite as badly frightened if it hadn't been for John Alexander of the British consulate. John has a talent for sniffing out intrigue, I think, inherited from his Italian ancestors, and he thought he was on the trail of a really dangerous plot against Wen and the magazine. Now I don't think, really, that the Japs cared whether *T'ien Hsia* made its monthly appearance or not. Save for one editorial every month which repeated in a stately literary fashion that Chungking was the berries and Japan was not, *T'ien Hsia* could not be called anything but a cultural publication, given to articles on oriental calligraphy, history, and books. That is what it set out to be and that is what it was. It was the happy hunting ground of such people as Dr. J. C. Ferguson, who is an authority on Chinese bronzes, and myself. Wen wrote a good article on *A Shropshire Lad* and his author and published it in *T'ien Hsia*. Sinmay published a poem in its pages, and I wrote reviews. Nevertheless, according to John, *T'ien Hsia* and its editors were in the gravest danger, and they believed him, and turned pale, and scrambled aboard the first south-going steamer to get out of it.

I heard an uproarious description of that journey from one of the typists. The editors were afraid of running short of money at first, because they hadn't been able to arrange for funds at the bank in their hurry, and besides, they thought it safer to disguise themselves as plain middle-class. So they took second-class tickets. Once aboard the lugger, however, Wen looked around and felt that his fastidious taste was being offended by the sordid surroundings, so he went to the purser and moved up to first class. Then Chuan Tsen-kuo said to Yeh Cho-yuan, "If he does it, why shouldn't we? After all, *T'ien Hsia* should maintain its prestige," and they too transferred to first class. It seemed too mean to leave the secretaries where they were, after that. Therefore the entire staff disembarked in Hong Kong like gentlemen.

They continued to behave in a manner befitting Chinese scholars. Wen, a graduate of Cambridge, felt all his Anglophilic tendencies coming back now that he was in one of the colonies of the Empire. Even in Hong Kong, he found, there were some young men among the British cadets and the government officials who admired China and Chinese culture. Wen met them all, went out to tea with them, talked literature rather than politics, and felt happy, happier than he had felt for years in Shanghai. The rest of the party acclimated themselves more slowly. They grumbled in letters to me about the high cost of living, but in the end they too decided to love the mountains and the beaches of the lovely island.

If I had known that *T'ien Hsia* was sending Charles to me with a letter of introduction I would probably have stopped resenting this flight. But of course I didn't know, and I resented it very much. I didn't think it had been necessary, and I missed them. I was lonesome, although Sinmay was still in Shanghai; I had liked the little office in Yuyuen Road. My comfortable world was broken up and I felt disappointed in Wen, and sore and angry.

Therefore I was short with John Alexander and Stella, his wife, one evening when I met them.

"We never seem to see Chinese friends any more," said Stella. "You probably know some interesting ones, Mickey. Will you introduce us?"

"You don't get any more Chinese from me," I retorted. "I'm not introducing you to any more. John would scare them away if I did."

Chapter 11

WE HAD gradually slipped into a state of affairs which would have seemed impossible a year before. We were living calmly, quietly, although we were completely surrounded by Japs. Up in Nanking were friends of mine in American and British diplomatic posts, people who had declared violently that they would immediately resign and go home if their careers entailed working among the Nips. Now they were to all intents and purposes stationed in the middle of Japan, and yet they were surviving.

We Chinese-conscious people in Shanghai grumbled, of course, about being cut off from China, though we still had many points of contact through Hong Kong, Ningpo, odd stations along the southern coast, and the guerrillas. Although with some delay, it was actually possible to correspond directly, through the Japanese-controlled post office, with Chungking after the government at last moved up there from Hankow. The Japs liked reading letters en route from the West so they let them come. I didn't do much of that at the time. I knew only a few newspapermen who had penetrated that deeply into China's west, and the Chinese who left Shanghai for the "interior" didn't write back.

The guerrillas were our chief topic of conversation during that period. Sinmay's brother Huan had joined a band of them which operated around Soochow. It was just the sort of thing he was good at; he hadn't found much to his taste in the life of Shanghai after he came back from Paris, but now he enjoyed himself thoroughly. Intrigue, exercise, authority—for Huan quickly became a general in the ragged regiment he joined—it was all better than the lazy, boring life to which he had been condemned by family exigency.

Before Huan joined the Army he had become involved in a silly romance with a maidservant in his father's house. It was the sort of thing that always happened to the Zaus when they were bored. It was complicated. A little penniless cousin in the house was in love with him and couldn't see any way of getting him, first because the family wouldn't consider such a disadvantageous marriage for the boy and second because Huan didn't care for her. She was a pathetic child, fifteen years old, badly treated by her stepmother and probably ill balanced. Huan was sorry for her and he tried to protect her from her stepmother's beatings, but when he began to discover her huddled on his bed of an evening when he wanted to turn in, he knew something would have to be done to stop it. He stayed away from home for a few days, down at Sinmay's, and the girl promptly took poison. They had to call in a doctor and use a stomach pump.

This was serious. Father bestirred himself, which he seldom did, and a reform was instituted. The little cousin went down to the country, to another household. Huan came home and found himself the seducer of a small maidservant of the house. He was so tired of it all that he immediately went out and married her. The wicked stepmother was pleased about this, because Father was angry and cast his erring son out of his house, and Huan, as next in line to Sinmay (who had been adopted out of the family by a rich childless uncle according to Chinese custom), was the heir apparent. Huan didn't care much. There wouldn't be much estate left to be done out of, anyway. He set up housekeeping in a dreary little bed-sitting-room with the maidservant wife, and when he had the chance to join up he grabbed at it: being a guerrilla chief was much more fun than that. His wife went back to his father's house and, it must be admitted, held her own against the stepmother as Huan's timid little cousin would never have been able to do. Such family quarrels usually blow over sooner or later, in China. In another few years it would be forgiven the girl that she had been a servant.

Officially Huan was out in the country from now on and should not have dared set foot within the city limits because there was a price on his head. In actuality he dropped in on the town fairly often, both for business and pleasure. He bought arms in Shanghai and took them up-river with him. Palms were greased all the way along, Chinese and Japanese palms both. It went smoothly as possible. Huan made the most of these visits, going to dancehalls and eating a lot and doing himself well. He even called on his wife once in a while, but she was having a baby and didn't go out with him much. One effect of his new career was that I was drawn into the middle of the crazy picture. Huan introduced Sinmay to many of his colleagues who lived in the little towns along the Soochow Road, and they decided to use my house for their purposes.

Sinmay's family now lived near me in another one of the cottages that occupied a compound on Avenue Joffre near the city limits. His own house couldn't be used for their idea because he was a Chinese tenant. Foreigners were neutrals, which was an enormous advantage. So they set up their radio station in the back bedroom of my second floor, confident of safety from police raids. It was a transmitter, the first I had ever seen close to, and although I never did learn what exactly it was used for, I knew it was in direct communication with Chungking. This, however, didn't necessarily mean the government. When we hear about Chinese guerrillas in America we are apt to think of them as one body, but we are wrong. There are many guerrillas and many leaders, and many ideologies behind the different bands. They have this in common, that each band accuses all the others of being mere bandits, but that is all they agree on. Huan's group was quarreling vigorously with another party that disputed his right to police the countryside near Shanghai. There was so much trouble over this petty argument that Sinmay reverted to his prewar philosophy and tried to wash his hands of the dirty politics he had stumbled into. He couldn't resist the game for long, though. It was all too exciting. So he maintained a watchful sovereignty over my back bedroom and the transmitter there.

The people who took care of the transmitter and who knew how to operate it were two young men and a girl. They all wore the blue dress of the farmer or laborer, which made them rather conspicuous going in and out of the house in Avenue Joffre; for this reason they didn't go out very much, but slept in the room and sent to restaurants for noodles whenever they felt hungry. It seems odd even to me that I should have permitted the transmitter to be operated like that, knowing nothing about it. I even had to take their word for it that they were in communication with Chungking. But I didn't want to seem intrusive, and I trusted Sinmay's politics, whatever I thought of his business acumen.

The thing was embarrassing, though. It made a noise, and sometimes people noticed it. One afternoon Malcolm Smythe, the police deputy commissioner, dropped in unexpectedly and had a drink downstairs. Suddenly he looked around curiously, his nose twitching. "Is your radio on?" he demanded. "I have the strangest feeling that somebody's broadcasting on a short wave or something. There it is again. Do you hear it?"

Yes, I did, all too plainly. Gaaak, gak, gakgakgak, gaaaaak. . . . I turned on the radio to drown it out and went upstairs as soon as I could to give them warning.

"Funny thing about these radios," Malcolm continued when I came downstairs again. "The Japs swear that we're harboring transmitters in the Settlement, you know, and in the French Concession too. I wouldn't be at all surprised, but how can we catch them at it? The Japs are trying to find them out by some triangulation process, but it can't find a transmitter accurately; the best they can do is locate it within a block's area. And of course in Shanghai a block holds a thousand people, easily. You can't arrest that number of Chinese just for investigation. I suppose the Japs would if they had their way, but we won't kick up all that hell for anyone, let alone Hirohito."

He seemed gloomy that day and out of sorts, and I wasn't surprised. The Shanghai police had a hell of a job those last few years.

Malcolm's visits and my report on the Japanese complaints frightened my new tenants. They lost their confidence in my immunity, and after a month or two they packed up their transmitter and went somewhere else. They told me that they did this every so often so that the Japs couldn't catch up on them. So they disappeared, the three young people in blue, and left the back bedroom to what was to be a long procession of roomers.

The first tenant after the departure of the transmitter club was Jean. I have written a whole book about Jean which a publisher is holding even now, waiting, he says, for the end of the war, "when people will be willing to face realities." This sounds very grim, which Jean herself was not, but I suppose her life could be described by that adjective. At least it was grim in spots. I had met her before. There was a man in town, a wealthy broker, who was eccentric and who loved Jean very much in his eccentric way. He called on me abruptly one day long before the war and said that he wanted to introduce me to a young woman who was stranded in the city without friends. "She has picked up a few men acquaintances around town—you know how it is," he said, "but she doesn't know any girls. If you could introduce her . . ."

Obligingly I had a tea party and invited Jean, sight unseen, to meet a couple of girls. It was not a success. Jean was extraordinarily pretty and she looked just like the others in the way she dressed, but there was a something in her manner that made me look at her twice. She wasn't at all easy in her mind. She kept moving around in her chair, and her accent was false and strained. And she seemed sulky, too; when the broker called to get her and asked her heartily how she had enjoyed the tea party, she seemed definitely sulky.

The broker, whom she called Deedee, took us both out to dinner, to a Japanese house. (This, I should explain, was in 1936.) The woman who served the dinner in her house was a well-known character among people who went in for Japanese massage; she was called "Buffalo San" even in the Shanghai telephone directory. She was an enormously fat creature and she took liberties with Deedee, and seemed to know Jean pretty well too. What surprised me more than anything about the evening, which ended with Buffalo San's giving us a massage all round, was that Jean spoke fluent Japanese. In fact, though I didn't know much about it, her Japanese sounded like a specially elegant kind. It was certainly complicated and prettier to hear than Buffalo's. But Deedee had told me that Jean came from South Africa and had been in the East a very short time. The whole thing was odd.

I saw her next during the hostilities, after the early curfew was lifted. She was dancing one evening at Farren's, with one of the visiting journalists, and she looked at me from under the brim of her excellently tailored hat as if she were not at all sure I would recognize her. I did, though.

Suddenly, soon after the transmitter left my bed and board, I heard of her again. Deedee phoned to tell me that poor little Jean had tried to commit suicide. "Things were just too much for her," he said sorrowfully. "They often are. It's living alone that does it; she begins to imagine that people are talking about her. I wonder if she could come and talk to you? It might cheer her up."

I still don't quite know why Deedee depended on me for this delicate job. He didn't know me well at all. Of course he was eccentric, and I am a writer, and people always assume that writers are easier than other people to approach for peculiar jobs. Or there may be another, more personal reason. I can put it in several ways. I could say, for example, that I am a sympathetic and receptive person and so people rush to me for help and advice, but this is not really true. I am not sympathetic: I am detached and hard, compared to most professional listeners. But I am receptive. I am a gossip, a good one. I like people and their activities. Therefore the persons who meet me, unless they are unusually reserved and resentful of prying, feel that there will be some reaction to their individual acts, the act each of us puts on for the external world. Tacitly I pledge myself to listen and watch. I give promise of being a good audience, and so—I get dragged into things. I could add to this summary, but Somerset Maugham said it all before me much better than I could. He pointed out that many troublesome people hope, secretly and shamedly, that they will be "put into books," and they hang around writers with the same half-terrified anticipation that women feel with psychoanalysts. Their egos are titillated. But this doesn't prevent them howling loudly when they think they have inspired something in print, in fiction. I said before that I like people, but I don't like that sort very much. If they have any chances at all of identifying themselves with a character in a story they keep a marked copy of the offending fiction to show their friends, they advertise it everywhere, and they talk wildly of outraged hospitality, libel suits, and plagiarism. Any writer knows what I mean, and anyone who isn't a writer can find out, not from me but from the Old Maestro, Maugham.

Am I claiming, you ask, never to use living people as models in my writing? Oh no. I use people. I use myself, which means that I use everything I find in my brain—experiences, impressions, memories, reading matter by other writers—everything, including the people who surround me and impinge on my awareness. Sometimes I am asked, "Do you think it's nice of you?" and I reply honestly, "I don't know. It isn't a question in my mind of being nice or not nice. I can't help it any more than I can help breathing. I am not apologizing or defending myself: there it is. I do it and I will always do it as long as I write, and it's no use trying to bring in the ethical aspects of writing. People who mind should stay away from writers. I think that they do, on the whole. People who don't mind but say they do will go on talking to me, and they are happy, so I don't worry about them."

I see that I am only recapitulating Maugham's statements; I can't help it, I suppose. It lies too near my heart to be dismissed lightly. Let me go on repeating him for a moment, then. I do not use people photographically or phonographically, setting down fact by fact what I see happen to them or what I hear them say. If I were to do this I would be inexcusable indeed: I would be dull, and a bad writer. I can't even tell a story as it happened even when I'm trying to. Unconsciously I add a bit of emphasis there, and cut out an obtrusive, unimportant detail here, and round the thing out until it is a well-turned anecdote instead of a true story. This makes people angry, and they call me a liar. I suppose you could call it that. But I just can't help it.

Jean was a liar too, but she was a different sort, much less common.

She just loved lying for its own sake. She probably lied to me the day she came to tell me her sad story, but perhaps not. You never knew with Jean when the mood would take her to spin tales. The tale she recounted that afternoon over the coffee cups was a simple and pathetic little one, and I think it was true.

For many reasons which are easily understood, Jean was afraid of most women. The prostitutes she knew didn't frighten her, but they weren't good friends. They were too much out for themselves. Also Deedee didn't like her knowing them; he was afraid they would try to keep her from going straight and he was probably right, because, said Jean, there weren't enough girls in the business now, the war kept new ones from coming to China, and a lot of madames were eager to persuade her to work for them. Deedee wanted Jean to keep away from that crowd. She didn't, as he pointed out, need the money any more; he was looking after her. It was time that Jean made other friends, from a different social circle. Deedee wanted her to be a good girl, and happy.

I think he had philanthropic hopes of doing the right thing by Jean, but by proxy. He couldn't marry her himself. His family had made that very clear, and he could see for himself that it wouldn't work out, not in a small place like Shanghai, his own home town. But he did love her quite unselfishly, and he wondered sometimes, and asked me in his inarticulate way, if it wouldn't be possible to educate his little Jean and fix her up until someone else married her. What did I think?

I thought that anything was possible in Shanghai, especially a marriage like that. It had happened before, often. From Jean's rambling stories it seemed that the biggest obstacle to the plan was herself. She was hopelessly sentimental, always falling in love with men who couldn't or wouldn't marry her, and when there were no men around for Jean to ruin herself for she fell in love with women. She had just made a mess of her affairs for the hundredth time by doing both. First she had indulged herself in an unhappiness over the newspaperman with whom I had seen her dancing.

"He asked me to help him get ready to go away," she recounted. "There I was with my heart breaking because I never would see him again. And because he said I ought to, I started to study at business college, and I was having an awful time with that terrible shorthand, and he kept telling me how much better a life it would be than I had before, working as somebody's secretary and finally marrying a clerk if I was very good. . . . And there he was, spending hundreds of dollars on rotten old curios to take home with him, all the while he was talking. So I went home and took poison. I often do. Veronal."

The newspaperman was flattered that such a beautiful girl had tried to kill herself for love of him. (Did I say that Jean was one of the most beautiful women I have ever seen?) He was so pleased, in fact, that after she had recovered a little he was very devoted, putting off his departure and bringing friends up to look at her, picturesque in the hospital. He paid the hospital bills, too: Deedee thought he should. He was so devoted that she stopped loving him. Jean was a consistent masochist.

Recovered in mind and body, she ventured out again and fell in love with a woman. This woman was not a prostitute but neither was she a member of the protected upper classes so desired by Deedee as a background for his protégée. We will call her Selma. Selma was one of those Russians you hear about in Shanghai: her morals were complicated by the fact that her desires were many and unconcentrated. She loved love. She was also ambitious socially. She had never ruined her social chances, such as they were—a Russian used to find it hard sledding in Shanghai at the best—but if you had wanted to you could have found out all sorts of things about her which wouldn't sound well in a drawing room. Jean, fascinated by Selma, yet found satisfaction in this fact. She was jealous. Selma was invited out on parties which didn't include Jean; she rubbed them in whenever she had a chance. Selma boasted of her successes (and lied about them) until it seemed to Jean that there was no justice in this world. Yes, she had been a bad girl and so it was only to be expected that people wouldn't invite her to parties. She accepted that. But Selma had been a bad girl too, in a flaunting and really extraordinary fashion; why, then, was she invited to parties? Jean brooded.

They really have minds like flibbertigibbets, these girls.

One afternoon the peak of misery was reached for Jean. She had given up the business school thankfully, but now she was left without much to do except wait for Deedee, never a very stimulating companion, or for Selma to come and play with her. Selma had promised to spend Saturday afternoon with her. Selma dropped in at the last minute wearing silver foxes (Jean had no silver foxes) and beaming with pride.

"I've just dropped in for a moment, my dear," she said. "I must fly. I've been invited to Sir Victor Sassoon's box at the races and I must *rush* —simply *rush*. Be a good girl and wait here for me, and I'll come and tell you all about it afterward. I did suggest to Sir Victor that he invite you, but—I don't want to hurt your feelings, dear, but the fact is, he didn't think it would be fair to his other guests. I mean, to introduce the ladies to a girl who—well, who used to be a prostitute. You understand, of course; I'm just terribly sorry. See you later."

She fluttered out, and I've often wondered where she was really going.

Jean sat and thought about it and thought about it, and then she took veronal again. "He called me a prostitute," she explained to the puzzled doctor who brought the stomach pump. I dare say he was not only puzzled but exasperated. Doctors in Shanghai have to use stomach pumps a lot.

Jean told me all about it, and you can guess what happened. She moved into the back bedroom.

But I liked having her there. Except when she had bitchy streaks and tried hard to fight with anyone in sight—it was usually Deedee—she was a charming companion, and we soon set to work on a book, the story of her life. This entailed long conversations about everyone in town who had ever visited her at Louise's, the high-priced house where she had spent two years of her professional life. Jean would come into my room in the morning after I came home from school; sitting on the bed in her dressing gown, she would tell me a story that she had thought of the night before. Sometimes it was true and sometimes it obviously wasn't, but it was always fun to listen to. I found out the most surprising things about a lot of acquaintances.

I think she enjoyed herself too. She wasn't lonely any more, and yet she was living in a milieu of which Deedee approved and which did not preclude the possibility of being married someday. People who came to my house to dinner found an exquisitely pretty girl there, a girl who sat in the corner with her hands folded and looked frightened. When she was drawn out and talked, she used that childish accent that had puzzled me so much when we first met, but after a while everyone was used to Jean and she was used to everyone. There were awkward moments, of course. I could always tell when they were coming. Jean hung over the banister of an evening, watching the guests arrive; sometimes she rushed into my bedroom to whisper hoarsely, "That man downstairs—I *know* him!" I would say, "Well, never mind. Come on down," and down we went, and I would duly note the start of surprise, the amazed expression on my guest's face as I introduced him. I liked it. So did Jean, sitting demurely in her corner.

She lasted almost a year. She was there the afternoon Charles called on me with his letter of introduction from *T'ien Hsia* in Hong Kong. He often told about that visit, later on. He had noticed my book reviews in the magazine, which occasionally published historical treatises of his.

"I like this woman's mind," he announced one day to Wen. "Who is she? Where does she live?"

"Oh, that's a very sad case," said Wen. "She's very nice, of course, but—well, as a matter of fact, she's madly in love with my friend Zau

Sinmay and he doesn't care for her at all. Really pathetic, don't you know."

Charles said that he would still like to meet me when he went to Shanghai, as he intended doing shortly, and Wen didn't like that. He was jealous of his real Englishman, now that he had come home after so many years in the Orient among Orientals. "She's terribly *American*," he objected tentatively.

It was Chuan Tsen-kuo who told Charles where to find me and gave him a card. Charles dropped in about tea time one day and handed the card over to Chin Lien, and was told to wait in the downstairs living room. I was upstairs with Jean and Sinmay.

"Blast," I said as Chin Lien gave the card to me. "Some silly British captain from Hong Kong. They've gone mad about limeys at the *T'ien Hsia* office. Let him wait."

Mr. Mills had heard the doorbell ring, and he now scrambled to the steps and pattered down to have a look. In the living room, Charles waited like a perfect gentleman.

"I heard someone on the steps, after a long time," he told me a few years afterward, "and I turned around—I'd been looking at your books —and held out my hand, saying, 'Oh, Miss Hahn?' And an enormous ape came down, wearing a red cap. It wasn't just what I was expecting. He swung around the curtains and stared at me until I was quite nervous, and then you came down looking rather blowzy—I'm sorry, Mickey, but you did; your dress was awful—and after that some blonde woman followed you up. Extraordinarily pretty she was. She sat in the corner and stared at me all the time I was speaking. It was nervous work."

I noticed that the captain looked rather frightened, but I was accustomed to that reaction to Mr. Mills. I didn't pay much attention. We had a drink. He told me that he liked my book reviews, which pleased me, and he said that he too was a writer. "In a way," he explained. "I write big historical books, very dull."

After a bit somebody else came to the front door, with another letter of introduction. It was a Russian-Czechoslovakian woman from India, who was interested in Indian dancing. She wanted to give a recital, she said, a dance recital, but she couldn't find Indians for an orchestra. Did I know how to help her out?

"There must be plenty of musicians among the Indian police," said Captain Boxer. "Why not phone the police commissioner and ask him to help you out?"

"That's a wonderful idea. I'll do it now," said the lady gratefully. "May I use the phone?"

Charles, who was joking, looked startled. As it happened his suggestion was a fortunate and fruitful one, and six months later Shanghai saw the dance recital. Just then, however, his expression showed that he considered the whole establishment crazy. When I had introduced him to Sinmay he stayed just long enough to be polite, and then, as the door opened to admit yet another caller, he fled.

"I had been given to understand," he told me when we were going over the history of the thing, "that you and Zau were actors in one of the great love stories of the world, so naturally I didn't wish to intrude. I was rather sorry about it at that, blowzy as you were."

"I remember," I confessed, "that just for a fleeting second that afternoon I too felt a certain regret. 'What a pity,' I thought, 'that I am involved in one of the world's great love stories.' . . . But it was very fleeting."

So Charles went back to Hong Kong and married an English girl.

Chapter 12

I FOUND OUT why Jean spoke such good Japanese. It is a crazy story and fortunately happens to be one of her true ones. She was born in Australia, and somehow or other when she was fifteen she was seen and coveted by the Japanese Prince Tokugawa. There are many Tokugawa descendants of the Shoguns who kept Japan under the family thumb back in the days when nobody was paying any attention to the Emperor. This one liked to travel in Europe.

Tokugawa was forty when he met Jean. I am not sure how it happened, because she is becomingly vague on the subject, but I think her mother or her guardian must have been delighted when he offered to take the girl off her hands. His daughter was Jean's age, and Jean's nominal job was that of companion to the little Princess. It was staggeringly romantic altogether. Jean, she assured me, was eager and happy to join the prince's household. She liked him. This is no sob story of betrayed maidenhood. I have always had the impression that Jean regretted the loss of Tokugawa.

Her life was merry and luxurious for a long time. The Prince had the sinecure of Minister without Portfolio and with his daughter and her companion he traveled around the world a couple of times. Jean learned how to behave at diplomatic receptions, and how to dress, and how to keep her mouth shut. At home there were scenes sometimes. Tokugawa was jealous and so was Jean. He was accustomed to jealous domestic scenes; almost any Japanese gentleman is. He liked them. Jean says that he once threatened to kill her with a knife; she woke up to find him standing over her with the weapon, then he flung it into the corner and wept loudly.

"I cannot do it," he wailed, "I cannot. You are too lovely."

Her eyes shone when she told me about it.

It all came to an end, though, when the household returned to Japan. The Prince's wife didn't like Jean at all, and Tokugawa didn't insist upon keeping her in the house. First she was farmed out to live in a geishaya, where she learned to dance geisha dances and to paint pretty pictures, and her Prince called on her there. But her noticeable blonde beauty attracted the unfavorable attention of the gendarmes, and she was sent out of the country without even saying good-by to the Prince. The gendarmes are like that—fiercely virtuous in fits and starts. They permitted her to take quite a lot of Tokugawa's money with her, however, and Jean gave most of it away to an Italian with whom she fell in love in Shanghai during the following month. Her sentimental and financial adventures in the ensuing years are too many to recount here, but they whiled away many a morning for both of us, in retrospect.

I hold no brief for Jean's politics, which are confused. The conquest by Japan of the territory around Shanghai excited and pleased her, and brought back vivid memories of happy old days, quarreling with her Prince. She was bright enough to realize that her own country and Japan would come to blows sooner or later, but she didn't worry unduly about that. Lingering on the roadside instead of hurrying to cross the bridge, she met Bob Horiguchi, the half-Japanese newspaperman who worked for Domei, and found him attractive.

This *affaire de cœur* started while Jean was living with me. (Bob's wife was away.) I didn't like it and I told her so. Her morals, while not exactly her own affair, were not mine. It wasn't that. I just didn't want Mr. Yoshinori Horiguchi in my house. Jean understood my point of view; we had no hard words over it, but she didn't want to give up Horiguchi. She thought of another plan. My house, she explained to Deedee, was too far away from town for her, now that she had once again decided to study at business college. Jean started learning shorthand on an average of four times a year, whenever some earnest young man had a good long talk with her and persuaded her to reform. Why it was necessary for Jean to be a secretary instead of some other kind of virtuous breadwinner in the busy treadmill of life I never understood. It must have had something to do with a movie she saw in one of her impressionable stages. Anyway, she was at it again, and Deedee let her move into a boardinghouse nearer town, where Horiguchi was free to take her out and to visit her at home.

There was another place where Jean might have met Japanese, now that so many were about, but I don't think she did. This was Louise's. Louise was one of the Shanghai characters that you don't hear so much about. The good old days for houses of prostitution were over by the time I reached Shanghai, and though the Kiangse Road district still had its famous addresses, the glory had departed from the business. A hundred years ago, when the British first settled a city on the Whangpoo mud flats, the foundation was laid for a brisk trade between San Francisco and the China Coast. I am not now talking about the kind of white-slave traffic that brings to mind South America and hypodermic needles: the "business girls" who came to Shanghai usually started secondhand from the Barbary Coast and came quite willingly, under their own steam. They were hard-boiled. Their names still live in Shanghai annals, and at least one or two of the girls themselves have married well and had settled down to happy old ages in the Orient until they were dislodged, like everyone else, by the war.

Some of the more righteous of our American statesmen out there, however, put a damper on the traffic a long time ago, and the old houses flourished no more, or used a different sort of bait for their clients. The personnel of the unsavory business before I left Shanghai consisted of Russian girls who were refugees from the Revolution or who were born in Harbin or Shanghai or Tientsin of parents who had escaped.

Jean, before leaving my house, took me to meet Louise. Louise was a large fat woman, a Canadian who had formerly been a trained nurse. Her place was reputed to be more expensive than the others, and it had a large clientele among the Chinese bankers who preferred white girls to their own kind. I can't understand such a preference, but the Chinese, like other people, follow the fashion in these matters, and for a while Louise's was the fad. Jean had been a great favorite of the bankers. They pitied her and made a pool to get her out of Louise's and into a little apartment where she could go straight. They paid the tuition, too, at business college. But that was a long time ago. Since then Jean had not stayed with Louise.

Telling me about it, she grew a little nostalgic for the old days, and decided to take me to see the place for myself. I was quite willing, but my first plan, to go there simply as a friend of Jean's and to be introduced and spend a few minutes in chatting politely, was not met with favor. Jean always preferred telling a lie if it was a good one. She telephoned

Louise and told her that she was bringing a friend to meet her who was down on her luck, an American girl married to a Chinese student who had forsaken her in Shanghai. My name for the purposes of the call was Mrs. Wong.

It was an idiotic idea, and if I hadn't fallen into the habit of indulging Jean like the child she was I wouldn't have done it. Jean had a lot of fun dressing me up. She made me wear slinky black, with a large hat and plenty of eye shadow. And so we set out for Louise's. I parked the car at some distance from her house, "where everyone always does," explained Jean, pointing it out.

The drawing room was done in a spare, chaste, modern style; not quite chromium-plated, because Louise liked her comfort, but getting near to it. I was amazed by Louise's own personality. I don't know what I had expected: the sort of madame you read about, I suppose. Louise was just a comfortable, chatty fat woman. She deplored bad language and dirty jokes, Jean had told me, and Louise bore this out by saying disapprovingly of some absent friend that her language was not ladylike. We had tea and chocolate cake that was very rich and heavy. Louise said her chocolate cake was famous. She and Jean talked of the girls, where they were and how they were doing. Nobody else came in that afternoon and we left before five. The only thing I thought at all out of the way was the appraising manner in which the houseboy looked at me as he let us out.

"He runs everything," Jean explained as we found the car; "I don't think Louise could manage without him. She says her boy friend helps her out, but don't you believe it. He just helps use the money. She's awfully hard up for girls, Louise is. She says the Japs are coming in quite often now and asking for new girls."

I lived to regret that silly prank. Jean had left our phone number with Louise, and the fat woman began to call up and ask for Mrs. Wong, and invite me down to meet some friends. I suppose Jean had expected that to happen; I know she was inordinately amused. At last I made a date with Louise, though it wasn't the kind she had in mind; I explained that I didn't like meeting new people but that I would be delighted to have lunch—just a family affair—with herself and Jean.

It would have been all right except for an unforeseen circumstance. We were waiting politely for lunch to be served. Louise's boy friend, a retired and run-down Shanghai policeman, made the cocktails, talking vivaciously as he did so of old days in India. So much Empire atmosphere staggered me a little and I reached out eagerly for my daiquiri. Louise, in the corner, was telling Jean enthusiastically about a new boarder she had just welcomed from Honolulu. "She's the prettiest thing," said Louise. "Red hair and such a nice disposition."

"Half-caste?" said Jean superciliously.

"No indeed!" Louise was indignant. "She's pure American. I'd introduce you right now, only she was a little bit homesick and Eddie—you remember Eddie—he took her out for a look around town, just to cheer her up. I expect they're still at Del Monte's or somewhere."

We had finished the cocktail when the new redhead came in with Eddie, and I froze with horror, because I knew Eddie. I gave scarcely a glance to the redhead, though she was indeed a vision, pure mahogany. I was wondering wildly if my black-eye-shadow disguise would hold. It wasn't as if I knew Eddie very well.

Louise introduced us, calling me "Mrs. Wong," and Eddie didn't look surprised or anything. I breathed again, and found myself listening to Jean's jealous whisperings against the redhead: "That's just like Louise," she said, "all over the girl, just because she's a novelty. You mightn't believe it, but *I* used to be the favorite here."

"Oh, I can well believe it," I assured her. "You're way ahead of that redhead."

Eddie accepted a cocktail and settled down in his chair, leaning back comfortably. He smiled at me in a friendly way.

"Seen Johnny Morris lately?" he inquired.

A much more publicized part of Shanghai's night life was the taxi dance. We have the same thing here at home on Broadway, but with an enormous difference. In Shanghai the dance halls are enormous and everybody goes, sooner or later, to all the better-known ones. It is not incumbent upon a visitor to hire a dancer, but they are important attractions. The Chinese think of their best taxi dancers as they used to think of their successful singsong girls, the hired entertainers at dinner parties, or as we think of our musical-comedy stars. Each dance hall has its Number One girl, and only the veriest tenderfoot would think of giving her only one ticket for a dance. The really proper behavior is to give her books and books of tickets, or to pay the management heavily for the privilege of her company at your table during half an hour or so. This is a good way to make yourself popular with both the lady and the proprietor. Gossip columnists for the Chinese papers watch the market eagerly and report it daily in their sheets. "Chu Wen-ching paid Old Lau three hundred dollars last night. Miss Golden Beetle entertained his happy friends for an hour." "Who gave the Hong Kong Beauty her new jade ring? The answer is not far away from the Majestic Hotel." We had dance halls that specialized in Korean girls, dance halls with Russians, dance halls with Japanese. The Frisco, a place beloved of sailors, was a dance hall with white girls of any nationality at all.

As women, we the bourgeoisie didn't know much about these places. Our men visited them, but I myself, for example, set foot inside the dance halls only when I was showing tourists around, or when the few cabarets had closed down and we still wanted good music on which to finish off a late evening. I had a friend, Betty, the tall, handsome wife of Victor Keen; she was working for the United Press and living away from her husband while she made up her mind to a divorce. We decided to investigate the mysteries and the technique of taxi-dancing. I can't remember now just how it all began, but I think we must have been drinking a little when we got the idea. I do remember how it ended. An insurance salesman, Betty's acquaintance, carried it through by applying to his friend, the manager of the Frisco, for permission for us to work there one evening.

"He'll have to talk it over with the regular girls," explained Buster, the insurance man. "If not, and if you're sprung on them cold, there's liable to be an awful row. But he's putting it up to them that you're only going to be there one night, trying to earn an honest penny to carry you on to India, and I don't think they'll mind."

I felt pretty silly about it when we started out at last, dressed in evening clothes. Betty was gloomy too, because she had a boy friend she cherished for one reason and one reason only—he topped her six feet two by another inch—and he didn't approve of the project at all. He was, she told me in exasperated tones, being stuffy.

The manager greeted us hastily and gave us our station, a tiny table just off the dance floor. All around the restaurant were other girls, sitting at inviting little tables that had extra chairs for clients. They stared at us and we realized that we were badly overdressed; the others wore shabby frocks, some short, some long, but all of them frayed at the hem and sweated out under the arms.

It was ten o'clock, still early for the sailors, who liked to go to the movies first. Pretty soon, though, they started to drift in. Our dresses may not have been admired by our rivals, but they worked quickly with the sailors. One of them joined us immediately.

He was a Briton, a cockney, and he didn't seem to have any money. We noticed that because he ordered no drinks and he didn't suggest dancing. Evidently it was wrong of him to take up space and time under these circumstances, and he knew it better than we did, because when the manager strolled watchfully around the floor he went away. After that the British contented themselves with sitting as near to us as they could get without joining the party, talking to us over the intervening space.

I had heard that the British and the Americans always had trouble at these places because of the difference in their rates of pay. The Yanks were wealthy and took what they liked, whereas the poor sterling-based British had to think twice before they ordered single beers. It was an obvious state of affairs and Betty and I commented on it in decently lowered tones.

In the meantime a few of the girls were dancing with special friends, old acquaintances who evidently came in every night. Still Betty and I sat there, resplendent in our dresses, with the non-dancing British sitting around us out of reach, if admiring.

"This is dreadful," said Betty. "It's just like my first party at high school. I'm being a wallflower. Do you suppose we are going through the evening without anybody asking us to dance?"

"Looks that way," I said gloomily. But the jinx was broken just then; an American Marine took Betty off to dance, and a moment later I got an Italian sailor.

Our conversation was on a high moral plane. After remarking that he hadn't seen me around before, the sailor said that the weather was mild but seasonable, and I said it was. He told me I danced well and I complimented him on his style. By that time the dance was over; they liked a quick turnover at the Frisco. My Wop didn't linger or buy me a drink, but he gave me five tickets. Betty's Marine sat down with us and set out to run up a bill.

After that we did fine. I collected a lot of tickets and Betty would have done better than I if her real boy friend hadn't suddenly marched in, a deep frown on his forehead, and planted himself at our table. The Marine who was sitting there at the time took one look at his face and withdrew, intimidated.

"Go away," said Betty. "You're spoiling everything. I told you not to come."

"Didn't I hear you making a date with that man?" demanded the angry swain.

"You did. What's it to you?" demanded Betty. I missed the rest of it because I was taken off to dance by a man who was, surprisingly enough, British. He was a Scottish engineer, and his first line was the same one I had heard about ten times already: "What are *you* doing here?" he asked.

I didn't want to cut in on the family quarrel at our table, so I accepted my engineer's offer thankfully and had a drink (cold tea with commission) at his. He was drunk. After a little while he asked for the story of my life. I gave him a pretty good one, concocted by Betty specially for the occasion. When I had finished the Scot announced that he was going to Take Me Out of All This. He was going to buy me a ticket straight back to the States where I belonged. What was more, he intended to come along with me and tell that stepmother exactly what he thought of her. Then he gave me a lot of tickets and went off to sleep.

I did pretty well out of the evening, but I would have done better if one American Marine hadn't cheated me out of my rightful earnings. He walked off without giving me even one ticket. I could have appealed to the manager, but I felt funny about it. Anyway, we didn't cash in on our tickets: we gave them to be distributed among the regular girls. Betty's young man took us home, in one of those uncomfortable silences. It lasted for half an hour, but he relaxed over coffee in Betty's apartment when we held our post-mortem. What cheered him up was our decision never again to enter the gay life.

Chapter 13

WAY OFF across the world, in Germany and the adjoining territories, Hitler was shouting and jumping up and down and bothering people generally. I can't remember now how many times he instituted drives to purge his land of the Jews, but we in Shanghai watched him with a special interest. Whenever people were kicked out of Germany in any appreciable number some of them turned up in China. There were few other places where they could go, and even these few places were beginning to turn them away. For two or three years Shanghai had been the last resort of these wanderers, and our society showed an increasing flavor of German. The ordinary Germans, of course, we had had always with us. They had their own school for their children, and as they grew less and less popular the diplomats showed a tendency to stay more and more to themselves, or at least to mix only with the Danes, Norwegians, and such. The refugees were more companionable.

I knew a lot of refugees who were now Shanghai citizens of fairly long standing. One of them was Horst Reihmer. In Shanghai he was one of the first to open a little *boîte* of the sort which later flooded our night-life districts. The walls were decorated by Schiff, another refugee. It was a good little place, the Maskee bar. Then they came thick and fast, as fast as the boats brought in refugees who had a little money and business sense.

Ultimately there was such a huge flood of Germans that the Shanghai Council, our administrative body, became alarmed. The rush of people was due to Hitler's last all-over drive before the Polish debacle and we saw immediately that this crowd was of different kidney to the preceding arrivals. They were poorer, more broken down, of a different type of education. Sir Victor, who with Speelman, a local Dutch financier, was working at the head of the relief committee, explained it to me by saying that most of this lot were "the sweepings of the country. They didn't have the guts or the brains to get out when they should have," he said. "They hung on as long as possible. Naturally they're not as likable as the others. This doesn't go for the old people or their very young relatives, but if you look at the young men in this crowd you'll see what I mean."

An emergency camp was fitted out, down near the city limits on the Hongkew side, and all around this camp there sprang up a number of little bakeshops and bars. There were bazaars to drum up money for the camp, and dozens of schemes to help put people into shops, and adjustment bureaus to find jobs for them—all the paraphernalia that can be found in any big town now that has received refugees in large number. We have learned the pattern. But in those days it was new to us and I found it hard to get used to the peddlers who came to the door all day with things to sell. I interviewed every one of them until I found that it was taking ninety per cent of my time. They sold everything from handbags and rugs and porcelain to shoelaces. All the moneyed residents of Shanghai went mad for Austrian glassware and china. Two or three exchange shops were set up downtown to accommodate the articles the refugees had brought with them out of Europe for sale: the Nazis had permitted them to carry with them household goods, and so the Jews had bought as much of the furniture and china and bedding as they could carry.

We reveled in good European cookery, cakes and preserves and goose. We had the best tailors in the world, I think—Leschiner and Jellinek. We all had Rosenthal dinner sets and elegant crystal. I spent too much on old-fashioned watches (but they came in handy later, when I myself needed money). The Jews, in spite of their appalling numbers, did so well that the Russians who had fled to Shanghai under similar circumstances back in 1917 became bitter and spiteful and frightened. Rumors began flying about; it was said that Sassoon and Hayim were sacking all their Russian doormen and bill collectors to give the jobs to the newcome Jews. These stories were indignantly repudiated by the financiers, and a newspaper editorial reminded the Russians sharply that there should be room in Shanghai for everybody. The Russians still muttered, though.

We had German entertainment in the night clubs; Germans trying to organize concerts and shows, German dancers, languishing mink-coated ladies looking for new sugar daddies. I knew an enterprising young couple who set up a gymnasium school, but they were perfectly willing to teach languages too, or higher mathematics or anything.

The Russo-Czech lady who had first called on me when Charles brought his card to the house kept up our acquaintance. Her name—at least the only one of her many names which I can spell—was Regina Petersen, and I called her Peter. Don't ask me why a Russo-Czech should have a Swedish name. Peter explained it once, but I have forgotten. She was an eccentric person, fond of refugees, Yogi, India and Indian dances —any number of disassociated interests. She took on an Indian name which she used when she gave concerts: Indra Devi. I don't know anything about India but I thought she danced awfully well, and her different saris were fascinating. Peter was in and out of the house all day, playing with the gibbons, trying in vain to make me take Yogi seriously, or indulging in one of her "days of silence," which days were dreaded by me because they made Peter such uncomfortable company. Instead of staying at home on these occasions she went out and did her usual business, shaking her head and placing her finger to her lips mysteriously if some uninitiated person spoke to her. Sinmay adored her in his own way; she appealed to his love of the bizarre. He could sit and watch her for hours, smiling to himself, now and then asking a question guaranteed to send her pelting off in pursuit of one of her hobbies. It was when Peter threw herself heart and soul into the cause of the refugees that I really lost patience with her.

I was spending ninety per cent of my time on them anyway. Peter added the missing ten per cent to my program, though I was not willing to be shoved into doling out more of the phony kindness that was all she could elicit from me those days.

"I'm a testy, selfish old maid," I would argue. "Please, oh, please let me alone. I can't help anybody more, not any more. There are too many of them."

But Peter only laughed and patted my cheek for being impatient, and brought the refugee. He was probably a very bright boy, but he irritated me so much that I could not be fair and study him impartially. It was all too evident that he had not insisted upon this introduction in order to be criticized, though he had brought with him a couple of manuscripts. He wanted me to admire him wholeheartedly.

It was a trifling encounter. I certainly never saw this Mr. Levin again: I was careful to avoid him, and to be adamant with Peter on the subject. But the fact that I have remembered him even to this day shows that he made an impression out of proportion to his weight, and I recall that my exasperation had an effect on my life. I took stock of it.

That afternoon, I told myself sternly, I had wasted more than two hours not just in being bored but in being *acutely* bored. It was happening more and more often these days. Either I was losing my zest for life, or the world was definitely too much with me. I saw too many people at the best of times, and at the worst they were mostly people I would rather do without. I went over a list in my mind of the individuals who had taken up my time that week: Don Chisolm for one. He was editor of a little advertising paper. I didn't like or approve of Don, or admire him, but he had begun to drop in on me with his Russian popsies and I was too lackadaisical to resist. Indeed, he was practically an intimate of the house. That was all wrong. Then there was Mr. Chen from Fukien. He was always taking me out to meet singsong girls of his acquaintance, hoping I would write them up and make them rich and famous through notoriety. I didn't particularly enjoy his company, but he enjoyed mine, I suppose—anyway, he had a lot of it. I had been too lazy to say no. And the women I knew, who dropped in to talk the precious afternoons away! It wasn't only Peter, by any means. There were dozens more. There were so many, and yet I can't remember their names. There was a blonde nurse who was subnormal mentally, but who just knew she could write a wonderful book if only she had the time. That woman victimized me, week after week.

What had become of me? Why was I such a patient slut? My foolish, insincere kindliness had let me in for all of this waste. It was certainly time to call a halt. To like everyone and to be happy with anyone was a virtue and its own reward, but I realized now that for weeks I had been feeling livery, impatient, restless. I didn't like everyone: I didn't like anyone, except perhaps Sinmay. It was time for a change. In the happy prewar days I would have settled the matter by purchasing a ticket for somewhere; now, surrounded by Japs, I could not run away. No, but I would do something.

Mr. Levin's image pursued me; I could not shake it off my mind. His silly, self-eager face, his boyish prattle, summed up for me all of demanding humanity. It seemed to me suddenly that all the clocks in Shanghai were ticking fast and faster, and my heart beat slow and slower.

Perhaps every woman who lives alone pays for her independence with these moods. I don't know. After a week of stewing around in mine I came to a decision. I would turn over a new leaf. Chin Lien would have to learn how to say, "Not at home." No more floundering about, letting things happen to me instead of directing the course of events that made up my life. No more petty tyranny on the part of all these no-accounts. The Marines, for one example: lots of them dropped in almost every day to play my radio, to sit around and tease the gibbon, to drink my whisky. Chin Lien must deal with them. That sad-eyed Pole who was always starving and always about to kill himself for love of a Chinese girl: I would beg Sir Victor to give him a job and then he would not have to come in at tea time. The other Pole who had a title and a bad case of kleptomania. That little tobacconist whose wife stayed the year round in Tientsin chasing Frenchmen. The whole cockeyed lot of them—out of my house, out of my mind, out of my life! I would keep only the ones I really wanted. And I would develop a sense of privacy. I would have a lock that worked on my bedroom door. I would stop lending money.

The result of all these cogitations was that I acquired shortly after that not one house guest, which had always been my quota, but two. Yet I did keep my vow to some extent: I learned to ignore the intrusive world when it all grew too bad. I became anti-social. Josie Stanton, wife of one of our nicer consuls, made a significant remark one day when I invited her and Ed, her husband, to dinner.

"Why, we'd love to, Mickey," she said cordially. Then, after a slight pause, she added, "Er—will you be there?"

Chapter 14

IT WAS a letter from America that settled the unrest in my household. The idea of a book on the Soong sisters grew out of John Gunther's book *Inside Asia* in two ways: first because it was John who named me as a likely person to do the job when he went home after visiting China, and second because a passage in his book so infuriated the Soongs that they made an important decision directly affecting me. I will explain.

The suggestion coming from the publishers attracted and frightened me at the same time. I knew no more about the Soongs at that period than I have already set down here. I had seen Mme. Chiang once at a distance, and Bernardine had taken me to a huge reception at the Kungs' house in Shanghai, where I shook hands with Dr. H. H. Kung and his wife and then passed on to the lawn and duly drank my cup of tea. In those days I didn't even know who the Kungs were. The nearest I had ever come to Mme. Sun, the middle one of the three, was in being introduced to Agnes Smedley at a time when the picturesque Agnes was rumored to be Mme. Sun's private secretary.

I would have to get their permission, I decided, before attempting such a book. The publishers' spokesman warned my agent that there had been so many frustrated attempts to write this thing that he had little hope of my success. Almost everybody who had ever published anything about the Far East had tried to do Mme. Chiang's life, and Madame had always replied with perfect logic to such overtures that she wanted to write it herself, someday when she had time.

It was Sinmay who made all the difference. "Don't concentrate on Soong Mayling," he counseled me, using, according to Chinese custom, Madame's maiden name. "Ai-ling is the one you should consult."

"Ai-ling?"

"Mme. Kung," he explained. "I know a good deal about her; many people do. My aunt is a very old friend of hers. They were girls together and they have kept up the friendship. I will ask her how to go about it. It is a really good idea, you know. You must do it, and become famous, and we will all live happy ever after. You are getting too lazy these days."

The last remark was too true for me to resent it. Instead I poked and prodded the lazy Sinmay until he actually did call on his aunt. She was out of town at the time—"In Hong Kong," he explained when he came home. "She is probably seeing Soong Ai-ling this very moment. We must wait."

That was China, so I waited patiently. When Aunt came home Sinmay took me to call on her and we had a long talk. She was a beautiful smiling lady—"My favorite aunt," Sinmay said as he introduced her. She wasn't at all sure that Mme. Kung would like such a book, but one could always try, she said. I spent some weeks asking around, getting a background through Sinmay's acquaintances, before I even wrote to the sisters.

I wrote a different letter to each of them. It would never do, I decided, to send a form letter like a mimeograph all around the family. Each sister lived in her own house, in her own individual milieu, and each milieu was as different as possible from the other two. My letters were individual too. I had no reply from Mme. Sun. I had a delayed reply from Mme. Chiang up in Chungking; she just said that although she liked the tone of my letter she was really too busy to bother about such things. But Mme. Kung was attracted by one phrase in my epistle to her: I had said that I wanted to write a truthful book. She suggested that I come down to Hong Kong and see her.

"Well, why not?" I said lightly. "I haven't been to Hong Kong for years. We'll both go and look the land over."

"It will be difficult," Sinmay assured me. "You have an impatient nature and this is going to take patience."

"I?" I was honestly amazed. "Why, I'm much more patient than anyone I know. I'm much better than I used to be. I'm so patient that I'm afraid to go home to America now. I won't be able to keep up with everyone else: I move too slowly."

Sinmay laughed at me without replying.

"We could go next week if there's a boat," I said thoughtfully. "Wait a minute while I find out. . . ."

"Why not tomorrow? It is almost time for the office to be closed."

"Oh no. I'm sure I can get somebody." I started to twirl the dial and Sinmay laughed harder than ever.

We embarked a couple of weeks later, in a small boat that took a good long time to arrive. Shipping had undergone a tremendous change since the beginning of the war. Nowadays we took whatever boat we could get. Our course was so erratic, there were so many stoppings and startings and returnings to small ports I had never heard of before, that I asked the captain for an explanation. Quite simply he gave it—he was running ammunition to the Chinese guerrillas. They had agents waiting at these obscure ports and they simply unloaded the guns and steamed off again.

It was quite an experience, after two years of staying in one spot, to go to sea again. I still remember how nice the blue ocean looked after we left the muddy Whangpoo waters behind, and the lift I felt, that old familiar, half-forgotten lift, that I was actually on my way to somewhere else. Sinmay didn't share my feelings. It was years since he had left Shanghai for any purpose except our jaunt to the Yellow Mountains, or to visit the family graves in Chekiang. He grumbled at the lack of comfort this trip entailed, and didn't brighten up until he remembered the experiences of an ancestor of his who had sailed away in a P. and O. boat to become a diplomat in Russia.

"He kept a diary I must show you when we get back," said Sinmay. "Oh, wonderful! He put everything down, and he was especially impressed by the way they kept changing plates at the table. He said, 'They bring a new plate for each different dish, and make a great fuss about it; yet when the food comes it is never enough.'"

Hong Kong was brilliantly sunny, quite a different place from the memory I had of a foggy, damp town in early spring. We took rooms at the Hongkong Hotel, startling and horrifying the local population to a degree I could not appreciate until I became a resident myself, years later. Not that Chinese didn't often book rooms in that rambling hostelry, although most of them preferred the smarter, newer quarters of the Gloucester, next door: it was Sinmay's appearance. Hong Kong Chinese were mostly brisk, Westernized people. The old-fashioned Cantonese didn't stay at hotels. They lived in their own homes, enormous rabbit warrens built on the hillside. Sinmay in his brown gown, drifting through the lobby of the "Grips," chatting amiably with me, arrested many a cocktail glass in mid-air.

The whole purpose of this trip was to interview Mme. Kung and, if possible, to get a start on the book. It had been an expensive journey, however, and we resolved to make the most of it; we planned to stay a month. Immediately we got in touch with *T'ien Hsia;* by a coincidence, we discovered, Mme. Kung had recently interested herself in that magazine to some extent. She and the original founder, Sun Fo (Sun Yat-sen's son), were friends. With the help of her brother T. V. they had managed to collect a lot of good solid advertisements from the big Chinese banks and firms. They were all on top of the world. A woman I had known slightly in Shanghai, Australian-born Alice Chow, was helping with the stenographic work of the office, mornings; in the afternoon she was Mme. Kung's secretary. So there we had a direct line straight to the Kung house out on Sassoon Road, in the Pokfulam District halfway around the island of Hong Kong.

We admired the offices very much. They were under the name, simply, of Wen Yuan-ning, who was doing other work for Chungking by taking care of all Hollington Tong's Hong Kong propaganda; not only *T'ien Hsia* but all sorts of printing jobs in English. (Holly Tong, if you don't know his name by this time, is the head of all Chungking "information" work, and a loyal slave to Mme. Chiang.) The offices were in the Hong Kong and Shanghai Bank Building, the newest and most nearly skyscraper type of office building that the colony possessed. It stood down on the harbor front just facing the town square, the one where all the horrible metal statues of British royalty were clustered around the nucleus of Queen Victoria, up on a high pedestal. I was to see that bank building many times later as the central figure of triumphant Japanese posters.

Sinmay had many friends in Hong Kong, old classmates who had trickled out of Shanghai little by little after the inauguration of the Incident. We were entertained every minute of the day, sitting first in this restaurant and then in that. Sinmay was charmed by the Cantonese custom of using pretty girls to wait on table, and I was equally delighted with Cantonese-style light lunch, where the waiter brings you tray after tray of small gadgets—fish cakes and sweet snacks and dumplings— from which you are expected to make your entire meal. Chuan and his sister Mei-mei gave a party out at Repulse Bay, hiring a cabana at the Lido, the new bathing pavilion.

"If you live like the Chinese," I admitted, "Hong Kong is not so bad."

"We are happy," said Chuan Tsen-kuo. "It's expensive, that's all. If you can arrange for money it's nicer than Shanghai. After all, the best Chinese have escaped from Shanghai. Try to persuade Sinmay to come down here with the family."

There were English people to look up. I was glad to run into Ian Morrison, a young man sometimes on the *Times* who had walked through on the Burma Road just before it was completed. Earlier, after teaching school for a while in Japan, Ian had taken a job as secretary to the British Ambassador to Tokyo. He came by his oriental interests naturally: his father was an old China hand and had had a street named after him in Peking. All this hodgepodge of his contacts, I decided, must add up to something: the usual something known among British as "Intelligence." They would never let a man like him slip through their fingers. Besides, Ian was awfully mysterious and thrilled about his work. Whenever he was asked what he was doing he hesitated palpably before replying, and when he replied it was with a palpable lie. I teased him about it when I knew him better.

"You are hopelessly young," I said accusingly.

"The Playboy of the Eastern World," he admitted. He wasn't the only one: there were a lot of young men in the same department, dashing around Hong Kong. Charles Boxer, the captain who had called on Mr. Mills and me in Shanghai, was the chief of them; he had been a language student in Japan, Ian told me, and was supposed to be the best in his line.

"Boxer, oh yes," I said. "I'd better give him a ring and meet his wife."

It was a nervous strain, waiting until the necessary formalities of an interview with Mme. Kung were completed. To fill in the time, I discovered, the parties with Sinmay were not enough. There were still long spaces of time when the Chinese talked their own language and left me alone to brood. I was in a dither about the book, and really anxious to make it successful. Probably this was because I had been reading in preparation, and inquiring around among the oldsters in Shanghai, until I had a fairly good picture of the period. My love affair with Shanghai made me eager to carry on with such a piece of her history; I was charmed merely with the possibilities of the background. Until you have fallen victim to the temptations of history you cannot understand what it is like, the rewards of research and the excitement of tracing down life stories and anecdotes through old newspapers and memoirs. Once you are hooked, there is no end to it. I was hooked, and now I was going to discover, once and for all, if I was to carry on with the work or drop it forever. It all depended on Mme. Kung. I was really jittery. Sinmay, probably in an attempt to encourage me by indirection, laughed at me, so I decided to take a vacation from Sinmay.

There were a few very young English people around town who were discontented with the city because it was slow and peaceful. They played golf, they drank, they played bridge, and two or three times a year they put on amateur plays. I knew some of them, and in a deliberate attempt to change my luck I called them up. I was a change for them too. I was a symbol of that delightfully attractive and wicked metropolis of Shanghai. They grabbed at me eagerly. I spent one or two evenings of sheer social boredom and I loved all of it, the rapid, gay, empty chatter, the drinks, the slow-slipping hours above the harbor, looking down at that beautiful stage setting of lights and mountains. This was the other side of Hong Kong which the Chinese didn't know. I wouldn't be able to stand it much of the time, I said to myself, but for a change how nice it was! And yet the British were foolish to cut themselves off completely from the native Chinese. Since their tastes were so different anyway, why couldn't they take the risk of being friendly? No Chinese, even if he belonged to their clubs, would spend such a completely vacuous evening, given his choice.

"You know a lot of Chinese people, don't you, Mickey?" inquired my host suddenly. It was almost as if he had read my mind.

"Why, yes. Quite a few."

"I'm wondering," he said, "if I oughtn't to try to meet some of them."

"It mightn't be a bad idea."

"But you don't know," he said eagerly, "how difficult it is here in Hong Kong. Nobody knows Chinese. I think I'll wait until I've been transferred to Shanghai. That would be better, don't you think?"

"The Chinese would probably be willing to wait," I assured him.

I was startled and alarmed to discover that Sinmay had gone into a bad fit of the sulks. It was my defection that had annoyed him.

"But why?" I asked. "I suppose you could have come along on these parties, but it never occurred to me to take you. You would have been bored to death."

"I didn't want to go," he said angrily. "It is just that they make me angry, these British. Look at this Morrison. He invited you to go out for a walk in the country on Sunday."

"But—you won't walk. You have always refused to walk. You say you have a bad foot."

"I don't *want* to go for that walk. I only want him to think of inviting me. If he were a visitor to Shanghai with a friend I would invite him just as I invite his friend."

"You never used to notice such things," I said helplessly. "What difference can it possibly make——"

"I hate these British," said Sinmay. He had never spoken like that before. I had always been amused by his loyalty to Cambridge, where he spent two years: it was Sinmay who insisted, whenever he went to Hangchow, on calling on his ancient friend Mr. Moule, the Englishman who lived there. It was Sinmay who mocked me whenever he had a chance because American literature was inferior to English.

"Hong Kong," I said suddenly.

"What are you saying?"

"I said, Hong Kong. It is this place that makes you so defensive all of a sudden. You never feel like this in Shanghai. It's the way they act about Chinese down here. That's why you are so angry. I've deserted you by going off with these English people and leaving you with the Chinese. I've stepped over the border. That's it, isn't it?"

"I believe it is," said Sinmay.

"We had better get back to Shanghai."

"Not so fast," he said. His good humor had come back as swiftly as it had vanished. "We have two dates. One is to see Mme. Kung on Thursday afternoon at three——"

"Oh no!" I cried.

"Yes, it is true. That Mrs. Chow telephoned while you were away. And the other is a luncheon which Captain Boxer is giving tomorrow at the Café de Chine. He is inviting all of us, you and Tsen-kuo and Yuan-ning and myself, and some officers from his department, and his new wife. Now *there* is a gentleman. He knows his manners."

Captain Boxer had invited a lot of people, enough for two big tables at the newest restaurant to capture Chinese fancy. He had already drunk two gimlets before we arrived, and was in a merry mood. (A gimlet is made of gin and bottled lime juice. It is the tipple of Hong Kong, as a gin sling is of Singapore.) In a maze of taipans and army uniforms and Chinese gowns I was introduced to Mrs. Boxer, a pretty, slender girl. "My husband makes me read all your articles," she said immediately.

It is all I remember her saying until the end of the luncheon, when she told Charles firmly, *"I am driving the car home."*

That, it seemed to me even in my advanced state of intoxication, was a sound idea. Charles had spent the entire luncheon going back and forth from table to table making us *kanpei* our wine cups with him. "Kanpei" is Chinese for "bottoms up," and the host is supposed to drink cup for cup with each guest, all the way around. He had been careful to carry on with the local tradition. I retained a memory of him as a brilliant, amusing, mad man, who had insisted on talking to me about the latest Chungking politics, of which I knew nothing, and harping on the approaching dissolution of the British Empire. When I offered congratulations on his marriage he said, "It always happens when one lives in Hong Kong, you know, more than four years. One either becomes a hopeless drunkard or one marries. I did both."

I was pleased when his wife phoned to invite Sinmay and me to cocktails later on in the week.

"You see? Now there is a real gentleman," said Sinmay again. "They say he has wonderful books."

"Never mind that," I said. "Tell me some more about Mme. Kung. What shall I say if she——"

We went on talking like that until three o'clock on Thursday afternoon.

Chapter 15

SINMAY CAME into my room to call for me at a quarter to three and found me sitting on my bed, shaking and clenching my teeth.

"What's the matter?" I demanded of him. "I've never been like this before. In another minute I'll start to cry."

"But she is not so terrible! I keep telling you. My aunt will probably be there; yes, she is back in Hong Kong. Why are you afraid?"

"It isn't exactly her I'm afraid of." Without talking any more about it, I picked up my bag and started out with him. I know now what it was. I realized that the interview marked the beginning of something important. I was going to have to stop playing and begin to work. My other work, writing and teaching and everything else, had been make-believe; this was the first job I had to get my teeth into. I was just about to dive into China, into the war and into real life. It was enough to frighten anyone.

Madame's house was set on a steep bluff above the ocean, with terraces and tennis courts around it. The taxi took a startling nose dive down the driveway and fetched up in the disconcerting way of Hong Kong cars, nuzzling the front door. A houseboy stood there bowing and smiling. Two bodyguards lounged in the courtyard next to the garage and glanced up as if they were expecting us, and didn't particularly care. They were big husky men.

In a very long room full of french windows that led to a veranda and a view Sinmay's aunt was sitting. She seemed quite at home, and indeed the house failed to live up to my frightened expectations of splendor. (Houses of rich Chinese always do, I have learned.) The furniture was chintzy and pretty, the place was not cluttered, but otherwise the whole effect was that of a modest Victorian interior. It wasn't even a very big house. I would have breathed easier except for the fact that Alice Chow came in just then, and she spoke of Mme. Kung in a tone of muted, frightened adoration that set me off shivering again. At last there was a light step on the stair, and I jumped to my feet.

She wasn't nearly as tall as I seemed to remember. But perhaps that was because Bernardine had made me notice with what dignity she moved, years ago at that Shanghai reception; perhaps I had had the wrong idea then. She looked now like a pretty little woman. Those are the exact words. She is shorter than I am, with incredibly tiny hands and feet. She has a smooth skin, darting black eyes, black hair piled high (because she doesn't like being small), and a good figure. As long as any of us may live in China I think we are still a little bemused by Chinese ladies, just because they are Chinese. We can tell ourselves that it is nonsense, but still we are fascinated by the romance of their Chineseness. It is something in the way they smile, perhaps; politely, never with abandon even when they giggle. Mme. Kung gave me her hand and smiled, and I was promptly bemused.

She carried a soft little feather fan. All the while we talked she waved the fan gently. I remember the fronds stirring in the electric fan's breeze, and I remember little else of that important afternoon. We didn't talk very much about the book—enough, but not very much. She told me that she had gone so far as to grant the interview, in spite of her dislike of publicity, because of John Gunther. John is a friend of mine, and I was sorry he had incurred such anger. In his *Inside Asia* he had spoken of her mistakenly, she declared. He had never met her, so how could he have known what she was like? In that book he had described her as a corrupt, scheming financier, striding like a tigress up and down her room when she was thwarted. Mme. Kung's voice shook when she talked about it. Her sister Mme. Chiang had been disturbed even more than she herself, she said. And I, Emily Hahn, had told her in my letter that I was anxious for the truth about the Soongs. The truth, she repeated—did I mean that?

I said that I did. I promised to be careful of my facts. I tried to explain to her how a newspaperman works: the roundabout ways he must go in getting his information. "What John wrote," I said, "was told him by people he met in Shanghai and Hong Kong. He thought he was getting the truth. He doesn't know China and he wasn't on his guard, I think, against the distortions that you find out here."

"But how can he take hearsay like that, when it means so much, and put it into print? It's wrong. It's wicked. My sister is very much upset, and we have decided that perhaps I have been at fault in not coming more to the front. I live a secluded life. I don't like going out in crowds. Well, this is my punishment. I know I have many enemies; oh yes, I have, Miss Hahn. Well, I must fight them instead of ignoring them. But I have always had a horror of newspapers and that sort of thing. My friend"— she put an affectionate hand on Aunt's arm—"says you are a kind woman and an honest one. I know you have helped Mr. Zau very much during the war in Shanghai. The family is grateful. If I could be quite sure of your judgment . . . I know I can trust your feelings. . . ."

"Suppose we arrange it like this, madame," I said. Later she told me she had been amused at my quick offer to protect her. She knows her power fully. "I don't want to hurt you. Let me start to work on the book and show you the beginning. I can't promise to let the Soongs dictate it——"

"Of course not."

"But I do promise this: if you don't approve of the book as a whole when it is finished I won't publish it. Is that satisfactory?"

I had made up my mind quickly. It wouldn't, of course, be the same sort of book that a person would write from the outside looking in. But such a book as that wouldn't have anything in it that you couldn't pick up in the market place anywhere. Anyone could write a hearsay book. If I had to err on the side of the Soongs—because what censor can be thoroughly ruthless about himself?—I would at least have much more information to offer, given me by the Soongs themselves, than could any historian who wrote a detached account of them from outside the city gates. I trusted Mme. Kung immediately. There was something about her that made me know how strong she was inside, with a toughness that makes for honesty. This strength was not belied by the softness and delicacy of her personality. It is not only strident women who tell the truth. If the Japanese hadn't ruined the word I would call her sincere.

We had tea, then, with American pie, and afterward we took our leave. I was ready to go home that afternoon before I might say something to spoil the atmosphere. I was still as careful of the situation as if it had been blown in thin glass. Even at my most pessimistic, however, I admitted that things looked promising. Mme. Kung had not said yes, exactly, but she had certainly not said no. Alice Chow, the devoted hoverer, was to see me later in the week to give me a definite reply.

"And you think it will be all right?" I demanded of Sinmay for the tenth time as Mme. Kung's big car drove us back along the winding road.

"Of course it is all right. Already it is settled. I heard from my aunt; she likes you very much and is willing. That is because of my aunt, who prepared Mme. Kung. Tomorrow we will go to thank her." He was silent a moment, smiling. "But she has charm," he said suddenly. "I did not realize that. One doesn't hear enough of Soong Ai-ling's charm. When she laughs and hides her face behind her fan it is very nice. A sort of flirtatiousness, not too much. I had an uncle who admired her as a girl and now I see why."

"Well," I said impulsively, "I love her."

I have never changed my mind about that.

Madame's mind worked away at one problem until she settled it to her satisfaction. There was never any nonsense of starting a thing and then dropping it because she was away after another interest. She figured out how to go about collecting the material I needed, and how to fit her sisters into the program. Any hesitation she still felt about the project she referred, as I heard later, to Mme. Chiang up in Chungking, because it was her youngest sister's desire that John Gunther's misconception be cleared up in the shortest possible time, and as completely as could be done. Only Dr. Kung and Soong Mayling, perhaps, understood how much those paragraphs had horrified and hurt her.

Up there in the foggy wartime capital, in absentia, I was instrumental in interrupting the work of the busiest woman in China. I get quite proud of myself when I think of it, because I know now what her office is like when she really gets down to business. I can imagine what happened; Donald, coming in with his notebook, ready to take down shorthand notes, was greeted by a question something like this: "Don, what are we going to do about this American woman—Hahn, her name is— who has got in to see Mme. Kung?"

"Never heard of her," Donald probably replied. So they turned the files over until they found my first request, and the notes that had been made on the matter. I can imagine that Mme. Chiang made a bitter remark about my persistence.

"If anyone is to write the story of my life," she said, perhaps for the millionth time, "I will do it myself. What do these people think?"

"Yes, but you won't get around to it for years," said Donald thoughtfully. (From now on I am not guessing; he told me about it himself.) "You know, there's something in what she says here. Somebody is bound to write this book sooner or later; you can't stop 'em. Why not let this woman try it, then? She's willing to co-operate. She isn't going to dig around looking for dirt as she would if she belonged to the other camp. I don't know—why not give her a chance? What can you lose? Nobody can write your autobiography, after all, but Soong Mayling."

"I should think not. . . . All right, if it doesn't take too much of my time."

So that was settled, and the job so many people had tried to get fell into my lap.

I met Alice a few days later at the Hongkong Hotel and she made the announcement with much drama. I like Alice, but in her emotional moments she is a little overpowering, and if I hadn't been very fond of Mme. Kung her worship would have put me off, just from sheer human orneriness. "I am to help you all I can," she said. "It is a sacrifice for me, I tell you frankly, because I have always wanted to write a book about Mme. Kung myself."

I murmured polite protests and assured her of my gratitude. The advisability of showing this gratitude, indeed, seemed to grow with each letter I had from Alice, written in her capacity as Mme. Kung's secretary. As each bit of information was tucked away in my notes I thanked her more extravagantly, until one day when I was with Mme. Kung she said:

"You needn't feel so grateful to Alice as all that. She isn't doing this purely out of kindness, you know. She's my secretary, after all."

Well, put like that, I could see her point, and I relaxed. Relations between Alice and me grew less emotional thereafter, and much more workmanlike. It was my first experience with one of the biggest difficulties one encounters when dealing with the great of this world— battling through the crowd of adorers. The great themselves are helpless to deal with the situation. I have seen things you wouldn't believe in Chungking, when one faction whose leading goddess was Mme. Chiang came to blows with another whose bright particular star was Mme. Sun. As chief custodian of Mme. Kung's claim to goddessness, Alice worked overtime, and she probably trembled in her boots at the suspicion that I was after her captaincy. I think she was probably not displeased when she had occasion shortly after the beginning of everything to write me a hint of a rebuke.

The Chinese, as I have said before, revel in gossip. Not only do they use it as a harmless pastime, but they know well how to make a weapon of it. Mme. Kung had a horror of being talked about; this may sound odd and inconsistent when you consider that she consented to a book about herself, but people aren't always consistent. At those early stages she had the idea that the public shouldn't know we were good friends. It would invalidate the book, she insisted. I argued that she was being unnecessarily squeamish, since it would be obvious in the text that the Soong family were co-operating with me, showing me private records, talking to me at length, and all that. In the end she lost her timidity and was much happier about all of it, but during that summer she started and trembled at the very hint of a whisper of conversation about her, no matter how innocent.

One evening we had dined and talked and it was still early. She suggested suddenly that we drive into town and see a movie. I accepted with pleasure, and the simple little expedition took place. The housekeeper came along too, and we slipped into the theater in the dark so that nobody would recognize us and make a fuss about her presence. Probably someone did see her, just the same, or another chauffeur recognized the limousine. Naturally I didn't speak of it around town myself, because I knew how touchy she was. However, a few days later I received a remarkable letter from Alice, telling me that the town was seething with gossip over the fact that we had gone to the movies, and that Madame was terribly upset. She reminded me that Madame's nerves were in a dreadful state anyway. She conveyed a reproach, delicately hinted, that I had been so crass, so mad as to broadcast to the world the secret fact that we had gone to the movies. I was warned. . . .

A similar incident is recounted in Ralf Sues's book, *Shark's Fins and Millet,* which ended on a more drastic note than did my experience. Myself, I just wrote to both Alice and Madame, assuring them of my innocence in regard to the base charge. Perhaps my impatience and natural anger with such foolishness showed between the lines; anyway, the teacup tornado blew over in a hurry. I used to rage when these things happened, and always I drove straight to the center of authority to get them ironed out. It was the only way to deal with the intricate windings of intrigue as she is played in Hong Kong. The British are as good as anyone at the stupid game.

"People work her up on purpose," I said once to Mme. Chiang, after her eldest sister had become agitated over some similar trifle.

"They do," she assented. "That's why I think this book may be good for her. Anything that will force her out of that unhealthy seclusion ought to be good. I know what all this is like. I have the same sort of problems in my own organization; I spend most of my life, it sometimes seems to me, settling household and office quarrels."

I am anticipating, however; all of this happened much later, on my second trip. During this summer month's visit in Hong Kong I saw Mme. Kung only twice, and the rest of our contacts were made through the mail. I was busily employed in collecting as much personal material as I could about her father, Charles Jones Soong, a remarkable man whose personality reached out across his grave and took hold of my imagination. I heard nothing direct either from Mme. Chiang or Mme. Sun, but I had the word of Mme. Kung that I would at least not be hindered by her sisters in my preparations. I might even be helped, she said. In the meantime I was to go back to Shanghai and see what sort of beginning I could make.

But what was this? I asked myself the same question that has been asked of me so many times since I published the Soong book. How could Mme. Kung speak so confidently on behalf of Mme. Sun? Weren't they bitter enemies? Mme. Sun's cohorts all said they were. Mme. Sun, they said, had shaken the sticky capitalistic gold dust of the Soong Dynasty off her tiny feet long since, when she first fled to Moscow, and wasn't Mme. Kung, even more than Mme. Chiang, the leader of the banking faction? Everybody in the Red group that I encountered in either port, Shanghai or Hong Kong, assured me that Mme. Sun was such a stranger to the family that she probably wouldn't know a Soong if it walked up and greeted her in the street.

I can only say that I found out very early in my biographer's career that this particular rumor has no basis in fact. None whatever. I have said it before in my book, but evidently not loud enough to pierce the ears of certain book reviewers. It just isn't true. The two ladies, Mmes. Kung and Sun—or, if you like it better, Soong Ching-ling and Soong Ai-ling—are good friends. They see each other often. They saw each other often before they were forced by the war's exigencies to live together too. I missed Mme. Sun by about two minutes at least twice when I went to the Kung house. I didn't always miss her; one day she was still there when I dropped in. Now, after some months, this statement of mine has been proved elsewhere, and there are so many photographs in support of it in the newspaper files that the most stubborn leftists can't argue them away, but you will find a lot of people still trying. When I first made the statement I didn't have public proof, and my way was made hard and stony. I was never allowed to enjoy my triumph either; as soon as Mme. Sun did admit that she was accepting Kung hospitality in Chungking the leftists began whispering, "She was forced to do it. . . . Not a free agent, you know. . . . Terribly difficult for her, poor sweet. Why, I tried to get into That House to see her the other day and I was turned away. It's like a prison."

Again I am anticipating. This time you will note that I speak with acerbity. It is the first chance I have had to blow my top in a good personal, untrammeled way. I wish to say good-naturedly that I have suffered a lot, and I often wonder in what cause. I believe it is just in the cause of plain scientific truth, because I have not sworn my lifeblood away to any political party. Without intending to do so, I ran slam-bang into the leftists and one of their legends by writing a book on the Soongs. This legend has been built up around Mme. Sun. If you want to know more about it, don't bother to ask me; look up Mme. Sun in almost any book on China written by an American writer with leftist sympathies. (You won't find the same thing in the Chinese books. Chinese writers don't bemuse as easy as we do.) At the same time exactly I ran slam-bang into the rightists and one of *their* legends. This legend has been built up around Mme. Kung. To know more about it you need only to turn to any of the cocktail groups of Shanghai, or Hong Kong, or Chungking, or Tientsin; you won't find much of it in books because of the law of scandal or libel. I can never remember which. Mme. Kung's legend is more diffuse than is the one about her young sister Ching-ling, because her husband shares in it, and so do her four children. John Gunther gathered his material from both parties when he prepared for his book, *Inside Asia.*

Part of my earliest work in preparation for *The Soong Sisters* was the gathering of all the vast amount of nebulous scandal that exists about the Soongs, sifting it out, classifying it, and then trying to trace it to a foundation in fact. I could write a big heavy book on that subject alone. I won't, though. If you, reader, know nothing about the Far East except what you read in books like this, it will mean nothing to you anyway. If you are an old hand from the Coast you probably already know most of the rumors I am talking about. Now you who know China, please do me a favor, because that research job is one which I hated to leave in order to write my book. Sit down and search your memory. Take your favorite bit of Soong scandal and look at it again, and trace out where it came from, and try to prove it to your satisfaction, and then if you have proof, send it on to me, care of the publishers. There are the stories about financial wanglings, and the stories about the vast sums which the Chiangs and the Soongs have piled up in American and South American banks, and the stories about Dr. Kung's private life, and the stories, never-ending, about squeeze. The only ones I ever proved were some of the squeeze ones, and they did *not* trace back to the sources the public expected. . . . I'll talk about squeeze in a moment. First I want to finish up the general subject of gossip in China.

If you ever go out there, be on your guard against certain types of stories which recur again and again and again. For some reason these tales have a special fascination for Chinese chatterers. Cheating in high places is the first. Espionage is the second. (You find the most elaborate allegations against the Generalissimo himself, for example: that he is in constant secret communication with Wang Ching-wei is a favorite. There are also people who will swear themselves orange in the face that Dr. Kung is a buddy of Hirohito.) The third is the good old execution story. Hardly a day went by in Shanghai that Sinmay didn't tell me of some acquaintance of ours whose head had been chopped off. The fact that these people invariably made personal appearances later on never discouraged him. He went on telling me about heads being chopped off, and he went on believing his own stories.

I think that this type of Chinese mentality is what led directly to the long period we had in Shanghai, after the retreat of the Chinese Army, when terrorism was king. I didn't realize until I found myself relaxing in the peace of Hong Kong how strongly that element was influencing our lives up in Shanghai. People were shot in broad daylight, out in the streets or in restaurants, for almost any suspected action, against the Chungking government, against the Japanese Army, or even in settlement for some private feud. The Japanese do not permit a similar lawlessness in their own country, but they were glad to use Chinese, accustomed to the idea of quick and violent revenge, to stir up their local type of excitement whenever it seemed expedient to remove patriots from their path. About half of the Shanghai assassinations of 1937 and 1938 were probably inspired by the Japs.

Now as to this word "squeeze"; it has become such an integral part of my vocabulary that I am apt to forget that I never heard it before I went to China. In private life it means the money taken out of the housekeeping funds for the houseboy's private use. Theoretically the house owner doesn't know his boy is squeezing, i.e., charging more for the meat, for example, than the butcher does. Actually the houseowner knows and condones, unless the squeeze becomes unreasonably high. There are other methods of domestic squeeze. Suppose I go out and buy a coat.

When the tailor brings it to the house my boy exacts a certain sum from him in the kitchen. The sum is fixed, a certain percentage of the coat's cost. The ramifications of this custom are endless.

In public life an official is squeezing when he takes a commission for some action committed in his public capacity. Suppose a Mr. Wan is buying airplanes for the Chinese Government; the companies offering him planes, if it is known that Mr. Wan is not averse to persuasion, will bid against each other on the bribe. The bribe is called the "squeeze." I thought of airplanes because of a story Dr. Kung told me. On his trip to England to attend the Coronation of the present King he made a side trip to the Continent, and in the course of this journey he visited Daladier. All through Dr. Kung's travels he was followed by a little shoal of munitions salesmen, and it may be that one of these astute gentlemen steered the conversations which the doctor had with Daladier into familiar paths. At any rate, Dr. Kung and M. Daladier did, ultimately, get around to the subject of airplanes. China wanted to buy planes and France wanted to sell them.

"But there was a woman in the deal," Dr. Kung said, "Daladier's secretary. She wanted a large sum of money from us for releasing these planes. She was greedy; she wanted much too much. I became disgusted and went away, and we bought no planes from France. It was not good."

I was impressed by his calm acceptance of the situation. The peculiar system by which France was governed just then, before the war, didn't seem peculiar to him at all. He was shocked not by the fact of corruption in high places but by the degree of it. That is the Chinese attitude. They face facts. They do not pretend on certain subjects as we do. We accept some things they do not; they accept some things we do not. That is why there is so much scandal, I think, in treaty ports where the two races mingle.

I was impressed also by something else in that story. I learned from it that the custom of government squeeze, even though we may not know the word for it, is not exactly new to Occidentals.

Chapter 16

SINMAY AND I came back to Shanghai in August, under the most delightfully melodramatic circumstances. He suddenly took it into his head to disguise himself, because he thought there might be trouble at landing. This was, as a matter of fact, quite possible. The Japs hadn't penetrated our daily lives as long as we stayed where they thought we belonged, which was within the limits of the International Settlement or the French Concession, but they hated us going outside that circle in any direction, and they had a chance to pounce on any arriving travelers who steamed up the Whangpoo past their occupied territory, even during the time such travelers should land at the wharf. Sinmay's record had become sufficiently irritating to the Sons of Heaven to make them take the chance of grabbing him if it presented itself. Therefore he blithely assumed another name.

On the *Maréchal Joffre,* which carried us back to our home town, he was known as Mr. Tsu. He wore European clothes for the first and only time of our acquaintance, and he looked perfectly terrible. I had never noticed before that his legs were too short, and his little beard looked so incongruous above the tweeds that he shaved it off. He used dark spectacles too. He speedily discovered about ten old cronies, and they spent all day sitting on deck, all wearing dark spectacles and all talking about how they were going to outwit the Japanese when the ship docked.

They were in an excited flurry when we arrived, and Sinmay was frankly disappointed that nothing at all happened to us. He walked ashore without being molested by anybody. The chauffeur was waiting with my car, and once we had passed the magic border around the customs jetty it felt as if we had never been away. Not quite, however, since these arrivals and departures always call forth comparisons with other journeys. I returned to my Shanghai with the eagerness of a lover, and that reminded me of the first time I arrived, bored and sulky and frowning, counting the days before I could sail away again. Now I recognized every street corner, and the very beggars in the downtown area were familiar to me. I looked eagerly at shopwindows while the chauffeur gave us the news, harmless domestic tittle-tattle and messages from Zoa that couldn't wait until we got home.

Yet it was a very different city now. It stood alone and beleaguered, surrounded on all sides by a greedy, watchful enemy. That cordon of uniformed spies at the jetty—it had had its effect on our spirits. "Someday soon," I said aloud, "we'll have to fight this out, you know. It isn't going to go on just like this indefinitely."

"It might," said Sinmay. "Things last a long time in China."

We went over and over the same old sayings: how it was to the Japs' advantage to leave our city the way she was, and how America was busy watching developments on the other side of the world and couldn't be expected, et cetera, et cetera. Sinmay never had much to say about Europe and Hitler. I depended on other friends for European-politico conversation. Sir Victor was always full of it, but he was over in the States just then, taking a series of massage for his bad hip. A lot of rich refugees, friends of his, kept me informed pretty well. I discovered soon after I came back that my life was becoming more and more full of European refugees. Failing the Chinese and Bernardine, that was all we had left. (Bernardine had gone to America and was busy building up a salon in Hollywood.)

It had been decided before we left Hong Kong that I would be coming back in the late autumn. I would stay in Hong Kong for a while, talking to Mme. Kung and making abstracts of such documents as the family was willing to let me see. They were generous with that information; Mme. Kung's help was hampered only by the vexing fact that some of her most interesting papers and all the old family photographs had been lost when the Japs moved in on the Kung estate up in Shansi, some months before. The pictures that were available I had copied quickly, before anyone could change his mind. I had compiled a list of names, Shanghai people Mme. Kung suggested for interviews. I was to polish off this part of it, go through the Shanghai newspaper files for various records of milestones in the Soong history, and fix up my house in preparation for a fairly long absence.

"You can work at your ease in Hong Kong," Mme. Kung had said. "Then later in the season, when my sister Mme. Chiang is not so busy as she is just now, organizing her girls' training schools, you will probably be permitted to see her in Chungking. There is just a chance, however, that she will come down to Hong Kong. I am trying to persuade her to do so. She ought to have her teeth seen to, and besides, she needs a general going over; she has never been the same, you know, since her accident in the motorcar that time she came down from Nanking with Donald. It would be nice for you to meet her here. It is a pity that you have to go to Chungking. It's an expensive trip and very uncomfortable, I believe, after you get there. I'm always so sorry for Dr. Kung, living there with never a break, working hard all the time, yet never complaining." She sighed.

"But I ought to see Chungking, don't you see, madame?" I said gently. "Even if Mme. Chiang does come down to the dentist."

She laughed. "You are too conscientious. There is nothing about Chungking to see but the caves for air raids."

"The government is there. The government, which is still resisting the Japanese after fleeing so many hundreds of miles. I ought to see the place just for that reason."

Mme. Kung was not convinced. I couldn't see the government, she reminded me. It wasn't a visible thing; it didn't convene all together except during the plenary sessions, and no lady would want to attend one of those. My eagerness to go tearing off into the muddy hills of Szechuan was incomprehensible to that gentlewoman. A writer, she had always thought, was a civilized stay-at-home sort of person; especially for a lady writer it should be unnecessary to behave like a traveling salesman. Why did I not seize the opportunity to stay in Hong Kong among friends, writing my book at my leisure? That was the way the other writers of her acquaintance behaved. Wen Yuan-ning and his poetry books, John Wu and his recent discovery of the Roman Catholic Church —they were writers. She had been led to believe that I was of the same kidney. She was growing more and more puzzled.

But she kept her word and went on working on my behalf. The result of her endeavors was evident after I returned to Shanghai. I had a telegram from Hollington Tong which arrived by roundabout ways so that it need not pass under the interested eyes of the Jap censors, over across Soochow Creek. In guarded terms Holly told me that if I should present myself at Mme. Chiang's door sometime in the following season of early winter, up there in Chungking, I would not be turned away. Not that they were in any particular hurry for me to arrive, you understand; the whole thing seemed to bore Holly and his department, as well it might. But anyway, I could see Madame. That was a tremendous step forward. You could almost call it a leap.

Mme. Sun would not make a similar gesture of hospitality. She has a small coterie of foreign friends among whom is Randall Gould, editor of the Shanghai *Evening Post,* who in his long career as a newspaperman for various journals, especially the *Christian Science Monitor,* has met her officially and socially more times than most people can claim. Her friendly attitude toward Randall is perhaps based on the color of his writings. He has written for the *New Republic* and the *Nation,* besides doing his own daily grind, and always in favor of the Chinese Communists. Ching-ling will not name herself a Communist. (I have never met anyone except an American, for that matter, who would.) But Randall, as a friend, was worth having and he could always get an audience with her. On one of his 1939 trips to Hong Kong he found her sitting with another old friend, an American missionary. Mme. Sun keeps up perhaps more than any other Soong with her foreign acquaintances. She is more in favor of internationalism than are the others. It surprised Randall at first that she should be so wrapped up in missionaries, because that is not the accepted idea of a Communist sympathizer. But, he recalled, Mme. Sun is much influenced still by her early days at a Methodist school in America.

"Haven't you had a letter from my friend Mickey Hahn?" he asked her.

Mme. Sun indicated that she had and that the matter was still under advisement. The missionary was galvanized into life at my name, and exclaimed in shocked horror that I had dared address myself to Madame. Were not the Soongs aware, she demanded, of my immoral record? Ching-ling requested—and got—highly colored details of the said record. She was suitably distressed. According to her intimate friends she is very squeamish about such matters: Hilda Selwyn-Clarke, who worked as her secretary for years, told me that she has never been able to make Mme. Sun say a word in favor of the birth-control clinic that Hilda founded in Hong Kong. "She looks pained and changes the subject," said Hilda. "I'm getting so that I dare not talk about anything remotely connected with sex when I'm with her. It's almost pathological."

Nobody can accuse Randall of being easily frightened by squeamishness. He promptly spoke up in opposition to the missionary and had the satisfaction at last of getting as a reply from Ching-ling the sort of silence (she converses in silences) that showed her mind was not closed, at any rate. I owe it to Mme. Kung that her sister's mind remained the slightest bit open, during the rest of the book's writing.

Getting ready in Shanghai, I decided to prepare for cold weather in Chungking. Perhaps I would have enough of it after a week end, but I doubted it. Things never move that swiftly. It would be bitterly cold there, especially in the houses. I duly bought long pants, and sweaters, and a padded Chinese gown which made me look absolutely cubic, if you can imagine a cube with bulges here and there. Zoa made that gown her special care, selecting deep plum color for the outside and a lighter purple for the lining. She said that I should really go the whole hog and order another one, padded only half as thick and done in a pastel color, for underneath. Chinese ladies did that, she said, when they were going into the interior, but it took up a lot of room in packing and we decided against it.

The most important purchase to my way of thinking was the boots. I have suffered from chilblains in cold weather ever since I spent a winter in sunny Italy, in an ancient stone palace without rugs on the floor. Therefore I ordered those boots which were to make me a laughingstock, but at least a comfortable laughingstock, in China's wartime capital. They were high boots like waders and they were lined with sheepskin. I've seen something like them since I came back to America, something that goes by the name of "stadium boots." But stadium boots are tiny, dainty things compared with the waders I took to Chungking.

The days were filled with noise and activity. Chin Lien had already left my employ, having saved up enough in years of slow, patient squeeze to invest in a little glass factory where he wouldn't have to work so hard. He called on me once in a while, bringing peculiar glassware objects as presents. It would not be so much of a wrench, now, to leave the house.

Looking over my letters home during this period, I am impressed by the way I seem to have stretched the silver cord almost to breaking point. It is true that I seem to have talked now and then, vaguely, of coming home for a visit. I discover an indignant outburst directed against my agent, who evidently had dared to suggest that I return for a while just to get in touch with the market again, to learn what America was like, and perhaps to furbish up my English. Obviously my feeble gestures toward America were not sincere. There is more sincerity in a plan I made to persuade my mother to come out and visit me. We almost put it over. She was to buy a ticket, round trip to Manila, on one of those cruises, which few people were taking now that the Japanese had moved in so close. The idea was that she should get off in Shanghai and pick up the boat on its way back; thus she would have a fairly long visit without being in danger of forgetting to return, as her daughter had done for the past six years. Something I said had worried Mother and I suspect that is why she was girding up her loins to make the trip.

One of your recent letters, Mother [I wrote], sounds very agitated about my idea of having a baby. Calm yourself; I hereby promise not to, until I can Give It A Name. All right? All right. I wasn't really serious, you know. Where would *I* put a baby? If you could only see how serious I am, and hardworking, and wholesome, and the old ladies' favorite, you wouldn't worry about me.

I'm not so sure Mother swallowed that. If my daughter ever writes a letter like that to me I'll probably pack up straightaway and come running to see what it is all about. Mother couldn't, though; there were too many other branches of the family needing her attention. In the meantime I couldn't have been thinking very hard about that hypothetical baby. Mr. Mills in the past year had given me a good deal of trouble, just worrying about his happiness. He slept indoors, in a movable cage, but during the day he swung around in his outside cage, and when it was cold he wore a fur coat. It was made up of bits taken out of my Chinese sable coat and the tailor never charged me for the gibbon's garments, but the fact that my pet wore sables made rather a scandal.

People seemed to resent something else about him too—his diapers. I couldn't understand why it annoyed them so much. To me it seemed the obvious way to keep him clean and comfortable. A gibbon is almost as easily housebroken as a dog. This was fortunate, because Mr. Mills lived a strangely civilized life. Sometimes he went downtown with me for lunch, and he attended so many cocktail parties that I received one nervous little invitation from an Englishwoman with a penciled note on the back: "Sorry we cannot extend invitation to Mr. Mills." I was unreasonably angry and didn't go to the party at all. The diaper idea, whatever could be urged against it, made him a much more acceptable caller. I suppose they didn't like it because to a lot of people the very appearance of an anthropoid ape is insulting. Putting such human-style clothes as diapers on the animal just points the insult.

I bought a female gibbon at an outrageous price, considering that she was old and tired and evidently ill. Once I saw the animal I couldn't leave her in the pet shop. She was chained by the neck to her basket, with only a foot-length of chain, and she was miserable. I bought her.

As soon as she came to the house I let her go and she climbed to the highest beam or curtain pole that she could find to sit on. After that we had to keep all the windows and doors closed, unless they were screened, for Mrs. Mills out in the open would just run away from everybody until she was shot or starved. She was a disappointment; her interest in Mr. Mills was that of a bored grandmother, and he wasn't interested in her at all, once he had discovered that she didn't feel playful. Little by little, though, she unbent. At first while I was romping and wrestling with Mills on the floor or the bed I would feel an iron grip on my sleeve, a sort of snatch, and I would look up to see Mrs. Mills retiring to her eyrie, making a threatening face at me. When she realized I wasn't torturing another gibbon her patriotic spirit was soothed. It began to look as if she were jealous of our games. She looked down on them wistfully. But never, never could she bring herself to join in.

I did tame her to some extent. Nobody else could groom her, but I could. She climbed down and leaned on my lap when she saw me. Once when Peter, the enthusiastic Russian lady, dashed in and kissed me, Mrs. Mills bit her savagely, sinking her tusks in up to the gums. I was scared to death, but Peter as a gibbon lover refused to complain. Mrs. Mills lived in the house as a strange gray wraith, drifting about and picking up her food whenever it pleased her to do so. Unlike Mills, she had black markings, an apron effect down her front that made her seem indecently naked. She would float like that supernatural man in *Dr. Caligari* over the table when we were eating, swiping bread or bananas. She much preferred the food she stole to anything we gave her. But soon she sickened with pneumonia. Sinmay and I put on gloves and grappled with her successfully, putting a warm coat over her naked-looking body, and once she was dressed she liked it. But the poor old lady sniffled and coughed and weakened for about eight days, and then one night, after having rallied and eaten too much, she died.

Sinmay and Zoa were surprisingly sympathetic. They had been cross with me for buying her, but when she was dead they were kind, and offered me a room in their house until her ghost should have left my room. Still, they began to look worried when a pet dealer called me up and said that Singapore was sending him two young gibbons, a male and a female, on which he would give me first refusal.

"Thank goodness you are going away," said Sinmay.

"But you can buy them for me," I said sweetly. "Can't you? I'll leave the money here, and my people can take care of them. All winter they had better stay indoors. They won't be used to this climate. I have ordered suits of clothes from the tailor already."

He moaned in anguish.

There was a round of parties in farewell. Sir Victor had come back. He was in time to see me off and to read the first tentative chapters of my book. I had collected enough already, in fact, to write all of the childhood history of Charlie Soong, and I was getting well into Shanghai and the birth of the girls when I handed the manuscript over to Victor. It was then that he did me an enormous favor.

I am not an introverted type of writer. On the contrary, I feel much better if I can have an audience near at hand. As soon as I have written more than five thousand words I want to rush off and show them to somebody, and talk about them, and get opinions, and defend myself. Up until then I had used my old friends from the Monday Night Club as victims, trying the book out on them chapter by chapter. They listened, appreciated, made a few gentle suggestions, asked a few questions, but kept telling me that it was too soon to judge. Victor was not so polite. He sent me my precious chapters with a blunt note: "This is dull," he said flatly. "It bored me to death. If I hadn't been in bed already, I would have fallen asleep in my chair, reading it."

Startled out of my conceit, I set to work on the book all over again. *The Soong Sisters* is still pretty dull, in my estimation. Thanks to Sir Victor it isn't even worse. I tore it all up and started again, in livelier vein, and before I left Shanghai he confessed that the second version kept him awake until one o'clock, anyway.

Then something happened that threw the whole pattern of my life, book and imminent trip and Mr. Mills's love life and all, into the shadows. The war began, over in Europe.

We were startled. We were distressed. We began remembering the other war, the one we had always thought would free us from any more in our generation. Probably in the back of our heads was the thought, "The really grim things, the big bombings and battles, never come out as far as the East. We fought the war at long distance last time and we'll fight it like that again. Our English boys will join up and sail away, and it is all very distressing, but it isn't happening here, not out in China. We will get off with our own tiny, slightly comic oriental war; that is our contribution."

This was in our minds in spite of what everyone told us on the radio over in America and England. I paused, sighed, looked wonderingly at the excited refugees, who were taking it very hard, and went on with my preparations. I was very angry with the government of Hong Kong for making a lot of silly new regulations about letting people in.

The shipping companies kept all their sailings secret, so my departure was simple and not crowded. Chin Lien saw me off.

"I'll be back in three months at the most," I promised everyone. "I'll stay just long enough to gather the rest of the material, and then I'll come back here to write it up. So long; I'll be seeing you!"

I never saw Shanghai again.

Chapter 17

FROM NOW ON my life was to be managed on a budget. I had made up my mind to put away the little extravagances of Shanghai, and as an earnest of good intentions I traveled second-class to Hong Kong and went to a definitely second-rate hotel when I got there. The cheaper hostelries of Hong Kong can always be recognized because they are built out of cardboard, and mine was no exception. The floor telephone was just outside the door of my room, and all day and all night the floor boy answered its ring with a long-drawn-out "We-e-e-e-ei!" that sounded like a newborn kid calling its mother. The entrance was on a steeply sloping street, and our whole building was tucked in next to the Matsubara Hotel, reserved for Japanese people. I used to peer into the next-door lobby with great interest as I climbed the hill to my own place. Officially the Japanese were still friendly with Britain, and many of them lived in Hong Kong; you saw their squat, bowlegged women sauntering about the mid-level streets, May Road and Kennedy Road and Mac-Donnell Road, all favorite residence districts for the Sons of Heaven.

Mme. Kung promised to get me to Chungking without a lengthy wait, although there was an imposing list of people anxious to travel up to Szechuan by the only short route left to us. In the meantime I played around: I bumped into Ian Morrison again, fresh from a trip through Indo-China, and spent a lot of time with Bob Winter from Peking.

Peking, like all the other never-never lands of the world, has its little collection of traditions and good stories, and its aristocracy of old-timers. Bob Winter is one of the old-timers. You will probably not read about him in the Peking novels and travel books that fill any Far East bookstore, but he is famous in his world nonetheless. A very long time ago he taught Romance languages in Evanston, but for the past eighteen years, I think it is, he has spent most of his time in Peking, working for the Rockefeller Institute and teaching at a university there. He is a big man with freakish glands or some other accident of physiology that has prevented him from showing any signs of advancing age. Perhaps his life has had a lot to do with it. Bob in all those years has been doing exactly the sort of thing he likes doing best. Few people can claim a record like that.

Like myself, Bob is an exhibitionist and would sell his grandmother if the transaction would make a good story. Or rather, he wouldn't bother to sell her; he would merely say he had done it and make a better story than the truth out of the old lady. Unlike me, though, he isn't a good listener, and our relationship developed along unusual lines. Bob did all the talking, which is not unusual, but I did all the listening and that is. I have since learned how to bully him into listening to me sometimes. There is a certain grim quality about all of our conversations, due to this unending struggle.

He had much more to talk about in those Hong Kong days, anyway, than I did. Peking had been under Japanese influence for some years, and the happy, peaceful life Bob led was threatened to such a degree that he had beaten the other lotus-eaters to the inevitable decision. He was giving it up until happier days. Farewell, then, to the Winter house with its famous flower gardens and the fruit-cats and pet deer which he kept in the gardens. Bob had decided to go in for a life of espionage. I am giving away no secrets when I tell this, because Bob wasn't like Ian Morrison and the other British Intelligence boys; he advertised himself directly instead of by implication.

Spy work is fun, of course, to anybody who hasn't grown old beyond redemption. Bob had a grand time. All his activities were thought up by himself, carried through on his own, and rewarded with nothing but an occasional thank you from the Chinese in Chungking. Bob was no government employee; he worked against the Japs purely as a side line, and usually as a personal favor to some friend in the guerrillas or somewhere. He never laughed at himself; he was deadly serious about it all. His methods were highly colored and reminiscent of Oppenheim or Sax Rohmer. There was the story of the white jade carving, a tiny bit of a thing which Bob carried around in his pocket. You see them in quantities in curio shops. There was some intricate business about a message and a radio for the guerrillas of Shantung: Bob kept a receiving set in his house which was to be given to the wandering soldiers, and the man who called for the set must be identified, so Bob broke the carving in half, gave one piece over, taught a password to the contact man, and there you were. When the messenger came for the radio he produced the missing half and the password, and all went well. Bob loved that sort of thing.

I have noticed it before about the people who live in Peking; they all seem to go in for lurid adventure along these lines. If they haven't fooled around with smuggling from Manchuria they have had a lot to do with the local wars. The Japanese venture, in their eyes, was just more of the same kind of excitement, but they were proved wrong in the end and the game went too far and was taken out of their hands. Not that it was ever in their hands. I have always thought it very nice of the Chinese to let Peking foreigners preen themselves on their "influence." Since those fabulous days when almost any missionary who happened to be around could nab a cushy job as adviser to the Ch'ing court it has been the same up north; the Chinese have handed little commissions over to us, small favors involving our passports or errands for us to run, back and forth between Chinese officials. We have been very useful to the Chinese of the old school, and they have been duly grateful. I don't think the new-fangled Chinese need us quite so much, or feel quite as grateful, but I think they will let us go on working for them as long as we want to. Romance in China is not yet dead.

Bob was this romance personified. He brought a large retinue down from Peking, including a Eurasian girl in search of her papa down in Indo-China (she carried The Papers in her girdle), a little Japanese woman whose Chinese husband was teaching in a university in Free China—this girl had always been very useful, Bob assured me, and she simply hated the Japanese—and the Living Buddha of Outer Mongolia.

This last item completely overshadowed all the others. The Delawah Butuktuk (the spelling is my own version of his Mongol name) was introduced to me at the hotel where they stayed, a Chinese hostel down on the water front, with mah-jongg parties going on all day and all night in practically every room but Bob's and the Buddha's. The Buddha was a new one on me but Bob assured me that he was a famous figure in Peking. For more than twenty years he had lived there, an exile from Outer Mongolia since the Russians had driven him out of his own country when they took that territory under their protection.

We are apt to think there is only one Living Buddha, the Dalai Lama whose picture, done up in gold paint, we saw everywhere when he was installed in office as a little boy of five. There are, however, at least seven of them. The Dalai Lama just happens to be more publicized than the others. Bob's Buddha was a man between fifty and sixty, with charming manners and a pock-marked face. According to Bob, he had decided that it was time to get out of Peking before the Japs grabbed him and incorporated him in their plans for a free, glorious New Asia. He wanted to go to Tibet, his spiritual home, a place he knew well, although in his present incarnation he has never been there. The Buddha depended heavily on Bob for guidance in this venture. He planned to go first to Chungking, to assure the Generalissimo of his preference for Chinese rather than Japanese, and then he would make his way south, around the coast, over India into Tibet.

Bob undertook to get him out of Peking. It entailed a disguise, of course, and disguising a Buddha is not a simple matter. Bob's first plan was to dress him like a Tibetan, and then to hire a number of ordinary Tibetans and to send them all together through the frontier guard in a Ford. The Buddha didn't like that notion. It seems that a Buddha must always wear a certain shade of yellow, regardless of what shape his clothes may take. Thus, though he was willing to wear Western clothes suitable for a Tibetan tourist of the middle class, these clothes had to be yellow. He appeared for the journey in yellow tweeds, with a yellow plush hat something like a Homburg. And here at last they were, safe in Hong Kong!

It would have been all right, probably, if Bob as raconteur had been satisfied with the story of the clothes and of the old man's retort when the Japanese emigration official asked him if he had been vaccinated: "Isn't my face enough for you?" he is alleged to have retorted. But Bob was proud of the fact that he had meddled with his divine ward's passport. I don't remember what sort of passport it was, but Bob had erased the date on it and substituted another one. He probably had excellent reasons for doing so, if he ever really did it, which is always a pertinent question to put to Bob when he tells stories. But he need not have boasted about this deed so much in Hong Kong, where all the officials were nervous and jumpy and very watchful. Bob forgot he had left China behind, outside the Colony limits. He was in British territory now, among suspicious imperialists. He and the Living Buddha couldn't get up to Chungking as quickly as they had hoped. They were detained and questioned. Rightly or wrongly, Bob put this delay down to Captain Boxer's address: we had all lunched together one day and everyone but the Buddha got intoxicated, and Bob thought Charles had squinted at him suspiciously or something. Anyway, the questions began next day, and since Charles was chief of Intelligence in Hong Kong the whole thing, in Bob's judgment, was obvious. Because of that man Boxer he and his poor old Buddha were being persecuted by the stupid, thick-headed, bureaucratic British.

I was cross with the British myself. But I didn't think it was Captain Boxer's fault; he did not seem to me the sort of person who would not appreciate the Living Buddha's special flavor. I defended him steadily whenever Bob went off into a typical Winter tirade.

"Anyway," I pointed out, "the Buddha is having a lovely time here. He has learned to go on the Peak tram all by himself."

"He has," Bob admitted. "He goes up every day. Yesterday he picked up another Mongolian, up on the top; he was awfully pleased about that, and I think it was remarkable myself. He likes collecting fountain pens too."

I gathered as much information about the old man as I could, for my private delectation. I liked him. Of course one is predisposed to like a person with such a history; it is just like being bemused by Chinese women and their charm. But I would have liked the Delawah if I hadn't known who he was. He had a sweet smile, a pleasant chuckle, and a halting delivery of Mandarin which was enough like mine to make conversation possible. He didn't like Chinese as a general rule, Bob explained; Mongols often do not. He found that he got on better with Europeans. He was doomed, evidently, to a lifetime of nostalgia for the steppes of Mongolia, although one human life should not seem long to an immortal, and our old Buddha didn't seem inclined to complain. Obviously he looked forward to the windy uplands of Tibet, which, as he remembered from another incarnation, was rather like Mongolia.

One day when I was wondering how much longer I was to live in that awful hotel I received a mysterious message from a Chinese official. The ticket for Mrs. Wang, he said, was all ready, and I was to drop in and get it that afternoon. For no reason which any Occidental could possibly figure out it had been decided that I was to travel incognito on the plane. Don't ask me why, because nobody ever explained it to me. That is simply the way things are done in high circles in China. I was writing the life story of the Soong sisters, and so I traveled under an assumed name, by special arrangement with the British and Chinese authorities. Everyone was duly apprised of this fact: Mrs. Wang's ticket was made out. I called for it, feeling uneasily as though I should have worn a thick black veil and come by night, instead of strolling into the CNAC office on a sunny afternoon. (Donald always used an assumed name too.)

The passenger planes flying between Free China and Hong Kong did as much of their traveling as possible at night. They started out from Hong Kong between midnight and two in the morning, and they started from Chungking or any other inland airfield at a time calculated to bring them over Japanese-occupied territory in the dark. None of us had forgotten the plane that was forced down into the Pearl River, when Woody, the pilot, had to swim for his life and passengers struggling with the river current were machine-gunned by Japanese.

The pilots of passenger planes were for the most part American. By the nature of their work they were thrown pretty much together. They all lived in flats near Kai Tak, in the most modern building you could find in Kowloon, the Eu Gardens. The pilots' wives saw each other as constantly as if they had been members of the same family. They lived the life of an American small town, glorified by the fact that out here in Hong Kong there was no servant problem and the "boys" made wonderful money, with bonuses whenever they went on extra trips. The women played mah-jongg all day, or bridge; they gave delectable lunches for each other and for the other American wives in town. They dressed in the American fashion and so they were the smartest women to be seen in town, perhaps the only smart women to be seen, because the young Englishwomen, though they tried, hadn't really learned yet how to dress. I couldn't keep up with them—I couldn't drink enough, or play mah-jongg well enough, or spend enough money, but just the same I was proud of them, on behalf of America. They kept the town stirred up. But they were their own club, with little communication with the outside world save through the medium of the American Club, over in the Hong Kong and Shanghai Bank. They were definitely one clique.

If you lived on the Hong Kong side of the harbor, setting out from Kai Tak airport at two in the morning offered a problem to the uninitiated. The ferryboats stopped running at twelve at night, I think it was —or was it? Dear me, the war has knocked all of that out of my head, and yet those ferry schedules used to be engraved on our brains in the old days. Anyway, the ferry didn't run late enough. An old-timer in Hong Kong would have known that you could always hire a little motor boat, called a "walla-walla," for onomatopoetic reasons, I think. I was not an old-timer and I fell for the plane company's suggestion that I go across early and register at some hotel on the other side. It was an elaborate and unnecessary program, but I fell for it. Mme. Kung was as kind as she always is, and arranged everything for the journey. She still maintained stoutly that I would stay in Szechuan only a week end, long enough for one interview with her illustrious sister. She laughed at my luggage, which was more plentiful by far than she considered necessary. But she helped.

One of the Kung bodyguards was told off to see me into the plane. He carried out his duties with unnecessary thoroughness and made me feel decidedly of another world. He accompanied me on the ferry and saw me to the Kowloon Hotel, a building later to achieve unsavory fame as a Jap concentration center for American and British prisoners. The theory of this hotel stop was that I should lie down and rest until it was time to go to the airport. I couldn't lie down and rest. I was much too excited. My head was spinningly full of Mme. Kung and Chungking and everything else. I packed my bags all over again, and when I started out to go just once more to the ladies' room I was astounded and dismayed at stumbling over the feet of the Kung bodyguard, who was standing in front of the door with his arms crossed, duly guarding me.

I had already tipped and dismissed him, with a secret feeling of relief, so it was a nasty shock to find him still there. It was worse when he came along with me to the lavatory, standing grimly on guard in the hall until I came out again. All the Chinese around there regarded me with becoming awe. I blushed and hurried back into the bedroom, cursing inwardly. At last it was time to go to the airport; the guard stood waiting, faithful to the last. As I climbed clumsily into the taxi I had a hopeful idea that he would now say good night, but he didn't. He got in too, next to the driver.

I climbed clumsily in and I climbed clumsily out when we reached the field, and there was a reason. Everybody who has traveled by plane in China knows why. And since everybody has also written about it in his memoirs I won't drag out the explanation. We are limited in our baggage on these planes but there is no extra charge for bodily weight. Therefore travelers usually wear as many clothes as they can, and carry whatever they can cram into their pockets, and also carry extra coats over their arms. I was taking an overcoat up to some young bank clerk whose old father in Shanghai had begged me to do him this small favor. The old man had stuffed all the pockets of the coat with socks, tooth-powder cans, bond certificates, and God knows what else that was contraband. I had my own clothes to worry about too. They had told me that Chungking was cold and I was taking no chances. First I was wearing a woolen dress and jacket. Over that I wore a cloth coat. Over that a fur coat of Chinese mink. On top of all that the Chinese padded gown of plum-colored silk. On my feet were the famous sheepskin boots, on their first trip and gaining fame by the minute. I looked like a deep-sea diver. I walked like one too.

There were lots of other passengers waiting to get aboard, but I was the star for the journey. I was expected. The bodyguard followed me through the necessary ceremonies, including the weighing in (I weighed one hundred and eighty pounds), and then before I had gone through the magic barrier that led to the field a tall man in ordinary clothes, with a drooping mustache and a British accent, invited me into the office room of the hangar. He was Moss, civil officer in charge of the airport. I came to know him so well later that I feel a slight shock as I write this account, at the thought that there was a first time for us to meet.

He and Sir Archibald Clark-Kerr were about the only public-office Britons I ever met who could get along on sensible, human terms with the Chinese. These two, who had very little in common otherwise, managed to cancel out a thousand snubs and unconscious stupidities perpetrated by less civilized colleagues. Nobody had told me about Moss, and I was puzzled but pleased at meeting him on the eve of my entry into Chungking; it was fitting, and a good omen. All the while we talked, while the plane was warming up, the Kung bodyguard stood just within the door in his now familiar attitude, arms folded, face sternly watchful.

"He's taking care of you all right, that chap," said Moss, laughing. "He's seeing you straight into the plane or know the reason why."

They telephoned up to the office: all was ready. Once more I put on the fur coat and the padded coat and the cloth coat and everything else; once more I shouldered the old man's banker son's overcoat, and I clumped down the iron stairs and was hoisted into the plane and wedged into my seat. I shook hands with Moss, I waved good-by, really good-by this time, to the bodyguard. He saluted. The plane roared, raced across the field, and suddenly was up in the air, heading into a dark but starry sky.

Chapter 18

IT IS HARD to estimate how many books of memoirs will be written about the Chungking of those days, and how many times you, reader, will go through descriptions of the Chungking Hostel. Quite a few on both counts, I should think, because we are living in a good age for writers, and almost everyone who has ever published an article gets himself sent into Szechuan sooner or later. On the other hand, you will get a lot more data on the Press Hostel than you will on my first stopping place, the Chungking Hostel, because I didn't rate as a newspaperman, and I had my reward: I didn't have to go and live under Holly Tong's wing. I fell into the same category as visiting plane salesmen and oil people. The Press Hostel was quite exquisitely uncomfortable, whereas the Chungking Hostel was just mildly awful.

I had a shattering experience the minute I arrived in town. I got myself lost. The plane dumped us, about eight in the morning, on a sandspit at the foot of a shabby-looking cliff on which houses were propped with every sort of wooden beam, strut, or stilt, sticking out from the rocky wall at any possible angle that would balance. Some of the houses looked fairly solid and stony, but most of them were built of reeds or other woodeny material. There was a shaky wooden pathway out to the sandspit, and there were sedan chairs waiting for us as we got through Customs. Nobody met me at the plane.

I walked out into the murky half-light that passed for daylight in Chungking and got into a sedan chair. My luggage was piled up in front of me and on my lap, and the coolies started straight up the side of the cliff, like mountain goats.

I have never gone through the phase experienced by most Europeans in China when they first see rickshas. I was always ready to admit that it was shameful to be pulled around on wheels by another human being when I was just as able to walk as he was. But, I said, why balk at a ricksha when you are doing just as much harm in every other way, merely by living like a foreigner in the overcrowded country of China? The shoes I walk in have been made by sweated labor; the shoemaker, beaten down by my bargaining, takes it out of his workers, and so they are being exploited (by me) just as much as the ricksha coolie is. The only difference between the shoemaker and the ricksha coolie is that I don't have to watch the former during his travail. The same goes for the farmer in the field, growing my rice, and the little boys in the kitchen of my favorite restaurant, and the workers in the coal and salt mines. And so, because I want to go on wearing shoes and eating meals and using coal and salt, I use rickshas too, without wasting time in insincere pity and oratory. But those chair coolies got me down.

They breathed in loud, stertorous gasps before we were halfway up to the first zigzag in the road. I saw how their shoulders had been warped into great lumps from the carrying poles, and their legs looked foreshortened and squashed with all their muscles, from being pressed downward. We hadn't gone very far when I yelled at them to stop.

Mandarin and Szechuanese have an occasional sound in common. They knew what I was saying, and they stopped and argued with me. I said I would walk for a while. They said never mind, they felt fine. I said never mind, I wanted to walk. They told each other I was a missionary and resignedly trotted along at my heels. For some time I hoisted my overclothed, overfed body up the steep track, much too winded to look at the view, which grew better with every step I took. At last my breathing grew louder than that of the coolies at their worst.

"You have walked," said the front one. "You have walked well. Now sit down again; we are in a hurry."

Then we ran into more difficulties. We couldn't seem to agree on where we were going. I said, "Chungking Hostel," over and over again, and at last in desperation I changed it to the Chinese for "American consulate." Nobody had told me that we had no consulate in Chungking, strictly speaking, because we had an embassy, and this embassy was across the river on the South Bank. The coolies knew it, though. They talked to each other awhile and then, resigned to fate, they started again at a brisk pace to take me straight into the Chialing River.

At least that must have been their plan. They were going down to the bank just as fast as they could, when all of a sudden I saw two English people, a man and a woman. They were so out of place there in that Chinese village street that I thought for a moment they had been cut out of a book, like paper dolls, and pasted down on this background. The man was smoking a pipe and wearing plus-fours and a tweed jacket, and the woman, palely blonde, wore a camel's-hair coat and no hat, and they had a Scotty dog on a lead. I shouted at my coolies to stop, I climbed out of the chair and rushed over to them. Their name was Milligan and they too were surprised at the meeting.

"Where is the Chungking Hostel, for God's sake?" I demanded. "My name is Emily Hahn and I come from Shanghai."

"It is just behind you over beyond that building," said the man, and the woman said, "From Shanghai? Did you know my brother Jack Crompton?"

I said, "Why, yes; he told me he had a sister in China."

"Our name is Milligan," said the man. "You were going straight into the Chialing River. There's no more roadway in this direction."

They set me down at the right place this time, and told me how much to pay the coolies, and went away. Waiting at the hostel was a worried little man who should have met the plane but had overslept.

You must have read about the hostel; it didn't have much future by the time I arrived. It had been put up for the pilots originally and for any official connected with flying, but now there was such a boom in occidental travelers that Dr. Kung had taken it over for them, and Chinese weren't supposed to live there. They were distributed among other places where there wasn't any running water and where the toilets were more primitive. We had nothing to complain about in regard to the plumbing; in such a flimsy structure it was really wonderful that we had plumbing. I was given a room on the ground floor next to the plumbing. It was a big room, much superior to the little cubicles upstairs where regular residents were salted away. Out back was a courtyard surrounded by more cubicles; the cook boys lived there and there was a big private assembly hall or dining room. The whole thing was built of cardboard, or, as Donald told me later, of lath and plaster. The government, expecting a lot more bombing, did not waste labor or stone on real buildings.

I was downcast by the darkness of the weather, but I didn't realize that. In Chungking for most of the year you must battle a weather depression that is something like the feeling an inexperienced person has in London. It is dark and moist and foggy in Chungking. This adds to the discomfort of the mud underfoot and the insufficient heating in wintertime.

After a while I got over it, just as I always got over it in London, but that day I was chilly and sleepy from flying all night, and I must have felt like hell because I can still remember it. I went to bed. It was possible to go to bed in that room, and it was also possible to sit at a table and typewrite, and if you had any clothes you could hang them up in a rickety wardrobe. There was one other chair, and that was all there was in this room, which was the best the town offered and which cost a very great deal. I don't notice comfort much or discomfort, but even I noticed that the bed wasn't very good. Just the same I went to sleep, and I didn't wake up until several hours later when Corin Bernfelt knocked on the door.

She was not pretty but she looked alert and amusing. She was small and skinny; her hair, light brown, fell around her shoulders long and straight and was held off her face with an Alice band. There was nothing to do about hair in Chungking, she explained, and without a good permanent she never could manage her hair anyway. She was English and talked exactly like my younger friends in London, rapidly yet with a drawl.

There is nothing in Chungking but the war and the people. Except for the native population, who are only waiting anyway until we can go away and leave them as they were, there is nothing there and no way to live in the cardboard houses unless you make your own world on that camping ground. You make that world, when you have learned your way around, out of the people who, like you, have pitched their tents there for as long as they must. As things turned out Corin was a good friend of mine and an important figure in my self-built city, and I should have realized at the beginning that we didn't think alike about people. It would have made a difference later on and it might have saved Corin's life if I had taken the lead in those matters. Although she seemed self-sufficient and downright she wasn't really. She was younger than I by a few years, and all alone in Chungking; she had drifted there by a queer series of circumstances.

She was working for Indusco, she told me. In those days we hadn't learned to call it Indusco, which was a name thought up as part of an advertising drive when its sponsors began canvassing for funds outside of China. We called it the "Co-ops." Corin was a "secretary" for the organization, and I never figured out just what she really did for them; she had a lot of little duties, really, that were bewilderingly varied. While we sat in my bare room and talked the rest of the regular inmates of the hotel came to meet me and to have a look.

Maya Rodeivitch was one of these, a girl who had come to Chungking along with the Chinese, from Hankow, retreating with them before the Japanese step by step all the way from Nanking to begin with. That was a real record, and I looked at Maya with respect when I heard it. I hadn't paid much attention to her at first because she had what I thought was a Russian accent, and I was used to Russians in China. Maya was Polish, though, and she wasn't just another outport girl. She had a job with the Chinese Government; she was another secretary. The place was lousy with secretaries.

In the course of the lunch hour I got a pretty good picture of Chungking society. Many of the Chinese personages and all of the diplomats rated houses of their own, and ran their lives in a fairly normal way with servants and kitchens, but the rest of the visiting population just did whatever they could, finding rooms with families and eating around at restaurants. The Chungking Hostel was a valuable part of life there, for you could eat foreign-style food in its dining room, and a lot of the Chinese had acquired a taste for foreign food. It wasn't good food but it wasn't half bad. I made the acquaintance of Chungking chicken right away. It is probably fundamentally like other chicken, but there is one disconcerting thing about it and that is its skin, which is coal-black. Until you have been reassured, it is startling to find black or navy-blue chicken meat on your plate.

Besides the Chinese who wanted to eat boiled black chicken I saw the other Westerners of Chungking, men from two rival plane-manufacturing companies, newspapermen who were taking a vacation from the dreadful cuisine of the Press Hostel, and an odd traveling salesman here and there. Also Fenn Lynch, who was adviser to Kung and the Financial Ministry. I had known him in Shanghai, where he had given a totally false impression of sober dignity. In Shanghai he dressed exactly like a banker and he looked like a banker, with his white hair and his clipped mustache. He sounded like a New York banker, too, because he had a slightly phony accent that was a little bit English and a little bit something else hard to describe, although a lot of people out East get it. We call it "bamboo American." I am tainted with it myself, I suppose. Anyway, some people have mentioned it now that I'm back here in America. It comes of talking a lot with foreigners and trying to enunciate clearly so they'll understand. Fenn had been brought up in foreign parts and so he had more reason than most of us for a special manner of talking, but it was fun to watch for his Irish accent. When Fenn started to talk Irish it meant that he was very drunk indeed. I hadn't known about that in Shanghai, but I learned it in Chungking. I scarcely recognized him when I first saw him there. He was wearing the shortest shorts I have ever seen in my life, although it was midwinter, and his face had a ruddy tinge and he was shouting Irish.

Little by little I got the community sorted out. Some of the luckier people were living in missionary houses. They were lucky because the missionaries, having lived in Chungking for years, were settled in and had spacious places, and kitchens, and comfortable beds, and cooks. Tilman Durdin and his newly wedded wife Peggy, charming people both, lived in a mission. Till was on the New York *Times,* and his office was in the hostel so I saw the Durdins a lot. I learned right away that distances counted for everything in Chungking, where the gasoline shortage had done away with all but the most necessary government motorcars. People walked everywhere, uphill and down through the valley.

Maya Rodeivitch did a fantastic sort of work: she broadcast in French at four in the morning and as far as I could see she did nothing else except on week ends, when she crossed the river to the South Bank and visited at one of the oil-company houses. Officially her secretarial work was for one of the Ministers, Chiu Chia-hwa, who had been trained in Germany, but I never saw her doing any secretarial work. I began to realize what her job really was, though, when she came to see me in my room alone. She talked, and she asked questions. She asked me what I thought of the Soongs, and she hinted that she didn't think much of them, and waited to see if I would bite.

"Now I wonder," I said to myself, "who she is working for. This is so clumsy and obvious that it must be that she reports to someone in the saddle. It must be the Kuomintang." Maya was quite harmless. Nobody ever said anything to the contrary, although a lot of people thought her much too noisy playing poker late at night, or coming up the stairs bursting with Polish energy and clumping her boots, or coughing. She coughed constantly and the foggy Chungking air was very bad for her.

There was a "hostess" for the hostel: Adelaide Yang, wife of Jack Yang —I mean Jack Young, the explorer. Adelaide's Chinese name was Su-lin (the Panda was named after her) and we all tried to make her use it, but it didn't come natural to her because she was an American-born girl. She was very pretty and always bemused people right away.

My first evening I was taken out to the Shanghai Restaurant around the corner by some of Holly Tong's office workers. Teddy White came with us. Teddy was new to China but had learned a lot of Chinese at Harvard and had been sent out by *Time* as a correspondent. He was very young and cocky, and knew simply everything about everything. Corin was with us, and so was an old Shanghai friend, Ma Ping-ho, an Irishman turned Chinese, who had struck up a friendship with Teddy on the basis of Chinese calligraphy, and who in my honor consented that night to speak English.

It was a queer little party. We sat in the upper-floor room of the restaurant, a cardboard room in a cardboard house where we scarcely dared stamp our feet. We shivered in the clammy air and drank a lot of hot rice wine until we were laughing very loud, even the saturnine Ma Ping-ho. The proprietors of the restaurant, exiles from home like so many of the Chungking residents, came up to peek at us through the cardboard doorway. Afterward we ran home through the mud, arm in arm under a moon that did a fairly good job of lighting us up, considering that it was not bombing season. It was hectic and merry, but I felt sad. I was homesick, and not for my house in Avenue Joffre with Sinmay and the gibbons, for Shanghai was part of China, and all of a sudden I didn't want to be living in China. I didn't want to be living in a war at all. These boys and girls were nice people, but they were living grimly. They had been grim for a long time and would have to go on just like that for a long time more. Corin's long lank hair depressed me. She was cut off from a hairdresser by hundreds of miles, I told myself, and she hadn't the money to get out of it all. (I was wrong about the hairdresser. In a few months there was one giving permanents right there in Chungking, in a cardboard beauty parlor.) Then there was Ma Ping-ho, formerly of Cork and Oxford and now growing dank and mossy in Szechuan. I dreamed about him that night in my damp room and I was still depressed in the morning. Definitely, it was time to do my work and forget about all these fancies.

A couple of young men in spectacles, young men I had known in Shanghai, called to tell me that they were now secretaries of Dr. Kung. He has always had a lot of secretaries and I suspect it is because he must find work for many old friends' sons. Mme. Kung had sent word that I would probably want to look at Dr. Kung, and that this should be arranged when I was ready to ask for an interview. Then Corin dropped in on her way to the Co-op office, and we huddled over the charcoal burner that would have heated the room if there had been fewer cracks in the walls, and exchanged the stories of our lives. I collected a lot of life stories while I was in Chungking, but none seemed less congruous than Corin's. She had lived in London and for a while she was an editor for *Vogue,* being especially hot on knitting patterns. She was really, she admitted modestly, queen of the knitters of London. We had a few friends in common; I had been sound in identifying her manner of speaking with my memories of that charming town. An unhappy love affair sent her wandering and, like practically ninety per cent of our young ladies who carried torches in the 1930s, Corin came to China. (I once drew a vivid picture of the docks of Shanghai. An ocean liner lay at the dock with gangplank down, offering the freedom of the town to a procession of young ladies. They tripped down the gangplank in endless procession, tall girls and short girls, fat girls and thin girls, blonde and chestnut. Each girl carried in one hand a portable typewriter and in the other, held aloft, a burning torch.)

Well, Corin came to China to visit friends, and there she stayed. She got a job on a news agency, and she fell in love, and she stayed on, and on, and on. The war came. Corin was in Peking and, like Bob Winter, she mixed in as much as she could, carrying messages back and forth for Chinese friends and having a wonderful time. But she got in too deep, or thought she did, and began to get that illusion of a Japanese Black List, with her name at the head of it, which haunts people who have been too long in the Orient. So when she was offered a job with the Co-ops she took it, and here she was, with her hair growing longer and straighter every month and nothing else happening at all. She wasn't even getting letters, she admitted, from her boy friend, who had gone home to America to visit his family. She was wondering if he hadn't forgotten all about her, and the idea made her unhappy, because Corin at thirty-two felt old and tired, and she wanted to keep house and have babies.

"Write and find out," I said immediately. No, Corin said, she couldn't do that. If he wanted to write her he would. If there was somebody else, no doubt he wanted to be sure before he wrote to her and broke their engagement. She would not hurry him.

It wasn't her way of doing things. She was not pretty, Corin wasn't; she had a long nose that she hated, and in spite of her quick mind and her training she couldn't manage her own emotions very well because that nose kept her uncertain. Sometimes because I was fond of her I wanted to give her a good shaking. Sometimes now I wish I had done it.

That afternoon I had a letter from the famous W. H. Donald, known to unoriginal journalists as the Power behind the Throne. My own pet name for him is Warwick II. All of us in giving Donald these names have played into his hands, because we are accepting the impression he is anxious to give. He would see me that afternoon, he said; he would send a car. Did I have time? Was I ready?

I was ready. I put on my padded gown and my sheepskin boots and my hat and trotted along out to the car. Under the heavy tread of my boots the cardboard room shuddered and all the furniture rocked on its legs as the door slammed behind me. . . .

Donald was waiting in the car with Jimmy McHugh. Jimmy gave me a bow and a secret, mysterious, sidelong look that meant nothing at all, as a matter of fact, except that Jimmy was in the Intelligence. He didn't mean to do it. He didn't do it consciously. Those boys just get into the habit. Later on in Hong Kong I acquired a new black gibbon that did all his talking out of the corner of his mouth in a confidential manner, and I called him Jimmy McHugh. That was because I was a patriotic American. There were lots of good British names I could have given him too.

Donald took us for a motorcar ride to look at his new house, half built at that time on the side of a steep hill just under Chialing House. Chialing House was a new, superelegant sort of hotel which was intended for extra-special government functions. It was way out on the only real road that led from town, overlooking the Chialing River, near Sun Fo's house; the fact that it was so far away from everywhere made it awful to get to but saved its existence later on when the bombing started. While my host bustled about from roofless room to veranda and back again I took a good look at him. I was still groggy and sleepy as newcomers always are in Chungking for the first few days, but he woke me up. He was more than sixty at the time and looked older because of his pure white hair, but though he looked old and had an old man's trick of repeating himself he still had vitality to spare. Some of it vibrated through the air and worked on me.

We went back to Donald's house, next door to the Chiangs' residence, for tea. It was not a cardboard edifice. Chungking in the old days had been the home of many retired generals and war lords who built themselves solid houses after foreign designs. Between the mushroom cottages that were being put up everywhere you came across these buildings, reassuringly firm and well built. There was a fireplace in Don's study and he gave a few orders to a Chinese girl in slacks who seemed to be running the place and then we had a fire. Don's study was full of maps and papers and here and there a book about China, but no modern books, just histories and geographies. While we waited for tea he talked, putting himself on the stage as he always did, showing me his best side, which I believe is also his only side. He is certainly a strange creature. He could only have come from Australia. He is hearty, honest, and completely without shyness. If he is wrong, and he sometimes is, he is totally unaware of it. Trying to sum him up, I find one phrase coming into my mind: Donald is a true democrat. It has never occurred to him to talk down to anybody, because he doesn't think of people in terms of intelligence. He talks straight, to coolies or statesmen, to Orientals or Occidentals, because he thinks that one language is enough for everyone. People in his estimation differ in only one way: they live on separate planes of honesty. He doesn't approve of dishonesty. He has a simple code and a very moral one. Perhaps that is why Mme. Chiang has kept him around so long; they are alike in that respect.

I read Ralf Sues's book and I liked it, but she irritated me when she said that Donald was Pygmalion and Mme. Chiang the statue, or words to that effect. I am sure Donald himself thinks so, down in his heart, but I am equally sure that Madame doesn't, and that the suggestion would irritate her profoundly, much more than it has irritated me.

Donald is not as subtle as Mme. Chiang, nor as careful a student of human nature, nor does he know as much about Chinese family relationships as she does. A knowledge of family and a sympathy for it is very important if you're going to have a hand in Chinese government. Donald could not hold Mme. Chiang's job down. He could not have built up Mme. Chiang out of nothing. He could not bemuse the world.

I came home in an improved mood. I had forgotten to be homesick, and I was full of Australian pep, and Donald had promised that I would see Mme. Chiang in the morning.

Chapter 19

I APPROACHED my first interview with Mme. Chiang much less nervously than I had gone to Sassoon Road. A few Chinese had done their best to give me the fidgets, assuring me that I would find the First Lady of the land less "human" than her eldest sister, but I wasn't impressed with the threat. What do people mean when they say "human"? Everything or nothing. Sometimes it means that a public person is not without his little vices, but that isn't what the gossips meant about Mme. Chiang and Mme. Kung. I think it really means "warmhearted." Certainly Mayling's heart is kept cool. She would like to be entirely steely and without emotion, I suspect, except in a large and patriotic way. She doesn't think that public personages should have any use for individualistic orgies of sentiment, either in love or anything else; she is as severe with her heart as a New Englander. That is what I thought after our first conversation, and I also thought that she was much fonder of her sister Ai-ling than she wanted to admit.

Partly because of Donald's careful training, every word Mme. Chiang gives to the press and every gesture she makes in front of a reporter is planned and weighed in advance. A few months after this, when the time seemed right for it, the Soong sisters made a public sign of family affection, and Mme. Chiang was free to promote her eldest sister as she really wanted to do. When I met her she was still careful of herself, still wondering what was best, but she was coming rapidly to a decision. That passage in John Gunther's book had done it. Her voice, like Mme. Kung's, shook with indignation as she talked to me about it.

Again I put in a word for John, and again found myself talking about Shanghai gossip and the cabal that was obviously in motion against the

Kungs. "It's an indirect way of getting at my husband," she summed it up. This shrewd remark started me probing after a bit of knowledge I was anxious to acquire. Was Mme. Chiang aware of her unpopularity among the older politicians in China? I wondered. I had my answer, prompt and clear: Mme. Chiang certainly was. She had been fighting ever since her marriage against the heavy, inevitable disapproval of old-fashioned China.

There have been about twenty descriptions of Mme. Chiang and the surroundings in which people interview her, so I won't bother about it. I have some of it already, anyway, in my book. She was used to writers and she put me at ease very quickly; we were chattering along like old friends when her husband suddenly entered the room. He hadn't been warned that she was not alone, and he was embarrassed at being in his slippers. I leaped to my feet. Even in his slippers the Generalissimo always had that effect on me; I found myself standing at attention whenever he appeared. His wife introduced us and he bowed and started to back out of the room.

"*Hao hao,*" he said, as she explained me rapidly in Chinese. "*Hao, hao, hao.*" The door closed on another bow. What he had said was just, "Good, good, good," and it means anything polite that you like to put into it. Madame smiled and said, "He didn't have his teeth in. Sit *down,* Miss Hahn."

I went back to the hostel feeling quite steamed up about the book. We had come to a clear understanding. Mme. Chiang—and by the way, al-though I don't know her well enough to do it in person, I'm going to call her "Mayling" in this book hereafter; I can't go on using titles indef-initely—Mayling was not opposed to the idea of the book. She admitted, though, that she wouldn't be ready or willing to help me if I were going to do only a long gush about herself. Why should she? She didn't need it and China didn't need it. If I emphasized Mme. Kung, however, and put her in the limelight, for a change and for a necessary balance against the malicious stories that were being spread over the Kung name, May-ling would give me all the information I wanted.

"You're fond of my sister, aren't you?" she asked.

I said that I was, and that such a book would be pleasant for me to write, as I could be sincere in concentrating on her sister. The question was how to go about the consultations. We decided that I should show the manuscript to the sisters as it was written or after a good part of it had been finished, and they would check it for facts.

"I won't do anything but that," she warned me. "I haven't time. At any rate you wouldn't want us to touch the text."

"Certainly not," I said warmly. "I don't expect you to do anything about my opinions, either. Even if you might not agree."

"That's arranged, then," said Mayling. "If you make mistakes, my sister or I will tell you about them. We will not comment on anything else. It's the only possible way such a book can be written. Otherwise it's so much propaganda turned out here at Holly's office."

She did not say, though, that I was to go straight back to Hong Kong. Instead she suggested several trips around the Szechuan countryside, to see her girls' schools, to inspect a stock-improving center and so forth. I had been quite right to bring my boots and all those coats, I reflected. I would have Christmas in Chungking, and the same idea had hit other people, evidently, because I found a couple of invitations in my room when I came home. Would I help do the Christmas broadcast? Would I go to see the War Orphans' Home on the day Madame distributed presents? Would I join the hostel party on Christmas Eve? There was more holiday spirit up here in the Chinese mountains than we had floating about in the foreign settlement of Shanghai. China's government really worked at being Christian; I found that out. I worked with them that year.

It was a queer time for most of us, the winter of the phony war. Our life in Chungking was full of the British. Although the city was a makeshift capital, it really was the national capital, and the English were behaving accordingly. They had nipped in ahead of everyone and got hold of the best house in town for their embassy. It was halfway between the downtown district of the city where the banks were and the part we lived in, where the two hostels and the Generalissimo's residence formed a nucleus for the rest of the circle of government people. I found some old friends among the British. The Ambassador, Sir Archibald Clark-Kerr, was to arrive soon, after one of his periodic visits to Shanghai. They were all excited because this time he would bring his wife, the "pocket Venus" whose exquisite miniature beauty had stirred up the diplomatic circles of the coast towns. Among all of the men I saw most of Morgan Crofton because he lived at the hostel. Morgan was one of the decoders, a young man who was always called "amusing" because he puzzled and bothered people, and they didn't know what else to do about him.

Like Charles, Morgan had written home and asked the authorities to take him out of China and let him get into the war, which as everyone knew was in Europe on the Continent, and not in the East, no matter what they said. He fretted his heart out in Chungking. He used to tell me about it when we walked over toward the embassy in the morning, his fat fox terrier running ahead of us and sniffing at the mud. Morgan had an abrupt manner and his sense of humor was violent and sudden, so that old codgers took a dislike to him, but he was really a Tory and his political beliefs were those of old codgers in clubs. He defended Chamberlain; we had a lot of hearty fights over that. He thought Churchill admirable in many ways, but dangerous. He had been in the Army in India, and bitterly regretted having resigned. If he hadn't resigned, he said, if he hadn't taken this footling job, he would be in the war where he belonged and no Foreign Office clerk could tell him nonsense about being needed more where he was. . . . All the young men from England were talking that way and feeling that way in the winter of 1939, out in the Orient. So many of them wrote letters home asking for transfer that the War Office lost patience and sent a mimeographed reply, reminding them acidly that Whitehall could not devote all its time to sending individual no's out to China and Malaya and Japan.

Except for the British, who had said flatly that they wanted to be in the town itself and never mind the bombing, the diplomats chose to live in the "safety zone" over across the Yangtze, on the South Bank. They found more room there and a neighborhood of more familiar quality. There was a very little town and most of the houses that amounted to anything had been built in the past, in the spacious days of peaceful trade. All the big foreign companies were represented there: Standard Oil, and Texaco, and Jardine's, and all the rest. One of the best was the APC, the Asiatic Petroleum Company, which was British. Some of these places were estates rather than houses. The APC House, which I was to know very well later on, had a large plot of mountainous ground enclosed by a wall and several wire fences, and there were two good-sized dwelling houses in the compound. Farther back in the hills, or upriver on what was known as the "Second Range," there were more and more houses built by foreigners and lived in by foreigners, mostly missionaries of one faith or another. Houses were at such a premium that people went a long distance from town to find them. The British embassy had its own launch to call for its people on the South Bank every morning and take them back at night. Those who could do it, like the tall young American consul who lived on the Second Range, walked to work in the morning and back at night—he was lucky because his office was on the South Bank too, but it was an incredibly long and steep walk. A lot of people kept their private chairs for the journey. A few kept ponies, but riding a pony to work was just as complicated as you would expect. The groom had to come along too, on *his* pony, and he had to look after it while you were in your office, or take it home again for the day and bring it at night, and the whole thing was much too elaborate for anyone who had an impatient nature.

Even the journey between the North and South Banks was too much for me with my impatient nature to face very often. Maya Rodeivitch dashed across the river every week end, and less enthusiastic souls went on Sunday for lunch, but I went protestingly, once in a very long while. You could go by day in the ferry, a ramshackle motorboat whose destinations on the riverside varied with the level of the water. Sometimes when the river was low the journey was doubly dangerous because of rocks that were exposed, and because of the increased fury of the current. It was never a safe journey at the best of times. But when the ferries were too full, or when it was late at night and they weren't running, you could hire a small boat, and that was really perilous. The boatmen hauled and toiled and poled in the mud until they were well upstream on the jumping-off side, then they poled themselves out toward the middle and let go, and as the boat went dancing and bobbing downriver they aimed madly to get across before it was too late. Sometimes they did miss and you had a long time poling or walking back on the other bank. It is an exasperating and a fearsome thing, that river. I knew a few people who were capsized and who saved themselves. I know another man who didn't survive the spring floods when his boat turned over. Now that I think back on it I am afraid, but at the time we didn't think much about natural dangers. We saved up our emotions for air raids.

I made the journey that winter only when I intended to spend some days with the Endicotts, and they didn't live on what we knew as the South Bank at all; they were on the other side of the river, true enough, but a long way downstream, at a tiny village that was noted only for their own house and the school where Jim Endicott had taught for many years. I met them through Mme. Chiang. Just about Christmas time—I forget if it was before or after the holiday itself—Holly's office sent me out on a day's journey to a school.

Jim Endicott was one of the men who came along with Mme. Chiang after we were deposited in the first classroom, waiting for the festivities to start. He acted as a guide during the exercises, whispering translations to me and now and then writing some explanation on an old envelope.

I talked to him a little on the long drive back, but we didn't really get acquainted until a few days later, when I was beginning to grow weary of trotting after Madame to ceremony after ceremony. How do public figures stand it? I have never been able to understand what keeps them going, for surely all emotional reactions disappear after the first few hours of oratory that is all alike? As an onlooker I lost all interest after a week of it, and vowed to go on with this program only when it would seem violently rude to refuse. That wasn't the sort of book I wanted to write. All Holly's office was writing that sort of eulogistic thing every day, and maybe it helped China and maybe it didn't, but I didn't intend to add to the bulk of such literature. I was muttering to myself as I staggered off the campus of the university grounds where poor Madame had just made her nth speech to a graduating class of girls, and Jim caught up with me, taking enormous strides with his long legs, and said:

"Just what is it you're doing here? I haven't got it straight."

It happened that that day I had overheard a passage between Madame and this Endicott which caught my attention. He was arguing with her. That was something worth eavesdropping on—a man, a European (to use our clumsy circumlocution for "white") arguing with Madame, disagreeing with her! The subject was the new Youth Movement among the adolescent school children of Chungking, and Endicott maintained that they should not be called on to take an oath of allegiance en masse, or rather in the presence of all the government officials who had gathered to watch this planned ceremony. "You are not giving them a choice," said Endicott.

"They aren't forced to do it," Madame countered quickly.

"Is any child going to refuse under such public pressure?" he asked.

"No, perhaps not. But no child is told he must swear; no child is penalized for refusing. The question doesn't come up, anyway. They all want to take the oath." Madame spoke sharply, but without surprise. She seemed to be used to this man's abrupt methods.

"It's like fascism," said Endicott. "There's no value in it. There's no individual thought."

The argument tailed off, interrupted by the demands of the ceremony, but my curiosity and admiration were whetted. Endicott, he explained to me now as we walked toward the road, was one of the many "advisers," their desire for which makes the government of China so peculiarly wistful. He had been asked to take the place of a man named Shepherd who had been the original "missionary adviser" to Mme. Chiang. "Think of the opportunities!" said everybody. But he wasn't the man for it, Endicott admitted. He wasn't tactful. He often irritated Madame; he couldn't help it. When he saw things going wrong he had to argue, and as a man with leftist tendencies he was always seeing things go wrong.

You can tell from as much of my book as I have already written that

I belong to that class which is instinctively and traditionally inimical to missionaries. The chief reason can be expressed in a simple phrase that always creeps into discussions on the subject: "Why don't they stay home and keep their noses out of other people's beliefs?" Actually that's a shallow and foolish question, and any wide-awake opponent could answer it a dozen ways, all satisfactory. Just the same I do feel that way about missionaries, that way and much more than that. Jim Endicott was the first one I met who was likable. I was to meet many more of the species, medical and teaching missionaries, and my liking of them has certainly removed the hysterical and unreasonable part of my objection to missions, whatever may remain of my more rational misgivings. Nowadays I don't feel called on to act the missionary whenever I meet a missionary. I don't agree with him, usually, but I don't want to kill him, or convert him. I live and let live, and the beginning of this broadmindedness in my make-up, the wedge that opened the door, was the Endicott couple.

I remember how they startled me, Jim and Mary, the first day I accepted a kind invitation from them and settled down to work in their attic. They lived an intensely domestic life, with four children just growing up, following a regular routine which Mary supplied pretty much by herself because of Jim's extracurricular duties over on the other side, as Madame's adviser.

Before they administered that shock they had already, quite unconsciously, given my convictions a pretty good shaking up. "If these people weren't missionaries," I kept telling myself, "I would put them down for any married couple in a university town. I've spent hundreds of hours of my life with people just like this.

"Their personalities should have nothing to do with your judgment of their usefulness," I told myself severely on the first evening, after I had gone up to bed. "Yes, so you feel at home with them. Yes, so they are intelligent in just the fashion you like, and they discuss matters in just the manner you prefer your discussions. Yes, so this is a charming room and their children are charming children, and the house is a nice shabby homelike honest house. You have seen nothing of the things that sickened you in the African missionary's house that one time you had to accept mission hospitality, where half a dozen underpaid Negroes were forced to work and make luxury for a spoiled, lowbred family of whites. No one but a bigot could accuse the Endicotts of exploiting the Chinese, personally at least. But what of the mission they represent? The actual, factual fallacy of missions still exists, regardless of the charm of the Endicotts." With that I went to sleep, pathetically grateful for a change from my hostel cot. It was the next morning that they shocked me so.

We were sitting in the attic, their workroom and mine. There was a stove there, an office typewriter, and unlimited copy paper. That morning, though, we didn't do much work. We talked for several hours instead. It was while they were telling me of the university crowd in Chengtu, an hour away by plane, that they began talking, I told them accusingly, in a narrow-minded way.

"You don't think we should disapprove of such behavior?" asked Jim. They had been condemning a man and a woman of the faculty for having an extramarital love affair.

"No, I don't," I said. "I think it's their own business."

"But morality," cried Mary, "surely it's the business of the community!"

"Conventions, if they are true conventions," urged Jim, "have grown up as they are needed. There is a reason for them."

"I can't agree," I said. "Often they are the result of unpleasant jealousies, and are built up in spite and frustration. I feel deeply that we should leave people alone when it comes to sex. And also in regard to God, for a man's god is his own business, just as much as his sex life is his own business. . . ."

"But it's the same *thing*," said Jim and Mary together, in great eagerness. "It's exactly the same thing!"

I was severely shocked. "Really," I said when I had caught my breath, "do you think that is the sort of thing your sort of person ought to say to my sort?"

I should like, just as a proof to myself that I can write, to give you some idea of Chungking. You must have your own ideas of it, because for a time, for a long time, it was a name headlined in the papers and mentioned in the magazines on almost every page. I stumble over it now in the books I have tried to read all at once now that I am home where I can get books.

The country is soft and green around Chungking. Somewhere I have asserted that China is an ugly, blank, treeless hunk of the world's area. I was talking through my hat. There are many lovely places in China that I hadn't seen when I sounded off like that, and Szechuan is one of them. Szechuan, at least the part I knew, is full of small fierce hills that make you smile and admire them as you do when you are confronted by a brave Pekingese dog. In everything but scale these hills are like the Rockies or the Andes: rugged in shape and running along in lines like ranges. They are thickly covered with trees. I am no botanist, but I was startled when I saw pines and banana palms growing together on a hillside. It is an ordinary sight in Chungking countryside. Szechuan is such a lush, moist, green kind of place that it is exceedingly fertile and has as many as four crops in one year.

But for all this greenery there is no joyful dancing of light and shadow, because of the fog which keeps the Japanese away, year after year, except for two or three midsummer months. And the city itself, built on a slice of land shaped like a flatiron or a piece of pie, is nothing to rejoice over. I used to hear about it before the Incident when I lived in Shanghai like all the other tenderfeet. Chungking was that town up at the other end of the Yangtze where the gunboats landed after they had gone through the Gorges. Chungking was a Godforsaken hole with a club in it and nothing whatever to do there but drink, ride funny little ponies up and down the hills, and play tennis wherever you could find a piece of ground level enough for a court.

Well, the war changed all that. Suddenly Chungking was much too big for itself. First came the august Chinese Government, and they filled the houses and populated the streets with strange, alarming people and wickedly beautiful women. Then came everyone else from all over the world. The native Szechuanese is undersized and pale and lacking in vitamins, and he looked with grave suspicion at all this beauty and fashion. Also, he is not a keen businessman. The business methods of the newcomers annoyed him, and jostled him, and fed him up. The rest of China is full of smiling people, but in Szechuan they pause in their work to look at you sourly, or they don't pause at all when you come by. The native costume includes a kind of towel twisted around the head, and I used to feel that I was in a hospital ward of convalescents, none of whom was happy.

Chungking. What does the name evoke in my mind? Air raids. Oranges. Szechuan food, good, full of strong pepper, probably to warm up the blood on the cold, wet, muddy days that come so often. Air always so moist as almost to drip. Houses either newly built of cards or old ramshackle palaces, damp and chilly. I can remember outings in the country when we rode pony-back and went swimming in a cold pool and came back merry and actually sunburnt, but they were exceptional. Yet Chungking is a place of flowers. You can have roses in your garden all the year round. I am not kind in my description of the rocky city, but I liked it. I was notorious in the foreign community for liking it. I suppose I liked it in spite of everything, because it was full of Chinese.

Chapter 20

It was not included in my plans that I experience an air raid during my visit to the capital. (And incidentally, it is high time that I get off my chest the inevitable expression we all use about Chungking: "the city built on rock." Something about the air-raid tunnels brings that out, sooner or later, with every visitor.) As I figured it, the Japanese stayed away from the place every year from September until late April or May. Only in the summer months did the milky, subdued radiance we knew as Chungking daylight become strong enough to show up the earth to Japanese bombardiers. That, as no doubt you know already, is why Chungking was chosen as the capital for refugees in the first place. In the second place, it is the ideal spot of the world's surface for air-raid tunnels. It's all solid rock, with enough steep hillsides to cut down the necessary engineering to a minimum. When I arrived the Chungking Hostel was just beginning to appreciate its newest possession, a private dugout with two entrances, according to all the latest rules for such hidey-holes. We discovered much later that it wasn't a good dugout at all. It was too shallow and the roof was not thick enough to sustain a direct hit. In the late months of 1939, though, we weren't yet tunnel experts, and we were very proud of our private one.

It wasn't quite finished. I was taken on a tour of inspection by Su-lin Young, the glamorous hostel hostess, and she showed me a pile of wooden struts which were destined to be put in place later on, to help hold up the roof. We crept down a long staircase chopped out of rock, and at the dark dank bottom our electric torches showed us an impressive cavern with benches and folding chairs waiting in rows for the hostel public, and several black puddles of wicked-looking water which had seeped through the walls. Su-lin told me what the whole affair cost; I have forgotten it, but it was an impressive figure, and somehow that bit of information made me feel even safer while I was below ground level.

Well, the very next day we had occasion to use the place officially. I was idling around in the lounge. I had put my portable typewriter on a desk, intending to write up a few notes, and the room at ten o'clock in the morning was filling up with hostel guests in search of warmth and company, when all of a sudden a loud, rude noise filled the air. We all know now what it sounds like, but it was my first air-raid alarm, for we hadn't run to such modern appliances during the Shanghai Incident.

"Wooooooo, woooooooo, wooooooo," sang the siren.

I swallowed hard and looked inquiringly at a man near by. "That's it," he said. "Maybe practice, maybe not. It's an unusually bright day for the season."

And it was; it was definitely possible, that day, to see ahead of you for as much as fifty paces. We asked the clerk, though, just to make sure. "No practice scheduled for today that I know of," he admitted. "It must be *them*."

Corin Bernfelt suddenly appeared, at least an hour earlier than she usually woke up. Corin slept an awful lot in order to save money which she would otherwise spend on breakfast, and which she couldn't spare out of her Co-op salary. Salaries in these organizations are always inadequate. She was an old hand at air raids. "Collect whatever papers you are especially fond of," she directed me, "and bring your typewriter."

We were led in a giggling, chattering procession down the stone steps and into the cavern. Maya Rodeivitch was already there with Choux, her Alsatian, saying *"Tais-toi"* to him without the slightest effect, for he had a fine baritone voice and he liked to use it. I could see her pretty well, as we were now lit up with electricity. Whenever Chungking's power station wasn't out of commission they were lavish with their use of it, I will say that for the hostel.

Peggy Durdin sat next to me, expressing disgust and annoyance because her work had been interrupted. She meant more than she said, though; her voice trembled as she talked lightly, and she smoked incessantly until we were told not to use up the air that way. She and Till had twice been bombed out of their flat the first week after they arrived, the bad month of May 1939, when Chungking took such a terrible beating. She hadn't been well since, had lost forty pounds, suffered in the climate, but steadfastly refused to go down to the comparative comfort of Indo-China and wait for her husband on week ends. A lot of people who have had histories like Peg's feel the same way. She was a missionary's child, which didn't stop her wholehearted attacks on the mission system. She was born in China and spoke fluent Mandarin. She had taught school in Shanghai, and naturally her patriotism was divided between America and China. Although there is no logical explanation for the feeling, Peg had a sense of duty toward Chungking. Even I, after a much shorter experience, acquired that sentiment ultimately. I was already slipping under its spell.

We waited down in the cave for about two hours that first time. The planes never flew over at all, but went to the military airfield. I've sat in so many caves so many times since that my memory is a bit clouded about my first raid, but I haven't forgotten P. C. Kuo, or, as I insist upon calling him, Kuo Ping-chia. I hate that way of dubbing Chinese by initials, as if they were so many Rotarians or bank clerks. Ping-chia would make a good bank clerk at that, to look at him. He was introduced to me by Corin, and he started talking eagerly about America, which he knows pretty well because he took a degree at Harvard. Ping-chia always talks eagerly to ladies anyway. He has a romantic nature and freely admits it. But that nature, and his romantic appearance to go with it, has not prevented him from developing his very good brain by a first-rate training in history. I consider him one of the best specimens of young China, as compared with Sinmay and tradition.

I forget just who detailed him to keep an eye on me, to help me when I was stumped for information or paper or typewriter supplies. I am very grateful, whoever thought of it. Without Ping-chia's help I should have taken a much longer time with my manuscript. Although he is ambitious and a hard worker, he was at loose ends just then and he found time to call on me at the hostel every day. He was paying his first call that day of the raid, and as we sat wearily through the long, long hours underground he and I began to discuss Chinese music. Now and then our discussion was punctuated by a bomb, far off on the airfield.

Ping-chia looks more like a Latin American than a Chinese. He is tall and broad-shouldered and he wears his Western clothes carefully. But this exterior is deceptive, for in his heart he dislikes the West and loves the classic arts of China. Not all those years at Cambridge could spoil his passion for the music and opera of his native land. When he was living in Hankow, teaching history at the university, he knew every little place in town where singsong girls gave selections from the old plays. He couldn't tell, himself, if it was the girls that attracted him or the songs. When he found out that I was interested in the custom, so strange to our Western minds, that educates and encourages prostitutes and singsong girls to learn classic opera, he poured out his heart.

"I do a little singing myself," he admitted. "In Nanking we gave many shows, and even in Hankow while the government paused there we put on one play, though I believe the authorities consider it frivolous and wrong to pay attention to music while we are fighting this war."

That was another interesting difference between our civilizations. Imagine Parliament or the Senate condemning grand opera because there is a war on! But in China the stage, being a pleasure, is naturally looked on as a frivolity as well. Those productions you used to hear so much about, those presentations of Mei Lan-fang, are considered by the dour authorities of the New Life Movement to be bathed in the same light we would shed on the latest Cole Porter show.

"Can you sing?" demanded Ping-chia eagerly. "Can you sing Chinese opera?"

"No," I admitted. "I haven't even seen many of the plays. Back in Shanghai Sinmay wouldn't go to the theater unless there was something extra-special. And of course in Shanghai we didn't have the best Peking players very often."

"But you did," said Ping-chia. "Shanghai is a wonderful city for the theater. I have heard some of the best plays produced in Shanghai. Have you heard any of the famous girl performers? Have you heard Lily Lee? She is really good."

Lily Lee! I remembered suddenly a girl Sinmay had brought to my house one afternoon, with a story of squandered fortunes. I had seen Lily again in Hong Kong. I told Ping-chia about it.

"We had dinner at Lily's house," I explained. "She's improved wonderfully in her English, hasn't she?"

He looked mysterious. "There was a reason for that," he said.

"Oh, I know." It was a romantic story that Lily had told me at the dinner table that night, while Sinmay drank rice wine and chattered with friends. She had fallen in love with an American she met in Hankow. After the latest exodus she had gone up to Chungking to see him. Followed a few weeks of loving bliss, and then she started back to Hong Kong, her plane ticket in her pocket, going in a sedan chair down to the riverbank, as befitted a great lady and famous artiste. But Lily Lee had never reached the plane. Chinese plain-clothes men took command of her chair coolies before she entered the airfield, and Lily was whisked off to prison for "questioning." She stayed in jail for five months without trial, while the young American made frantic endeavors to get her out. The government was very suspicious of Lily, and accused her outright of being a spy. As to what sort of spy, they were rather vague. I suppose they thought she had been planted by the Japs, and then her fondness for the foreigner was not so good, either.

"I was not uncomfortable," Lily admitted. "But one bad old official, he pretended to set me free, and when I realized what it was all about I was living in his house. He wanted me to live with him, to be his concubine, and when I would not they put me back into the jail. I was never tried at all. My boy friend was very good about it. After I got out of jail, after I came to Hong Kong, he lost his job. I am going to America to marry him."

I thought of all this while I talked to Ping-chia, and he nodded excitedly several times.

"That is it. Yes, it is that Lily," he said. "I was very much in love with her in Hankow at just the same time, before she was arrested. It began one evening when there was a moon. We had met during rehearsals of a play, and that night Lily came to my garden and serenaded me. Out there, under the moon, she sang to me. . . ."

"You must have been much distressed, then, when she was put into prison after the government moved up here?"

Ping-chia sighed. "She wrote to me from the prison," he admitted. "She sent me a Christmas card. But of course I dared not answer."

"Whyever not?"

His big brown eyes looked startled. "Why, they would have put me in jail!" he cried. "I would have been implicated! . . . She was a beautiful girl, Lily was. I loved her very much."

In the course of the air raid he decided to teach me a Chinese song. When he spoke of songs he did not, of course, mean the amusing little jingles that Sinmay taught me when we were playing with his children in his Shanghai house. Those songs, like Japanese songs, were not unlike our own; they had a familiar rhythm and they rhymed after their own fashion. So too did the poems that my teacher taught me to chant, like little children learning their first characters at school. We had made translations of English nursery rhymes, and often when we went to the movies I would see how our simple American popular melodies caught on with the Chinese. "Oh, Susanna" was such a success in China that Sinmay insisted it was originally Chinese. Sometimes our songs puzzle them, especially the ones in two or three parts. They don't understand harmony until they grow familiar with it through us. Ping-chia's songs, however, were completely different. They were dramatic monologues or dialogues; the music of the song depended completely on the words. Each word had to be sung in a certain way, following a pattern of music that has been set down rigidly for centuries. You cannot fit other words to the music. Words and music are the same thing, inalterably tied together. Each artist has his own interpretation of the song and there are many subtle changes from one performance to another. All this Ping-chia tried to tell me, down in the dugout.

"I will teach you a sympathetic one," he decided enthusiastically. "We will now sing 'Ma Tso'—'Scolding in the Palace.' It is a very popular song. I will tell you first what the words mean. The speaker is a queen, very angry with her stepson because he has poisoned her husband, the king. . . ." He went on and on, telling one of the familiar old stories of blood and intrigue. Then he began singing.

At first, though I tried politely to follow him and to sing the same notes, I confess I felt very silly. It meant nothing to me. It sounded like caterwauling. Ping-chia's face looked simply funny in the dim light of the cave, and it was hard to believe that anyone could get aesthetic pleasure from those discordant, thin sounds. Then, after I had gone through it with him two or three times, the miracle happened, the miracle that has made such a difference to me, ever since. I don't know what it was. There was a sort of click in my mind; my ears opened. I liked it. It made sense. It had melody. I remembered it. After that, whenever I heard Chinese music it made sense and I liked it. And belatedly I recalled a scene in the Congo, on the broad veranda of the African house, when we played records on the little gramophone of an evening. We had a collection of songs from all over the world, and I used to marvel at the Negroes because they actually liked the Chinese records best. Those black men with their wonderful voices, and their songs that are the forerunners of our own melodies, those black men loved Chinese opera. They would crowd around the machine and listen raptly, and when the record came to an end they would beg for repetitions. Now I understood. I opened my mouth and sang lustily. The time hastened as we sang over and over, Ping-chia and I, "Scolding in the Palace." . . .

"Mickey, for God's sake!" It was Peggy Durdin speaking. She had obviously failed to follow me into the new realms I was discovering.

"I say so too," grumbled Maya.

"Do you mind changing the record?" demanded Ed Pawley, the usually genial plane manufacturer from Loiwing.

"We wouldn't mind," they all chimed in, "if it were real music you people were singing, but this stuff—a joke's a joke."

Astonished, I glanced at Ping-chia. "Never mind," he said. "We know. We can practice some more after the raid."

The All Clear sounded and we hurried up the steps into the fresh air.

Mail came very irregularly from the outside world, especially mine. Because of the time lag everywhere in mail delivery my family in America continued for a long time to write me in Shanghai, and the letters I did receive came in sudden quantities, after long silences, from the Shanghai house, with a covering note, usually, from Sinmay. I had been so long in the rigorous, comfortless atmosphere of Szechuan that these letters came as rather a shock. Sinmay was indulging in one of his bad moods, and it went on and on, lasting from one mail delivery to the next, until I found myself growing very irritable with him.

To begin with, he had somehow forgotten, from the sound of the correspondence, why I had gone to Chungking at all. In Shanghai he had been eagerly co-operative. Without him I could never have gotten into contact with the Soongs. Later he had been eager to dig up local color for me, and to find people who could give me those trifling remembrances of the Soong family that make all the difference in a biography. Even when I packed to come away on this, the most important trip of all, he had been charmingly helpful. It was a disappointment to me that he refused to come along.

"It will cost too much," he had argued, "and you won't be gone such a long time as all that. If I stay here you won't be tempted to stay so long."

"It will be worth the money," I insisted with sincerity. "How can I get along without an interpreter? I always thought you meant to come with me. I'm afraid to go without you. China isn't like Europe."

"No, no, don't be afraid. You are all right now. I couldn't leave my press for such a long period of time, and really, it is too expensive," he said with finality. "I cannot do it. If I were to go to Chungking, besides, the Japanese would know it and they would make trouble for Zoa."

The last argument convinced me. Still, with the memory of that conversation fresh in my ears, I thought it unfair of Sinmay to take the attitude he now maintained, which was that I was far away in one of the gayer of the nation's capitals, dancing and drinking and whiling my life away generally, while he kept the home fires burning in faithful loneliness. Never did he mention the book. His letters seemed to have been written with an eye to posterity, and they drew a stark, simple, unlovely picture of a sort of forsaken merman. Sinmay was cuddling a broken heart. Why, he wanted to know, wasn't I hurrying back? What was the attraction in the hills of Szechuan? He had had a dreadful dream, he said, on Christmas Eve. He was sure I had found my true love at last. There could be no doubt about it; plunged again into the world which I forswore for his sake, I had forgotten all about Shanghai and my Chinese family.

"I have been hearing things," he said darkly. It was an old one and I recognized it, but just the same I was a little hurt. I had been looking on myself in quite a different and much more heroic light. I had thought of myself as quite a he-woman, carving out a career against tremendous odds.

Then too, Sinmay wasn't getting on very well with the German refugee, who for a year had been living unobtrusively in my house. "Your housekeeper," as he called him, was stirring up trouble with the servants and had vowed a vow to get rid of my inoffensive old amah. Wolf wasn't co-operating in the liaison which had always flourished between the two households. They were squabbling over my car, and they were squabbling over my money. I had left a certain amount, calculated to cover house-keeping expenses and something more for Sinmay, because Sinmay was always needing money unexpectedly; now there wasn't enough. And on top of all these little pinpricks, they weren't following my directions about those new gibbons. You remember the gibbons? The pet shop had promised me a pair of young ones, but they hadn't arrived when I left. Now, evidently, they were there and Sinmay had followed my instructions by going to inspect them, but he was disobeying me. I had agreed on a price. Well, Sinmay thought I had agreed on too large a price and he was trying to beat the pet-shop man down.

I was obsessed during those days with the notion, no doubt erroneous, that the whole world wanted my gibbons. I had horrid visions of a host of people creeping up behind Sinmay and snatching those gibbons out from under his nose. I need not have worried, and I know it now, having had a certain amount of experience in trying to dispose of gibbons, but in those days I was not so wise. I talked all over the hostel about my gibbons. I cursed Sinmay. I sent telegrams, once every day:

BUY GIBBONS IMMEDIATELY.

DO NOT HAGGLE COMMA BUY GIBBONS.

BUY APES DO IT NOW.

HAVE YOU BOUGHT GIBBONS?

RECEIVED LETTER DATED FOURTEENTH NO MENTION GIBBONS HAVE YOU BOUGHT?

And then at last came the answer, fiendishly worded:

GIBBONS BOUGHT.

Could anything be more maddening? What did the man mean? Had *he* bought the gibbons at last, or had somebody else done what I so greatly feared, and sneaked in and bought them before Sinmay got there? It took some weeks to get the proper answer, and I was furious long before that. All was well and the gibbons were even then making a happy mess of my back bedroom, but I didn't know it. All I knew was that Sinmay kept on asking for more money. It was not a request calculated to soothe my angry breast.

What I didn't know was that Sinmay himself was suffering real doubts. He was truly the victim of his moods and I shouldn't have been so quick to accuse him, as I always did, of cooking them up to get himself out of awkward situations. I think that he shared my moment's vision in Hong Kong when I foresaw the end of my Shanghai existence, that long-ago summer afternoon. Time moves on and takes us with it, though the

Chinese would like to stop everything short and keep it just as it is, like a still picture in the middle of a movie. It wasn't my fault and Sinmay was unjust in scolding me for it, but Shanghai was over for me, and I suppose in his bones he knew it.

But I didn't. Up in Chungking, alone in my bare cold room, I swore at Sinmay and paced the floor, smarting under his rebukes.

"As soon as I get back to Shanghai," I vowed, "I'll make him sorry for this. I won't stand for it. Just as soon as I get back . . ."

Furiously I sat down at my desk and wrote him a check.

Chapter 21

THE LIVING BUDDHA was still in Chungking, and thereby hung a tragic story. His trip from Hong Kong had been ill advised. I don't know, now, if it was his own idea to go and pay his respects to the Generalissimo or if one of his friends had been too officious on his behalf, but the result was very bad indeed for the poor old divinity, for he was now a prisoner. True, he could go out of doors if he wished. He could even visit neighboring cities, such as Chengtu. But whenever he tried to get out for good, to continue the journey to Tibet where his ranch and a quiet, peaceful death awaited him, the Mongolian Commission or whatever they call themselves would not let him go. They made all sorts of polite excuses, but I am afraid the truth of the matter is that they consider him in the light of a valuable prize, representing as he does thousands and thousands of Mongolian worshipers. He is being held as a hostage and a bank, I believe—at any rate he is being held, definitely against his wishes.

One day he telephoned and asked me to come with Corin to see him. We were very glad to go, and only doubtful that we would be permitted into the building, but after a little delay that ticklish matter was arranged by Holly. God was sitting comfortably in a large room overlooking a hanging garden, and he had acquired a Mongolian servant to look after him. But he was bored—"I have nothing to do all day," he said fretfully, "but chant the Sutras"—and his gouty foot was troubling him, and he was running short of his special clothes, for he had left most of them in Hong Kong at a Mongol boardinghouse. Bob Winter had gone to Yunnan and he intended to stay there with his university connections for a long time; the old man felt lost and deserted without this last link connecting him to his past. Just before Bob left we had all four spent a pleasant Christmas Eve together at a restaurant down in the town. We ate a lot and we talked and sang. I sang some American cowboy songs to God, and he sang some Mongolian cowboy songs for us, songs from his own homeland. One of them was especially nice; it was to be sung while milking a cow, and God went through the gestures and smiled sweetly as he sang in a fine, resonant voice, and afterward he looked miserably homesick. Twenty years is a long time to be exiled from the plains of Mongolia when you are a cowboy at heart. And now he was worse than an exile; he was a prisoner.

"I was informed that I was Buddha," he said to Bob, "at the age of six. Since then, you know my life. It has been a good life on the whole, not as stormy as some of my former incarnations. . . . But with conditions as they are, sometimes I wonder if I shouldn't seek different work." Or, as Bob put it, "I wonder if I shouldn't look for a different job."

After Bob left, Corin and I tried hard to keep the old man happy and interested in life. We were permitted one day to take him out on a picnic. Holly provided the car, a big favor in that petrol-hungry village, and we set out happily with only two bodyguards accompanying us to make sure we did not elope with our valuable friend. There are not many roads around Chungking; we took the one that leads to the governmental summer resort, and when we arrived God said that his foot was not paining him at all and that we must take a walk. It was a pretty place, the tiny collection of Chinese houses scarcely jarring at all with the mountains surrounding. God led us swiftly up a mountain path, so that we young women were panting in a few minutes, though he hadn't turned a hair. We picked flowers and branches. We watched the birds, and he named them for us. The fresh wind blew down the hillside and gave him energy, and his face was flushed; we sat on the edge of a bluff and he picked a broad grass blade and made a whistle, and then blew on it so that you would have sworn a cuckoo was calling.

It was a happy afternoon, one of the best Chungking afternoons that I can remember. If only more people could speak his own language, God said, he would not be too badly off in Chungking.

It was much later in the year, in midsummer, that he determined to visit Chengtu. He was wretched during the bombing season, and hated to sit in the Mongolian Commission tunnel, or in any tunnel for that matter, for hours and hours while the Japanese planes prowled through the clean sky looking for their prey. He said so, frankly, and Corin was shocked.

"But why shouldn't he dislike air raids?" I asked her on the way home.

I loved going home from his house, because our chairs glided through the hanging garden and from there we had a magnificent view of the town and the river and the green hills beyond. Besides, after seeing God I always felt twice as alive and keen and calm as I was normally. "Why shouldn't he feel the way we do?" I continued. "You hate the raids yourself. You come out in spots during a raid season, you hate them so much."

"That's different," said Corin, "because I am a human. It is natural that I should be afraid to die. He's God. *He* shouldn't care." She meant it, too: she was really shocked.

The Living Buddha determined to go on his vacation in August, and he asked me if it were true, as he had heard, that the Japs, although they did sometimes bomb Chengtu, observed the laws of neutrality and refrained from aiming at the Canadian university campus. I said that this had been true, with an occasional exception which was no doubt due to accident or bad aiming. He explained that he would plan, this being the case, to go straight to the university grounds whenever he heard the warning siren. But nobody knew him in Chengtu, and he knew nobody, and perhaps the gates to the campus would be closed during a raid, in order to prevent mobs from flooding the district. Could I give him a letter to some of my friends there, who could see to it that he would be allowed to come in?

Yes, I said, certainly. By that time my friends the Endicotts would have moved their household to Chengtu, as Jim was not renewing his advisership to Mme. Chiang and had been assigned to an English professorial chair at the university. A letter to their address and to the other missionaries would give the old man a contact, and he could do the rest. I sat down to write the letter for him, and I found myself at a loss.

After all, what was I to say? I was in effect committing to the care of a Christian minister one of the seven Living Buddhas of the Orient. The underlying ethics of the matter were unusual, but offered no real problem to my conscience: it wasn't that. It was only that I didn't know the polite way to put it. Anyway you write it, it looks odd. In the end I went at it bald-headed, desperately, with the following result:

Rev. J. G. Endicott
Chengtu

DEAR JIM:
This will serve to introduce to you my friend, the Living Buddha of Outer Mongolia. Anything you can do for Him will be greatly appreciated.
Very truly yours,
EMILY HAHN

Chapter 22

SPRING WAS BEGINNING to make the outlines of the Szechuan hills even more fuzzy than they usually were. Spring brought rain in earnest instead of in the halfhearted drizzle that kept our clothes messy all winter, and we plowed through the streets with mud above our ankles. The rich farm land of Chungking bade fair to swallow our houses completely. Pigs rooted about the streets and one even saw an occasional cow. The famous Chungking rats, enormous beasts, went to ground. There was an impression of warmth and a thinning of the fog, out of doors; indoors it was still cold and choked with charcoal fumes.

For a long time I had been carrying on a queer correspondence with Ma Ping-ho, the Irishman who had turned Chinese and now had an office in Holly's little hive of industry, over at the Press Hostel. I hadn't seen him much, but Teddy White kept me informed. Teddy was often at our hostel, chiefly because he loved to chatter with the Durdins, but also because he liked coming in to see me. Teddy was a large part of Chungking as far as the Fourth Estate was concerned. I started out disliking him rather, because he was obviously a bright, precocious boy, and he knew it. This is an unfair reason for disliking anyone and I got over it. Teddy had learned to speak Chinese and to read and write the classical language before he left Harvard, and for this reason *Time* made him a Far East reporter. He was conscientious and in his work he had a broad clear field, without rivals. He came out East full of illusions and warm hopes of the leftist party in China, and although he still holds many of his early convictions he has had to go through a period of bitter disillusionment. Nowadays I think we ought to consider Teddy as a leading expert on many of China's lesser-known territories, and we can trust what he says, *almost* completely. Then, I thought that his reports were too highly colored by what he wanted to see rather than what he actually saw. He made a trip that year to the northwest, through country which few white people had managed to get permission to visit, and he came back to Chungking and promptly wrote a book about it. The book was bespoken before he wrote it, and Teddy collected an advance on it which he needed, but when he had finished—and for this I respect him deeply and warmly—he decided not to publish it after all.

"I read it over," he explained, "and I realized that it was all padding except for a little bit, most of which wasn't true. A book like that isn't worth printing, so I withdrew it."

Very few of our fraternity would have been as honest as Teddy in like case. He would have been safe in publishing it, for nobody could argue with his statements. He would have made an early success—he was only twenty-six, and the world was eager to read about China's mysterious northwest. He had worked hard on it too. I like Teddy a lot for that decision. It marked his entry into the adult world. But he wasn't an adult when he talked to me about Ma; he was a mischievous schoolboy, peeking out at Big Sister from behind the parlor curtains when she was entertaining a beau. He insisted on considering Ma Ping-ho my boy friend. I wasn't pleased at this conception: Ma was no prize. He was far too dirty and eccentric.

A couple of days after I arrived I received the first letter of the series. Ma had written it in thick, crabbed black handwriting on soft Chinese paper on which the ink spread. It was an amusing and erudite attack on something I had said at the party. It was quite sane and civilized, and I answered it promptly. After that I found a note on my desk almost every day. Though through the weeks I never saw their author, I was glad to get them and amused enough to reply. Usually they were normal in tone, but sometimes they sounded a little vague and disturbing. That was only to be expected, from what Teddy told me. Ma was a good man to have in Holly's department, according to Teddy; his Chinese was wonderfully fluent and his work for the most part was steady. He helped arrange propaganda broadcasts in Chinese. But there were times, said Teddy, when he grew too eccentric to be of any use for a few days. Holly made allowances for him, and went so far as to keep an eye on his physical well-being, buying his warm underwear out of his own pocket (for Ma gave all his salary away to beggars) and seeing to it that he ate more or less regularly.

In all the time of my first visit to Chungking I saw him only twice. Through the medium of the notes he made a date with me to come out for coffee, early in the morning after one of his all-night sessions at the broadcasting studio. He came by the hostel, where his appearance called forth puzzled stares from the servants, and we plowed through mud down to a shop where they actually served coffee and hot cakes. He chattered cleverly, sounding exactly like any Oxford undergraduate who liked his books. It was difficult to believe in him when I looked at his gaunt, bearded face with the wen on the forehead, his grimy, faded blue gown, his bony wrists, his blackened teeth. Difficult and sad too. In one of the letters he had revealed a tragic terror that his mind was slipping.

He had not begun to doubt his sanity because of any of his own actions, which of course seemed quite rational and ordinary to him, but because his grandfather had ended his days as a lunatic. I did a lot of thinking about Ma Ping-ho, wondering how to talk to him and help him out. Whatever I did in the end, as it turned out, was not worth the trouble I caused him. I need not have meddled.

A few days after the coffee drinking he called for me without warning and said, "Come on out for a walk. It's spring."

It was, a lovely day for Chungking. Still I hesitated. He looked even odder than usual, and I was busy, and I didn't want him to get into the habit of pulling me away from my book. But he was insistent and persuaded me.

We started out along the road by the Chialing River, toward Pei-pei. He strode along in his English way, fantastically unlike the slow stroll of the sages he wanted to imitate, and we covered the ground so briskly that in a short time we had left behind even the new village that was growing up at the outskirts of town. It was well on toward noon before I suggested that we turn back.

"Not yet," he urged. "We'll sit up here on this grave and talk."

Off the main road he selected a high mound with a dry sandy patch on the ground near the little rock fence that marked an important ancestor. We sat down there and I rubbed my blistered heel ruefully.

"Why isn't Zau here," he demanded abruptly, "taking care of you?"

"He didn't know I would have to stay so long," I said.

"But he should be living here," said Ma Ping-ho. "The time for Shanghai is past."

It was very much what I felt myself. "You know the Chinese," I argued. "They don't give up their homes as easily as we do."

"I *am* Chinese," snapped Ma, and I was silent. Then he went on talking in an incoherent way. He said that we were destined for each other. He didn't talk at all about love in the ordinary way; I should have begun screaming, I think, if he had; but the burden of his argument was that he, Ma Ping-ho, by virtue of his own emotional history, was obviously my mate. We were both pilgrims to the shrine of China, as it were, forerunners of mankind's new caravansary. Exalted, his cheeks bright red, he talked on and on, and I forgot to be detached and wise and all-understanding. I was tired and nonplussed and a little frightened.

"Now," I said as he paused, "I'm going back."

Oh no, said Ma. I was not going back. I was never going back. What was the sense of that? We were going on, and on, and on. We were going straight along that road into the future, and it was time to be starting.

He held out his hand to help me up so that we could continue the journey. I was wearing woven sandals and my feet hurt. Vexed and hungry, I argued with Ma more emphatically than was wise. His mood changed and he became ugly, but after a bit, when I insisted on calling a ricksha coolie, he capitulated. It was miraculous luck that I should have sighted a coolie at all, out there in the country, and Ma admitted that Providence seemed to be in favor of my return to town. I rode back at a good clip, and he ran alongside the ricksha, his long bony body enveloped in a cloud of dust. How he did it I don't know, but he kept up with us all the way to the corner of the street where the hostel was.

I got rid of him at the door and went to my own room in a bad state of nerves. I had missed out on lunch.

After that I managed to avoid seeing Ma any more. Unfortunately he retained an acute awareness of me. One evening at the Press Hostel Teddy happened to speak of me. I don't know what he said, and whatever it was, he assured me later, was trivial, something like "Mickey says she hasn't had any mail for a month." Anyway, much to the public alarm and amazement, Ma leaped to his feet and slapped Teddy lightly on the cheek.

"You have insulted the woman I love," he said, shaking with passion. "You have spoken her name. I challenge you to a duel," or words to that effect. Teddy was really his closest friend among the foreigners, and his champion to boot. It was an awkward and painful situation. Holly smoothed it over for the time being, and gave Ma some work out of town so that he might calm down at leisure. Holly was worried, though, and displeased with me, which was natural but unfair. He didn't know what I had been up to with his difficult protégé, but he suspected the worst.

Teddy hurried over to make his report to me and to find out what had been going on. "Did you correspond with Ma?" he demanded.

"Certainly I did," I said. "So what?"

He moaned. "Oh, you shouldn't. . . . He might show those letters around," he said. "He isn't responsible."

"But there's nothing to show," I said. "Let him show them if he likes. What's the matter with you, Teddy?"

Teddy, an innocent boy in spite of all his ambitions, had the hot and easily fired imagination of all innocent boys. He stared at me with moist bright eyes. "Did you make *love* with him?" he persisted.

"Either get out of here, Teddy," I said, "or talk about something that makes sense. Have you ever looked at his teeth?"

Teddy is very difficult to convince away from something he hopes is true. We settled down to a half hour of poetry. I always enjoyed those sessions because Teddy let me read aloud as much as I liked, and what is more, he listened. But I still felt ruffled. I was getting just a bit fed up with Chungking.

One day toward the end of March I found myself being jolted out of the routine forever. At least I thought so then. Donald telephoned me and told me he was leaving town. I had to coax and tease him a bit before he would go any further, but at last I elicited the information that Mme. Chiang, too, was leaving town. Anybody else would have put it the other way around—Madame was going and so, therefore, was Donald—but that wasn't his way. For some months she had been hinting that she would give in to Sister Ai-ling's pleading and go down to Hong Kong for a visit, but she had put it off again and again. When it wasn't a group of her girls graduating and needing her to make a speech it was a misgiving that she had no right to take time off from the rigors of war, when all the soldiers were suffering so. It was the state of her teeth that settled matters. Other doctors could be brought up to Chungking to do their stuff, like Dr. Harry Talbot—Harry had so impressed Madame by his treatment of her sinus that she made him operate on practically everybody in the family before he went back to Hong Kong. There wasn't a Soong sinus infection left in Chungking. But dentists were different. They need their gadgets and their offices. Mme. Chiang couldn't put it off any longer, unless she was willing to cast herself on the mercies of a Chungking dentist, and she wasn't. She was particular about her teeth and very wisely didn't trust British dentists either, but imported an American from Shanghai to meet her halfway.

"That's disturbing news for me," I said very crossly. "Here I am and she goes and runs out on me. What am I supposed to do now?"

"There is nothing to prevent you copying me," said Donald blithely. "I have been given to understand that an ordinary passenger plane, leaving at about the same time as Madame's, has one place still available for a passenger."

"Oh."

"Yes," he said. "I didn't forget you, as you can see. But don't talk about this to anybody. There's always a good deal of unofficial interest when Madame takes a trip by plane."

"Is it possible that she's going to America?" I demanded. That was a hardy perennial rumor, and it had many guises whenever it appeared. "If so, will I be permitted to go along? If so——"

"She's going to Hong Kong, so far as I know," said Donald, "and that's all. Now you'd better go and pack."

You don't do much packing when you leave Chungking. There is an unwritten law which has never been broken by anyone, to my knowledge, except Wen Yuan-ning, and that is never to take anything away from the capital which can be used by anybody remaining there. It is almost impossible to get clothes and toilet articles up to Chungking for the market, because airplane transportation is the only method they have for getting supplies, and the available airplane space is needed for much more important things. A dress which means very little to a woman in Hong Kong or India makes all the difference in the world to a woman in Chungking. The same goes for men's clothes, shirts and ties and braces and shoes, all those things. Departing journalists and oil men hold "pot latches" in their rooms when they go, and I did the same.

There were rules already laid down for my clothes. Most of them had been bespoken long since. I put aside those for Corin and those for Maya. I made as fair a division as possible of my few drops of perfume. I handed out the toothpaste, the stockings, the hats. Nobody seemed interested in my padded gown and I kept that, but even my Chinese mink coat was eagerly snapped up by Corin, though it was so old and badly tanned that the fur kept splitting.

I had left, when this was finished, my typewriter, the clothes I was wearing, my toothbrush, and my hairbrush and comb. I had still another toothbrush, but Kuo Ping-chia kept that. He said he could boil it and use it for a long time. Foreign-made toothbrushes were hard to get. I even left my empty luggage except for one faithful square hatbox which has been with me for twelve years and has never yet carried a hat. Fenn Lynch was invaluable on occasions like this because he had a car and government petrol. He always took people down to the plane. We got there in ample time, with Corin and Ping-chia, my faithful allies, accompanying me as far as they could. The airfield, that famous battered strip of sandspit, was Fenn's own stamping ground and he careered happily around it, introducing me to Woody, the pilot, and talking to everybody. Ping-chia shook hands vigorously. Corin cried. Fenn, as the plane roared off, saluted dramatically. It was all quite poignant, because I thought that I would never be back again.

"And I'm sorry about that, too," I said to myself, flattening my nose against the window to look my last at the roofless fire-whitened houses of the old city, and the rapids where the rivers ran together at the point of the flatiron. "It's quite a place, Chungking is. How I hate to leave Corin! She didn't cry because I was leaving; she cried because she is staying behind. Can't I dig her out of there before she melts into the fog entirely? Get her a job or a man or something? Can anyone make up for someone else's deficient vitality? Oh, stop it, Emily Hahn; you can't manage other people. Look what happened to you with Ma Ping-ho."

The trip grew a little rough, and the Chinese were noisily sick. They often are, on planes, because they think it is expected of them. One thing led to another and finally I found myself, very much out of character because I am not mechanically minded, piloting the plane with Woody keeping a sharp eye on my technique. It couldn't have been flawless work, for the manager back in the passengers' compartment noticed the difference right away. He wrote us a note, commenting on the shakiness of the plane since I had taken over, but I sat up there feeling important and doing what Woody told me to do until we reached Hong Kong, after dark.

How lovely it looked! We had not gone in for blackouts in Chungking as yet, but in retrospect I seemed to have been living in darkness. Hong Kong's red and blue neon lights and the brilliant yellow illumination all along the face of the Peak grew more and more beautiful as we circled around, lower and lower. It had been a foggy day but as soon as we dropped lower than the clouds the air seemed crystal-clear.

"I've been breathing fog and mist for more than three months," I said joyfully to Woody. "Now I can live again."

"Going to stay here long?" he asked.

"No, just long enough to finish up the book," I said. "Then back to Shanghai and my gibbons."

"That'll be nice."

Little Billie Lee, the faithful secretary of *T'ien Hsia,* had been clamoring for me to keep an old promise and stay in her flat for as long as I could spare the time. It was late in the evening when I got there. With a Eurasian girl named Mavis Ming Billie occupied a ground-floor flat of four rooms, out in Happy Valley.

Happy Valley, out where the racecourse is, strikes a pleasant sort of average for white-collar workers and bachelor girls like Billie. She could get in to work on the tram or the bus. She could afford one servant, an amah who did all the work of the house for seventeen dollars a month. She shared expenses with Mavis and with any third girl they happened to get to help out with the household; at the moment they were alone.

Billie did practically all of the real work that was done at *T'ien Hsia,* lived in a state of suspended exasperation with Alice Chow, and saved a little bit out of her ridiculous salary every month. Mavis, a stenographer for the Co-ops, had an absorbing and important hobby: she conducted a

gymnasium class which had headquarters in England and was known
as the "Women's League of Health and Beauty." Theoretically Mavis
should have been able to live on her profits from the League, but it
hadn't worked out very well. The pure white ladies of the town didn't
take her seriously because she was Eurasian, even though they were
obsessed with reducing, and the Eurasian girls couldn't pay very well
for their classes. So Mavis divided her labors, and she too put by a little
money every month.

I sat down on my bed. "Now tell me about you," I invited. "What is
all this about getting married?"

"Yes," said Billie, blushing. "Last December it was, soon after you
went to Chungking. You met him last summer at the beach—remember?
Paddy Gill. He's a soldier."

I remembered him. He was an Irishman, prematurely baldish. A
sergeant or something, I recalled.

"It's a good thing Mamma died last year," said Billie. "It would have
been an awful shock to her, me marrying a soldier. We don't think much
of soldiers in our family. But after the war Paddy is going to get out of
the Army, and he was going to be sent away soon, and he had been
after me for more than a year, and I wouldn't have been happy marrying
a Chinese. I'm too foreign in my ways. So we were married secretly. You
were the very first one I told, honestly, Mickey."

I yawned widely. "I don't mind soldiers myself," I said. "How are the
Boxers getting along, speaking of soldiers?"

"Oh, all right, I guess. Mrs. Boxer's been helping out at the Co-operative
office, Mavis says. Mavis says she isn't much help though; she doesn't
come in regularly. It's always that way with volunteer help, and these
society ladies don't understand how to do regular work, I suppose."

The girls showed me around the bathroom and left me to my accu-
mulated letters. Vaguely I noticed that Billie was getting rather thick
around the waist. Still, in wartime and with these sudden marriages,
those things were likely to happen. I would wait until she talked about
it herself. I yawned again and started to undress.

Billie poked her head in the door. "I forgot to tell you," she said, "that
this neighborhood is full of sneak thieves. Don't leave anything near the
window where they can reach it through the bars. Mavis and I keep
hockey sticks by our beds just in case anything happens: I lost a dress
last week. Blue taffeta it was, and it cost eighty dollars: I was just sick.
They use long poles with hooks on them. We haven't enough police in
Hong Kong, you know, now that the town is so full of refugees. Well,
good night."

Chapter 23

THE GIRLS had a host of friends. They knew all the Eurasian and Chinese and Portuguese secretaries and stenographers in town. Billie kept in touch through her friends with all the downtown firms and all their private business, including the private business of the employees and employers. There were no secrets from me in Hong Kong, no facts or rumors kept from the keen eyes of those little girls, who recounted them all at home. They were also in touch, through Mavis' job at the Co-op office, with the leftist element among the Europeans, and through Billie's job at Wen Yuan-ning's with all the visiting journalists. For girls with their limited background they managed to develop an unusual sense of what was going on in the world outside the tight little colony. They were well ahead of the other stenographers; instead of merely grousing vaguely, as the others did, about the unfair system that kept them underpaid and underfoot, they investigated the whys and wherefores of this state of theirs and saw a future when these injustices might possibly be wiped out. Mavis was fiery and resentful, but Billie was gentle and her feelings were easily hurt. Both of them really discussed the problem; they didn't just blow off steam and then forget about it.

"Write us a book," urged Mavis. "I'm sick of all the nonsense they print about Eurasians. Write us a good book."

"It might help," said Billie hopefully. "I'm thinking about my baby. Paddy says he'll be all right in England, but I don't know."

Every day I listened to them giggling and chattering and talking on the phone to their friends, and I felt very old and motherly. When breakfast was over and they had rushed off to catch their bus, and the amah had cleared off the table, I would bring out my typewriter and the manuscript and get down to work grimly, for I was at that stage all writers know when I was near the end but just couldn't seem to get there. A whole lot of things stood in the way, chief among them this visit Mme. Chiang was making to her sister. Mme. Sun had joined in the reunion, moving outright to Sassoon Road, and the three of them were having a great time, acting like schoolgirls and sinking all their political differences and even refusing to quarrel—for the time being. It was a nice sight, but it was bad for my book, because even the faithful Mme. Kung was too busy to help me out and answer questions.

Bored and worried and feeling stale, I turned for comfort to society. I didn't know many people in Hong Kong; the young couple who had contributed to Sinmay's distress were back in England on a visit, and Ian had gone to Indo-China. I missed Sinmay acutely but, remembering what had happened before, I dared not press him to come down to Hong Kong, and I didn't want to go back to Shanghai too soon, not before I had wound up the Soong reunion. If it had been possible to telephone Shanghai by long distance this book would have a very different plot from now on. As it was, my only news of Sinmay was a long letter remarkable in content. For five closely typed pages he accused himself of having been a son of a bitch and worse. He went into details and lashed himself into a perfect sweat. He was more than honest in his analysis; he admitted having been lazy, selfish, neglectful, and even spitefully jealous of my capacity for work. As I read it my heart grew more and more light and gooey, like a slowly baking meringue, until I came to the last page. In the final paragraph he asked me for five hundred dollars, quite simply, and then in a postscript added:

"If you want to know why this letter is as it is, it is because I have been reading, *How to Win Friends and Influence People.*"

Damn the Japanese, who wouldn't let me bring any of my old letters from China. The missive was a perfect description of Sinmay from his exasperating best to his charming worst. I groaned when I finished the last page, because there was no one there who would appreciate it with me, and because I couldn't reform Sinmay, and because I knew that I couldn't, couldn't, couldn't go on with the Zaus. It was beyond my power; we stood on opposite sides of a suddenly swollen river. I felt it, as clearly as I saw myself in the mirror. But still . . .

"I'll have to go back," I resolved, "and talk it out face to face. There are things to be arranged; we have to get all disentangled on that printing press and everything. And I owe Sinmay a personal explanation. He won't really care; he doesn't mind anything in the end. It's my loss, not his." Now that I had made the decision I was unhappy. It was tempting to hope that I could be persuaded to change my mind, back in Shanghai. Sinmay had always persuaded me before. But Chungking had made a difference in all that.

Oh, why couldn't I relax, I wondered, and let things just drift along? Five years earlier I had made up my mind and chosen my place and selected a life and a burial plot in China. Why should I now feel that I must undo everything, smash the edifice I had built, throw myself out onto the road again? I didn't exactly know. I had never before stayed in one place so long, and the familiar routine of starting out fresh did not seem so familiar any more. Nor was it attractive, after all this time.

"Am I going to go on doing this forever?" I demanded, growing frightened. Again I didn't know, but I did know one thing. If I had a child I would stay put, somewhere, somehow. The idea was there, a certainty standing all alone in the middle of my mind, and how was I to guess that it was just as big a mistake as my other ideas?

The only people I knew who were still in town were the Boxers. I telephoned Ursula.

"We must have you to dinner," she said, planning aloud. "Wait a minute while I look at my book. . . ."

I felt a little thrill of displeasure at those words. People should not need books to tell them what their dates were, I said to myself severely, fresh as I was from the sparse social atmosphere of Szechuan.

"Here we are," came her voice again, high and shrill and English. "Can you come alone—that is, are you—er—*with* anybody this trip?"

I recalled her frightened glances at Sinmay's brown robe whenever he wasn't looking at her. "All alone this time," I said blithely. There was a definite note of relief in her reply.

"Oh, splendid. Would Thursday suit you?"

Yes, Thursday would suit me fine.

I met Alf Bennett at the Boxers'. Alf was an RAF officer, at once deliberately comic and knowingly glamorous. He had an incredible mustache, curled at the ends like Father's in the Clarence Day play. He had high blood pressure and a growling voice; he roared, and drank, and knew poetry, and fancied himself a picturesque figure, as he was. Picturesque and privileged. Everybody knew Alf, and women were wistful about him, but a little afraid.

He was comparatively new to Hong Kong and to Charles Boxer, but Charles was delighted with his absurd appearance and his capacity for liquor. "Isn't he good?" he kept demanding of me, as in the course of the evening Alf became more and more an ultracivilized buffoon. We all drank heavily: cocktails, wine with the elaborate dinner, and what we wanted afterward.

Well, so there I was launched all over again in Hong Kong, and now I had things to do of an evening. One afternoon Charles decided that I must go to a cocktail party to which "the office" had been invited. An ex-civilian flier who had joined the RAF and given up his job as Moss's assistant was the host, and when I suggested tentatively that he might like to know I was coming Charles scoffed at me.

"Old Max won't care. He invited everybody in town, anyway, and Alf's boss; Max won't dare object even if he wants to," he said. "Alf will bring you. So long, Emily Hahn."

Max Oxford had a precise drawl that sounded just like his name. His house in Kowloon was one of the new Spanish-style white stucco cottages that were growing up near the Kai Tak airfield; the Japs loved them later on, and squabbled bitterly over their shining newness, for each officer wanted a cute cottage all to himself. But this was back in 1940 when nobody dreamed of such a situation. The Empire stood solid and firm at Max's cocktail party. There were naval officers there, and willowy young girls, and Moss with his wife, and Ursula, smart and expensive in black, and the two Canavals, doctors, man and wife, that everyone was swearing by. There was Alf getting drunk in one corner, and Charles getting drunk in another. I looked at young Major Boxer, whose graying hair was even more disorderly than usual as he chattered and drank gin. He drank earnestly these days, and whenever he was a little drunk he talked of the end of the Empire.

"Don't you agree, Emily Hahn, that the day of the white man is done out here? Russia or no Russia, we're finished and we don't know it. All this is exactly like the merriment of Rome before the great fall. We are assisting in the death throes of capitalism. It's a very nice party too. Have another, Emily Hahn. Nonsense, you don't have to go yet."

But he had to go, Ursula insisted; there was a dinner party across the bay and they were late. Alf and I suddenly found ourselves the last of the party. We adjourned to the Peninsula for dinner, drunk and giggling, and in the stately dining room of that dismally expensive hotel we drank sparkling burgundy and waltzed wildly, round and round and round, under the crystal chandeliers.

At last the silence of the Soongs was broken. Mme. Kung sent for me one afternoon to give me a hot tip.

"My sisters have persuaded me to come out to dinner," she said excitedly. "We are going to dine at the Hongkong Hotel tonight, and I thought that it would be worth seeing us all together. It would be interesting, don't you think? Would you consider it interesting enough for the book? Then get somebody to bring you to the main dining room at eight o'clock, or earlier than that if you want a good table."

I asked Alf to escort me to the Hongkong Hotel for my scoop. We took the little table next to the pillar just in the middle of the inside room, well in view of the Soongs. They were there, sure enough, with Moss and his wife, Donald, and one of the younger brothers who are always fated to be compared, disparagingly, with T.V.

"So now you have seen them," said Alf. "Is this all there is to it? We may now feel ourselves free to pollute ourselves and enjoy it, if so."

Once again we waltzed, round and round and round. Alf was a good dancer. I kicked up my heels: my long skirt flew out in a bell as I whirled.

Over at the Soong table Mme. Sun, sober in black, looked at us appraisingly and said to Mme. Kung, "There's Mickey Hahn. I suppose that's Mickey Mouse she's with?"

The ladies were so tremendously busy with their shopping and their family affairs that I suddenly gave up the whole thing. I didn't fancy the position. I felt increasingly self-conscious, hanging around in a British colony when there didn't seem to be any more material forthcoming from my models. I didn't blame them; they had been admirably patient all along. It must have been irritating to have a person trotting after them everywhere, snapping up crumbs of information, studying their characters as well as their histories. And I wasn't too happy, myself, in Hong Kong; I felt out of things. My place was in Chungking; failing that, in my beloved Shanghai. I would go back there. There wouldn't be much more to be gleaned from the ladies, and we could do it by mail.

I made arrangements speedily, all unaware that Fate, with her eye balefully fixed on me, was lying in wait just around the corner. The ticket was bought for a ship sailing next day. The bags were packed. I didn't wire Sinmay, on purpose. I said good-by to Wen Yuan-ning and the office. I should have called up Mme. Kung to say good-by; it was the natural thing to do, but I was just a mite peeved with Mme. Kung. I was probably a little jealous too. She had deserted me for her sisters. I wrote her a good-by letter and gave it to Alice Chow.

Probably in the back of my mind was the thought that Wen Yuan-ning would report my departure to her anyway. I failed to take note of his manner when I went in to pay my respects to the staff: Wen was sulky with me, resenting my growing friendship with Mme. Kung, with Charles, and "the office." He felt that the British as well as the Kungs were his own property, and he also had a very conservative, ultra-British feeling against the crude Yankee. He tried to express it one day to the Alexanders, soon after it became evident that Charles preferred my company to his: "Mickey's so *pushing*," he complained. So he said good-by to me with secret relief and pleasure, and did not go out of his way to mention my name to the Boxers or to Madame.

Billie and Mavis saw me off. We weren't told just when the ship was sailing, because this was war and such things were better kept secret.

That accounts for my error in timing. I had expected to be out on the high seas by three at the latest; Alice, with my letter in her purse, would not arrive at Madame's house for her afternoon work until the same hour. But Madame read the letter and flew to the telephone in an attempt to call me back, for reasons which were evident later on. Nobody answered, and she bundled Alice into a car and sent her direct to the dock. The ship was still there and looked likely to be there for some hours to come. Alice ran up the gangplank, discovered my cabin easily, for there were only two or three other passengers aboard, and landed in my presence all breathless and panting. Mavis and Billie were still there, saying good-by. We all turned around and stared at her in amazement.

"Mme. Kung—says—come immediately," panted Alice. "Never mind your things. Come right away, to her house."

Wonderingly, I dropped a dress half draped on its hanger and obediently started out. "What is it?" I asked meekly as we climbed into the car.

"I don't know." Alice had caught her breath and now began to put her hair in order. "I don't know a thing. The house out there is a luna-tic asylum; they're having their pictures taken this afternoon and the place is full of reporters. But Madame didn't mean for you to meet the reporters. We're to go in the back way."

"I can't help worrying," I said thoughtfully, "about my boat. And my clothes. I'm not used to this sort of thing."

"The captain said you won't sail before dark. Don't worry."

Mme. Kung didn't keep me waiting very long, though it seemed long to me, anxiously huddled in the small dining room. Through the closed double doors came familiar voices: Spencer Moosa of the AP, George Giffen of the *Telegraph,* and then the sputtering of a Russian photog-rapher I had met. That bubbly voice was Mme. Chiang; the slower, deliberate accents of Mme. Sun were for a moment unfamiliar to me because she was actually giggling as someone made a joke. I didn't hear my own Madame. After a while she came in and joined me, looking reproachful.

"You were going," she said immediately, "without saying good-by?"

"But you were so busy. I didn't want to be a bother."

"I spent the morning," she said, "with Mr. Zau's aunt. She has just come back from Shanghai."

"How are they all?" I asked eagerly.

"Quite well." I thought she hesitated, and I was right. "Have you noti-fied them that you are coming?" she asked.

"As a matter of fact I haven't. It isn't much use these days; you can't put the name of the boat or the sailing date or anything, so why bother? I thought I'd just arrive, and then telephone."

Mme. Kung asked a few idle questions about the boat and my cabin, while I wondered why she had brought me so far. A farewell note would have been easier for both of us, *much* easier for me. . . .

"Do you think they can do without you?" she asked me suddenly. It was so near to my own recent cogitations that I was very much startled. "I know," she said. "I know you've been wondering the same thing. I'm not a mind reader, but from a few things you have said lately I knew what was in your mind. I talked it over today with his aunt, who is fond of you. This is what I thought: you are alone here in China, with no family to take care of you." That was characteristically Chinese, I reflected: I could never have explained to her that I was alone in China because I had run away from my family.

"I don't want you to be exploited by China," continued the amazing Mme. Kung. "If this happens, if Mr. Zau takes advantage of you—oh, it would be unconscious on his part, but I know that Chinese tendency—you will end by hating us all. Yes, I think you will. I know China and I know America. You will go away from China without complaining, but you will feel bitter. Isn't it true?"

I sat there without answering.

"I don't want this to happen," said Mme. Kung. "It's not too late. Forgive me for interfering, but I'm sure it's for the best. Don't go back to Shanghai yet. Think it over first." She smiled at me. "You have already been thinking it over," she reminded me.

"Yes, I have," I said when I began to catch my breath. "I have."

She sat there, looking kindly on me. I sat there staring at her as if she had stepped out of *The Arabian Nights*. I was certainly for once in my life knocked off my feet. In the next room was a dead hush, then there came a flash of light through the cracks of the door and a sudden babble of voices as the photographer told his subjects to relax.

"Well then," I said, suddenly lightheaded, "that is that. I won't go back to Shanghai. Oh dear."

"It's for the best," repeated Madame. "I know how you feel. I love that city. It's my home. But we have to wait until the end of the war, and if you're allied with us you shouldn't really be going back anyway. Should you?"

I sat there gloomily contemplating life in the Crown Colony. "I don't want to live in Hong Kong," I said. "It might be better to go home to America, but I'd get stuck there."

"Really? Why?" There spoke a lady accustomed to traveling easily, without fretting over passports or bank accounts. "Nowadays it is so easy to travel," she said innocently. "But it wasn't my idea that you go home so soon—although no doubt your mother is getting anxious about you. No. You can write her a reassuring letter and explain to her that I too have many children traveling over all the world in these sad times. It can't be helped. I had thought you might go back to Chungking."

I had thought so too.

"There's a secret I'm going to tell you," she said, looking excited. "You mustn't tell anyone yet, but we're all going to Chungking!"

It was a day of surprises. "Mme. Sun too?" I asked.

"Mme. Sun too. My youngest sister has been begging us to come back for a visit. We've been talking about it ever since she arrived, and now she says that I made a definite promise to go and must keep it. You see, she can't stay any longer. There is always so much work for her up in Szechuan. But it seems a pity to cut our reunion short, and besides, I do owe it to my husband to go and see him, since he can't come here. Mme. Sun has consented to make it a real family party."

"That's the part I don't understand," I admitted. "Is that to show that the Reds are really reconciled at last?"

"It's a personal visit," she said, "as far as I know. She's going to stay with us rather than at the Chiangs' house because we have more room."

"Oh."

"Now about you. I thought that this trip would be a good way to end your book."

"Good? It's the perfect ending. You couldn't have arranged things better, madame, if you'd done it on purpose for me."

There is a quality possessed by few people in the circles frequented by Mme. Kung, and it is usually called "consideration" or "thoughtfulness." Neither of those words is really descriptive, is it, when you come down to examine it? We mean "considerate of other people," or "thoughtful of other people": we really mean, to take it further, that the person with that quality is not too full of himself to be aware of the outside world. I have sometimes wondered about the mentality of professional philanthropists. I am told that many of them are dried-up recluses, people who rather dislike to be impinged upon by other egos. Rockefeller was like that. You wouldn't call him "thoughtful." Perhaps he was, but it wasn't his reputation. Mme. Kung's surprising quality was her warmth. When she did something for me like this, going out of her way to set me in what she considered the right path, I was aware of the personal effort that went into that action. She had expended genuine emotion on my case. There was sweetness in what she had done. It was *good*. It was also more than that, because it was characteristic: I was no particular favorite. She would do as much for anyone she knew.

The argument her enemies advance is that she does these things *only* for the people she knows. A person in public life, they tell me, should deal in large numbers and think of his people in terms of thousands. Mme. Kung is nothing, officially speaking: she has no official position in the government. But as Mme. Chiang's sister, the head of the house of Soong, the wife of Dr. Kung, she is a force. If she fails to use her power for the best, say her hostile critics, she has failed in her duty.

I am not going to argue by saying that you can't hold her responsible for her position. China is called a democracy, but it is a far cry from that structure of society to the government we have set up in Washington. In many ways there is no basis for comparison. Nobody knows that better than I do. Mme. Kung *is* a power in China. But she does think in large numbers; she does try to work for the people, and I think that her interest in her friends is an asset rather than a liability. The impersonal approach to reform leads to all the evils of social service as we see it working out in our own organizations. We could use a few more brains with the feudal point of view when it comes to rearranging our world. In our high places we are a little short on human sympathy and understanding, and on the courage to admit human responsibility. Mme. Kung is not. She has greatness.

In case you ever have occasion to cancel a seagoing passage at the last minute, remember that the forfeit on your ticket is one third its value. I dragged my half-unpacked bags down the gangplank just in time and returned to Happy Valley to surprise the little girls and send the amah scuttling into the kitchen in dismay to cook more rice.

Next day I set about winding up things in Shanghai, and the job was made easy because I met an old friend from there in the lobby of the Hongkong Hotel.

"I'll take your house," he said eagerly. "They're terribly hard to get, I hear, what with the town filling up with German refugees. I'll break the news to the refugee that he must find another place. I'll give the gibbons to Horst Reihmer for the summer; he can keep them out in Hungjao Road in his new house and it will be grand for them. Later on when you decide what you want done with them, just let me know. Don't worry, I'll fix it all." And he did.

The refugee, incidentally, was plunged into despair, and a lot of letters went back and forth between us. I could never figure out just why I felt so guilty toward him. After all, what had I done but take care of him for a year or so, and then withdraw my help? I'll admit that there is a sort of debt which attaches to that kind of relationship: you might say that I had pauperized him because I took him in in the first place; so now he was my responsibility. That's the way he seemed to figure, anyway. In the end he found a job through the Alexanders, broadcasting for the Allies in German, but I doubt if he has yet forgiven me for the wrong I did him, though he did come and stay with me for a bit, later on in Hong Kong. Old habit, I suppose.

Sinmay never wrote to me at all. Or perhaps he did, and forgot to mail the letter. He sent an indirect message one time, though, through a girl we both knew; he said that he wasn't angry with me, that he hoped I was happy, and that I possessed many of the qualities of a good Chinese woman. I think it was a compliment. I even think he meant it to be.

There were five or six days to get through before I went back to Chungking. I was fidgety and, following my usual pattern, I rushed about and saw people so that I wouldn't think too much. There was an amazing afternoon when everything happened by accident but nevertheless we made history of a sort. I don't know just how it all began. I was having a drink with Alf in the lobby of the Grips. That is what the English called the Hongkong Hotel, because they give nicknames to everything. Well, there we were, and we met someone else, and we drank a lot of "ox's blood," which you make by mixing champagne with sparkling burgundy, and there is brandy in it, too, I believe, though I'm not sure. I was supposed to go to Mayor Wu Teh-chen's house for dinner and poker that evening, under the wing of General Cohen. The general was playing his role of Picturesque Old China Hand those days. He would sit in the lobby of the Grips day after day, slightly drunk, cheerfully ready to fasten on anyone who came by. He didn't have many troubles: Mme. Sun paid him a pension and he played a lot of poker, usually with Wu Teh-chen, and dabbled in various real-estate deals and so on just for the fun of it. It was a sort of hazard, getting through the Grips lobby around noon. If you didn't run into General Cohen you were apt to fall in with One-Arm Sutton.

I was to meet Morris Cohen on the Kowloon side at the ferry station at five o'clock. But I was still drinking at five o'clock, at Alf's flat, trying to talk sensibly with his French teacher. It was nearer seven when Alf drove me in his car over to the ferry. He was wearing his uniform cap, but no coat, and the general cocked a wise eye at him as I got out, full of apologies.

"Think nothing of it," he said largely, hailing a taxi.

Wu Teh-chen, who had been Mayor of Canton before they drove him out, was waiting dinner for us. ("Ask him what happened to that blood he was going to shed the last drop of," Charles had said unkindly when he heard where I was going.) It was a good dinner with a lot of whisky and also plenty of guests. I knew them all, pretty ladies and important gentlemen in Chinese society. I sobered up a bit. After dinner when the poker began, however, I wasn't sober enough to refuse to play, and I solemnly took my seat with the best sharks in the Far East. It was then that Morris Cohen won my everlasting gratitude. He let me play just one minute before he said, "Get out of that chair and go upstairs, Mickey."

Meekly I obeyed him. Up in the ladies' room I found all the pretty ladies, doing up their faces and chatting about their children. I must have been quite drunk. I don't often get that drunk. One of the women, chatting politely with me, pointed to a young and handsome lady who was combing her hair and said, "How old do you think she is?"

"Oh," I said, "about twenty-two."

"Thirty-five," said Elsie, "and she has nine children."

At this I burst into tears. "What is it?" asked Elsie, alarmed. "Get some water, somebody. What is it?"

"She has nine children," I sobbed, "and I haven't any."

In an embarrassed but sympathetic silence the ladies allowed me to get out of the room and downstairs to a taxi.

"I'm so awfully sorry," I said next day to the general. "Honestly, Morris, I'm terribly sorry. I called up the Mayor this morning."

"That's all right," said Cohen. "You was all right. You was cute. You was adorable."

"Yesh, I can imagine." I brooded sadly and held my head.

"Honest you was all right," said the general. "Nobody would of known. But that boy friend of yours, that RAF, now he was polluted if you like. Boy, did he have a load on. In fact, the only reason I could tell you was drunk was that you was lettin' him drive."

Charles and I were seated next to each other at a Chinese dinner, where Max was host. Charles was making life hideous for the unfortunate Max, who hoped to glean certain information from Ed Pawley, his guest of honor. He wanted to know just how much private aid was going into Chungking from Americans, in the form of planes and suchlike appurtenances of civilization. But every time he came near the ticklish subject, while Ed listened gravely and silently, Charles would call irreverently from our side of the table, "Got the old pump handle working, Max?"

It was enough to discourage any earnest beginner in the art of snooping for King and country. Max glared at Charles; Charles toasted Max.

Little by little we weeded ourselves out. The Americans went home. Ursula went home, but Charles didn't. Alf was suddenly possessed of a familiar conviction that often came over him when he was in his cups: he thought he could fly. He got up on the table and walked across, his arms held out stiffly, his big black eyes glassy. When he came to the edge of the table he went right on walking, straight off into space, and as he went down his boot caught me in the hand: I have the mark to this day. It was a special occasion, for two out-of-town officers were with us that evening, Kenneth Millar from Shanghai and Robert Scott of the Bureau of Information down in Singapore. A Hong Kong member of "the office" took me home at the end of it all, and some of the men accompanied Charles to his flat and went to bed on the floor.

"It was queer, the way Ursula went off," I said inquisitively to my escort. "She just came over to Charles while he was talking to me, with his arm around me—you know how he gets; it's a little embarrassing— and said, 'I'm going home now,' and Charles just said, 'Yes,' and she went. Like that."

"I know," he said. "Quite a common occurrence. What number is your house?"

Some of us met the next day for a post-mortem drink at eleven, in the hotel lobby. Charles was pale and wan. "I haven't done much today," he said. "I took a large sheet of paper and wrote across the top, 'Secret,' and that's the extent of the day's labors, so far. After tiffin I might possibly go back and put ahead of it the word 'Very.'"

I dined at the Boxers' the night before I flew back to Chungking. Ursula was going away soon on a long trip, she said, to Australia. She hadn't been well since her marriage, she complained, and she was thin and tired. It would be a long trip. . . . She glanced at Charles and he studied the pattern of the hearthrug, but he didn't say anything.

"I'm afraid he'll get into mischief, too," continued Ursula. "When he's with Alf he is apt to do anything."

I said, "If I were going to be here I'd volunteer to keep an eye on him, but I'm off to Chungking myself."

"You'll be back later, though, Emily Hahn," said Charles. "Nobody stays in Chungking forever."

"Probably."

"You take care of him, Mickey," said Ursula. "Do. I wouldn't trust a blonde."

"All right," I said amiably. "I will."

Chapter 24

TEDDY MET MY PLANE, which was a kind and thoughtful thing to do on a cold, muddy morning. In the past six weeks nothing at all had happened to improve Chungking's climate and I needed the little warm glow I felt when I saw him shivering there. The town was more crowded than ever, he told me. There was a joyful reunion with Corin and others.

"I said I'd come back, didn't I?" I demanded swaggeringly.

"Yes, but we didn't think you would really be so idiotic," said Corin. "Still, it's nice to see you. Give us the news from the world."

I said that the most interesting item for our group was that we were getting a new member of the journalistic crowd, the relief for Pierard, Havas correspondent. "Jacques Marcuse," I announced, "a man I met once in Shanghai, years ago. He isn't French, by the way; he's Belgian like Pierard."

"What's he like?" demanded Teddy.

"Tall, skinny, sloppy, attractive to some women," I said rapidly. "In fact he's attractive to lots of women."

Corin's thin, ugly face looked thoughtful. "Intelligent?" she demanded. "Political, or just sort of continental?"

"Political when he has time, I should think."

"Oh, that sort." Corin dismissed him scornfully.

The Press Hostel was a sort of an estate, surrounded by a fence which was more theoretical in those days than visible. (Since I left they have really enclosed the place and put a detective guard on the door.) There were two or three biggish buildings including the stone one which had offices in it, and a bit of broadcasting apparatus. There were two long lines of cubicles, plain, boxlike bedrooms or offices for the overflow from the original hostel building, a pretty lath-and-plaster edifice, now insufficient for the many press people who had come. Here and there over the ground—everywhere but in the huge crater left spang in the middle of the place by a bomb the summer before—were smaller buildings. One of them was a delightful little hut all by itself, near Holly's own house where his wife and children shared his existence. This hut was for lucky Betty Graham, the one unmarried lady journalist in Chungking in those days. Betty was to become a sort of hardy Chungking perennial. Sometimes she worked for Reuter's, sometimes AP, sometimes Havas: she didn't care which as long as it was a newspaper job.

There is nothing particularly unusual about unmarried lady journalists, but Betty's presence was a sore point with Holly, whose wife told him that a girl should not live in the hostel alone with all those rough men. Holly listens to his wife. And so, just to preserve the conventions, this special detached hut was built for Betty. I avoided the whole question by taking the easy way and spending much, much more money at the Chungking Hostel.

Mme. Kung didn't keep me waiting long. It was delightfully easy to go to see her in that town of long distances and no transportation. All I had to do was trot next door.

Mme. Sun was living with her in the Kung castle: she had been given the third floor of the main house to herself. For the first time since I began writing the book I saw something of her, the mythical third sister, and heard about her activities. The young people of the town and the leftists greeted her arrival with glad, thrilled cries, and she was being treated like a combination goddess and queen by this faction. She tried to avoid their attentions, for she is shy and cautious. She granted a few special interviews to old, faithful friends, but put off most of the yearning worshipers, using as excuse a half statement, which was never quite expressed, that she was not her own master in that house.

This hint was immediately pounced upon and quoted as proof that the unfortunate Red princess was being held prisoner by her wicked capitalistic sister and her vicious banker brother-in-law. In my capacity of reporter outside the palace gates I saw and heard this legend, watching cynically as it grew, and grew, and grew. Mme. Sun, I knew, was really at liberty to see whomever she wished to see and to go wherever she wished to go. She was on excellent terms at the time with all her family, including Mme. Chiang, her natural and triumphant rival for the coveted title of First Lady. She didn't even *want* to live as an enemy and a rival. But however quietly she went about her business—appearing at a reception as the Kung guest of honor and being photographed with the Generalissimo in the act of toasting him—her admirers, especially the foreign ones, insisted that she was being held in durance vile. They gnashed their teeth as they thought of their beautiful Madame in such a tragic situation. It is an interesting study of public opinion, stubborn and inflexible once it is formed. And there is no doubt that it was also a useful situation for Soong Ching-ling, who was able to turn away a lot of people who bored her, whom she didn't want to see, or who had shocked her sense of morality, without hurting their feelings. "Her sister wouldn't let us in," said the disappointed aspirants as they retraced their steps from the Kung house. "I know she'd love to see me—we were such good friends in Hankow. But that terrible sister won't let her see a soul. It's terrible."

In the Kung castle Soong Ching-ling was saying to Mme. Kung, "*That* woman? Why, I understand she has lover after lover. I don't want to see her, ever again," or, "I'm not at all satisfied with his stand on Russia in his latest articles. We'll just send him some cigarettes and say I'm not well."

The picturesque trio was being worked to death. All the women in town—statesmen's wives and Y.W.C.A. workers and teachers, and college girls and statesmen's daughters—all wanted to do honor to the Soong sisters. The public dinners were much of a muchness and I didn't bother about them, but when the sisters went on tours of inspection of factories, hospitals, et cetera, Miss Hahn as biographer was there, along with the reporters and the photographers. It was pleasant to watch the sisters together. They really did enjoy themselves. I grew sentimental when they giggled and chaffed, thinking of their lives long ago in the school down in Georgia, before they had given a thought to marriage and rivalry. My book waxed fat and was further from making an end than ever, but I didn't mind.

Rumors multiplied and flourished. The whole town showed the effect of those three women on the local legends within a week after they arrived. One little gossipmonger came into the hostel one day with even his spectacles gleaming, so happy he was over the latest report. "Isn't it true, Mickey," he demanded, "that Dr. Kung's summer house is just next door to a girls' school?"

"His summer home," I said emphatically, "is all by itself on a mountaintop, out at the hot springs. There's not a school, or a girl for that matter, for miles around. It's all forest."

"Isn't it true," he continued, not having heard a word of my speech, "that Dr. Kung watches the girls doing their exercises every morning? And isn't it true that he presented the school with a fund of three hundred thousand dollars in appreciation of those morning exercises?"

I sputtered furiously and denied the nonsense, but his spectacles still gleamed; his ears were closed. He was a reporter in pursuit of the Truth, and he would not be contradicted. . . . "Hi, Till!" he shouted. "Have you heard the latest about Kung and the girls' school?"

My social life, independent of the Soongs, proceeded according to plan. A birthday party for Corin took place around the corner from our hostel, in a house occupied by an amiable plane salesman who was willing to lend it for the occasion. It was at this party that Corin, pretty and excited in a dress left to her by the departing Butterfield-Swire wife, danced steadily throughout the evening with Jacques Marcuse, the Havas correspondent. Jacques is in many ways a remarkable man. He was remarkable that evening, for he danced indefatigably in spite of his heavy cowhide boots. His long blond hair flopped round; his agile bottom, in brown corduroys, presented itself impartially to the room as he whirled in circles across the floor and swung the fragile birthday girl in his arms until she was dizzy. But she loved it.

"He's not at all the way you described him," she said to me.

"Oh yes, he is," I said, "but let it pass. . . . Haven't you heard from your American boy friend at all, Corin?"

"No," she said, looking stubborn. "No. He never wrote again."

"Then write to him, for Pete's sake, and find out why."

"I don't have to. It must be another woman. No, that's over," said Corin, and went out to dance again with Marcuse. I felt quite cross. But anybody, perhaps, would be better than the nobody with whom she had been spending her last tortured year, and anyway, I could do nothing. I never did do anything from that time on, anything in the way of a warning. It would have been no use, would it? Would it? I wish someone would tell me flatly, "No, it wouldn't." I would feel better.

One day while the two sisters Mmes. Kung and Sun were strolling in their garden there came the crack of a rifle. Mme. Kung insists that she heard a "swish" of a bullet, too, traveling past them, but although the entire household searched earnestly they couldn't find it. Mme. Sun didn't seem to mind that incident very much, but she was distinctly nervous when the first air raid arrived.

The Japanese had been irritated beyond control by the loud noise of rejoicing in the Chinese press after the sisters made the public gesture of unity by coming together to Chungking. It was definitely annoying to their propaganda experts, who had spread themselves on the thesis that China was coming to pieces from internal disagreements in the Soong dynasty. Probably that accounts for our early air raid, first of the season, which came along two or three days after the sisters arrived. It was really more of a warning than a raid; they did much better later. But for a demonstration it wasn't so bad, and a few bombs fell, though wide, near the residential section where the government officials, *and* the sisters, were living. I dropped in that evening and found Mme. Kung laughing at Mme. Sun, who was frightened and wanted to go back to Hong Kong.

I was surprised, because I would have expected the elder sister to be the more nervous. She scouted the suggestion.

"It was much worse at the beginning," she said, "last year when we didn't have the signals straight. Poor Dr. Kung!"

Now that the season had officially opened there was a flurry on the part of the municipal authorities to clear the town of its surplus population. Now, an older and wiser woman by two years in occupied territory, I know how that sort of thing can be done. It is done by the Japanese, who are not squeamish in their methods. But the Chinese would probably object to the Jap system, which is direct and unsentimental: when Japs want to get rid of people they simply go around town, rounding them up, and then cart them out and dump them at a safe distance. The Chinese authorities couldn't do that in Chungking. They couldn't even take a fair census; they didn't really know how many people were crowded into the ancient, rebuilt city. Nobody would register, for fear of being told he was inessential and ordered out again. The government sighed and did the next best thing: they went on digging air-raid tunnels. "One or two really bad raids, later in the season, will get rid of them," said Mme. Kung wisely. "They'll start moving out into the country then."

The trouble was that as soon as a group did take the initiative and move out into the country a busy, big community would begin to spring up. Relatives followed and built cottages near by. Wandering peddlers settled down and set up shops. Other shops sprang up and other people came along and liked the looks of the place, and before you knew where you were there was a flourishing village, big enough for the Japs to bomb. It happened over and over again.

The early raids left only vague memories with me. There was a time during the full moon when the raiders came every night, as soon as the moon was out. We guests at the hostel got up and sat outdoors on the lawn, peering up at the starry heavens and waiting for something to happen. We were foolhardy in those days because we didn't know any better. The bombing, which had at first been concentrated on a distant military airfield, drew nearer and nearer, until a British officer came upstairs one night and hauled me out and insisted that I join him and a burly RAF officer who was his superior in a downstairs room at least. There came a time when they bombed so very close that I didn't need any more arguments, but ran down into the tunnel just as quickly as anybody. Nowadays, knowing what I know and have seen since then, I shudder at my idiocy, but we all went through that foolhardy phase. Until you see it happen you just don't believe in it.

Those moonlight vigils out on the lawn were actually pleasant, once I had stopped shivering and yawning. There were a lot of people living in the hostel just then whose company I liked.

An exception was an American with a loud manner of talking, who said he was in the hide-exporting business. In actuality he was a secret agent and everyone knew it. We knew his real name, and his reason for keeping the German mistress who hung around the hostel. Once when we were caught suddenly by the blackout she was noticed by Morgan sneaking into the hostel when we had all been ordered to stay out of doors. She must have crept up the steps during the raid and indulged in her nefarious trade in the room of a German soi-disant refugee. A few nights later the refugee was arrested by Chinese soldiers. It was just like a movie: the German protested he had nothing to hide, though they searched his room and found a transmitter there. He chewed up a paper and tried to swallow it. It had a code on it, *exactly* like the movies.

Everybody was badly shaken by the scene. Hitherto we had accepted him as a perfectly pukka refugee. He had introduced himself to me, naming several friends of mine in Shanghai as reference. My only reason for avoiding him had been that he was such a bore. I had put him down as one of those heavily Teutonic artistes from Munich, and he looked the part to perfection. But that night when he was arrested I wasn't so sure. He didn't seem surprised at the arrest, or even very indignant. He was angry and violent—he pulled a gun on the soldiers, and there was a struggle—but he wasn't surprised.

"Let me get dressed, will you?" he said. The soldiers let him dress, tied his hands with rope, and then marched him out past all of us, standing there in our pajamas in a row, our mouths hanging open. He didn't look at any of us. That was queer too. If it had been me I should have appealed to the crowd, but he didn't.

Next day several people at the hostel were all for Taking Steps. There was an uneasy feeling that we Europeans should stick together, and that no doubt it was all a fantastic oriental mistake. I didn't share the sentiments of the others in so far as they were based on race discrimination, but I did feel a little sick. Suppose it was a mistake? Allegedly he had been tortured by the Nazis before he escaped from Europe. So how could he possibly have been a spy for the Axis?

I have never heard the end of the story. When I left he was still in prison. We heard all sorts of other stories afterward, the most reasonable of which was that he hadn't been spying for the Nazis but for the Chinese Reds.

Certain newspapermen, as usual, acted as if they knew all about it but weren't talking. The American secret agent certainly did know, but he isn't talking either. I wonder if he tells his friends the things he used to tell us while playing poker. I shouldn't think so. Most of his conversation in those days was about women, and everyone in the hostel knew exactly what money he was giving the German lady, and for what specific services. He didn't talk about those visits upstairs during the blackouts, though.

A month of Chungking under fire was more than enough for Mme. Sun, and about the beginning of May she and her eldest sister went back to Hong Kong, where it was peaceful and quiet. Mme. Kung felt guilty at leaving her husband there, but he kept putting off his vacation for an indefinite period and she had promised Ching-ling not to outstay her in the capital. In our last conversation she said:

"You had better stay here, after all. I've changed my mind. You certainly work faster here than in Hong Kong where there are distractions. My sister Mme. Chiang has promised to be more co-operative on the book, now that she has time. Stay here and finish your book: I want it to be a success for your sake. And then build a new life," said Mme. Kung.

"It *is* nice of you to help me," I said sincerely.

"I feel guilty," she admitted, "because I've been interfering again. But I'm sure it's all for the best."

"And as for the new life," I said, "don't let that worry you. I'm used to building new lives."

"I hope so," said Mme. Kung, but she sounded dubious.

Chapter 25

As THE MISTS dried out of Chungking's atmosphere, leaving a hard bright world baking under the sun, so did my mind lose its dreaminess. This was an advantage in a way, not only for the good of the book but also for my new job which I took on just as the Soongs flew away, back to Hong Kong. I began to get worried about funds. I was taking much longer on the manuscript than the publisher and I had first intended. This wasn't a surprise to the publisher, and it was less surprising to me. You can't go on chasing people all over China these days without using up a lot of time. New York obligingly pushed the deadline forward about six months, so that was all right, but the advance which had been supposed to cover the calculated period of gestation was now running short. Perhaps you laymen don't realize what a gamble a book is for the writer, who always does his year's or two years' work before he has any idea if it is going to give him returns. There comes a time for me during every book's writing when I tell myself that I am an idiot and that I must find another job with a Saturday pay check. This time the impulse overpowered me and I actually found the job, with Havas.

So nowadays I spent a good deal of time in the Press Hostel, and could have insisted on my rights as a journalist in good standing to live there altogether. I didn't, though. I wasn't tempted in the first place by the exquisite discomfort of the Press Hostel, nor in the second place by the jolly, quite maddening lack of privacy that prevailed there, nor in the third by the worse-than-primitive plumbing. (We used to have better plumbing facilities in the Congo than obtained at the Chungking Press Hostel.) There was another reason, too, that I didn't move in under Hollington Tong's wing, and that was Ma Ping-ho, who spent all his time with Holly's crowd. Nobody was allowed to mention my name in Ma's hearing, or to let him know I was back.

No one really works very hard as a foreign correspondent, and since Marcuse and I were dividing the job we had a lot of freedom. He wasn't a perfect person to work for. He had his bad moments. We had a couple of rows, when he forgot who did what, and when, and where; but they blew over. More serious was the phase we went through when Marcuse, a newcomer to Chungking and unacquainted with air-raid procedure, bawled me out for leaving the office and going into a tunnel during raids. "You must Stand By!" he shouted. "What? Go into a dugout? I never heard of such a thing. You're yellow!"

My reply was brief and emphatic, and supported by the combined protests of whatever other gentlemen of the press overheard him. A few days later, when the whole office was bombed and came tumbling down, Jacques stopped talking that way and we had no more of his heroic nonsense. But then his mind at the time was mostly on Corin.

The rapidity with which that friendship developed was the cause of great anxiety to Holly. He couldn't very well station himself at the door of Jacques's room in the main building. He didn't want to reprimand the representative of Havas, either. But he didn't like that sort of thing going on in the respectable precincts of a respectable government building, either. And Marcuse, who dominated Corin completely, was mischievous. I often suspected him of going out of his way to shock Holly and the others. In the early days before the raids grew really intense, while he was still trying to insist that I stand by my typewriter during the bombings, he saw that Corin was in a bad state of nerves. She had a respect for bombs which Jacques refused to recognize. When the Japanese flew over he wouldn't allow her to run for shelter, or, rather, he refused to go and so she couldn't. There must have been some strange scenes aboveground. When the All Clear sounded and I went up to knock on his door and to get my cables for the day, I would find Corin with traces of tears on her cheeks, and Jacques puffing one of his clay pipes and looking masterful.

Being a sort of benevolent aunt to the lovers came natural to me. Corin would drop in during the afternoon while I was working and we would have a pleasant visit, if the Japanese didn't interfere. She was looking well and happy except when the scenes over air raids upset her. Jacques was attentive and complimentary and he gave her no cause for uneasiness. To be sure, there was a girl in Shanghai who refused to accept the congé he tried to send her by mail; Jacques made no secret of his dilemma but proudly showed her frantic telegram around the hostel, and asked advice from everyone, and talked it over with Corin. It was going to be awkward, Jacques said to Corin, and she agreed that it was going to be awkward. But of course Jacques loved *her* now. He loved *her,* and all of the other affairs were over. They would go to Shanghai as soon as his term in Chungking was finished, and they would be married.

Then the European blitz came along.

As Havas correspondent, I listened in on the successive stages of that incredible moment of earth's history. We would read the terse sentences and stare at each other, wondering if it wasn't just a bad joke. It couldn't happen, it couldn't! Why, in all our lifetime it had never happened. Everyone knew how good the French Army was, didn't they? And we couldn't afford to let France fall: what would happen to the world if France fell?

Chungking was seething. The Dutch Minister fell away before our eyes; he must have lost ten pounds in a few days. His two boys were in Rotterdam. And the Nazi Army smashed ahead, crossing rivers over whose unfamiliar names I toiled as I made out the day's flimsies. When the Havas sources closed down and fled, before they set up their new offices in Vichy, we got our news from a French gunboat that was stationed there in the Yangtze. When the Belgian King capitulated the Ambassador in Shanghai published a repudiation of the surrender and declared himself for the refugee government. When the smoke died down and we looked around there were the ugly facts—French resistance finished, and the retreat from Dunkirk accomplished.

I do a lot of picking at the British, but I have the usual American sentimental feeling for them, after all. It has nothing to do with principles, and not very much to do with politics. We have their literature and their language, and we have borrowed a lot of their law. You can't argue yourself out of that close a relationship without working at it. I had no desire to work at it. I suffered too.

In a way I was lucky. We were all lucky in Chungking, because we heard the news in a peculiarly exact way. We heard the German side and the Allied side, just as it came through from the offices on the spot, unmarred by editorial comment and uncolored by radio announcers. I have often sighed since for that clean, uncluttered sort of reporting, smothered as I am by extraneous voices in my newspapers and on my radio programs.

We still didn't realize how bad it was until the Germans bombed Paris, and I remember meeting a Frenchman, Leo, in the hostel corridor, early in the morning, en route from the bathroom. I was clutching soap and towel, and holding my bathrobe together in front; Leo, similarly attired, was going to try his luck at the men's bath. But we stopped to talk.

"Paris bombed!" he said. "But it is terrible, *hein?*" It was the only time in six years' acquaintance I had seen Leo wholly serious. "Bombs falling on Paris, I cannot believe it," he said. "My sister is living there; I have dispatched a cable. Ah, ah, ah." A lady in peignoir and slippers drifted past us in the dark hall and Leo looked after her appraisingly. "Who is that?" he demanded. "Not bad at all." Then he remembered again and his plump face resettled in lines of anxiety. "Terrible, *hein?*" he added.

Over at the Press Hostel we gathered and shifted and gathered again in busy little groups. The American young men—Mel Jacoby, Frank Smith, Teddy White—felt uneasily that it was time to stop playing around the Far East; time to enlist somewhere, probably in England. Marcuse, the one European of our group, said that he was going immediately to join the Free French, which sent Corin into yelps of protest which did not cease until I reminded her that Jacques would have to wait, anyway, for formal release from his post.

I don't think I had any strong urge to join up in anything, but there was a sort of premonitory prickle at the roots of my scalp, and I felt guilty that the States hadn't gone into the war as yet. I don't think I realized how strong the isolationists were at home. I had fallen out of the habit of believing anything I read in the news magazines (and I didn't learn my mistake for years). I was certainly out of touch with my country, without knowing it; those stories and photographs of America First meetings which I was to see in the following months registered themselves in my brain merely as typical exaggerations, cooked up to fill the columns with something readable.

It is odd when you come to think of it that I accepted without question the necessity of our entry into the war. I had been brought up in the age of pacifism. We were taught in school that war was wicked and totally unnecessary. All the more "enlightened" educational groups took that attitude. We were filled with statistics of the munitions industry and with the conclusions our seniors drew from these figures. We were given new propaganda regularly in the popular magazines, warning us against warmongers. . . . It worked, evidently, on the minds of many of us, enough of us to slow down our actions by some years. I suppose it didn't work on me when the time came because I was outside the country and had a different point of view. The same goes for anyone used to traveling beyond America's limits. But I had doubts, up until the last minute and even beyond. I didn't doubt that we should be fighting, but I regretted the blind manner in which so many of the English hurled themselves into the fire.

"Morgan Crofton is wild to get back to Europe and join up," I said disapprovingly at lunch one day at the Clark-Kerrs' table. Sir Archibald pricked up his ears.

"You don't think he should feel that way?"

"He should join," I admitted, "but he shouldn't *want* to join. He shouldn't *enjoy* getting into a war."

We had a long argument. I think it very likely that I was talking nonsense, but I can't remember what we said. I remember instead that the Clark-Kerrs were having servant trouble; Sir Archie wanted to live on Chinese food and Lady Clark-Kerr couldn't seem to convince the cook that she meant it. She was just as pretty as rumor had said, but fantastic as an Ambassador's wife, whom one expects to look like a large burlap bag filled with flour and tied around the middle with rope. "Tita" Clark-Kerr is much more like a doll, with golden curls and tiny perfect features. The trace of Chilean or Spanish accent in her speech adds to the baby-doll effect and totally belies the dangerous truth that she is an intelligent and well-informed woman.

It was soothing to lunch with those people. If the British still functioned through their diplomatic channels so smoothly, perhaps the civilization that I had become used to and fond of, with all its faults, might yet survive. Sir Archie, Tita, John Alexander—they all did seem to know what they were doing, though at the moment all they were doing was to concentrate on Tita's poor forehead, which had a big painful boil on it. Between gossip and political discussion of a light, large sort, Sir Archie applied hot compresses to his wife's brow. But we did talk, and he talked sense. He wasn't optimistic. That too was soothing. I don't know anything that upsets me more and makes me less sure of our survival than the hearty sort of Briton who tells me that they are bound to Muddle Through, and that they Lose Every Battle but the Last.

After lunch Sir Stafford Cripps came in for a visit. I beat a retreat as soon as he got there, but I saw something that amused me before I went. Sir Stafford, a lugubrious, parchmenty person, looked at Tita's boil and said, "What's the trouble?"

They told him about it, and he brightened up in a ghoulish sort of way—Sir Stafford knows a lot about doctors and bad health.

"You don't want to use hot water, you know," he said authoritatively. "It spreads the infection. You want to bring it to a head and lance it, don't you? Use cold water, the coldest you can get."

Immediately the Clark-Kerrs ordered cold water and changed their treatment. Just like me, I reflected as I rode downhill from their house. I'm a pushover for any sort of medical treatment, no matter who suggests it. There is a moral in that anecdote if you want to find it, but I haven't time.

It was decided that Corin should break her connection with the Co-ops and let somebody else, whose personal life was less full, take on the task of saving the Chinese. It was also decided by me, with the hearty concurrence of Jacques, that my connection with the Fourth Estate come to an end when June did, and Corin could take my place. Meantime none of us did any work worth speaking of, because the Japanese reflected their ally's success in Europe by giving us a burst of activity hitherto, as they say in the papers, unprecedented.

As I remember it, life for a month or so was just one rush to get into a tunnel. The walk between my place and the Press Hostel was always anxious because if I was caught halfway it meant a long way to run before I got to a safe place, either end. The chief danger wasn't the bombs, but the local police, who had ordered all residents to be off the street before the second alarm, which we called the "Urgent," and which meant that the planes had arrived at the city limits. Anybody out after the Urgent was to be shot. Some people were. We really couldn't complain. The watch system was good.

We always had the first alarm fifty minutes before the Urgent, just as the enemy planes crossed over the border of Szechuan Province a long way off, out on the plains, and fifty minutes was enough to get into a tunnel anywhere in town if you ran, and if the tunnel authorities knew you and would let you in. For the Chinese there was a regular system, which was later applied to us. They were given tickets and told where they were to run to. We just went, by virtue of our whiteness, into the nearest hole. But the public ones weren't very nice; they were overcrowded and you had to stand up. Our hostel dugout, as we have seen, had benches and chairs, and a limited attendance. I liked it better than the press one, but experience was to show that it wasn't safe.

Early in May it became evident that the Japs knew where the Chiangs lived and were trying to destroy their house. This was too bad for the Chungking Hostel because we weren't far away from the palace. One day a bomb fell in the front garden where we had so often whiled away the moonlit nights looking for bombers, and a few tons of rich mud were thrown out into the street and our roof was slightly cracked. We went on living there anyway. But we couldn't trust our dugout: the roof was sagging dangerously. It was duly condemned and after that all the guests went to Kung's tunnel.

Often on Sundays I broke my old rule and consented to go over to the South Bank for lunch. I was much more inclined to accept invitations of the sort nowadays, for the South Bank was safe from bombs if you stuck to the diplomatic district, which was supposed by the rules of war to be immune. The Japs dropped leaflets, warning all third nationals and diplomats who still lived on the North Bank to move over to that charmed neighborhood before they were blown to bits. The British embassy said, "Pooh, pooh." We still felt somehow safe in that stately building. I walked over there early one morning and found that Tita Clark-Kerr had come down for the day with her husband. Time hung heavy on our hands, even after an air-raid signal sounded, and we decided to wash our hair. The two of us went upstairs to one of the luxurious bathrooms that looked so good to me, and got to work.

We had finished washing and were setting our locks, Tita doing wonderfully well with her pale blonde ringlets, when the Urgent sounded. We paused and looked at each other questioningly.

"Shall we?" I asked. After all, it was her embassy, not mine.

"No," she decided. "We'll catch cold down there and I look a fright." So we went on pinning and chattering. All of a sudden there was a whirling sort of noise and Sir Archie stood there, red in the face with haste and anger. "Go downstairs *immediately*," he said in an awful voice. "The idea!"

Complaining bitterly, but under our breaths, we obeyed him. It was just as well we went when we did. That day bombs fell almost on the lawn. We felt the concussion and didn't like it at all. Later—but it happened a good deal later, and I will wait for the proper time to tell it.

I ought to take time off here to talk a bit about my emotional reactions to the Japanese, but I didn't have any after the first few raids. At first I did; I felt hatred and defiance and a furious impotence, crouching in a hole in the ground without the chance of even hitting back. Later I lost any personal feeling about it. Subconsciously I put the raids into the same category as earthquakes and measles. They seemed more like acts of God than deliberate attempts on the part of human beings to kill me. This was due, no doubt, to the fact that we didn't see planes as much as we had done at first, in the carefree, daring days when we stayed aboveground and took risks. I was still afraid. A big "crrrump" sounding near by always put my stomach out of order and was followed by a strange desire on my part to go to sleep. Sooner or later in a dugout I always went to sleep. But my fear was not an angry fear.

I regained all my personal animosity that day that I washed my hair, however. In the afternoon, after four hours underground, Morgan Crofton and I walked back together to the hostel, and we had a hard time getting there. Many city streets were in flames and the way was blocked, so we had to crawl roundabout through back alleys and over fences to get home. We saw no dead bodies; casualties were growing less because the people were learning to take shelter. But the destruction was enormous and I was hot with anger.

"I would laugh," said Morgan, "if we were to find the hostel spread all over the ground."

Well, we did.

Chapter 26

ONE HALF of the building, the back part, had disappeared completely save for pieces of the walls and roof which were lying on the slope of the hill back of the hostel. There was a lot of debris spread out in the street in front of the door too. By the time we arrived they had cleaned up quite a bit of it, so that traffic was able to get through, and we were allowed to go in the front door. My room was still there, open to the sky more or less, but there. All my belongings, however, were thickly coated with plaster dust. All the guests who had come out of near-by dugouts were there, doing what Morgan and I were doing—salvaging our property. We decided that the rooms were still habitable, at least until something else could be rigged up. Why, the flush toilet was actually still working! It is true that the bathroom door had been torn from its hinges, but if you propped it up again the room was usable.

We spent a rather grim evening. Although the bombers hadn't yet hit the electric power plant and we had light, everyone was wondering what the rest of the season was going to be like if the spring had brought so much variety into our lives. The hostel manager bustled about, getting us to pack up whatever we didn't need so that he could put it into safety. Really valuable things, he promised, he would place down in the dugout where they would be out of danger of rain and bombs. Everyone had in mind going over next day to Chialing House, to see what could be done about taking rooms there.

Chialing House was an imposing plaster edifice out along the main road some distance from the hostel. It had been built with loving care and a lot of expense by a government group headed by H. H. Kung, for the purpose of entertaining distinguished visitors who were not foreigners and who couldn't stay in the hostel. Kung also used it for big official parties. That was where he gave his cocktail party and reception for Mme. Sun. There were tall red pillars in the main hall, and lots of windows overlooking the river, and hanging terraces. But when it came to rooming facilities, Chinese tradition in hotelkeeping had triumphed. The rooms were small and uncomfortable and there weren't as many of them as you expected when you looked at the place from outside.

I went to bed early, tired out as I always was after a long bombing. An air raid leaves you, for some strange reason, aching in your bones, as if you had been walking for many miles instead of sitting in a stuffy little cave all day. Probably I wouldn't have waked at all, in spite of a lot of noise and thumping that trickled from the real world into my dreams, if one of the men hadn't come in and pulled my arm.

"Get up, get up before you're brained," he called, and hurried out again. I sat up, tangling myself in the mosquito net which appeared to my fuddled senses to be sopping wet. I heard a queer noise that came again and again: "Smack. Smack." Then I realized I, as well as the net, was soaking, and that a heavy rain was coming down from heaven, right through the holes in the ceiling and onto me. The smacking noise was plaster that was getting wet and falling in slabs from the mangled remains of the roof. It was really dangerous to stay there. I groped around in the dark and got a dressing gown, and hurried out, slipping on the slimy floor.

Downstairs everyone was huddling in the lounge and the lobby, look-ing cross. There was a good deal of comforting helpful efficiency on the part of the hotel boys. They put me to bed with Maya in a small dining room, stretched out on tables and wrapped in blankets. It was about midnight, and I dozed off, in spite of the noise and the glaring lights, until falling plaster woke me again. This time it was no joke, for the rain had soaked through the floor upstairs and now large gobs of plaster were falling on the first floor, all over the place except the middle of the lobby, which was protected from upstairs by a strip of intact roof. We were herded into this safety zone and stood there miserably, sharing umbrellas and looking sour.

It was all so awful that we became hysterically silly. Morgan was brew-ing hot soup with bouillon cubes and a thermos of water, and he insisted that we drink the stuff. Some American boy brought out a jug of local wine and we had a bit of that, though it tasted like fusel oil. We laughed and whooped and sang, and our blood began to run again, and I was feeling better until Maya said, "Thank God for a sense of humor."

As soon as morning dawned Morgan jumped into his battered car and drove over to Chialing House and booked rooms. He helped me move most of my things that morning, just in time, for the hotel was filling up with people from all over town who had been bombed out.

"They'll bomb here next," he said, "but for the time being it will do."

I went to Holly's dinner party that night, a gallant effort considering that half the roof of the dining room was gone. Guest of honor was Wu Teh-chen, deposed Mayor of Canton. I hadn't seen him since Hong Kong days and he greeted me with enthusiasm. Wu's English is good but just a trifle academic. "Well, well, Miss Hahn!" he cried, shaking hands. "How are you after all this bombing? Still intact?"

It is a tribute to the Pawley family's peculiarly original flavor that more people haven't heard of them. They have a long and fascinating history which dates back to the last generation, when the father of the four boys settled his family on an island in the West Indies and brought them up to do business in a big and imaginative way. I suppose Kipling had the Pawley type in mind in his earlier phase when he was enthusiasti-cally fond of Americans for their initiative and poetry and practical sense of values. Nobody could have lived long at the Chungking Hostel with-out noticing that there seemed to be rather a lot of Pawley around the place, popping in and out. The thicker-set one who didn't say much, and who rather drawled when he talked, was Ed. The thin nervous one who talked a lot, rapidly, and swung his watch chain round his finger was Bill. At that period we saw only those two Pawleys, but more were to follow. But it was Bill who told me about their factory in Loiwing. They came and went, Ed spending more time in town than Bill. I was slow to realize what an enormous thing it was that they had done, building an entire city in the jungle at the Burma border, bringing large numbers of American engineers and mechanics out there to live, and giving them all the comforts that could be thought of to make them happy about being thus cut off from home. I wanted very much to see the place, but it wasn't to be my destiny. First I couldn't afford the time, then I couldn't afford the plane fare, and in the end (1942) the Japs found Loiwing and wiped it out, all the hygienically screened bungalows and the employees' dance hall and the Capehart and the movie house and the hospital and, of course, the factory and the planes. The Pawleys were always spectacular in a modest way. Once they flew a panda from Chengtu: not a giant panda but a regular one. It looked like a surprised raccoon with the tail of a red fox.

Ed was missing his wife and four children more and more acutely as time went on and his duties kept him away from his home in California. He is charmingly uxorious. And so one day Bill, flying through America, stopped off to see his sister-in-law and on a characteristic impulse scooped up the family, put them into a Clipper and brought them to Hong Kong. Ida, Ed's wife, came on up to Chungking as a pleasant surprise. The Pawley ensemble happily took a wing of the hostel and made it vastly more comfortable than were the other cubicles, with a remarkable addition of a pair of V-spring mattresses.

When the hostel was bombed the first time the mattresses were deserted by Ed and Ida. They went over to the APC House on the South Bank, where they decided to stay until things quieted down a little. Ed foresaw that there would be a rush for that South Bank safety zone soon, and he made his arrangements accordingly. The man in charge of APC in Chungking was Teddy Gammell, an Englishman, and with permission from the head office in Hong Kong he agreed to divide up with the Pawleys on the house and expenses. During her short stay at the hostel I learned to like Ida very much. People always like Ida. She is a gentlewoman and exceedingly nice to look at, with a lovely face, prematurely gray hair, and pleasing clothes. Visiting their wing was a refreshing relief from the grim facts of existence as we wrestled with them in the rest of the hostel. There was actually extra furniture in their living room, and there were flowers in vases, and pictures of the children in silver stand-up frames, and all the little amenities that depend so much on transportation. That was how the Pawleys had come to know the APC personnel so well; the European young men of the town trooped to their rooms for bridge games of an evening, even all the way from the South Bank. Though I don't play bridge I would be there too, drinking real whisky and luxuriating in civilized comfort. I missed them now.

Living in Chialing House was just like living in the hostel except that there were no Pawleys and I had a longer walk to the Havas office every day. The dugout was further away, and you always had to run for it. Many a time did I toil up the face of the rock cliff where that Chialing House dugout was located, puffing and blowing and sobbing for breath before I fell into the cave's mouth, just as the Urgent went off. Life was more complicated now, however; one of my suitcases had been lost over at the abandoned hostel and this was a serious loss. My manuscript was in that bag, my photographs, cuttings, and practically all the impedimenta of the book except the current chapter. I was awfully worried. Every day between raids I went over and pestered the people who were sorting out the rubble. It took time. At last I was permitted down in the condemned dugout and allowed to root for myself. I quickly found the suitcase in a small cache there, covered with green mold but undisturbed.

We had been told that we could probably move back in a couple of weeks, when the indefatigable Chinese had rebuilt the place. I was much relieved because my claim on Chialing House was soon to expire: there were dozens of people on their waiting list. One day there was a real humdinger of a raid. When it was over I looked at my watch and discovered that I would still have time to keep a date I had made with Mme. Chiang at her house, if I hurried. I duly hurried, along the road from Chialing House, noting with interest as I passed the Press Hostel that a whole lot of the front structure of the place was now down in the road, mingled with blocks of stone from the built-up bluff next door. Just as I started to cross a particularly muddy street, in a spot I knew well, the Generalissimo came along in his car going the other way. I turned around to look at him as he sped past, and at the same time I went on walking across the street with vague intent to dive through a shallow mud puddle which I had navigated only that morning in safety.

Alas! Since I had crossed that street a bomb had fallen on the same place and the puddle which had been shallow was now a deep crater. I couldn't have known. It still looked the same from the top. I walked bang into it. The passers-by were much edified.

No Chungking pig could have been filthier or thicker with muck than was I when I climbed out of that hole. What was more serious was that I had skinned my knee badly. There was no time to go back. I had to finish my journey and present myself to Mme. Chiang all dripping and stinking as I was. I did it too. Madame didn't care very much, for she was having her own troubles that afternoon. The Japs had got the range of her house at last and knocked a piece off the corner, and her husband had given orders to move outright to their country house across the river. Everything was in a confusion of packing. I had my interview, washed my knee, and went back to Chungking Hostel just to see what was up. It was on the way home, anyway. As I had expected, nothing was left at all, this time. The hostel was gone.

There was Ed Pawley, with the office car, loading it up with his handsome luggage and the now sodden V-spring mattresses. Helping him was the APC assistant to Gammell, a cheerful young giant named Gidley Baird, famous in European circles for his size and in Chinese circles for his habit of taking on a chair coolie's job whenever he felt facetious. Gidley was an enthusiastic bridge player and an old acquaintance of mine from the Pawley parties. Both men set up a cheerful shout when they saw me.

"Get your traps," said Gidley, "you're going home with us."

"Just the girl we want," said Ed. "I promised Ida I'd bring you."

"What is this?"

"We think you had better come on over to the South Bank," they explained. "This bombing is going to get worse and worse, and you'd better beat it while the beating's good. You'll be very happy at the APC House."

It was a wonderful invitation. There were people who were rushing around offering their eyeteeth for a similar chance, but nobody wanted eyeteeth. They wanted houses.

"Why?" I asked suspiciously. "You don't love me that much, surely?"

They side-stepped the question, telling me to hurry up and get ready. It took a little more work to discover their reasons for such a sudden burst of hospitality, but I dug it out of them at last. They wanted me purely and simply to help push out another guest who was quartered on them and who was unwelcome. To get rid of that person they told him that I had arranged before his arrival to come over and live in the last available APC room. "And so," said Ed, "you've got to do it, to back us up. Besides, we'll be awfully glad to have you, of course."

"But I can't come over here every day to my job and go back every night," I objected. "What with the ferry and everything it takes two hours each way."

"Quit your job," said Ed.

"I did," I admitted. "I've only three days to go. . . ."

"Well, then! And Ida needs another woman in the house."

"Your Madame's moving to the other side," urged Gidley. "I heard about that today from the bank."

"Yes, that's true. . . . Well, okay, and thanks a lot."

"You can come over and go back with me for the three days," Ed assured me. "I've got a private boat."

"You would!"

"No sense being niggardly," said Ed. It was a saying he often used, and an attitude which was extremely irritating to people more inclined to be economical. Ed never knew how peeved he made Englishmen with that habit he had of paying high for what he wanted. But then lots of Englishmen peeved Ed too. Terribly.

Joyfully I hurried back to Chialing House, a place I hadn't learned to love, and gathered up my belongings. They weren't much of a bother already. I had lost about half of what I brought to Chungking. I still wonder what coolie picked up my opal brooch from the hostel rubble, but it served me right for having left it out in an air raid. We drove the car over to one of the ferry stops and started down to the river. It seemed a long time since I had first climbed that cliff so as not to be cruel to the chair coolies. Now I knew every step of the way. Parts of the path were chopped out of the rock and parts were built up of planks, zigzagging down across the face of the bluff; some of the stairs were protected by railings and some were really dangerous to navigate. Here and there we passed a temporary house built of wood, perched crazily on the steep slope. In spring, when the water was high, this house would be swept away. After the subsidence its owners would come back and build it all over again.

We walked past the public ferry, a crazy little river steamer already sagging with the weight of blue-clad country people on their way home for the night. Down on the muddy beach Ed's boat was waiting, a superlarge rowboat with a specially picked crew. Now that the raid was over for the day most of the traffic was going in the other direction. Every bright morning nowadays a lot of the Chinese got up early and crossed the river and went out into the country, to squat there in the open until the planes had visited the town and gone away again. Now they were coming back to see if they still had houses.

The beach on the other side was equally crowded with chairs, with the picturesque addition of a line of tethered ponies for anyone who preferred riding a real beast of burden over the hills to his house. Chungking ponies are a special breed. They are small and bad-tempered like the little Mongol ponies we race and ride in Shanghai, but their lives on these hillsides, going up and down the stone staircases that have been

constructed everywhere, have made them as sure-footed and deliberat
as mules. Often when I was riding one I felt as if I were going dow
into the Grand Canyon.

We piled our luggage into a chair and climbed the hill on foot. It's
long, steep climb and it leads through the courtyard of the Chungking
Club, where most people stop to rest and drink. Not that there was muc
there to drink, but sometimes the head boy managed to stock a few bot
tles of locally made "gin" or "vodka."

From the moment I set foot on the South Bank I knew I was in
different atmosphere. I had left the new China and stepped back into the
old. I was in the safety zone, the magic circle drawn by the once omnip
otent Europeans. All this ground was leased by some foreign firm o
other: all these big houses had been there from the old days, the day
when gunboats traveled unhampered up and down the Yangtze, through
the rapids, from Shanghai to Chungking and back again. And even I
nowadays, was an old China hand and could think back to the dul
peaceful times when all the foreign population turned out to greet the
boys from the boat as they traveled, bringing news from downriver
having drinks at the club, going to parties at the BAT House and the
APC House and all the other houses.

Gammell was charmingly hospitable. I had a real bath in a real bath-
tub, and changed my dress, and bandaged my knee, and came down
for dinner. We sat in cushioned chairs and drank cocktails, waiting for
dinner to be announced. It grew dark and over on the other side a few
lights blinked and wavered from oil lamps, for the power station had
been damaged and the electricity had gone off. Here, with our own
dynamo, we had our electric light. We were still privileged foreigners,
living in a safety zone.

I sipped my gimlet and looked over at new China, waiting there in
the night to be bombed again, a hopeless, battered mass of darker
shadows in the dark. Here I sat on a screened veranda, clean and comfortable and waiting for dinner, two miles off. I was out of it. How much
longer would I be safe? I looked around at my hosts. They were laughing and talking together, and they didn't look at all worried. They looked
like people who had been sitting on that veranda for years. But we knew
it would not be much longer.

Chapter 27

Still with me, ghost? Then for another hour
We'll stand beneath the sky, the iron shower.
One puff of smoke follows the insect flight,
One latest crash comes echoing from high——

The Germans took another town last night.
The Germans stand again on Flanders mud,
And I am sick, captive and sick, and I
Am powerless to choose my place to die.

I wander through the streets: torn bodies lie
Sprawling: the gutters run with alien blood.

O ghost, stay with me yet awhile; I must
Suffer before I join this Chinese dust:
Once more with face uplifted to the sky
Must call for bombs and fire to cool my blood.

I SCARED Morgan Crofton to death by starting to write poetry in Chungking. He was a proper, upper-class Englishman and he knew it was not the thing to do, but I couldn't help it; the insecurity of life had joggled me up and I was back in the adolescent phase of bewilderment and lightning changes of mood that with me always results in poetry. It was the first poem I had written in years and it weighed heavy on me. I wanted to get rid of it. I typed it out and sent it to Max Oxford in Hong Kong, because he was interested in air raids, as an RAF officer.

Max showed it to Charles Boxer, who began to worry gravely about my state of mind. He thought it sounded as if I were cracking under the strain, which in his guilty frame of mind (because he felt like a slacker) he imagined to be terrific for all of us. He sent a message, through Max, that a trip was being scheduled for both of them and that they might be descending upon the British embassy any time now. I was delighted with the news, and promptly went into a reverie wherein I showed Chungking to the two men as it ought to be shown, and not as the embassy would do it, with luncheon at all the embassies and legations in turn, and expensive drinks at the club or the consuls' mess. I would take them for walks, I resolved. I would round up the few moth-eaten ponies available and take them out along the road to the secret mint in the valley beyond the Second Range. Perhaps we might even get a car to go to the temple at the hot springs, and smell the pine forest there. All of these visions left out the air raids and the probable fact that the young men would be coming on official business, without leisure for such jaunts. Besides, there was a peculiarity about my reverie. Max as an unmarried man should have been the central figure of these dreams, but he wasn't. I kept wondering what Charles would have to say about Chungking. For a woman my age I was certainly going through a phase remarkably like adolescence.

Actually the visit didn't take place during my term of residence in the capital, though Charles's other Chungking friends urged him to hurry up with it. He was a Japanese expert and didn't know China very well. His sympathies, non-political and sentimental, were with Japan, for he had spent years there, serving a term in their army as a special compliment, and he spoke that language fluently but knew nothing of Chinese, except in so far as he could read the written characters that are common to both nations. I would shake my head over this failing and make resolutions to bring him around to a more sensible state of mind.

Sir Archie had his way until the last possible moment. In spite of Japanese warnings the British embassy stayed nobly where it was, near the seat of the government, on the north side of the river—and incidentally in the most comfortable house in town. There was a grassy lawn there, and the department had already started to Branch Out, as they always do. Houses on either side of the embassy had been rented from their Chinese banker-owners.

On the Sunday after I arrived we scrimshankers over on the South Bank took a walk. The APC owned a lot of outlying places, and one was a bungalow far off on the Second Range, which had been used in the old days by engineers and their families. We packed our lunch, made careful arrangements, and started out, a large party, for a day in the country.

The Japs couldn't resist the weather, which was ideal for bombing—clear of fog and innocent of clouds, a cerulean sky. Just as we got to the bungalow about eighty enemy planes flew over. (The Japs really spread themselves in those days. They had hopes of crushing Chungking definitely, that year, with bombs alone. It was an interesting lesson to people who overrate the efficacy of air power.) Of course there was no resistance. It is pleasant for me now to realize that times have changed and that there is a good deal of resistance today, but my own eyes have never seen the Japanese as anything but unchecked, happily flying wherever they like and dropping bombs with a gay abandon. The occasional forlorn "pop, pop" of an anti-aircraft gun meant nothing, to us or to them.

The entire party of us, feeling fairly secure because we were a long way from any concentration of houses, stood on the hilltop and watched. Sometimes it was too much for our nerves anyway and we crouched close to the ground, instinctively, but nothing fell anywhere near. It was a remarkable scene. The bombs were dropped in a straight line and many of them fell into the water, and an occasional incendiary missile flared up harmlessly on the beach, but most of them fell on the town where they were intended to go. The main feature of this particular raid, as far as we were concerned, was that they got the British embassy. We saw it. A bomb falling on a Chungking house never finds much resistance, and the effect is gaudy—there is a fountain of black debris and smoke, spouting incredibly high in the air, and then it calms down, and then it goes on again, playing in the air like water, but now it is less opaque because it is only smoke and dust, the heavy stuff having fallen out of the spout. Little by little the smoke loses its black color, fades out, becomes white, and after a long time the whole thing is over and you see tiny figures of coolies working in the ruins. And so the embassy came over to live on the South Bank in spite of Sir Archie's resolution, and they commandeered a smaller APC house near us.

I spent less and less time on the North Bank. It wasn't necessary any more, and the air raids were coming so often that we could depend on a certain schedule. The Japanese were methodical and saw no reason why they should vary their program. It went like this: four to five days of intensive bombing, when eighty planes at least, and sometimes close to two hundred, flew over the city and bombed it everywhere. Then there would be two or three days when they didn't come. The RAF officer explained to us that they were reconditioning their planes, over in Hankow where they came from. Then it would start all over again. The weather through the short Chungking summer is monotonously clear and bright, and we didn't look for rain very often to give us surcease. Under these repeated attacks the city dwellers gave in and admitted that they had better make the best of it until autumn and foggy weather. Some hardy souls continued to cross the river every morning and trek to the countryside, then come back at night. But it was an unpleasantly difficult and long procedure, especially getting back on the crowded ferry of an evening.

If I had been living on the North Bank I could never have finished my book as I did that summer. Even where I was, most of the day it was impossible to work. Actually I must have done the bulk of it after the first signal during raids, waiting for the Urgent. Then the house was quiet, and nobody was in a mood to disturb me. I would type away like mad on the side veranda, while the Pawleys and Gidley and Teddy played bridge or did their office work, all of us keeping a nervous eye on the heavens and listening for the warbling note that meant business.

We learned how to make week ends more pleasant, though. The APC had an installation a few miles downriver. It didn't do any business any more because there was no oil to sell, but the houses and grounds were still kept up, and sometimes we went there in the company boat on Saturday and stayed over until Monday morning. There was a British gunboat anchored there, prudently out of the neighborhood of the military objectives of Chungking. We took our own servants and food and liquor, and while the others played bridge I read or fooled around with those of the guests who didn't like cards. On Sunday we would lunch aboard the boat. It could have been a much less pleasant existence. I blessed the day I had been bombed out of the hostel, and I wrote my book, and flourished under the protection of the safety zone, though I still had anxious moments.

Mme. Chiang's house was a long way off, but I could get there by chair across the hills and the fields, and occasionally I did. She lived on a high hill, in a house hidden by trees, hidden even from the sky, which was after all the most important aspect of hiding. I had some enchanted afternoons with Madame in that hot bright weather.

Gidley Baird lent me his chair for the trips, because it was a special chair and the whole household felt that my mission, too, was quite special and warranted attention from the public. He had twice as many coolies as most people needed because he was a big heavy man, and I gained much face when I went riding in such style. We cut across country to get to my destination; we plodded through an emerald-colored valley and for a long, long time we were completely out of the world. There were no houses in sight, no roads. Only the bright green paddy fields, bordered with straight little clay pathways, with here and there a stunted tree. A range of pleasant little mountains enclosed us. I would jog along like a princess in the sedan chair, chatting with the coolies, observing with pleasure that they didn't sweat or suffer like the less fortunate ones who carried ordinary chairs. I looked my fill at all the mountainsides and the trees that softened their rocky outlines. I put on dark glasses to protect my eyes from the brilliant sunlight bouncing off the young rice and the clear unsullied water that stood around its roots. Then I adjusted my enormous straw hat, took off my glasses, and settled down with the *Oxford Book of Light Verse* which I had borrowed from Mme. Chiang. All that summer I was reading poetry. I had discovered that rhyme and rhythm are soothing when you are waiting for Japanese bombers. Later in Hong Kong I remembered my discovery, and a heavy anthology of British and American verse shared my flight throughout the hostilities and saw me through the unforgettable weeks that followed after. But if those weeks are unforgettable now, they were unbelievable then. Japanese or no Japanese, one achieved a sense of peace and beauty on summer afternoons, jogging across the fields to Madame's house, all among the stone graves and the young green shoots.

Old trees kept the building damp and cool even in the hottest of the summer days. Once I counted the stone steps that led up a steep hillside to Madame's door, but I have forgotten how many there were. She complained sometimes that she felt cut off out there in the safety of the countryside, though a telephone ran not only to her study, where she tried to compose her soul in patience by translating the classics into English, but even to the main room in the tunnel under the hill.

Of all the houses I've seen Soongs in, I liked that one best. Like the APC House where I was living it was an old building, a relief from the lath-and-plaster bungalows that now mushroomed the Chungking hills. Even the stone wall that guarded the foot of the hill, and the guards in uniform who popped out from behind it to challenge me when I arrived, and the new telephone poles that led up the stone staircase—even all of that couldn't spoil the peaceful, aged quality of the house itself with its garden. The living room had comfortable furniture in it, like all Soong living rooms: they share my horror of Chinese chairs. There was a chummy little dining room where Soong Mayling gave me new kinds of marmalade to try. She likes making marmalade in Chungking, where she can get all sorts of citrus fruit, including a thick-skinned grapefruit I've never seen elsewhere.

Madame's nervous habit of working couldn't be overcome, even out there in the dreamy, shady quiet of her summer refuge. She wasn't well. She suffered pitifully from migraine. Vicious headaches had been coming on ever since her accident with Donald on the Nanking–Shanghai motor road, back in 1937, and though a chiropractor in Hong Kong had been able to give her some relief it wasn't sufficient. As if migraine isn't enough for any one woman in one season, she also had urticaria. I am something of an expert on hives. I had them unremittingly for three years after coming home from Africa and I've often wondered why I used to think they were a joke, in the days before I started getting them myself. I was most awfully sorry for Soong Mayling. I still am. And she was thoroughly likable, out in that summer house. She lost her last mistrust of the book and of me, perhaps because she had already looked over the manuscript; as one craftsman to a fellow, she talked enthusiastically about writing and reading. It wasn't my place as a biographer to say so in the book but I think she enjoyed those afternoons too. They were relaxing, and there was no harm in them. No politics interfered with our mutual dissertations on ethics and literature. We were not concerned with means but with ends. We talked like idealistic schoolgirls. It was nice.

One day was different. Sometimes by a fluke we people on the South Bank heard the world news first in town, in spite of the monopoly on telegraph lines into Holly's compound, because of the American gunboat *Tutuila,* which sat at anchor all year round on our side of the river. The *Tutuila* had a receiving set, and one day the young commander, Bob Germany, climbed the hill swiftly to bring us an item he had just heard from the air. The United States were applying an embargo at last on the sale of high-octane gasoline to foreign powers, i.e., to Japan.

In the living room we of the house assembled to talk it over. It might be very important, important enough to cause an accidental bomb to drop on us there in the safety zone. Then again, it might mean nothing. The fact that we were still selling heavy crude oil was ominous and disappointing. However, I was glad to carry the news that day to Mme. Chiang.

She hadn't heard it, and the news cheered her a lot. It was one of her bad days and she was lying on the chaise longue, wrapped in blankets. I hadn't been there long when the Generalissimo came home unusually early, and Mayling called to him before he entered the room.

"Is it true that there's an embargo on gasoline in America?" she demanded excitedly. Chiang Kai-shek, having seen that there was company, turned away at the door after bowing, and started up the steps. Over his shoulder he made the noise that signifies cheerful assent in China—it is like the last sound in "yeah." I can only spell it "—eah."

"No, but really?" insisted his wife. She spoke Chinese with him all the time.

"—eah," repeated Chiang amiably, halfway up the steps.

"But isn't that marvelous? Isn't it?" she demanded.

Chiang wasn't thrilled as she was, I felt. He was thinking about that crude oil. "—eah," came floating down the stairs, and then somewhere a door closed.

There was one evening when I stayed *chez* Chiang a long time, long after the hour I always set for going home. (Mme. Chiang was strict about her routine, but that evening her husband wasn't expected home until late, and she didn't like being alone. Bodyguards, evidently, are

ot the best company in the world.) The chair coolies knew where they
were going, though, and we weren't worried. We borrowed a lantern
from the Chiang kitchen, said good-by, crept carefully down the stone
staircase to the foot of the mountain, and set off along the road.

Crossing by way of the rice paddies was out of the question on such
a dark night. The coolies explained this to me and then set off at a good
brisk trot along the newly built road. I don't really know why I bother
to tell this incident. It has no value as an anecdote. I only want to evoke,
if I can, for my own sake, the sensations of that night. I have known
China so thoroughly, all her scents and noises and colors, that it is easy
for me to bring back the feeling of a familiar moment there. The streets
of Yangtzepoo in Shanghai, for instance, or the dust-choked air of Peking
in summer. The wet pathways of Hangchow along the lakeside, and the
drifting silence of one of those flat boats with canopies. The hard sharp
rocks and the soft gliding clouds of the Yellow Mountain. It is easy to
think of these. I could draw pictures of any of them. I would know at
midnight where I was if I should wake up in any of these places; I would
recognize the smell of it and the sound of it. But that night in my chair,
gliding along the dark road from Madame's house, was a special moment.
It had no familiarity. It was not China, and it was not me. Somehow we,
the coolies and I, had become new people in a different universe. We
trotted along at the bottom of a deep, dark canyon of blackness and all
the exciting pleasures of the afternoon, my talk with Mme. Chiang, the
poem we had read, the sunlight on my neck as I crossed the field, the
flowers I was carrying even now, in the back of the chair—they were not
there. I had it all in my mind, like something I had read in a book, but it
was no more real than that. My whole life was just that: a book I was
reading. That moment, then, that was the proof. Once and only once,
for the first time, I closed the book and laid it aside. I sat back in
the chair as it jounced and joggled along to the soft pats of the coolies'
feet on the road, and wondered: Now what?

Along the edge of the world which we approached there was the faint-
est possible glow of rosy light. We padded along in the blackness and the
glow grew stronger. I had really forgotten what book I was reading or
who I was now that it was closed. I didn't care. I watched, curious in a
mild way, as we drew nearer to the glow, and then we topped a rise in
the road and we were in a village. It was late. Nobody came out into the
road to look at us. We swung along strong and quiet through the dimly
lit street. Then all of a sudden, off to the right and behind a hill, there
came loud singing. It must have been the music of a Chinese talking
picture, one of the many that they make nowadays in the studios of

Chungking. It was turned on high, so loud that the world was full of it. Chinese voices sang words that I didn't understand, but the music itself was familiar. They had borrowed a waltz from us. They sang it slowly, chantingly. It was amazingly loud and full of meaning there in that valley between the mountains, and at night.

It came to me with a little shock, not unpleasant, that I had opened my book again. It might have been different. Down in the blackness of the valley I might quite possibly have opened another volume and emerged as a different individual, but no. I was still Emily Hahn, going home to Chungking in a chair, after dark.

There was a monotony in getting scared every day. The Japanese had a contemptuous way of holding to their program without varying the timetable, since it made no difference, after all, when they came; there was no resistance at any time of day. We could expect the first alarm soon after ten in the morning, and all through July, except on those pleasant days when the planes were being reconditioned, we moved into the dugouts for the better part of the morning and afternoon. That is the people on the North Bank did. We on the south side had much more freedom in our safety zone. Theoretically we stayed belowstairs, out of danger, but actually we didn't. I would lie on a bed on the veranda, reading and eating peanut brittle if I could find any, until I heard the planes, when I would run along with the others to the cellar downstairs. After they had bombed and gone, long before the All Clear signal, we acted as if it were over. The bridge game was resumed, or work continued in the APC office, and I heaved a sigh of relief and went back to my manuscript. We always got awfully hungry, waiting. Nobody had lunch for about six weeks, that summer.

In general the war was languishing. We heard news occasionally of battles here and there, and along toward August we became anxious because the Japs were reported to be moving in on the lower reaches of the Yangtze, the other side of the rapids, at Ichang. That meant that they would have large airfields within a short bombing distance of Chungking. We feared that this would mean less warning for our citizens, and so it worked out. By the time the enemy had the field in condition to be used, though, the sunny season was almost over. The Japs themselves were getting tired of the mass raids, and began using fewer planes in a more supple way, swooping low over the town and strafing the place with machine guns.

For some reason or other I had to cross the river one day, but I can't remember now why I took the risk. Perhaps Dr. Kung had some material

or me that I was to call for in person, or maybe Mme. Chiang—but she,
like myself, stayed as much as possible on the South Bank. I can't remember what it was all about, but I do recall my feeling of utter helplessness and panic when the alarm went off, catching me alone near the
ferry.

The helplessness was due to the fact that I was alone in a strange
neighborhood and had no dugout to go to, and no way of getting to a
better place on that side of the river. It was a contingency I had often
imagined and always avoided. The panic is harder to explain, but I'll
have a stab at it. I am not a neurotic type; at least I don't think I am. But
I did have one neurotic notion at that time. I hated crowds. I had a
real terror of crowds. Well, now, all of a sudden in Chungking I was in
the middle of a mob. After a moment, when I stood in the middle of the
road, I got a grip on myself and started to run with my fellow men, under
the warbling of the siren, down to the river.

We were trying to catch the ferry before it went to the other side.
Always when an alarm sounded the ferries loaded up as much as they
could carry and beat it for the South Bank as fast as they could fight the
current. All three available boats would do this, and once they reached the
other side they stayed there until the raid was over. If you missed the
boats, or failed to get aboard because of the crowd, you were out of luck.
Either you ran back up the hill and took refuge somehow, or you hurried
a long way down the beach to some rowboat and bribed a boatman, if
you could find him, to take you away. It was highly desirable *not* to be
near the ferry station: the Japs always bombed it. It was also imperative
not to be near the staircase up on top, for the same reason. And it was
just as well not to be aboard the ferry in midstream when they came
over, either. They loved to sink crowded boats.

I tried to get aboard the ferry. This meant speed, running along the
street to the staircase and rushing down the cliffside, in company with
about eight hundred racing Chinese. Halfway down I was negotiating a
bad spot where there was no railing, only a narrow set of stone steps
overhanging a sheer drop. I was on the outside of the crowd, and I
couldn't fight against the pressure of bodies. I felt myself slipping, being
shoved off the side.

Then a coolie grabbed my arm, pulled me back on the step—I can
still feel the iron grip of his skinny fingers—and was away down the
steps before I could thank him. Quickly, then, I arrived at the ferry. A
narrow plank bridge stretched from the shore, balancing across the one
or two rocks and up on the flat platform from which one got on the
boat. There again I was almost off; there again a coolie saved me at the

last minute. In that short time I lost for good my horror of crowds
They were a crowded mass, but they were good-natured. We were a
uncomfortable and, I suppose, frightened. But we laughed and felt like
good friends. Even at that moment I could feel that my heart had light
ened and an old trouble melted away.

The first ferry was full to bursting and moved off clumsily, lurching
as it hit the strong current toward midstream. We watched with bate
breath. It happened every so often that a boat turned over, and once you
were caught in the stream it didn't matter much if you could swim o
not. Well, the first boat made it and the second was chugging up. Would
I be able to get aboard? And if I got aboard, were we going to get to the
other side before the planes arrived?

Yes to both. I pushed my way on. We started out. We made it, and the
planes didn't come over until I was halfway up the South Bank hill to the
APC House. Teddy was waiting anxiously with his binoculars, watching
the beach across the river.

"I knew you were somewhere near the ferry," he said. "I remembered
how you hated crowds, and I was worried. I tried to see you with the
glasses, but you're wearing blue and so is every coolie in China, and i
just wasn't any use."

They made a fuss over me and I was pleased and comforted, especially
when they brought out one of their rare bottles of beer and opened it
I was the brand saved from the burning, the temperamental artiste whose
soul had been harried. . . . "Poor Mickey," said Teddy, "when you hate
crowds so much too."

"But I don't," I said, draining my glass. "I love 'em."

Then the planes arrived.

The situation deteriorated rapidly toward the end of my stay. Each
summer, according to the people who live there permanently, they used
to think that a fortnight more tacked on to the bombing season would
finish off Chinese resistance. The raids grew longer and longer; there
were fewer and fewer places to live, less and less resistance in the soul
of the people. You can be bombed out just so often and then it ceases to
be amusing to pick up your bags and move to another place. Even that
wouldn't be so bad if one could only sleep, but the Japanese began a
round-the-clock campaign, and that meant sitting up all night as well a
all day in the dugout. It was certainly bad. But I still don't think tha
another fortnight would have done the trick.

One lady whose husband was a Minister, and who had been a famou
young hostess in the Shanghai period, was bombed out so completely

that her house was simply a mess of bricks and broken furniture. We all turned out to help her salvage what we could, and it is quite surprising what can be recovered from ruins if you go about the job scientifically. Patricia recovered her piano, a box of chocolates, and two unbroken bottles of Rose's lime juice, while her clothes were scarcely damaged at all. I had occasion to notice that fact about clothes quite often. My own wardrobe, flung to the four points of the compass, was nevertheless all right when I gathered it together again, though a lot of it simply disappeared. I remember that Maya and I had a brisk argument over a stocking which had draped itself over a neighboring roof after the hostel received the coup de grâce: we both claimed it, but neither of us ever recovered it.

Until quite late in the season, long after the rest of us gave up our stubborn foolhardiness, Fenn Lynch refused to go down into cellars. Fortunately for him, he was in a fairly solid building on the day the Japs decided to polish off the downtown district. He was in his own Bank of China, at his desk on the ground floor. Everyone had gone down to the vaults, but not old Fenn. A bomb came down spang on the middle of the house. Concrete and steel reinforcements held out pretty well, and Fenn escaped being brained by falling plaster, but only just. He probably stood still for a little while until the noise and echo had died away, because he showed the signs for a long time afterward. He was dazed, and more respectful than he had been formerly of bombers. He did a good job that same afternoon, though, of sending panic-stricken crowds of refugees from a collapsed dugout, through flaming streets, to a safe cave. Fenn had guts and self-control when he needed them. He moved over to the South Bank too. Everyone moved over. There just weren't any houses left for them in the city. Our week-end parties became bigger and better with every week of bombing.

Chapter 28

ONE DAY I began to type faster and faster, hunched over the baby Hermes that had made my life miserable by breaking down every week. I breathed fast. I worked like a crazy woman. I always do, just as I am getting close to the end. It would be a tremendous thing, that business of writing the last sentence. It wasn't just that another book was finished. After all, that is nothing remarkable in this distressingly literate age of

ours. Nowadays the remarkable people are those who don't write books
No, my excitement this time was due to surrounding circumstances
This book was not only another book, it was my life. That sounds melo
dramatic, but it was literally true. Because of the book I had left my
home, broken up my house, deserted the gibbons and Sinmay, and lived
under conditions of acute discomfort for nearly a year. The manuscript
had done that, leading me around by the nose for eighteen months. The
fact that I had no place I could call home—that was the manuscript. My
luggage, ravaged and torn and moldy, and my belongings, lost and scat
tered—that was the manuscript. Myself, a neglected-looking female with
worn-out shoes, with teeth that called for attention—*that* was the manu
script.

"What else exists of me?" I asked myself in the queer hidden cellar
of the brain that goes on thinking no matter what you do on the surface
"Nothing else," replied my brain; "nothing else. In America my name
means something to my mother and something—less, but still something
—to my sisters and brother. Here and there in the files of old magazine
you can see it, that jumble of letters, EMILY HAHN. The name means a lo
to me, but that is all it is."

A staggering fact, the aloneness that sweeps over us at times. I always
have it when I am finishing a book.

I wrote the last page, my legs beginning to tremble. It was at eight in
the morning and I had known for several days, actually, that it would
be finished soon, but still I was surprised. I had been on that job a long
long time.

I shouted, pulling the sheet out of the roller. "Done!" I yelled through
the door to the Pawleys, who were still at breakfast. "Done!" I yelled
over the railing to Gidley Baird, who was getting the office ready for the
day's work. "Teddy," I called down the corridor, "did you hear me?
I've finished the book!"

I don't usually make quite such a public noise about my work, but
that summer we were all soaked in the community spirit. Even the close
mouthed business folk had become expansive and confidential, and dis
cussed their business in the presence of the whole household.

My book was a group problem. Nobody had read it and nobody was
particularly keen to, because they weren't a reading crowd, but the ab
stract fact of the book, and the presence of a writer in their midst, made
a pleasant change for our household. I had already promised to hand out
autographed copies all around. It stimulated Gidley to reminiscences of
other writers he had known. Teddy remembered successful journalists
who had stopped over and got drunk in the club in Manila when he was

there. Ida wondered if she shouldn't do something with that article she once wrote. They all took a pleasantly paternal attitude toward my opus, and their pleasure and excitement when I made my announcement were genuine. It was almost sufficient to cancel out the inner misgiving that would be my constant companion until I started on another book.

There were certain matters to be accomplished now that my mind was clear. A complete copy of the whole thing to be made and sent over to the States, whither I had been sending chapter after chapter as it was done. I was at least six months overdue with the thing already, so time was an item to be considered gravely. And there were other things to decide, chief of which was—whither now for myself, on this long pilgrimage?

A month or so before that morning I had received a mysterious cable signed "Pat." Just Pat, nothing more.

ARE YOU CONTEMPLATING VISIT TO STATES SHORTLY OR WHERE WILL YOU BE AUGUST THIS YEAR CAN MEET YOU CAPETOWN OR INDOCHINA

This is a remarkable message, especially when you are not sure of the author's identity. I know about six people, males and females, named Pat. It was more than likely, however, that the sender was Pat Putnam, because something in the sound of it was characteristic of this old friend of mine. That I had heard nothing from Pat Putnam in five years would not rule him out; he is like that. The whole family is like that. Once Pat Putnam's mother sent a telegram to me in Shanghai: CAN YOU MEET ME JUBA NOVEMBER? She was more than sixty at the time, and she went to Juba, too, though I couldn't make it. This must be Pat Putnam. I wanted to reply PITCAIRN ISLAND OR NOTHING, but if it was Pat Putnam he would probably call my bluff and turn up at Pitcairn Island. I preferred not to risk that. Besides, the cable on second thought seemed quite reasonable; why shouldn't I meet him in Capetown? It wasn't as if I had another date in August. I replied to this effect, and we arranged the following program (under difficulties, for the cables took a month each way): I was to take a boat from Hong Kong with my gibbons, and Pat would meet me in Los Angeles. He is fond of apes, and he meant to bring his car along on purpose to transport them across the country with me. After arriving in the East we could talk over at leisure where to put the gibbons. It would be nice to see Pat again, though we would probably quarrel. We always do.

In the meantime the boarders at the APC House were naturally intrigued by this interchange of messages. The Pawleys were full of similar stories. Bill Pawley travels everywhere by plane and thinks nothing of whooshing around the world three or four times a year. I got jealous listening to stories about him, and protested that, though I travel the hard way and it takes me much longer, I get there, too, just the same.

"Which reminds me of what happened in 1932," I said, "while I was still in the Congo. I had two friends who married each other while I was down there. They wrote and told me that if I would arrange my voyage home accordingly they could probably meet me somewhere en route. Would I, they said, pick out somewhere feasible? So I sat down and telegraphed them that I would meet them in Zanzibar. It's a beautiful name, don't you think? I've always liked it. . . . Zanzibar . . . Well, I sent my telegram and then I forgot all about it. I didn't really take Desmond and Leona's intentions seriously. They were a merry young couple and they changed their minds a lot. And the weeks went by and I didn't get any answer, and I assumed that they didn't like the sound of Zanzibar. I went off to Ruanda-Urundi instead and put them out of my mind.

"When it was time to go home I shipped from Dar es Salaam, in Tanganyika. It was a bad year for shipping and I had to wait a long time there, and this used up my money, so that when a ship did come along I didn't ask questions as to her ports of call, but jumped aboard third-class, and sailed off for Genoa. She was an Italian boat and didn't stop anywhere before Cairo. I did notice a mass of land on the left as we steamed north, and I asked some officer what it was, and he said 'Zanzibar.' But that stirred only a faint memory in my mind. I had a lot of other things to worry about. I was broke as usual.

"Well, I arrived in England, ultimately, and I had to scurry around to get money, and what with this and that I still didn't think of my friends until one day the phone rang. 'Is this Miss Hahn?' a polite voice inquired. I said, 'Yes?' 'Miss *Emily* Hahn?' insisted the voice; 'Miss Emily Hahn, the famous writer?' And I said again, 'Yes, yes, who is it?' Then the voice said, 'Well, you can bloody well go to hell, Miss Hahn,' and I said, 'Oh, hello, Desmond; what's the matter with you?' He said 'We went to Zanzibar. We sat there in Zanzibar, waiting for you, for two months. I lost my money in a gold mine, we both had malaria, Leona's pregnant, and it's all your fault.' But I don't think it was, do you?"

"Certainly not," said my audience stanchly.

This time when I got ready to go away there was no doubt about it. I was going for good. I even bought my ticket to the States. I knew that this time I oughtn't to put the U.S. off again. Not only was there the inducement of Pat and the car, and a sympathetic reception for the gib bons, but there was Mother. Of course for almost seven years she had been writing the same kind of letter, telling me that the family missed me and it was my duty to come home, but in Chungking I found myself agreeing with her, for the first time. It was indeed time to go home. I had fought off the conviction for months, even years. I had flown into passions of rage when my agent wrote me that I was Losing Touch with America.

"As if anyone could lose touch nowadays!" I stormed. "Nowadays when the radio makes it impossible to cut yourself off from your own civilization, even if you wanted to! Nowadays when we have magazines and movies and long-distance telephones and air mail! The man's talking nonsense."

But he wasn't. It takes more than radio and television to bridge the gap between China and America. I had been away too long, and the fact that I talked that way was proof of it, if only I had known. But wait a minute. When I say "too long," what do I mean? Had I been away too long for my own good? Or did I mean that I had been away so long that my individuality was being lost? If the latter is what I mean (and what my agent means too), then I think that, after all, my long stay in the Orient wasn't a bad thing. I am not at all enamored of the individuality I lost. I was a crass young person, overeducated and underexperienced, like most Americans. I was a smart aleck. It wasn't a bad thing at all, leaving that young woman at the bottom of the Whangpoo or wherever I had dropped her.

There were few ships sailing direct to San Francisco or Los Angeles by the time I deigned to look them up. The ticklish political situation had played hob with shipping on the Pacific. All I could find was an extremely dubious chance of a berth on the *Coolidge* or passage in a cabin liner that traveled every month through Manila and Shanghai, and thence to Los Angeles.

The whole colony on the South Bank was changing. Gidley's "relief" had arrived, traveling overland from Indo-China and bringing because of this a beautiful lot of luggage for everybody: clothes and furniture and liquor that had been ordered months before by various diplomats. Everyone was eager to get as much in as he could as soon as possible; you never knew when that route too would be closed to neutrals. With the arrival of Mr. Powell, Gidley started to pack and get ready for his trip down to Hong Kong. He was going to join up, like most of the young Englishmen in China. Then Corin and Jacques came along with the news that they too were pulling out. The breakup of Jacques's country, Belgium, and of France had changed his plans to stay up in Chungking at the Havas office for a full year. He wanted to get into something that would be more useful for the Allies.

"So you're getting out of here at last," I said to Corin. "That's grand."

"It might be," she admitted cautiously. I looked at her, trying to sum up the situation, and I didn't like what I saw. That first happy bloom she had possessed during the early months of the love affair had vanished. She was thinner than ever, jumpy, and a bad color. She should have been happier about her release from the Chungking backwater, where she had been forced by her oddly twisted conscience to crouch in abject miserable poverty all these past months. "I'm worried about money, as usual," she said. "I'll have enough to pay my plane fare, but it will just about clean me out."

"But Jacques? Or do you still feel feministic enough not to take his money? After all, Corin, it's because of him you're going away from your job——"

"No, I don't mind sharing with Jacques. That's all right." Corin shut up for a moment. "If we have to, can we borrow from you in Hong Kong?" she asked. When I said yes, she wandered away, leaving me worried.

Allow me to pause and think China over, sitting on my hatbox, waiting for the boat that will take me to the plane on the emergency airfield. I have half an hour more of China. Then the plane will fly me down to Hong Kong and the beginning of a completely changed existence. Although I don't know it, sitting there on that suitcase, I am saying good-by to what remains of myself. But I carry with me six years of China, uninterrupted China, and I have in my brain certain impressions which may be worth a little thought.

That was 1940. I am writing this book in 1944, in New York, four years down the line, looking back at a scene that grows clearer as the details disappear. Yesterday I had tea with a fellow refugee. "Do you know," she said, "wherever I go, whoever I meet, I am asked the same questions. People ask me about three things in China: the guerrillas, the Communists, and the Co-operatives. It gives one a strange idea of what they think of China, over here. What is one to answer? You tell me, Miss Hahn. We should understand a little. You've been there nine years and I've been there fifteen. How is one to explain to these people that there are no more Communists in China than there are here in the United States? How can I convince them that in all my time there I never yet saw a Co-operative? We have as many Co-operatives here in America, but very few people see them. And the guerrillas——"

"Well, I did see evidence of guerrillas," I said. "We don't have those over here, you must admit."

She had something there about the Communists and the Co-ops, though. Do you know where the trouble is? It's in the books you have been given about China, the books and the articles. You can't help it, but you have a distorted picture of the truth, and I'm not surprised at it when I look over the literature that they've been feeding you.

I haven't a word to say against Edgar Snow. But when you have read *Red Star Over China* you begin to expect much more of the Reds than you have got. I haven't anything but praise for the Co-operatives—I mean Indusco. But it was overadvertised. The people who sponsor it wanted you to know what a good thing it was, and they wanted you to help, too, with money. So they wrote a lot of articles about it, and published a lot of glowing photographs in pamphlets, and as a result the idea of Indusco, over here in America, has been blown up to amazing and quite false proportions.

Then the people who fought with the guerrillas. Well, they did fight with the guerrillas. They spent many months with those gallant bands, and it was a terrific experience, and they were burned up with admiration for the guerrillas. They wanted to tell you how gallant and brave and deserted these men and women are, so they, too, wrote books, and you bought them, and there again is something which can't possibly live up to its reputation.

The average American today, the one who takes a sympathetic interest in China, is full of hooey through no fault of his own. He thinks that the guerrillas are the only soldiers who do any fighting at all in China. He thinks the woods are full of them. Actually the regular soldiers of China can put up a pretty good fight too. Actually, though as a symbol the guerrillas are inspiring and invaluable, the great burden of resistance has rested on the regular Army. What else can you expect, considering the small handfuls of guerrillas and the material they haven't got. Much of their effort is lost, anyway, because of interguerrilla arguments and jealousy and hijacking. *I am not trying to run them down,* Agnes Smedley and Ed Snow and General Carlson and the rest of you; I'm only trying to undo some of the harm you have unwittingly done your friends. You have worked people up into a state where they are going to be awfully mad pretty soon. They are heading for a big disappointment.

Now the Communists. That situation is due to the peculiarity of most American newspapermen in China, who are nearly all of them inclined to be leftist, out of a frustrated sense of guilt, a superior viewpoint of things as they are, and a tendency to follow the crowd—of newspapermen.

Most newspapermen don't know any more about the Communists in China than you do. They hear rumors. They try to get permission to go and see these people, and once in a great while somebody does. But the chances of seeing what really goes on among the Chinese Communists are even less than those of seeing the inside of Russia. If you live in Chungking you can always interview Chou En-lai. That is what he is there for. But if you think China is going to give you all the answers you are as innocent as—as an American newspaperman.

Me? No, I don't know anything about the Communists. The difference between me and you, over there in the Press Hostel, is that I admit it. Long ago I grew tired of hanging around the people who were supposed to know. They put on too many airs for me. They acted so mysterious that I came to the conclusion, which has since been proved correct, that they didn't know anything either.

As for Indusco, I won't meet with any argument. Indusco is a marvelous idea. It's too good an idea to be killed even by the people who are trying to kill it just now. It can't be killed even by the well-meaning people who tried to boost it, and who boosted it too much. The Chinese Co-operatives are languishing. They are nearly non-existent. There never were such a lot of them as you were told, to begin with. All the while I was in Chungking I tried to find some, and the Indusco authorities kept putting me off. "They're not so good just around this district," I was told. "You ought to go to Paochi." Yes, but we in America were told that there were thousands of them, flourishing ones, all over Central China. I visited Chengtu, which was a center, supposedly, and even there I met with disappointment.

That isn't the fault of the Co-ops. It's the fault of the advertisers, who were so eager to give them a hand that they told lies.

The day of judgment is overtaking China just now, on all these points. Everywhere I go in New York I am running into dissatisfaction and an impatient feeling on the part of the public that they have been fooled. It frightens me. Is it too late to start telling the truth?

If only they had realized it, China doesn't have to depend on exaggeration. The truth would have been good enough.

Chapter 29

I'M COMING NOW to a difficult part of this egotistical history. How can I explain the sudden change that took place in my plans? I don't want to write too much about Charles because it will sound sappy. Once in print, fond reminiscences have a way of changing horribly. That is why love letters sound the way they do in a courtroom. It would be especially unfair to Charles to take advantage of his absence. He is in a place where he can't control my writing just now. And he is exceedingly British; he hates publicity about his own feelings or mine. He doesn't even like me showing my poems around; he thinks that poems are personal, private things, nobody's business but our own. It is obvious that I'm not like that at all. I print my poetry whenever I get the chance, because once a thing is written it ceases to mean anything personal to me. Anyway, if I have a deep conviction it is that a good story must be told. I can't understand Charles's attitude, and he can't understand mine. When he writes, he writes safe, impersonal histories. I shall try to hit what I think is a fair compromise; I will talk about myself and make no attempt to explain him or his emotions. That's a difficult thing to do and in places will fall short of my intentions. But I'll try.

I went out to dinner with Charles and Max the evening after I arrived in Hong Kong. I was feeling on top of the world. The book was finished and sent off, I had bought two new dresses, I had a private bathroom at the Gloucester with really hot water, there would be no more air raids, and my hair was cut and permanented. Everything was perfect, if a trifle unsettled. Yes, that was still there, sticking like a burr in my head: I was *unsettled*. Now that I think back over my years, that feeling has always been responsible for my more outlandish decisions; it was as if I had to plunge into things, take steps which I couldn't retrace, just to get myself settled. As an experienced observer of myself, I should have realized that evening that I was set for mischief. Perhaps I did. Perhaps that is why I chattered so happily, and ate and drank so earnestly, and looked at Charles with such pleasure.

I did like him a lot. There was a good deal to tell him. I was surprised that I hadn't written to him from Chungking, telling him all those things throughout the summer. We drifted about that evening, dining late and wandering further afield until we ended up where Charles always did fetch up after an evening's drinking, in the Tokyo Hotel down on Connaught Road. It was not my idea of relaxation to sit on a Japanese mat and talk to geisha, but Charles liked it and there was no arguing with him. He called in the old woman who ran the restaurant and solemnly introduced us: "This *okusan* (lady) has come from Chungking."

"*So des nei!*" exclaimed the madame, opening her slit eyes wide.

"Yes, *so des*," I said, glowering at her.

"And were there many Japanese airplanes coming?" asked Madame.

"Many," I said cheerily, "every day. Every day I hid in a cave."

Max heaved a deep sigh and lay down on the mat and went to sleep.

"What I like about you, Mickey," said Charles, who always gets earnest in his cups, "is that you have guts. Yes, you have guts." He always gets repetitive too. The more he said it the more I liked it.

I don't know why I have always had so little conscience about married men. It can't be Mother's fault; she brought us up very carefully. Of course if I were put into a corner and forced to defend myself in debate I could do it. I am full of all those tag lines we learned when I was a girl, such as: Marriage should not mean possession. When a man wishes to be unfaithful to his wife the mischief is already done. A woman who can't hold a man doesn't deserve to keep him, et cetera, et cetera. There are other unarguable facts, however, which also have something to do with the case, and in my younger days I failed to take them into consideration. In general (of course all these generalizations aren't of much practical value) it is unwise to go poaching among married people, because then society doesn't like you. It doesn't seem fair, either. Men are so easy that it's not quite sporting to wade in and grab off a married one; what married woman wants to spend all her leisure watching her man? Oh I've been careless and unsporting in my time, but I have one defense to offer: I didn't know any better. Little by little I learned. There were faults in my philosophy and it took time and experience to show them up.

And besides, there was one very good reason for me to spend my time with married men. It was a selfish reason, I grant you, but we savage youths of that generation were selfish, and from my point of view I couldn't have done better. I didn't at all want to be married. We won't go into the why of it, but I didn't. Therefore it was wise of me to avoid taking risks. I couldn't marry a married man, and that was that.

All of which doesn't serve to explain why my conscience let me down in regard to Charles. To begin with, I didn't feel particularly aware of his marriage. He said that it was over. He had decided that it was over months before, which was why his wife had gone off to Australia. She hadn't been willing to wind it up without a trial separation, but he decided for himself, just the same. They were arguing it out by letter. If Charles had been ordinarily married and contented, if he had only wanted to indulge in an extramarital affair because his wife wasn't around, I would have run away. I wouldn't have been satisfied. I was serious about Charles from the beginning, from before the beginning, and that was a completely new departure for me. I told him so. We never talked seriously, but I told him so just the same when I had fortified myself with whisky.

None of this fitted in at all with my plans. We hadn't yet come to a decision, and it was time for me to go off to Shanghai if I wanted to have a decent visit before my boat left for the States. Charles didn't like to talk about my going away, but he stirred himself at last.

"Why go to Shanghai at all?" he demanded. "Why not take the last month here?"

"But the gibbons. I'll have to arrange about the gibbons."

Then Charles astonished me for the first time, though not the last: "Bring them down here," he said.

"You mean—you don't mind gibbons?" I was incredulous. "People always hate them," I explained. "It's only fair to warn you. Only a few crackpots like myself and Peter, that Russian girl, can bear them."

"I don't suppose I'll love them," he admitted, "but I won't be living with them. You can put them up in the Dogs' Home, I should think. And then you'll have no ties left in Shanghai." He spoke with satisfaction. I dashed off to the telegraph offices and started to make arrangements. It developed that if I waited for the gibbons that would put off my departure for the States too. Their keeper wrote to me rather crossly that he couldn't simply dump them onto a southbound steamer. No captain would consent to such a cargo. The gibbons would have to wait about for a proper chaperon, and people willing to chaperon gibbons for a week on the high seas are few and far between. He was looking around, but I would have to be patient.

I was. More cheerfully than I would have expected to do it, back in Chungking, I changed my ticket again. I was now booked to sail in November instead of October, and Charles was awfully pleased. "I can still get home for Christmas," I explained.

One evening we set out for a party that promised to be out of the ordinary run of Hong Kong parties. It usually did seem to be that way when I went out with Charles, but this was stranger than ever. There was a man working for his office who had a queer history. He was Chinese but had been born in Mexico and brought up in Japan, and when he came back to his native land he didn't marry an ordinary Chinese girl, but a Eurasian.

"It's the old lady, his mother-in-law, that I want to meet," said Charles. "She's English. She married some Chinese out in Australia and went to a little town with him, somewhere near Canton, and they had about twenty children. This chap says she's never gone back to England in forty years. I thought you'd be interested."

I fell for Mrs. Lee right away. She may not have been back to England in forty years, but you wouldn't have known it to look at her. She was British from top to toe. She dressed like a cockney and she talked like a cockney.

"Forty years over here, my dear," she said to me. "I wouldn't know the old town now, they tell me. Oh, I've had a life, I have. Helping my husband's family thresh the wheat, just like any farmer woman, and me six months gone with my first. . . . Oh, I've had a life."

The conversation was bewilderingly polyglot. Charles and the son-in-law chattered in Japanese, Mother-in-law and Mickey chattered in English, Mickey and Daughter chattered in Mandarin, and the young couple talked to each other in some other language, probably Shanghai dialect, while now and then Mrs. Lee said something to her offspring in Cantonese.

"I'll have just a little of that wine," said Mrs. Lee. "My daughter can tell you that I never drink, nor smoke either. But tonight's rather an occasion, meeting the major and all. And you, my dear, how does it happen they didn't ship you off for the evacuation? Did your husband the major put his foot down?"

"I was in the interior," I said evasively, "and got a visa to come back after the evacuation ship had left."

"Aren't you the cunning one," said Mrs. Lee.

I realize that it is time to explain the evacuation, before we go any further. We are in Hong Kong now to stay, and we must understand the situation clearly. In May, while I was still up in the Szechuan hills, the political developments between Britain and Japan must have taken a turn for the worse, though the public didn't know about it. Charles and a few other experts recommended to the colonial government that the service women and children be sent away. This is always done in British colonies when things get ticklish. The Hong Kong government accepted the suggestion with alacrity, but they went further than any such government had ever gone before. In a way, they repeated the behavior of the British diplomats in Shanghai, back in 1937. They ordered the evacuation of *all* women and children.

A lot of confusion ensued. To begin with, the order wasn't clear. Just what women and children, asked the public, were meant? The reply was ill considered: "Pure British," said the government. This implied that the thousands of Eurasians and Portuguese who held British passports were not considered worth saving from danger, though the non-Asiatic women and children were. These Asiatics, always sensitive and considering themselves badly treated (which they were), blew up. The officials who answered their charges got in deeper and deeper. "You natives," they said in effect, "are at home here. In a pinch you can go into Free China. Our women from England are in a different category."

Now of course this wasn't true. Most Eurasians born in Hong Kong have been brought up like English people. They wear foreign-style clothes, speak English, can't write or read Chinese, and consider that they are as British as anyone. After all, that is what they have been taught all their lives, though they are snubbed too. They took the decision hard. They were very much insulted.

The Portuguese had a beef too. Although they come from Macau, they hold British passports and feel entitled to all the privileges pertaining thereto. And they are as sensitive as the other Eurasians.

"We can't help it," said the harried authorities. "We are giving free transportation to these women and children, all the way to Australia. We can't send every woman and child in town down under. Australia couldn't cope with them. It would cost far too much. And we would have to take the millions of Chinese too, if we start accepting Eurasians. It's out of the question."

It was a bad mess. On top of all that there was trouble with the "pures," as the other Hong Kong citizens began bitterly calling the English-born people. Most of those women didn't want to go. They didn't want to leave their peaceful, luxurious houses. They didn't want to leave their husbands. It would be for an indefinite period, they knew. Hong Kong was not in danger, they said, and anyway, what if she was? Weren't they perfectly capable of seeing it through? Why must they be sent away like useless appendages? They were furious and disturbed and unconvinced and stubborn. Not the service women of course—they are used to being shipped around—but the ordinary women of Hong Kong.

"Go to Australia?" they cried. "Do you know how difficult it is to get maids in Australia, or cooks? Who's going to help me with Baby? Why do I have to go if those Eurasian women can stay? Why must I go and leave my husband free to play around with Chinese tarts? What about my house? Why, this is my home. If I were living in England would you make me go away, just because there's danger of an invasion from the Germans? And who says we are in danger here, anyway? Didn't you say you could manage those silly little Japs?"

The husbands shouted, "Who's going to pay the expenses of double households for me? Can you guarantee that my wife will behave herself? There's a law, and I stand by the law."

There began a great spectacle of shuffling and evasion. Although one of the officials threatened and stormed and said he would load the women on the evacuation ships forcibly, carrying them aboard kicking and screaming if necessary, he never gave the order. Some women went away quietly enough. Many who didn't want to go managed not to go. They signed up as "essential war workers," as nurses, or as some other sort of helper. Other women simply wouldn't go, and when bullying and cajoling and threatening failed they were left undisturbed. Hilda Selwyn-Clarke, the wife of the director of medical services, caused a scandal by slipping out of town and taking her four-year-old daughter to Canton, where she remained quietly until the registration of the women was completed, and then she came back equally unobtrusively. On that wangle she was bound to get away with it.

Other confusion lay in the fact that women like myself, who were not British, were allowed to stay as we liked. The government didn't consider itself responsible for us. If the American Government should order me out, that would be a different matter, but the American Government, according to our law, couldn't do any such thing even if it wanted to. I was all right in Hong Kong. Nobody cared at all. On a Saturday night at the Grips you could see all of us, the Americans and the French and the Dutch and the Eurasians and the Chinese, not to mention quite a few Englishwomen who had got out of going. We were popular because we were becoming rare. It was a fine time for the girls.

Indirectly the situation was responsible, too, for Ursula's protracted absence. She had gone to Australia all right, according to plan, where she stayed with Charles's cousins and didn't like it at all. As soon as she could she started back to Hong Kong. When she arrived in Singapore, however, the blow had already fallen and the evacuation had taken place. If Ursula had been in Hong Kong at the time she would no doubt have managed to stay, as so many of her friends did. She might even have gone with her friend Vera Armstrong as far as Manila and then come back again, as Vera did, full of rage at the idea of being cut off from her house for any longer period. ("My husband's a lawyer," stormed Vera, "and he says they can't make me go away; they can't.") But as it was, she was in Singapore. Singapore, too, was having evacuation troubles. Ursula decided not to risk being sent back to Australia. She quickly grabbed a job with a government department which entitled her to stay put, and sat down to wait for a later chance to get back to Charles. Well-meaning females began to write hinting letters to her, and Ursula hastily wrote Charles, asking him what mischief was afoot.

Now we can go back to Mrs. Lee and the Chinese restaurant.

"Babies are dear little things," she said, "though I did have too many meself. . . . Have you any babies, madam?"

"No," I said, solemnly shaking my head. "No, I can't have any children."

"Oh, isn't that a pity!"

Over on the other side of the table, Charles pricked up his ears and looked at me.

"Yes," I said to Mrs. Lee, "I'm sorry too."

"Nonsense," said Charles crisply. "Of course you can have children."

"As it happens, I can't," I said, and I thought I was telling the truth. "I've been told so, often, by doctors. I can't."

"Of course you can. I'll bet you anything you like."

"What is this nonsense?" he demanded in the taxi, after we had sent the guests off to the ferry. "Is that why you carry on so about children, weeping at Wu Teh-chen's and keeping gibbons and all that?"

"Oh no. I don't want children. I never did."

"All women want children," said Charles with amusing certainty. "But see here; do you really want a child? If so, I'll let you have one."

"Huh?"

"Let's have one," he said. "I'll take care of it. It can be my heir. Just to make things all right, if I can get a divorce and if it all works out, we might even get married. If we want to, that is, and after a long time for considering."

"Do you mean it?" I asked after a pause. I knew already, though, that he did. He was being flippant, but that is the way Charles is; he just is flippant. It didn't alter the fact that he meant it.

"I never heard such nonsense," said Charles indignantly. "Can't have children! Whatever will Mrs. Lee think of me?"

"All right," I said, "let's try."

"And you can turn in your steamship ticket," he said. "You had better do that tomorrow."

Chapter 30

WHENEVER I think back on September 1940, which is often, I am freshly surprised at the simplicity that marked our deciding. It was an important decision, but we settled it all in a few sentences; we must have been thinking it over, each of us, in a hidden way for a long time. If you are a writer you know how your brain seems to work sometimes all by itself, unbidden, and on company time. Then all of a sudden out comes a finished piece of work, well turned and neat and a complete surprise to the conscious level of your brain. That's how Carola was planned, and though I may not have much in my life to be smug about, I recommend the method. I found it thoroughly satisfactory. It must have been right, too, because for the next year and a bit of time over I was happy. I have been happy before, but not like that, in such a solid way.

I don't know how Charles felt. I don't understand him at all and I don't try to, because that is an impertinence I resent between lovers—poking and prying around in one's emotions. But if I had worried on his behalf I might have been less selfishly happy. British folklore and Charles's family history are rich in examples of women who were noble, who understood their men, and who denied themselves love when it was necessary for their mates' careers thus to deny. I'm afraid I didn't give it so much as a thought until my doctor scolded me, much later—too late. Even then I didn't care as I should. I suppose like the young savage I was I felt that it was his career and his lookout. If he didn't care, why should I? The doctor wouldn't believe that Carola was Charles's idea to begin with. Most people won't believe it. Most people, naturally, think she was an unavoidable accident. They don't know from nothing!

Then too I felt that as a career the Army wasn't really very close to Charles's heart. Not that he neglected the Army; he was supposed to be damned good at his work. But he hadn't exactly picked it out for himself. It was foreordained. All his paternal ancestors were service people, just like those families we make fun of on the stage: Charles's brother was in the Army, they meant Charles for the Navy, but he was too nearsighted and so he went to Sandhurst instead. It was taken for granted. Otherwise his tastes and talents would have made him a don in a university. Even after he had his commission, universities offered him fellowships, and he had to reject them, though reluctantly.

At the age of fourteen Charles was deeply immersed in Portuguese and Japanese. It is a combination that led him inevitably to sixteenth-century studies in the Far East. A great-uncle was captain in the Opium Fleet and lies buried now in Macau. Charles read a paper to the Royal Asiatic Society when he was seventeen, and no doubt his interest in Asia is the direct result of that uncle and of the library that the family collected afterward, based on Nunky's exploits. Decidedly he isn't a straight military type, and I should be excused that I have never thought of him in that way. Yet he looked it, God knows, even when he wasn't in uniform. He walked and talked and drank like an Army officer.

We never talked about his career. He would have snorted and spat if I used the word. He didn't think much of the British setup out there.

"Hong Kong is the dumping ground for the duds," he said. "Including me. Any old fool who can't be used elsewhere is dumped out here in Hong Kong. Look at them!"

Naturally we didn't announce our decision to the city, but when I canceled my passage to America the word went around, as such things always did in that little gossiping community, and people wondered why, or, less delicately, who. Visitors from Shanghai were puzzled, too, and did a good deal of sniffing, trying to locate the rat. I embarked on a long series of cables home, asking my brother-in-law to find out how difficult it was, after returning to the States, for a woman to get permission to get out again. He knew what I meant, of course; none of the family had any illusions that I would want to stay home once I had got there. He looked it all up and answered frankly that my chances of getting back to the Far East, unless things cleared up a good deal, were slim. All of that correspondence softened the disappointment Mother felt when a letter came at last, putting off my return home yet again. For the first time, now that it was irrevocable that I was not going, I felt genuinely homesick.

I made plans. No bride could have gone about fixing up her home more calmly. The more I recall it the more I wonder now at the utterly natural way I went into the proposition. Maybe there are times in our lives when, in spite of all our civilization, we are capable of following instinct blindly. There was only one time I know of that Charles pulled back and took a look squarely at the difficulties of the situation.

He was always busy. You must think of the following year as one of hectic activity on his part. He had to be within reach of his office all the time, all day and all night, and he tried to arrange the week so that nothing would be neglected. On his free evenings he did his own work, reading and writing historical articles, and he wanted to be absolutely quiet and undisturbed at those times. He allowed himself one or sometimes two parties a week. When he was busy I did as I liked, but it was understood that Saturday was the one afternoon and night that he could spend with me without office work or any treatises on sixteenth-century Japan interfering. And Wednesday afternoon. Charles was always methodical.

This was on a Saturday evening. We were dining out and I was waiting for him, though it wasn't time for him yet, when he called up. (I was still living in the Gloucester.) "I'm coming ten minutes early," he said with a false sort of briskness. "There's something I want to talk over before we go out." It was just like him, and like the pressure of his work, that he had to plan hours in advance for ten minutes. He came in looking impossibly picturesque in his uniform mess jacket, strapped trousers, and cap. Hong Kong was full of such pleasant frippery in those days, when we were at war and yet we weren't. I probably looked picturesque myself; I can remember how I loved that dress. It had a full, full skirt; it was a printed chintz, with enormous poppies sprinkled around it. The two of us looked like a scene in *Cavalcade,* but I don't think we sounded like it.

"About this baby," said Charles. He was walking up and down the room, not looking at me because he was embarrassed.

"Yes?" I said. I was sitting on the bed, looking straight at him for the same reason.

"Have you thought," he said, "that if we have this baby it'll *show?*"

I replied, after a short pause, that the idea had, as a matter of fact, already occurred to me.

"But then you can't go to cocktail parties," he said, very worried. "You can't go around looking like that."

I said, "I don't have to go to cocktail parties when it comes to that point. I won't want to."

"You wouldn't expect me to take you out to the Sheko pool?" he insisted.

"No, I'd much rather swim in the ocean. Anyway, when it's that far along I'll be hiding out somewhere, won't I?"

"Oh, we'll manage," he said, cheerful now that the problem was off his chest. "We'll take a small house on the Peak or somewhere. By the way, you'll be wanting a flat soon, won't you? This hotel is all very well for a bit, but it would be more convenient if you took a place. Now I just heard that there's a furnished flat going in the building near Abermor Court"—he lived in Abermor Court—"and I think you'd better have a look at it."

I picked up my handbag and we started out for the dinner party. "And another thing, about the baby," I said, "remember, I still think I won't be able to have it. The doctors have always said so."

"Pooh, pooh," said Charles. "Nonsense."

Corin and Jacques came to town. My days had been taken up pretty well, ever since my arrival, with other transient friends from Chungking: Gidley had already passed through, and so had a few tenants of the Press Hostel. But these other people heralded their arrival with loud squawks of joy, wasting no time getting in touch with me. Corin and Jacques avoided me for a day or so. After that I wouldn't be avoided, and they couldn't keep it up, because like everyone else they had to come and live at the Gloucester. Corin and I went shopping and she bought some dresses and cheered up under that unfailing tonic. She also borrowed money from me for Jacques. The strangeness that I had felt when they got there melted away after a day of activity, when Jacques had gone on ahead to Shanghai, and I felt that we were back on the old footing.

Charles and I went out for a week end at J. J. Paterson's place at Fanling which is a long way in on the mainland road, the last Chinese village before the border is reached. J.J. is a famous taipan who had been in China all his life, and who preferred to live miles from town, in a bungalow from which he could go out shooting or walking in his garden, or playing golf at the Fanling Country Club. He is a large red-faced man with a sense of humor well above the average, and a style of exhibiting it all his own. Once in a while, when his chosen mode of living all alone palled on him, he sent out invitations to everyone he liked, and had a real bang-up party.

Sunday was a fine hot day. As Charles said afterward, it felt like the last gasp of capitalism, and well worth it. We all met at a swimming beach at Castle Peak in the morning; that is on the mainland. We had sandwiches, and drinks in thermos flasks. Then we drove to the Fanling bungalow and drank some more, and did gymnastic tricks on the lawn. It was brilliantly sunny: there is no weather like that of Hong Kong in autumn. It was perfect. We ate again, and drank again, and played on the lawn or slept in the shade if we wanted to, and the day dragged on with pleasant idiocy until dark.

After supper I found myself mixed up with a captain, name unknown, who had been following me about for a few hours and who was now firmly determined to take me out walking in the garden. J.J.'s bungalow fronts a broad expanse of turf, and a double terrace drops down just below his house-wide veranda. I was unfamiliar with that irregularity in the ground. We must have halted just above the first dip, looking for the moon, when Captain Unknown grabbed me and became violently amorous.

I was startled, and instead of talking him out of it, or calling indoors so that others would join us and scare him off, I just started to push him away. He wouldn't be pushed, and I backed up and fell straight down the terrace, my left foot doubling up under me. I have always been an awkward cow of a woman. The wedge heels of my cork-soled shoes were as much to be blamed as the captain. I thought it was only a turned ankle, and though the pain made me dizzy I put that down to its being a joint injury, and made light of it. The captain made less of it than that. He paid no attention whatever to my foot. He was feeling amorous, not helpful. Under pretense of giving me his arm and helping me to a chair, he led me swiftly further and further away from the house and at last put me down somewhere, I rather think in the vegetable garden, and there resumed his suit. As Charles had said, it was all exactly like a Roman orgy—too much so at the moment to suit me. When all else failed I used force and hurried back to the house, hobbling on my injured foot, with the wicked captain in hot pursuit. It was definitely irritating to find Charles cozily chatting away to some people in a corner, not at all interested in my injury. Nobody was. I stood there in the middle of J.J.'s admirable drawing room wailing, "It hu-u-u-urts!" and nobody evinced the slightest reaction until some man happened to glance at my ankle.

"Gosh, it is swelling," he admitted. "I'd better tie it up for you." He found ice cubes and a big handkerchief, and until the party broke up I rubbed the swelling with these. Charles first noticed that I was in trouble when I climbed carefully into his ramshackle car, though we had all shouted at him for about an hour. When he enjoys himself he concentrates. "It looks bad," he said in surprise. "What have you been doing out there in the moonlight? If it goes on being painful in the morning you'd better ring up Tony Dawson-Grove. He's a good doctor, I think, and a nice chap. You'll like him."

I did like Tony, who was struggling into the front rank of medicos in the Colony despite his really remarkable childish good looks. I didn't realize that morning when he came into the hotel room that I was going to know him as well as I knew anyone in the ensuing months, but I did like him straight off. He arrived while I was being entertained by one Lieutenant Jones of the Royal Scots, who at the age of thirty was getting a reputation as a Character. Jones twisted his handsome military mustache when Tony entered, and said, "Ha! Dawson-Grove, I believe?"

The doctor nodded. "How are you, Pansy?" The lieutenant drained his whisky glass, for which I had paid—he hated treating people unless it was absolutely necessary—and left, making one more careful quip at the door. We heard his voice down the corridor: "Haw, haw, haw!"

"So you know Pansy Jones," said the doctor, opening his bag. "We were up at Oxford at the same time. You were there too around that time, I believe? . . . Now then, let's have a look at it. Good God!"

The foot and ankle had turned a choice plum color with brown trimmings.

"I couldn't sleep," I complained.

"I should think not. How did it happen?" I explained. "Do you mean to tell me," he demanded, "that nobody gave you first aid? Nobody even attempted to bandage it? Who was at the party?" I gave a hasty list of as many names as I had known. . . . "At least two of those women," said

Tony impressively, "have completed their V.A.D. courses in the past two months. This looks like a first-rate sprain. It should be all right in ten days."

That was why I didn't even look at the flat in Tregunter Mansions before I moved in. Billie Lee went up instead and inspected it, and reported satisfactorily, and I took it. The rent was high, I thought, but I didn't know anything about general expenses in that part of town. It wasn't. May Road, where Charles had lived since his marriage and where my new flat was located in a building next door to his, was the highest street of the "mid-level" district. Hong Kong's arrangement physically is simply allegorical. The island is mostly a high mountain rising slightly off center. The first settlers probably were satisfied with sea-level dwellings, but when later traders began to make money they built themselves mansions at the top, from where they could look all around at the isle-dotted sea on one side and utilitarian, flat Kowloon, on the mainland, on the other. The difficulty of getting up and down was enormous, but the prestige made it worth while, evidently, for everybody who could afford it in the ensuing years lived on the Peak. The Peak became symbolic of social eminence. Before the funicular Peak tram was constructed Peak dwellers used sedan chairs to get up and down, or horses, or even, during one colorful period, camels. Automobiles made it much easier to be socially proper. For at least four months of the year the Peak is covered with clouds. You can't see the view for the fog. The Hong Kong taipans have always paid heavily for their glory. But the summer, after the spring fogs are driven off, makes everything worth it, for Peak air is delightfully clear and fresh.

Lots of people like Charles, who worked hard and with long hours, compromised on their social standing by moving in at mid-level. May Road, Conduit Road, Robinson Road—they were built up with houses from one end to the other. Here was where you found the young men and women, the rising vice-presidents and officers, the sons of company presidents, and newlyweds from the Peak. Whereas Jack MacGregor of the liquor firm of Caldbeck MacGregor lived on the Peak as he had done since the days of the camel, in a house full of Victorian comfort and bric-a-brac, his son Robin occupied a smart little modern flat in St. Joan's Court at mid-level.

If you were less than forty and had no children, that was what you wanted: a modern flat not too far out. If you were middle-aged or old or had offspring you moved up the hill to the fogs and old houses and glory. It was the ambition of all right-minded young wives, though, to get up there just as soon as it could be done, along with government servants and millionaires. May Road may have been good enough, but it wasn't quite Quite.

I was shocked at the difference in expenses between my new apartment and the place I had shared with Billie and Mavis down in Happy Valley. Whereas one amah had been quite enough to keep our house clean and to cook for three of us in the Valley, it now appeared that I alone couldn't do with less than three servants: a cook-houseboy, a coolie to help him, and a wash amah to do my laundry. It seemed unnecessary and I protested. True, I had used that many servants in Shanghai, but there the dollar was only a quarter the value of the Hong Kong yuan, and I had had more for my money anyway.

"I don't need a wash amah all the week," I said in surprise. "And why does a cook boy need a coolie when he's cooking for one?"

It was Charles's turn to be surprised. "Why, everyone has that many servants," he said.

"No, they don't," I retorted, my mind on the Happy Valley flat. "What do I pay the cook?"

"Thirty dollars."

"Thirty dollars? But in Billie's house we gave the amah seventeen, and she did all the work."

"In May Road," said Charles, as if that settled everything, "you pay thirty dollars. You won't get a cook for less. I have a man if you want him. I meant to give my own boy the sack and take this fellow, who has good references from a man in our office, but I've relented and I'm going to give my people another chance. Want him?"

Fortunately for my entire future, I said yes. That is how Ah King came into my life. It was the luckiest hiring I ever did, but at the time I didn't appreciate it. I was grumbling to myself at the expense of life as a lady in Hong Kong. I was accustomed to scraping and saving; I had held myself on short rations for the past year of traveling in the interior, and old habits die hard. I had the money but it scared me to spend it on non-essentials. Charles seemed to take this style completely for granted; in his world people just did spend that much, and I didn't like to go on pointing out to him the fact that most of the humans in Hong Kong, as a matter of fact, lived on much less. It was not the time to pinch. I had to live near Charles so that we could spend our rare free times together without delay. I didn't like to protest. His own flat, with its magnificent, dramatic view over the harbor, cost much more than mine.

Ah King came into the hotel to show me his credentials. I was stretched out on the bed, my bandaged foot on a pillow. It was getting on to the ten-day limit that Tony had set, but it wasn't feeling any better; moving around was increasingly agonizing. I liked Ah King's grave face and his dignified presence. Most Cantonese are small and wiry; Ah King impressed me favorably by looking like a northerner. Is all this boring? It wasn't to me. I loved it. Ah King went to get the flat ready; I wanted to move in on December first.

I called up Tony and complained with vigor about the foot, and he took me immediately to have it X-rayed. The anklebone was broken. A small piece was flopping about under the skin without making the slightest attempt to anchor itself.

"Oh, damn," said Tony in heartfelt tones, "oh, damn. It is all my fault. One should always X-ray a sprain. We'll have to put you in a cast."

The cast would last at least four weeks more, he admitted. Charles cursed it and so did I, but at least when I was fitted out with a large white plaster boot my ankle didn't hurt any more, and that relief was worth a good deal of inconvenience. My awkward self, stumping around the streets, became a familiar sight. I was carried by auto, cast and all, to the beach on Wednesday and Saturday afternoons to watch Charles swimming happily in the surf. Or we went to the club at Sheko and he dipped in the pool while I sat disconsolate on a chaise longue and made conversation with golfers. It was a long way from the rowdy existence of Shanghai. Viewed on the surface, I had made a bad bargain, but we don't exist on the surface. I took surprisingly well to the stuffy routine of Hong Kong, and talked gently and patiently and contentedly with the wealthy bourgeoisie. I had an exciting secret, something they knew nothing about. When I thought of the adventure Charles and I were sharing I didn't care what sort of people I had lunch and tea with. It didn't matter at all.

"But nothing's happened," I complained, on the eve of my removal to May Road. "All these preparations are all very well, and Horst writes me that the gibbons are coming soon, and that is nice. But I'm still not having a baby. I think I can't."

"Yes, you can," said Charles. "I'll have you know that I *always* get girls into trouble."

Chapter 31

ONE of the irritating things about the British point of view which you noticed in the Hong Kong residents was their stubborn refusal to consider the Far East situation. The war meant to them the war in Europe. That they took very seriously. The women, as I said, learned how to do nursing so that they could stay in the Colony, the young men all joined up and wore uniforms, and there were bazaars and benefit balls one after another, to collect funds for airplanes. The airplanes, however, were all to be sent to Europe and used against Hitler; that was the theme of all the propaganda we were given. Hong Kong, unlike Shanghai, has always been a place where people planned to live permanently. Old people who had spent their twenty-five and thirty-five years in the Colony built houses on the Peak and sat down on their pensions, intending to end their days in a warmer and more comfortable climate than obtains at home. They lived at less expense than would have been possible in Europe, even in the cheaper Riviera towns, and they lived an ideally British sort of life. They had their golf and their races and even their hunts, when they wanted to make the effort. Charles was somewhat contemptuous of the people who went in so knowingly and enthusiastically for horses in Hong Kong when they had never done anything of the sort at home. But they loved it, and it was all harmless enough. There was sailing. There was tennis; that goes without saying.

But nobody among those British ever gave China a thought. You could go through the day, from the eleven o'clock drink in the Grips through lunch at someone's house and tea somewhere else down to dinner, stately on the Peak with plenty of cut glass and damask linen and heavy silver, and nobody would talk of the war in China except as a far-off exotic manifestation of the natives. In Charles's office, it is true, there was a group of young men who made the natives their special consideration. One officer was good at Cantonese and so they nominated him to be a sort of liaison man with the local Chinese. His job, theoretically, was to be friendly with the people who made up most of the town's population, to keep in touch with their trends and ideas, and to write reports on all this. The difficulty was that he was too British ever to be particularly friendly with anybody at all. His one close friend among the Chinese was the ultra-British Harold Lee, whose name was rapidly becoming famous for his quaint Oxonian mannerisms. Harold is a charming fellow, but you could search throughout China without finding anybody less typical of his native land. One of the Englishmen ran into him one day in an office building belonging to the Lees, who are wealthy landowners. "Hello, Harold," said the Englishman. "Do you work here?"

"Vaguely," said Harold in languid tones.

He lived in the family mansion and was embarked on a promising career in the law, besides keeping an eye on all his family affairs. He was a brilliant man and pretty well settled in Hong Kong, though it had been a shock when he first came back from Oxford, where he had done particularly well at soccer and had been popular all around. In Hong Kong stupid, vulgar merchants treated him like a native and Harold didn't like it. He didn't mind being Chinese, you understand. He liked that, and hated it when I told him he was English. But naturally he objected to being patronized by some fat beer merchant or other. Ultimately he settled down with a few good English friends like this officer, and a doctor in the government, and a *very* few Americans. But he must have been surprised at the general lack of interest the British showed in their own rather precarious situation. I know that I was.

I found an entirely new (to me) kind of Chinese living in Hong Kong. The Cantonese who make up the bulk of the population have stubbornly resisted change, and in Hong Kong you will find many old customs and traditions flourishing in a lively manner which you can't find anywhere else in China. Perhaps this is because the rest of China has been exposed to the progressive influence of the Chiangs and their sort; I don't know. The streets of the city were always full of long funeral processions, gay with costumes and discordant with brass bands. There were still brides carried about in sedan chairs, their faces hidden. Now and then I even saw a naked baby with a little lock of hair braided into a queue on the top of his head.

We went out a lot with the gayer young British people, or with French or Dutch residents. (Charles's gift for languages made him an unofficial expert on all "foreigners." Most of the other Army people were simply terrified of them.) The general hated entertaining, so he left all that to Charles. This let us in for a lot of big cocktail parties in the Hongkong Hotel. It was much the existence I would have been leading in London, save for the fact that with a few exceptions the people we saw were not as amusing as those I could have dug up elsewhere. I didn't mind it as much as I would have under different circumstances. I enjoyed it. But after a few months I was homesick anyway, for China.

There were plenty of respectable Chinese about. Charles liked them and I took him to their houses, and they liked him, I suppose, though I found a strong anti-British feeling among the upper classes. Still I was homesick for the China I knew.

I missed the pleasant, lazy disorderliness of Sinmay's house. My servants were Hong Kong servants, May Road style, respectful and distant. Ah King didn't exactly disapprove of me—later he was to like me a good deal—but several things about me were already startling him a lot. My Chinese guests, for example. Before me I don't think he had ever entertained Chinese for his masters except at large, stiff, formal receptions when oriental diplomats would not be out of place. Then one afternoon a Sikh policeman from Shanghai dropped by for tea, and both Ah King and Gunga Singh were embarrassed. In the Indian's case it was that damned Hong Kong atmosphere, which had had such a bad effect on Sinmay.

"I don't know what's the matter with this town," he said fretfully. "I'm staying with a cousin down in Happy Valley, and I mentioned that I was coming up to tea with you and I asked him if he knew you. He said, 'You're going up to May Road? Why, that's on the Peak. They won't let you go up the Peak. You'll be turned back.' What's the idea, Mickey?"

I shrugged it off and we talked about other things. But Ah King, perfect servant though he was, peered fearfully at the turbaned Gunga Singh when he brought in the tea tray.

A Chinese boy who worked in one of the news agencies in Chungking took me one evening to an "escort bureau," where he had a girl friend. You may not be aware that prostitution doesn't exist in Hong Kong. It has been abolished by order of Parliament or something. Once upon a time there used to be prostitutes there, as there usually are in seaports, and a government doctor examined them every week, and the venereal disease problem was fairly well under control. But along came an idealistic lady writer named Stella Benson, and she was horrified to discover that such things existed in a crown colony. (Actually what she took exception to especially was the slave-girl setup, but she went the wrong way about abolishing it.) A lot of other idealistic English ladies turned to with Stella Benson, terrifying their menfolk into legislation, and prostitution was abolished. So afterward no government doctor went around inspecting the women, and the venereal disease problem, though it had no official existence, was really very bad. And instead of prostitutes, Hong Kong had "escort girls." They lived in crowded places upstairs in the houses along the harbor front, and these places were known as "clubs." The place young Chang took me to was an athletic club. Like other houses of its kind it had a catalogue, a printed leaflet with photographs of the girls who lived there or who dropped in now and then as they made their rounds. If you had just come in from out of town, as many Chinese countrymen did, you telephoned this club and explained that you wanted a guide, or escort, to show you around. You made your choice from the photograph and the girl came to call on you, or if you were an intimate of the place you dropped in and played mah-jongg there, and kidded with the madame. But it wasn't prostitution, no indeed. The police visited the clubs periodically for their tips, but even when the managers paid squeeze regularly the government occasionally

made trouble. My athletic club, for example, when Chang first introduced me there, was a dark hovel, long and narrow and built something
like an old-fashioned Pullman, with cubicles up and down the hall and
an open space in the back for mah-jongg. Each cubicle had a wooden
bed in it and not much else. One of the periodical purity drives came
along soon afterward, and when I called in again there were no cubicles;
they had been abolished by order of the police. All the partitions had
been taken out, and now when anyone wanted privacy they just put
movable screens up around the chosen spot.

Chang's girl, Ying Ping, could speak good Mandarin and I needed
practice. Not many people in Hong Kong did speak it well enough to be
good for my vocabulary. When you are talking with someone who is not
a teacher you get along better, for a teacher, whether he wants to or not,
usually confines his talk to certain dull subjects and talks down to you,
in a stilted fashion beyond which you seldom progress. The people at the
athletic club, Madame and the man who made the dates at the telephone,
and the girls, and Ying Ping herself, all thought me slightly mad for
calling on them at all, but I didn't care. Ying Ping didn't either. I took
up time that she couldn't have used more profitably with male clients
because I always came early, in the afternoon, after one unfortunate
experience which I'll describe in a minute. I paid her the regular rates for
"entertainment" and we just sat there in the crowded, noisy, cheerful
room, talking Mandarin. After a few visits I got to know all the girls
by sight, and a few who could speak English would hail me cheerfully
when we met in the street.

That unfortunate experience was all my own fault. It happened that
one evening after dinner, while I was still living in the hotel, I had nothing to do, and I thought I'd walk down to the escort bureau to see Ying
Ping. When I arrived I realized, even before I went upstairs, that I might
be making a mistake. Before when I had called, by daylight, it was all
dull and quiet. I would go along Queen's Road, past the big market, until
I came to an open-front shop that sold toothbrushes and such odds and
ends. Next to this shop was a dark, narrow staircase up which I went,
past a sinister-looking dentist's office and on to the top floor, which was
the club. In the afternoon it was somnolent there. Old amahs shuffled
around with buckets, for there wasn't a drop of running water in the
building, nor any toilet. That condition was not unusual in Hong Kong.
Girls slept soundly on the beds and couches scattered about the long
room. They slept as they had fallen in the early morning, dressed in their
tinsel finery, their faces smudged with enamel. They slept in crowds,
piled on top of each other, anywhere, like kittens. About three or four

they would begin to wake, yawning and stretching. I watched with amusement as they dressed over again for the evening, for the wardrobe was communal and they pulled dresses out of drawers any old place, wearing anyone's that pleased them or happened to fit.

That night Queen's Road was jammed, though, with a different sort of crowd, not a shopping crowd but a lot of young men looking for pleasure or mischief. When I had climbed the staircase next to the toothbrush shop and entered the club I knew I had made a mistake in coming. Lights blazed over the room and a lot of men were crowded around the mah-jongg table with some of the girls, playing. Chinese playing mah-jongg make a terrific noise. It's not at all like the quiet ladylike games we used to have in the States. They try to be noisy. They slam the tiles on the bare table and shout their signals, and everyone screams with laughter. A girl was playing the "pip'a" and singing. I was blinded and deafened. Unfortunately my entrance caused a lot of commotion and Ying Ping spotted me and rushed over and made me sit down.

She was all dressed up, thick with paint and looking like a different woman. In the afternoon she was a spotty sort of slut, amiable-looking but not alluring. Now she was ready for action and none of the spots showed, and her hair had been greased and carefully arranged. The girls went to the beauty parlor every evening to be combed afresh on contract, ten cents a time.

We sat halfway down the corridor from the mah-jongg game, near the door, while I tried to think of a graceful way to get out. Suddenly the door blew open and two husky young men staggered in and started down the hall toward the mah-jongg table. One of them glanced at me, paused, went on, and then turned around and came back. He tossed an apple in my lap.

"Hello," he said in pleased surprise. Then he spoke in Cantonese, and when I blinked at him uncomprehendingly he turned back to English. He reached out and grabbed my hand and pulled me to my feet, saying, "Come on and have a drink."

There was great consternation among the little girls. They fluttered around us like butterflies, explaining to him that I was not part of the club, but a client like himself. He didn't quite understand, naturally, but after a bit he apologized, sat down, and made polite conversation. I got out soon, though, without any more protest from Ying Ping, and hurried home to the Gloucester. I never again went back after dinner to the club.

Agnes Smedley was in Hong Kong. After some years of wandering about with the guerrillas, working in a semiofficial capacity with Dr.

Robert Lim for the Chinese Red Cross, her health forced her to come
back into civilization. Here and there I had run into Agnes quite often in
the course of five years. When I first met her it was in Shanghai. She was
living then in a self-chosen prison, occupying a miserable little cell high
up in a Chinese house near Mme. Sun, for whom she was doing a sort of
secretarial job. She lived in seclusion partly because she had her own
reasons, considering the affiliations she then had, and partly because
Mme. Sun has even more than her share of the Soong passion for mysterious privacy, alternating with a passion for publicity for her "causes."
I think of Agnes necessarily in terms of phases, because our acquaintance
has always been interrupted by long periods during which she changed
greatly. That first time I was introduced to her I think she was in an
unhappy phase; she looked like a tortured person and her face was
heavily lined. I know, too, that she must have been pitifully poor, for
she was thin and very shabby. The woman who introduced us was actually surprised that Agnes had any capacity for merriment.

"One day," she said, "Agnes turned up for a newspaperman's cocktail
party and she was actually dressed up, making jokes with one of the
men. I was never so surprised in all my life. She's usually so tragic and
sour."

When I think of that remark now I laugh very hard, because Agnes
is anything but sour, and when she is tragic I always suspect it's because
she is enjoying herself in that role. But at that time it was true. I didn't
see Agnes again for three or four years, and then I met her in Chungking
fairly often. Then she was feeling vigorous again, and happy. She was
working as she wanted to work, and for Bobby Lim, whom she adores.
Until now Agnes has always come to blows with the organizations with
which she was temporarily connected, usually on a point of principle.
A devil of discord drives her. In the case of the Red Cross, though she
has found plenty to disapprove of, she has so far swallowed her first
impulses to go and smash somebody in the nose unless that somebody
has happened to be opposed to the Red Cross, when, of course, she goes
to town, with a whoop of relief. Agnes likes a vigorous life.

She was laid up in hospital when I went to see her, looking most incongruous in a peach-colored satin nightgown that Hilda Selwyn-Clarke
had hastily bought for her. Agnes' head is a noble one, but it goes better
with a Roman toga or a bishop's surplice than it does with hand-
embroidered lingerie. (The toga is my own idea, but Agnes has been
seen and even photographed in the bishop's outfit. That, however, is a
story that happened much later.) I found her entertaining her friend
Dr. Eva Ho, whose full name is Ho-tung and who is an M.D. and the

daughter of old Sir Robert Ho-tung. A lot of women are daughters of Sir Robert, but nobody else is an M.D. or much like Eva in any respect. She was wearing navy slacks that afternoon and talking about her coming trip to Kweiyang. Agnes was trying to keep her mind on the subject, but she broke off to chuckle.

"I've met an amusing man," she announced. "The government doctor who examined me. He tells me that I have a simply *fascinating* gall bladder."

There was prevalent in government circles an uneasy feeling that Hong Kong should not be too hospitable to Agnes Smedley. The Peakites felt that she was a dangerous woman. They weren't sure in what way, but all those Reds and anarchists, they agreed, were best left alone. The police had been on the case, and only the fact that Agnes was a close friend of Mrs. Selwyn-Clarke, wife of the director of medical services, saved her from being requested to leave before her gall bladder could be attended to. Agnes had promised not to make any public speeches or otherwise disturb the peace of the Colony, and now she was being left more or less alone.

Her patron, Hilda Selwyn-Clarke, was another source of uneasiness to the old guard. I had heard of her for years from Freda Utley and from other people who had encountered her in Hankow, and I had not forgotten her name. One doesn't forget anybody who stands out so remarkably in her community as Hilda did. I have already spoken of how the rank and file of my acquaintances remained peacefully unaware that China existed. Hilda was completely different. She worked hard for several Chinese organizations and was secretary even then for Mme. Sun, in the China Defense League. Corin hated her.

"I've been introduced to her three times and she still doesn't recognize me," said Corin. I kept this in mind the third time I was introduced to Hilda, and gave her back a walleyed, oblivious stare to match her own. Also I gravely accepted the introduction as though it had never before taken place. Hilda looked startled. Months later she explained: "Mme. Sun had told me never to get intimate with you," she said. "She was suspicious of your politics and thought you might spy on the League. Which is ridiculous. But at the time, of course, I tried to obey her. It was Agnes who laughed me out of it."

They called Hilda, inevitably, "Red Hilda." She had red hair and was a member of the Socialist Party, which in Hong Kong was understood to be dangerously radical. She mixed into politics, too, and with her husband tried to reform things. Dr. Selwyn-Clarke was a man who was feared and usually disliked in the Colony. I heard of him a lot before I met him. I was always seeing his name in the paper, and hearing of him. The Peak called him "Septic." The British are always giving nicknames, as you know. I wonder why they didn't nickname the Selwyn-Clarke child while they were at it—but then she wasn't in the papers as much as her parents. Selwyn in those days meant nothing to me but the man who was all mixed up in a local battle about night soil. That is an interesting bit of history which I had better describe.

The Chinese have certain habits in farming which are not our habits, and one of them is that of using human excrement for fertilizer. Selwyn once explained to me that this system isn't as dangerous as we used to think it. He didn't seem to think that the dysentery and cholera of the Colony owed its prevalence to the use of that kind of fertilizer as much as it did to flies and careless preparation of food, though he was still fiercely opposed to the use of uncooked food in any form. Anyway, the drainage system of Hong Kong owed a lot to this custom of the natives. The job of carrying the city sewage out of our ken was done by a certain guild of coolies, and just about the time I arrived in Hong Kong there had been a reshuffle of the city contracts. Another guild had been given the commission. The local name for excrement of that sort is "night soil," and you had to know it to understand the newspaper stories of the ensuing argument.

M. K. Lo was a local lawyer, prominent in his own right and a member of a prominent family. The Los are related by marriage to the Ho-tungs and like the Ho-tungs are of mixed blood. Also like the Ho-tungs, there are many of them. M.K. in the night-soil quarrel was against Selwyn's faction, and though I don't know the ins and outs of the fight, you can take my word for it that the town was rocking with it. One day I was walking downtown, strolling along easily, and as I neared Government House I found myself inextricably mixed in a procession of black-clad women and shouting men, carrying banners. It was impossible to get away from the parade. When I crossed the street, so did they. When I took to the middle of the road, so did they. I didn't shake them until we reached Government House, when they turned off to make a demonstration before the gate in protest, and then I realized that I had been implicated in a parade of the Night Soil Coolie Carriers.

All of these bits of publicity made me interested in the Selwyn-Clarke family. When Agnes got well enough to come out of hospital she took up residence in the house of her new but excellent friend, Ronald, Bishop Hall of Hong Kong. (Hall was known as another dangerous radical.) The bishop had a country house out in Shatin, a small town on the New

Territories road to Taipo at the border, over on the mainland. Theoretically Agnes was supposed to live out there, but of course she came to town quite a lot, and then she divided her time between the Selwyn-Clarke house and mine. She insisted that Hilda and I become friends, and as a matter of fact we very quickly did.

Agnes liked Charles. She had heard of him from Freda Utley before, and was already prejudiced in his favor. I had been rather careful of talking about my private project, but I did tell Agnes, and she had a suggestion to make.

"Hilda knows all the medical men in town," she said. "If you think there's some reason you can't have this child, why not be examined? Yes, I know it's difficult under the circumstances, but Hilda will know what to do. I'll talk to her."

Hilda did know what to do, but she wasn't sure she ought to do it.

"Gordon King's your man," she said immediately. "I'm sure he'll know what the trouble is. I went through all that myself, you know, before I married. But, Mickey, are you quite sure? Think it over again. There seems to be a period that all of us professional women go through, in the middle thirties, when we want children before it's too late. But have you considered what a problem the child will be in your work? Are you sure this isn't simply an emotional urge that will pass?"

"My work," I scoffed. "I don't think that is cosmically important, do you? Yes, I'm sure."

So Hilda made an appointment for me with the doctor.

Chapter 32

NONE OF IT could have been done, I realize now, without Hilda's help. Although she was mildly radical, she had all the power of the most conventional of British women in a colony because of her husband's position. The Governor, Sir Geoffrey Northcote, liked Hilda and admired her, and after he left he probably recommended her to the attention of the acting governor, Norton, who was there when I arrived. Hilda was the highest "ranking" wife still in town, as no officials higher in rank than Selwyn kept their wives with them after the evacuation. I've explained how that all came to pass. A lot of men were now very bitter with Selwyn. They felt that a good Englishman, even if he didn't agree in principle with the evacuation, should follow the crowd and thus, paraoxically speaking, set an example. The rank and file of England always eel like this and I don't see it, but never mind. I heard lots of criticism f Selwyn and Hilda. They didn't understand their man at all. If Selwyn ad merely wanted to keep his family there for himself he would un-loubtedly have sent them away. He castigated himself constantly. He led uch an inhuman life of intense work that he wasn't aware of their exist-nce, personally, at all. There had been a time, Hilda told me, when he nade an effort to remain in contact with his little girl, Mary, but by the ime I arrived even that indulgence was slipping into desuetude, and he vas beginning to skip their Sundays together.

Selwyn kept his wife and child there because he felt that Hilda could do some good" with her Chinese affiliations. Also, like Charles, he felt trongly that the British should not whisk their own families away just ecause it was in their power, and leave the Asiatics to face the music ecause it was not in theirs.

"We get these people into a mess," Charles said once, emphatically, we set ourselves up to govern them and we get them into a war, and hen we take away our own women and leave them to deal with the ituation. No! I don't like it. If you were my wife, Mickey, you'd have o go. That happens to be Army regulations and hasn't anything to do vith the case and I'd have no choice. But as it is, we're fortunate, and you an do as you like."

Without Hilda I wouldn't have dared interview Professor King. He vas the best gynecologist, perhaps, on the Coast, but he had in his past een a missionary. When I first interviewed him I was thankful that Iilda had broken the ice in advance. A tall, lean man, he gave an im-ression of utter dryness. He was compounded, it seemed to me, of equal arts of principle and professional technique, and only an interesting ngle to his work, or a chance to play the piano undisturbed, could stir im to enthusiasm. He inspired confidence, but he was not a man you ould get gushy with. I told him that I wanted a child and that I doubted iy ability to conceive. I gave him my reasons, and whatever medical pinions I had collected on the subject in the past.

"You are married?" he asked.

Now was the moment. I said simply, "No." I had meant to say much tore, but that was before I saw him. This word was enough.

"You intend to be?" he asked. Then, swiftly, so that I wouldn't have answer, he started his examination. At the conclusion he said, "I can't e anything wrong with you at all. On preliminary examination there ems to be no reason why you shouldn't conceive. I suggest a small peration." He described it.

"Does it often work?"

"In twenty per cent of the cases it works."

I came home feeling hopeful, but something happened about then tha disturbed me. Charles had written his wife as soon as we decided tha I was not going back to America. He told her that we were living to gether, and asked for a divorce. Now Ursula's reply had arrived: sh refused to divorce him.

I looked at Charles in alarm. "You think she'll come back?" I de manded.

He looked uncertain, and I realized that he was very much afraid o her himself. "I hope not," he admitted, "but she may work it. We'll trus to the government. Don't worry."

So now, faced with such a threat, we were both glum. Charles foresaw the old regime of conversational breakfasts and a wife who refused t speak to him if he overdid it at a cocktail party. I drew unpleasant pic tures in my mind of lonely evenings during the ordeal of the take-over And the baby. What of the baby?

"Oh, don't worry," said Charles. "I didn't mean to worry you. We g on as before."

Up in Shanghai, my friend who had taken Mills was getting franti with the gibbon problem. He had a strong disinclination to bring tw gibbons (the new female had died) into his apartment in town. Just a the last possible moment he found an Australian lady, a soldier's wife who was being sent down to Australia for the duration. She agreed t chaperon the animals on the ship, and he joyously loaded them aboar in the required crate and hurried away to send me a wire.

I smile tenderly as I remember the sunny morning they arrived. On of the CNAC pilots, Woody, the man who let me pilot the plane from Chungking, had said that he wanted the gibbons. Because he lived i Kowloon and seemed eager to keep them, and because I didn't quit know how to keep them with me, I agreed to give them away.

Woody was so enthusiastic that he came with me to meet the boat It was anchored in mid-harbor, and we had to hire a motorboat to get ou to it. We were late arriving, too, and the Australian lady who had kept a eye on the gibbons was fretfully pacing the deck, anxious to hand ove her charges and rush to town on a shopping tour. We approached th ship, bouncing over the bright blue water, under the bright blue sky. saw her at long distance hiking up and down. I climbed out to the pro of our launch and waved wildly. The plump figure hesitated; you coul see hope stiffening her frame as she watched us coming. She pointed questioningly aft, where I saw the crate. I nodded vigorously. She slumped in enormous relief and crossed herself just as we approached the companionway.

"Oh!" was her greeting, in a burst of relieved sigh. "What a time we've all had! I tried to take 'em out for exercise, but I was always so afraid they would escape, you know. . . . Junior did, once, and got into the galley, and we had such a time catching him, you can't think. Here you are; here's Bybie's clothes." She handed me the diminutive leather trunk that held the entire gibbon wardrobe. "And God bless," she said. "I'm off to the shops."

It was a highly emotional moment for me when I stooped down before the cage and looked in. Gravely, my Mr. Mills looked out at me. At first I meant nothing to him, though he stuck out a tentative hand and pulled my skirt, just for the devil of it. After all, it had been more than a year since I saw him.

"Mills," I said. "Mills, old boy."

My voice did it. Recognition spread slowly over his face. He made no outcry, but he began to bounce up and down, and when I opened the door he walked out straight into my arms and cuddled down. It was perfect happiness. . . .

"The little guy," said Woody, "has escaped."

And so he had. A small, wiry, black beast with a white forehead, Junior was now going hand over hand toward an upper deck.

"Hold on," I said to Woody, "he'll come back. Look." Gripping Mills, I climbed down the companionway to the launch, and Junior followed, and grabbed Woody and clung to him. Somebody handed down the evil-smelling crate after us. Mills looked around the little walla-walla and didn't like it. He let go of me suddenly and crawled back into the crate. If he had been able to close the door after him he would have done so. Junior followed, and so we got them home.

But I see that the Freudian censor has intervened. I haven't mentioned the fact that both of them, in the excitement of the moment, had dirtied us pretty thoroughly first. It was this fact, which seemed trivial to me at the time, that decided Woody definitely against adopting any gibbons, and without argument he helped me take the crate and the animals straight to something known as the Dogs' Home, over in Kowloon at the town's edge. I walked into the place blind, myself. I didn't know, then, that I had made an important choice. The society vet was a Mrs. Hogg, on the Hong Kong side. It was Mrs. Hogg who usually clipped wire-hairs in the spring, and de-ticked the toes of spaniels and so forth for the Peakites. Mrs. Loseby ran the Dogs' Home in Kowloon, but free. Mrs. Loseby did it for the Blue Cross (SPCA) and for love of animals. Mrs. Loseby was much aware of the fact that she wasn't an accredited vet. I didn't know that, nor did I care, but if I had known a few things about the situation in general I would never, never have called her Mrs. Hogg—which I did, alas.

Mrs. Loseby was a very fat, very pink woman, and very English. She bristled first when she heard my American accent, and she bristled second when I called her "Mrs. Hogg," and she bristled most of all when she realized that even Woody was a Yank. It looked like a thin time for the gibbons, until she saw them. Then, being English, she fell in love with them.

"Oh, the beautiful!" she cried. I beamed, and Woody rubbed at the spots on his coat and muttered under his breath. Mrs. Loseby now thawed. She explained that she was used to much more difficult propositions; she often put up giant pandas en route for the U.S.A. She hastily cleaned out a large cage and we put the gibbons in, and they went sailing happily around, and it was all highly satisfactory. Especially to Woody, who would not now have to take them home and lock them in his garage, as had been his misled intention. I shook hands with him and thanked him warmly, and said good-by, practically forever, and went home to take a bath.

Next day when I took Charles to see the gibbons we found a large sign on the gate of the Dogs' Home: BELL OUT OF ORDER: PLEASE KNOCK. Mrs. Loseby hurried to open to us.

"They fused all the wiring in the place, the pets," she said fondly.

On his first introduction to them, I watched Charles anxiously. How was he going to react? Would he crab the whole show? Quietly, with the corners of his mouth soberly downturned, Charles sauntered into the cage and let Mills swing over and sit on his head. In a moment he was scratching Junior's stomach, still very soberly, but I knew it was going to be all right.

"I dare say," he remarked on the way home, "they're as good an imitation as you could find."

Although I was never told what he did, Charles went on being busier and busier, along with the rest of his office. They now embarked on a series of dinners that were something new, I think, in Hong Kong government circles: they were given in honor of various Chinese dignitaries but they weren't dignified. One, for example, was for Admiral Chan

Chak, known as the héro of Bocca Tigris. Chan Chak was working for the British, I found out later, with the approval of Chungking, and he was the most important Chinese in town, so far as Charles was concerned. But he didn't speak much English and Charles had no Chinese, and so I was a welcome addition to the party. It was given at one of the big restaurants, the Golden Dragon. We all drank a lot and had a good time, and I found myself talking raptly with young Cooper about Irish poetry.

Cooper the poet. He looked just like one; he was young enough not to mind that. He was about twenty-five; he had a long, sorrowful face and a deep Irish voice, and he really didn't give much of a damn about anything but words. He was fluent in Icelandic and Swedish, "and so," as Charles would say blithely, "he was sent to Singapore." Now he was in Hong Kong, as a sort of exchange for Alf Bennett, who was going south soon. Cooper was also getting pretty good in Cantonese and Japanese. Already he knew more Chinese characters than I did. He wrote poetry and jingles, pottered about with his languages, did a lot of mysterious work for Charles's office, and looked exceedingly pained, not to say dignified, when Charles accused him of being a genius. He had a house way out in Shatin near the bishop's house where Agnes Smedley was staying, and he ran a fantastically old Rolls-Royce which used too much gasoline.

In October of that year came the Chinese Moon Festival. On one night the moon was biggest of all the year round, and Cooper gave a moon-gazing party and invited some of the Chinese intelligentsia, Charles and me. The house in Shatin was glaringly new, white stucco, a Chinese country villa built on foreign lines. Cooper had rented it from a Chinese, without noticing that the plaster was still damp, and though he had been in it for some weeks it still looked unoccupied. We had a Chinese dinner that was rankly bad, and Charles criticized Cooper loudly all through the meal for having had the cheek to do such a thing when he was inviting Chinese guests. Cooper didn't seem to care, even when he committed the *gaffe* of serving the rice wine unheated. We all howled lustily at that, and made the servant take it out and warm it up. I remember—I remember a Siamese kitten on the table, wandering about and eating what it wanted. I remember how we sat in the garden afterward and looked obediently, according to tradition, at the great orange moon that hung like a stage prop or a ripe fig in the sky. I talked about poetry with Chuan Tsen-kuo; for many happy years in China, by that time, I had talked about poetry with Chuan Tsen-kuo. I remember that

I was feeling warm and quiet because I had written a poem to hand to Charles after dinner, where he read it in the light of the moon.

> In mirrors, lakes, and in a lover's eyes
> We seek our lonely being, and this is love;
> This and this only. Poetry and flowers,
> Music and moons, the sweet swift pace of hours
> At night, all frame self-portraits, all are lies,
> The tissue of that famous velvet glove.
>
> Narcissus died of self-desire, not knowing
> The secret of our love, the vital breath.
> We needs must live upon each other, growing
> On that reflection, self-reflection glowing
> In lovers' eyes, or love must come to death.
>
> Then must I die? In fright my blood is flowing.
>
> Within your eyes law fails, the word's untrue.
> I cannot see myself, but only you.

Then, walking back along the Shatin road in the white dust, in the white light, the green night, we strode swiftly down the hill ahead of the others, crunch, crunch, crunch in the silence, saying nothing.

Chapter 33

CHRISTMAS was riotous that year. Charles and I always invited everybody to our parties, and accepted practically all the invitations that came along. Later Charles usually grew more sober about the outside parties, but he never regretted or reneged on his own—or on mine. One time he stampeded my flat with the entire personnel of a large drunken stag cocktail party, at eleven in the evening. For Christmas Eve we blithely made three dates, which we didn't discover until it was time to sort things out and compare notes.

Never mind. We decided to do them all, pausing only to settle on one house for dinner, so that we could notify the other hostesses in time.

"If you don't mind," I said hesitantly, "I thought we might eat dinner at Vi Chan's. I'll tell you why. I know Vi is sort of fantastic, but I'm fond of her sister Anne. Now Anne has gone and divorced her husband and married Hubert Chen, which shocks all the old-fashioned people in her set, and she feels her position. If you and I went there to dinner——"

"I can't keep track of all these Asiatic scandals," said Charles amiably. "It's okay by me, baby. I don't see just why *we* should make her feel any more acceptable socially, but——"

"Just so she won't feel everybody is letting her down," I said sentimentally.

We started out on Christmas Eve with the best of intentions, as you can see. I was still doing my face, the amah dithering around behind my chair, when Charles came stamping in with Cooper in close attendance. "I brought old Snooper in for a drink," he announced, and he called Ah King and ordered old-fashioneds. "We have time for one or two." Everyone, as usual, was in the bedroom while I finished my toilette. Everyone always is. Sometimes I wonder, a little fretfully, why. I think I inherit the tendency from Sinmay's household. After one old-fashioned Billie Lee dropped in to leave her Christmas gift, and Charles wouldn't let her go again. We had another one all around. Charles wouldn't let anybody go by that time. He wouldn't even let me go to Vi's house. By nine or ten o'clock he had decided that we could take Cooper and Billie with us to Vi's.

"Of course there'll be room," he scoffed. "You can always add another bowl of rice to a Chinese dinner, can't you? Old Vi'll be *glad* to have Snooper and Billie."

"Of course," I said cheerfully. It all seemed perfectly logical. So there we were; me in long black lace, Charles in his mess jacket, Cooper in filthy tweeds, and Billie still dressed for the office, trooping into an absolutely frigid Chinese drawing room, hours after dinner should have been served.

Vi Chan has always taken her position merrily, but seriously *au fond*. Somebody else will have to write her story because I haven't the room here, but it must be done. I dare not say how old she is, but she doesn't look it. With an entire family (and in Cantonese circles that is saying something) she had managed, for years, to live on the forbidden Peak territory in a huge house which looked surprised at itself, and with reason. There was a swimming pool, a tennis court, a Victorian-British exterior, and then you stepped indoors, into a mass of teakwood and Chinese screens and this and that, with Vi waiting to greet you all dressed up, usually in Western evening dress, and always with a large bright flower in her hair. Usually there were Westerners at her parties, with a large preponderance of American Navy men. Tonight, though, she had evidently planned just the one thing I would never expect of Vi, a small *intime* affair. And, boy, was she mad!

Chinese dinners take place at seven at the latest. They are planned with an eye to the size of the table, too. You have tables for eight, tables for six, tables for four, but you can't very well have tables for more than twelve, because then the circle is so large that the guests on the diameter can't reach to the dishes with their chopsticks. If you want more than twelve you just set another table and dish your food out twice. Vi had planned a table of six. And there we were, with two extra strangers, and a couple of hours late in the bargain.

If it had been me I wouldn't have noticed, because I am an American barbarian; Vi was near enough to being a similar character to be all right on her own, but there was that complication of Anne and Hubert, who were sensitive anyway. The family elected to feel insulted. And so, save for Charles's happy and oblivious chatter, the meal progressed in stately silence. Billie was quiet as always, sitting there showing her dimples and unaware anything was wrong, and Cooper had sunk, as usual, into a philological coma. It wasn't the jolliest Christmas dinner I have ever eaten. We got out before midnight and traveled on to the next place, where we thawed out.

The evening ended at a typical bright young colonial party, with discreet flirtations everywhere, sleek, beautiful women and dashing young men in uniform, all being incredibly childish, so it seemed to me, and playing charades. I can't romp the way they do. Or maybe I can. I put up a pretty good imitation that winter. I used to work hard at it in a quiet way. At the beginning of my Hong Kong residence it was never comfortable when I went to one of those parties, for anybody. Only the outstanding bad hats, the people known unfavorably as "crackers" or "intelligent" or something like that, were at ease with me. The others, the pretty blonde girls, the gallant young men, had a way of backing into corners and staring at me rather like rabbits at a tigress. But all that passed, because they were kindly young people really, and bored, and because the British are easier and more tolerant of eccentricity than are most people, and because, anyway, I had begun to develop an assurance that was to come in handy. We played our charades, we drank at the funny little bar, we giggled, we saw Christmas in. Half the men I remember that night, horsing around, are dead, and the girls are standing in line at Stanley with cup in hand, waiting for a handout of thin rice stew. Does that sound banal? It isn't. It hits me sometimes like a slap in the face. It has no implications; I'm not moved to philosophy when this happens, but there it is. It dazes me.

It shouldn't amaze me as much as all that. Charles, standing behind his barbed-wire fence in Argyle Camp, is not being dazed; I'm sure of it.

He kept telling me in his off-guard moments. There was one afternoon when he dropped in after a walk. Sometimes when he had the time after work he would change his clothes and go striding up to the Peak and down again at a pace nobody else could keep up, and he stopped in on the road down for a glass of beer. One evening he said:

"You'd better go away. If you're having a baby you won't be able to run very fast, will you?"

"Run from what?"

"The theory is that it would be the maddened populace, before ever the Japanese got in. Personally I believe that if the Sikhs were first there wouldn't be much left of any of you, even for the Chinese. But that's only my own idea." He added, as he always added, "But it's entirely up to you of course. . . ."

I said impatiently, "Darling, the whole world's going to hell anyway. Suppose I go now; it may catch me wherever I am. Let's take whatever time we have left right here. I like Hong Kong."

He looked at his beer and said, "All right. It's up to you."

"Did you read," I asked brightly, "in that book of yours—Rowland-son—about the British and what they did to the Indians after the mas-sacre of the Englishwomen, during the revolution? They made them lick up the blood in the roads."

"Yes," said Charles, "I read it."

On Saturday afternoon we would go to the Dogs' Home and take the gibbons out into the country and let them play. It was a long way from home, though, and we couldn't well afford the time entailed in getting the car across on the ferry to Kowloon. My flat had the usual Hong Kong veranda, and I decided to fence it in with chicken wire and take the gibbons home. Charles was amazingly amenable to the whole thing. He liked them. He always said that he wouldn't have them in his own house for a million pounds, but he liked them at my flat.

Familiar trouble started immediately. Now and then one of them would get out and roam around the neighborhood, scaring people. When we went to the bathing beaches it wasn't so bad, because nobody but ourselves went swimming in the winter and we had the place to play around in without interference most of the time. I must admit that there was rather a contretemps on New Year's Day. It was cold and foggy, but we packed a lunch basket with picnic food nevertheless, and took the gibbons and Cooper out to Middle Beach. Unfortunately a Chinese party was going on in one of the shacks on the hillside, and Mills was attracted by the noise and gaiety, and he went up to investigate.

I suppose I didn't realize that Mills was getting to be quite a big boy. He weighed about thirty pounds and stood as tall as a six-year-old, and when you're not used to gibbons it might be a little startling to have one drop playfully on your shoulders as you're taking a quiet walk by the sea. I mean, I can realize that now. At the time I was just intolerant, I suppose. That afternoon, for example, I considered it definitely unreasonable of the Chinese party to object to Mills's presence in their house, or, to be absolutely factual, on their roof peeking in here and there. I watched with impatient disdain when the party closed the doors and the windows and then sat there in what must have been a very stuffy bungalow, screaming for help.

"Oh, go and get him," I snapped at Cooper. "Tell him lunch is ready. Those *idiots*. . . . Really, the Chinese have no talent for animals, have they?"

Charles ate a whole tomato sandwich at a gulp. "I," he said, "have nothing to do with this at all. I wash my hands of it. Go and get him, Snooper."

Cooper said mournfully, "I don't see why it's always me." But he started up the hill toward that vociferous bungalow. Mills, on the roof, yawned and scratched himself under the left armpit. We lay out in the pale sunlight, comfortable on the sand, and waited.

"Who do you suppose keeps those awful monkeys?" asked Charles lazily.

After a while the yapping on the hillside stopped, and a while later Mills loped up to me, saying, "Oop, oop."

"They were angry," reported Cooper. "One of them yelled, 'Your monkey is trying to rape these girls!' I borrowed a leaf from your book, Mickey, and replied with all the dignity I could muster, 'It's not a monkey, it's an ape.'"

"What utter rot," I snorted. "Did they *look* at him? Anybody who could be raped by Mills rapes awful easy."

"The Chinese are going away," said Charles.

"Let them," I said. "We don't want 'em, do we, Mills?"

"Junior is lost," said Cooper dispassionately.

It took us two hours to find Junior.

It was on the cards that Charles should go to Singapore. He had had a narrow escape once about Christmas time, but the general decided at the last minute to put the trip off. Charles for his own secret reasons was to go down to Singapore and consult with the military authorities there. We learned about it definitely in February; he was to go in March

"I don't like it," I said.

"I hate it," said Charles. "But I'll have to face her sooner or later."

We had a birthday party for Charles at Mme. Kung's, and Cooper asked me to marry him. It was nice of him, because I was feeling increasingly ill, and very much worried about Singapore.

"Don't you let him go down there," said Agnes Smedley.

I couldn't very well help it. The general had told Charles to go, and of course he had to face Ursula sooner or later, anyway. But I couldn't marry Cooper, certainly not, just at that time. I explained to him.

"I don't think you are," he said. "You're just nervous. If you've never had a baby before, why should you be having one now?"

"But I don't feel well. Not at all."

"You're nervous," said Cooper. Charles had left us his car to use in his absence, and we drove out into the country and watched the working sea, and talked about poetry and Cooper. "I ought to be married," he explained. "Obviously, somebody should take care of me. That's why it doesn't matter that you are older. It would be that sort of relationship with anyone."

"But——" I stopped. I didn't want to say outright that the prospect of taking care of a genius did not attract me. Besides, I felt a bit insulted. "Why," I said to myself, *"I'm* sort of a genius myself. *I'm* entitled to a nurse or mamma too." Not that I wasn't very fond of Cooper; I was. We always had much more to talk about than Charles and I did. Charles noticed it himself.

The days went on. I taught school and felt sick. It wasn't the way I should have felt sick, though; I was sick all the time, but never very much. I didn't want to eat. Cooper practically moved into the guest room and took very good care of me. I didn't hear from Charles. We had agreed that we wouldn't write, under the circumstances, but I regretted that. I found another gibbon, a dainty little female one, and I bought her and brought her home. Then Cooper and I found yet another one, very small and charming, like Mills in his youth. We named it Tertius and it was Cooper's darling. He carried it everywhere, to the office and to the beach and into the Grips, hidden under his coat. He wrote poems about the gibbons, all of them lost now but the ones I can remember.

There was one about an afternoon we had spent at Repulse Bay with Chinese friends:

> They went to Mr. Quock's for tea.
> Junior was one, the other Mills,
> Two gibbons quite well known to me.

> *Because we thought they'd like a spree,*
> *Believing boredom almost kills,*
> *They went to Mr. Quock's for tea.*
>
> *How quickly they dispelled ennui*
> *And made the guests forget their ills!*
> *Two gibbons quite well known to me.*
>
> *Chatter of wars, finance, T.V.,*
> *Gave way to far less distant thrills.*
> *They went to Mr. Quock's for tea.*
>
> *They swung among the crockery*
> *And thought them in their native hills.*
> *They went to Mr. Quock's for tea,*
> *Two gibbons quite well known to me.*

The house turned into a small, exclusive zoo. There was nobody to keep us in hand but Ah King, and it was all beyond him. Gibbons wandered at will, and we read a crazy mixture of Donne, Joyce, the modern Americans, Edward Lear, and our own efforts. We didn't go to bed sometimes for a few days, and then we didn't get up for longer than that. It seems like a dream now. It was a dream, and not always a good one. There was a pain somewhere between my backbone and the wishbone in front, and I couldn't eat.

I wanted Charles.

Chapter 34

CHARLES CAME BACK just a month from the time he left. He had gone down by boat, then flown to Chungking and had a riotous week there with some of our old friends, but I didn't know that until he told me afterward. I just went on with Cooper, teaching school in a misty way and complaining about my back, or was it my chest? The day before he came back I went to Tony Dawson-Grove for an examination. Tony had an ulcer, and he decided that I had an ulcer too. Anyway, he said, it was probably the beginning of one. Then he examined me some more, and I realized from his expression that it wasn't my imagination after all.

I thought I would say it for him, because he was looking terrified. He is younger than I am. "I might possibly be pregnant," I said in an offhand tone.

There was a long chilly silence, and then he said, "You oughtn't do this to a man like Charles."

I bristled. "Why not?"

"And to yourself," said Tony hastily. "Have a cigarette. . . . You don't know this town, Mickey; I do. You can't. You'll have to go away."

I said, "What do you bet?"

We stared at each other. "I don't understand you," said Tony.

"I didn't mean to drag you into it," I said apologetically. "You'll have to check up with Gordon King. Have I really an ulcer, do you think?"

He brightened when he knew that Gordon King was in on it, but he held firmly to the ulcer. "You've been fretting over Charles's wife," he said, "and fretting helps an ulcer. I'm always much worse when I worry over my cases. I won't sleep a wink tonight," he added in angry tones. "It's early days to say definitely, anyway."

I dragged home, told Cooper, who was sulky about it, and went to bed. Charles arrived that night but didn't telephone me until morning, which was a plain indication of what had happened in Singapore, and I knew it. It was Ah King who gave me the news, straight from Master's own houseboy, that the major was back.

He called in the morning, crisp and cheerful. "Where the hell's my car?"

"Cooper should have sent you the keys last night," I said. "The car's down the road. We stopped putting it into the garage because Cooper kept locking the keys in with it."

"I'll drop in after work, shall I?"

"Yes. Oh, Cooper says, can he have the car this afternoon?"

Charles said, "Well, if he likes. . . . But doesn't he intend to do any work?"

"He's rather got into the habit of taking me around instead," I explained.

"I see. Well, I'll give him the keys before tiffin."

I went downtown after my lecture and had a hair-set. Then, feeling much better and dressed in new navy blue, I called for Charles at the office, complete with car and Cooper. He was undoubtedly pleased to see me. "I'll drive," he said, smiling. "Cooper, I think I'll take a walk and then stop in to see Mickey. When are *you* coming up?"

Cooper looked at me and I said, "Well, we ought to be through fighting about six-thirty. But telephone first."

He walked off into the crowd and we drove home. I chattered all the way, without asking that one question that had to be asked, and we duly separated at the bottom of the steps. Nothing could have been more admirably civilized, or sillier. I feel quite detached about it now, and I see that. Charles took his walk, and I changed into the housecoat he had given me for Christmas, and waited for him. And he came in, civilian-looking and sweaty in a blue shirt, and ordered beer, and we sat side by side on the sofa like the lady and gent that we were, and made conversation.

"And how's Ursula?"

"Oh, fine."

"Well?"

"Well . . ."

"Did you live with her?"

"Oh, of course I did," said Charles impatiently.

I looked down at my beer and tried to keep my lips still. "Well, what do you want to do?" I asked.

"It's up to you, Mickey."

"But it isn't. Not now."

We were both quiet. "She was perfectly furious," he began explaining. "She was going to have you kicked out of the Colony. I had to keep her quiet. Besides, she wanted to."

"She couldn't have me kicked out."

"I don't know. . . . I was afraid."

"Is she going to have a baby?"

"I don't know. She tried to. She didn't tell me that for some days. And then when I said, 'Do you think that's wise?' she said she wanted to have a little Frog anyway. . . . She always calls me Frog. Don't cry, Mickey. I love you much better than I do her. I told her so. She kept asking me, and I kept telling her."

I said, "Wait a minute," and went into the bedroom and lay down. I wasn't crying. That is the advantage of being older. I was just wondering what to do. I also felt pretty sick.

He looked miserable and badly frightened. Something had certainly happened to me in the years I spent in China, because I didn't get any satisfaction at all out of that. I have said I won't probe into Charles's motives and I will stand by that, but I'll go so far as to say that I think I know what it was, and why we felt so differently about the thing. He had just acted like one normal single person, taking the easier and pleasanter way. I was being two people, myself and the baby. I was thinking half the time like that unborn child, a fact that probably mystified him. We didn't quarrel. Charles and I never quarreled except once, after the surrender. We didn't quarrel, and we didn't talk about it endlessly, and I didn't even nag him—much. We couldn't talk any more that evening anyway, because Cooper came in and Charles went home. I told Cooper and said I had a bad headache. Naturally he blew up. He was righteously indignant. But I went to bed, and I slept.

There was to be a cocktail party the next evening. In the afternoon Charles invited another girl to come with us, swimming—and Cooper, of course; always Cooper. I had come to a decision. "We'll have to talk it over with him, Art," I said in the car. "We'll have to pin him down, to see what he wants. Just one talk."

"Certainly," said Cooper, and after Vera had been taken home, sunburnt and gritty with sand, he leaned forward to Charles in the driver's seat and said impressively, "Mickey and I wish to talk with you. With your permission we'll come into your place early this evening, before it's time for the party. Is that satisfactory?"

"Quite," said Charles. Later he told me that he said to himself, "This is it. They're going to be married. They'll announce it tonight."

So there we were, dressed up and ready for the party, except that Cooper was wearing Tertius, the youngest gibbon, firmly clinging to his shirt front all through the interview.

I have never actually seen a shotgun wedding, though I've made plenty of jokes about them, but that interview must have been exactly like one. I've laughed about it a lot since. At the time, though, I was feeling tragic. I don't know how Cooper felt; he looked like a Methodist minister. And Charles was airy as all hell. As if we were acting in a drawing-room comedy, we settled down in our chairs and ordered drinks with meticulous care, and made polite chatter. Then Charles said, "Well, shoot," and I said, "Well, what do you want to do about things?"

I really didn't know. He never talks about the way he feels; he's afraid to. I suppose if Cooper hadn't been there we never would have been able to talk it out, but Cooper was there, and taking the leading role. He cracked the whip. He asked questions. He made Charles talk, and he made me talk.

I said I couldn't go on just like that, having a baby that had been deserted. The fact that Charles was considering a permanent reconciliation with Ursula meant desertion, I said.

No, said Charles, no indeed; he was not considering a permanent reconciliation. I was wrong there, absolutely wrong. He had only gone back to her because she had wanted him to, and it seemed the easiest and simplest thing to do at the time.

But if she had a baby? I cut in crisply.

She wouldn't, he said. Anyway, what if she did? "I can afford two children," said Charles.

Cooper and I both gasped at that, and I started to object in strong terms, but Cooper now took the stage. Charles, he said accusingly, was being absolutely immoral in his attitude toward his wife. He didn't seem to care how he lied and wriggled, as long as he kept things pleasant for himself. He was being even less fair to her than to me, said Cooper. It was a point, and it hit Charles between the eyes.

"But I believe she really loves me," he said. "I didn't before, but——"

"Boooooo," said Cooper and I.

"You didn't tell her *I* was pregnant?" I demanded.

"No, because I wasn't sure. I——"

"Really, Charles."

We finished our drinks and ordered another round. "I'll admit I've done everything wrong," he said. "I went down there to clear things up and now they're worse than ever. I still think I managed her rather well; she was going to kick up a hell of a stink. As it is, things are quiet and pleasant. But you don't seem to understand. If what I've done is such a terrible crime, I can only suggest that you get even. Go off with somebody yourself. Go off with Cooper for a couple of weeks. I won't like it, but I can see it's only fair."

"You are incredible," said Cooper icily. "Do you really think we could live together while Mickey is having your baby?"

Charles blinked at him and took another draught of old-fashioned. Of course he hadn't really thought so.

"I have another suggestion," said Cooper. "Mickey, will you marry me?"

Well, naturally I loved that. So I said, "Yes."

"I've got to go down to Singapore soon," he resumed. "I've been transferred, and I can't put it off any longer. You will have to do something about the baby, if it's not too late—if it is, never mind; it will be considered as mine. Then you'll follow, and——"

"I'll have to get all sorts of permits, remember," I said, very much interested in the mechanics of the case. "Nowadays it isn't easy to get an entry permit into the colonies. It will take a few weeks. When do you think you're going?"

"In about a week. We're waiting for a boat——"

The forgotten Charles now cut in, and his voice was admirably light and casual. "The time and the place are matters of complete indifference to me," he remarked, "but what I would like to know——"

Nothing could have been more effective. There was an infinitesimal pause, and then we all roared with laughter. We laughed, and laughed, and laughed, and somehow everything was all right again. Then we went to the cocktail party.

"You used me, you know," said Cooper.

"Maybe," I admitted, "but I swear I didn't mean to. It all happened that way; I didn't plan it. Charles admits that all through the—the shotgun interview he was saying to himself, 'I won't let Cooper get away with it.' He didn't give me a thought; he says he just turned into a complete cad, and he was damned if he'd let you win out. So there you are. He's finally written Ursula everything, and he said that, no matter what, he won't ever live with her again. Well, that's that. She'll get tired in time."

Cooper thought it over. "You used me," he repeated, "but anyway, there is always Tertius."

"I'm too old for you anyway."

"You *are* ridiculous about that. . . . Charles is conceited, and childish, and he has no sense of responsibility, but one forgives him everything. That remark about the time and the place, you know. Sheer genius."

He sailed the day after, smuggling Tertius aboard against all the laws of the sea.

My agent sent word that the publishers had a new idea for the next book. They thought I might do a history of Singapore and of its founder, Raffles. Everything seemed propitious for such a work; the newspapers at home were playing up Singapore as the impregnable fortress on which the Far East depended to maintain the status quo, and there I was, almost on the spot, and well in training for another book on Asia. I liked it too. I had developed a fondness for historical research while doing *The Soong Sisters,* and the more I read of Sir Thomas Raffles the more I like him. He founded the Regent's Park Zoological Society, for one thing. He kept a gibbon, for another, and the gibbon's name was Mr. Silvio. The day I found that out I was so excited that I telephoned Charles at his office to tell him. The Hong Kong Club had a library that was a monument to Victoria, and although it wasn't the most stimulating collection of books in the world for a general public, it was full of what I needed. And Singapore itself—the history of Singapore is ninety per cent that of the Eurasians who make up the city. I had that fixed idea of the Eurasians in the Far East already in my mind, and it looked like the ideal chance to do something about it. I worked hard and happily on Raffles. By the time Pearl Harbor came along I was almost ready to start the book; all that remained was to go down to Singapore for a look around. But I'm anticipating.

The determined though well-bred silence on the part of the public was getting on our nerves. I had time to think all sorts of things, and though it was late in the day for that I did at last give some thought to Charles's career. I inquired around, discreetly. There were people in on the secret because we had told them; there was an old lawyer who had drawn up Charles's will in favor of the baby, and a few people like that. It seems that the British Army is more practical than you might think. Just at that moment the British Army needed Charles. We assumed that they would ultimately put things down on a record and talk it over after the war. Fair enough. In the meantime, "The general hasn't said a thing," said Charles.

One man in all the Far East could be depended on to be reasonable, and that was Sir Archibald Clark-Kerr. He came down into town just about that time, flying from his ambassadorial post in Chungking for some reason or other. We met for a drink at the Grips and I told him.

"Oh well," he said, "the general's a reasonable fellow. If things get too hot, come on up to the embassy in Chungking; we'll be glad to have you. By the way, things may get hot anyway, if the Japanese attack; please don't hesitate to come on up the minute it looks bad. You'd be better off even there—we have pretty good hospitals now."

"P. T. Chen's wife died of childbed fever in Chungking," I said.

"Yes, shocking thing. . . . But that's better than being bombed."

"It's a moot point, Sir Archie. Do you think Charles will get into bad trouble?"

"I doubt it. We need him too badly. I can't see any way out of this, Mickey, but war."

"Oh lordy."

"Oh lordy, indeed."

"How much does Jack tell you about his work?" I asked Vera Armstrong in the ladies' room. Jack Armstrong was Charles's regular attorney, who had taken care of his marriage settlement and who was now in his confidence about our baby. Jack was a perfect man for such work: he never said anything to anybody, though he chattered as lightly as the next man.

"He never tells me anything," said Vera crossly. She patted her hair and powdered her nose. Vera has red hair and eyes of different colors, one blue and one brown. Otherwise, too, she is out of the ordinary. She has a quick intelligence that was always stubbing its toe in Hong Kong. She didn't know what the trouble was, herself, but she was too high-geared for her friends. She has French blood and was born and brought up in Japan, and although she thought she was just another May Road matron, she wasn't. It made for trouble. "He never tells me anything, the rat," said Vera.

"Then you don't know I'm having a baby?" I asked.

Vera studied me, her eyes lightening with interest. "My dear! Well, now that you mention it, I did think you were letting yourself go rather shockingly. . . . How perfectly amazing."

"Not at all," I said stiffly.

"Well, I do think Jack might have said something. Oh, do let me help. Have you bought anything yet?" Vera has two children of her own.

"No, and I haven't the slightest idea how to go about it."

"I'll do it," said Vera. "Everybody will think I'm expecting again, but never mind. I say, this *is* one in the eye for old Ursula. We had the most frightful row on her wedding day—did Charles tell you?"

"No, he didn't. How fortunate! And will you really help me with the nappies and all that?"

"I'll go down to Kayamally's in the morning," said Vera. We un-locked the door and joined the gentlemen demurely.

Chapter 35

THIS PROGRAM was all intensely personal, and for the first time in many years I really shut China and the political situation out of my mind. I made gestures of keeping up with things. I read the papers, and the work on Singapore and Raffles kept me in touch, in a remote, his-torical sort of way, but in actuality I had slipped back into one woman's life, like the Chinese themselves, and I busied myself with my own thoughts and my own affairs. Even Agnes Smedley couldn't jounce me out of it. She was roughly sympathetic, in her own way, about the baby; she oversimplified the matter. "You take your child in your arms and tell 'em all to go to hell," she counseled me.

"But I don't have to, Agnes. They're not being mean. Everyone has been awfully nice, so far," I said. She stared at me, uncomprehending. The world to Agnes is full of dragons, familiar dragons which she is for-ever battling. A world of easygoing people just doesn't exist in her conception of things. She didn't worry about it, though. There would come a time, she knew, when I would need a champion, and then she could do her job.

Agnes carried with her, always, an atmosphere of tenseness. It could be as calm and gentle out of doors as anything, and yet when she came in you thought of blowing winds and flying sleet and snow, and clouds whizzing past the mountaintops. One evening I was sitting peacefully at my desk, and I'll swear it was as sweet a spring evening as you'll find anywhere along the Pacific. Then suddenly the door burst open and Agnes stamped in, frowning. She shook snowflakes off her sturdy shoulders. I could almost hear the stamp of the horse outside and smell the sweaty saddle leather, and the frosty pine needles that they had bruised in their headlong flight. . . . "I've brought a chicken for you," growled Agnes.

"I'll have to tell Mme. Kung," I said to Charles. "I'll have to tell her before she can see for herself too. I tell you what: *you'd* better tell her. She likes you, I think."

"I won't," said Charles flatly. "I'm afraid."

"So am I. I don't see why you need be so mean about it."

It stayed like that until one afternoon when I was in her car, taking a ride with her. She was busy in her own way, but she felt imprisoned sometimes and then she just went out and told the chauffeur to drive around the island, while she sat well back in the deep car so nobody could see her. Sometimes she asked me to come along, and this was one of the times. It was difficult, but I told her.

Her reaction was typical. There was a little silence, while I held on to her hand firmly, possibly for fear she would slap me, and she stared straight ahead at the back of the chauffeur's head. Suddenly she giggled. I dropped her hand and turned around to look at her. She giggled like a little girl.

"My sister," she said, "will be *furious* with me."

Then she scolded me, gently. She scolded me like a Christian and a law-abiding woman. She told me that she had always defended me when people said I wasn't a good girl.

She then lapsed into deep thought, and I interrupted it. "I think we'd better cut this off," I said. "Being my friend after a bit will be embarrassing for you. Don't you think so?"

No, she didn't think so. She then dropped all of that, and started giving me medical advice. There was a certain tea which I must drink a good deal of. I must try to develop some sort of religion; nobody should have a baby, she said, without God to help. (Madame is practical.) Was there any chance that Charles's wife would let him go? We discussed that, in a sensible hardheaded manner, until it was time to go home. I'll swear I don't know yet if she was thoroughly horrified or if she didn't get just a bit of a kick out of it. Anyway, she was thoroughly kind, of course, and from then on she managed to send encouraging messages and strengthening food whenever she had a chance. Also she cautioned me against thinking of Ursula or getting upset at all. "You may regret it all your life if you hurt yourself now," she said.

"She's right," said Charles heartily.

But my mind did start working for me. I suppose that sort of thing always happens. Sometimes at night when my back kept me awake I lay there and wanted my mother. I wasn't unhappy, but I did want my mother. Just the same, I couldn't very well have her. I couldn't even tell her. Agnes was preparing to go to the States, because she smelled the war coming and she didn't want the Japs to catch her, and it wasn't propitious to go back into China just then. I asked her to carry the word to my sister. I didn't dare write this direct because Hong Kong was an inconveniently chummy little town, and the censors were all women I knew intimately. Of course they would have to know later, anyway, but I didn't feel like announcing it just that way. What I said to my sister, I felt, was nobody's business.

The appearance of *The Soong Sisters* in the middle of all this was sufficiently exciting, but my first enthusiasm was a little damped when I looked at the advance copy that was sent me. The embossed Soong character on the cover was upside down. It was a natural thing to happen in America, but it was unfortunate, because it could mean awfully bad luck to the Chinese mind. I sent a frantic cable to the publishers, and everyone scurried around to put it right, and there was a sarcastic little mention of it in the local sheet, and that was that. Later reports of the book's success came pouring in. Charles was proud and I was proud, and everything was fine.

"I read it all last night," he said one day, "and I must say, it wasn't as bad as I'd expected. Clever girl, Mickey."

We waited and waited, and still nobody said a word. We got so nervous at last that we resolved to give a reward to the first member of the general public who said anything about it; a box of cigars if it was a man, and a box of chocolates to a lady. Soon after this—and I think it was well on to the end of July—it happened. I met Hal Sweet, of the CNAC, in a shop. Hal is an American; all the pilots were American unless they were Chinese.

"Come and have a drink," he said. We did, and once we were ensconced at the table he said it. He cleared his throat a couple of times first.

"Uh—have you been married lately?" he asked.

I said, "Well, you get the cigars." Then I had to explain. What he said accounts for a good deal of what happened later, between me and the other Hong Kong Americans.

"All right, but, Mickey—why a limey?"

That, it seems, was the general sentiment. People had been talking for weeks, and comments were varied, but among my compatriots the first sentiment, evidently, was outraged patriotism. It amazed me how much the international complications of the affair seemed to matter to people. My old friend Mrs. Loseby, the Dogs' Home lady, had turned bright red with anger and said:

"Some women will stop at nothing to bring discredit to our nation!"

Disquieting reports came from Shanghai about Corin. Then one day I had a letter from her, a long and extraordinary one. She had put herself in the care of Dr. Halpern, the clever mental specialist who had opened a hospital for Chinese patients. Corin was like the rest of us in this generation: she ran to the doctor to ease her heart, and like the rest of us when we do that she found some sort of substitute for what she wanted. But she must have been in a precarious state, just the same. The letter was like that of an Oxford Grouper, confessing her sins toward me. She said that Jacques had cut her off from me; Jacques had been madly possessive and resented all her friendships; Jacques had forced her to avoid me in Hong Kong, and only let her see me when he wanted her to borrow money. Would I forgive her?

I was upset, but there wasn't anything to do except write reassuringly and, I hope, sensibly. I asked her to come to Hong Kong if the authorities would permit it, and stay with me. I even said I needed her, which wasn't true, and I was a little afraid she would come. I knew she didn't like Charles. But of course she wouldn't leave Jacques. Then I got in touch with other friends, and they wrote and told me their viewpoints. After all, we don't help each other really. None of the letters sounded as if Corin were anything but very much alone in the world; each one was about the writer, and not about the tortured Corin at all. I know she wasn't normal. She was probably a bore. I know that people did everything they could; they gave her work, and kept her going, and advised her, and kept her seeing the doctor, and even then in the end it wasn't any use, but . . .

You see, I failed too.

Charles spoke about the general situation only once more. It was when we were having tea.

"You might think of going away," he said abruptly.

"I wouldn't," I said. "Why?"

For once he tried to put weight into his light voice, and he looked straight at me. "You know that if it happens I can't help you," he said.

"Yes, I know."

"I'll be busy in the war. I can't stop and look after you and the baby."

"Of course."

"You could go to Singapore, perhaps. Cooper thinks it's criminal of me not to make you go."

"But you can't make me go, can you? I'm American."

"No, I can't."

"And Singapore, and Manila—they're all in the same boat, Charles."

"You could go to America."

"With this baby?"

He was silent.

"How do you know America will stay out of it, anyway?"

"That's so," said Charles. "Well, I'll have a beer."

Tony had a try too. *"Now* will you go?" he said pleadingly, when the news looked a little rocky.

I said, "No."

"All right. Come in the same time next week."

American service men were ordered to send their wives away and there was weeping and wailing in all the pretty little houses where they had settled down.

"How's Sandy?" I asked an American Navy captain one day, just before the exodus.

"Not so good," he said. "Somebody showed her a dishpan and a washtub, and she's scared to death."

Then the Chase and the National City banks sent out orders for the wives to be sent away. The Peak houses were hastily packed up, and there were tearful leave-takings, and the men went back on a bachelor basis. After a while the only American woman I knew was Charlotte Gower, doctor in anthropology, and professor out at Ling Nan University, which was maintaining a sort of double life, half in Canton and half as a refugee institution in Hong Kong, in borrowed classrooms at the university there. I love Charlotte. We had met through Dr. Jim Henry, president of Ling Nan. Charlotte had once written me a note suggesting that we meet at the American Club for lunch, and I wasn't at all pleased.

"A missionary anthropologist? Lummy," I grumbled. "Well, I guess I'll have to." I accepted, and turned up more or less on time to find Dr. Gower waiting for me with another woman. They looked forbidding, and my heart went down to my french heels. They both had high collars, short haircuts, and rather scholastic-looking spectacles.

"Will you have a drink before lunch?" asked Charlotte. I glanced from one to the other, and then committed one of those social crimes which are occasionally necessary.

"A tomato juice," I said primly.

Charlotte said over her shoulder, "One tomato juice, two old-fashioneds."

I have often blamed her for this and maintained that she can never make it up to me, but it is the only thing I wouldn't forgive Charlotte.

Charles asked her to come and live with me the last six weeks, and she did. I think she had a row with the faculty over it, but she did. Charles heaved a sigh of relief and went back to work. We would talk in the evening, Charlotte and I, while the sun set over the Pacific with a rather disappointing lack of color—sunsets in Hong Kong are nothing to brag about—and upstairs the pianola played a song which I should think would curl Carola's hair whenever she hears it. It was the same song, night after night, and I don't know the name of it, but whenever I hear it even now my back aches a little, and my blood races, and again I am sitting heavily in my Hong Kong living room, waiting for the Japanese to come and bomb us.

Chapter 36

I BEGAN asking around, among experienced ladies, the same questions that we all ask when the time comes. "How will I *know?*"

An interesting point was that everybody had a different story to tell. I have never heard two firsthand reports of childbirth that sounded remotely alike. The only thing that all women seem to have in common on this subject is a kindly desire to reassure you, the novice, and a natural tendency to discuss it over and over again. I was lunching one day with two Chinese women, Billie Lee and Elsie Soong.

"It's going to be quite all right," Elsie said. "I've had five, my dear, and I know all about it. It's nothing to worry about, nothing at all. Don't believe anybody who tries to frighten you. Oh, how well I remember my first. My mother hung a knotted towel over the head of the bed, you know, so that I could hang on to something, and my hands were in *ribbons,* my dear. It took almost three days. I'll never forget it as long as I live."

Billie, watching my face, interposed hastily. "Don't you give it a thought," she said. "Look at me, small as I am, and the doctor said he'd never pull me through, but it wasn't bad at all. Not at all. Easy as anything." Her vivid little face took on a reminiscent look: "Of course," she admitted, "I do remember saying to the nurse, 'Kill me, kill me, I want to *die. . . .*'"

I went home and read a good book.

Suddenly my life seemed full, overfull, of kind ladies coming in to sit with me. I couldn't imagine where they had sprung from. They didn't leave me alone for a minute, and I was bewildered and grateful and annoyed in turn. I didn't have time to read any more, or muse, or listen to that pianola upstairs, or wonder what was going to happen, or anything. It took me quite a while to find out why. Charles had done it. He had been going around saying, "I do wish you'd look in on Mickey if you have the time. She's alone so much, you know. I can't do it myself, but I would appreciate it if . . ."

It was very nice of him, very touching, and the only evidence I had of the worry he was undergoing. Then I complicated matters by forgetting I was pregnant. I was going downtown to see the doctor, then have lunch with Hilda in the Parisian Grill. We were celebrating my book or something, and I had asked the proprietor, Emile, to put a half bottle of champagne on ice, and I took a taxi down. As sometimes happens, I forgot all about the baby. I was sitting down and didn't keep in mind the fact, which Gordon King was always telling me, that my center of gravity had shifted. So when the taxi stopped in front of Tony's office I jumped out in the old lighthearted way, and I fell over and sprained my ankle.

A crowd immediately gathered, mostly of eager Chinese who all too evidently expected me to have the baby then and there. They hovered over me and asked questions, picked me up and helped me into the Gloucester, kind as can be, and started telling each other about their aunts and cousins who had lost progeny in the same way. I bless the unknown name of the amah who massaged my ankle with something that smelled of wintergreen. It kept me from fainting, and I managed to reach Hilda and then get my foot tied up, and we took the champagne home and had it there. But until Carola arrived that ankle stayed sprained. Very uncomfortable. It was the other ankle, too.

Ah King was getting pretty mad at the whole thing. He said I ought not go out so much. He said I ought not eat fruit at all; every sensible Chinese knew that, he said, whereas I didn't eat anything else. It was most unorthodox and dangerous. I had never known him to be so talkative before, but now I learned a lot about him. He had a daughter, and once upon a time he had had a son, but the son quarreled with him and ran away, and joined the Army, and Ah King hadn't heard from him since. That summer trouble came to what remained of his family. His wife and daughter, living over in Kowloon, fell ill and wouldn't get well again, and at last Ah King told me about it.

I made Tony visit them. Owing to an outrageous landlord's ruling, servants weren't allowed to keep their families with them in our house, and he found the two women in a little hovel, crowding unspeakably with a lot of other people. They had typhoid, and Tony managed to squeeze them into the government hospital in Kowloon, though all the hospitals during those years when refugees flooded the Colony were pitiably crowded. After a bit they recovered and came home, to my place: I said to hell with the landlord. It wasn't a legal ruling anyway. I paid the hospital bills, which were very low; about twelve Hong Kong dollars altogether, as I remember. That is what it cost me to buy Ah King's lifetime devotion; that is what saved my life, and Carola's, later on. Not expensive, was it?

Gordon King looked at me with a dead pan, as usual. "You have lost ten pounds in the last few months," he said.

"Why, that's wonderful," I said brightly. "Isn't it?"

"Perhaps."

The room at hospital had long been waiting for me. Tony was nervous as a cat; he had expected the baby earlier. Gordon waited and waited, and finally tried to induce things, and still nothing happened. Charlotte and I chatted about everything else in the world, and still nothing happened. At last Gordon said that he would take me into hospital anyway, on a Sunday evening. Charles was to be ready with the car at five. He had to rush for it. There was trouble at the border with the Japanese, and one of the police over in the New Territories thought he had discovered a secret munitions road on British ground. Charles hurried over to the mainland to look at the road, which was a false alarm, and then hurried back. In the meantime things had at last started. Three o'clock, I think it was.

"Charlotte," I said, "this is it."

"Are you sure? You've had two false alarms, and made poor Mrs. Armstrong rush over——"

"No doubt about it," I said. "This time, I know."

One does forget. I can remember only that I was excited and glad. I felt drunk. I chattered like a magpie to Charles as we drove to hospital, and timed the pains the way the doctor had told me to. In the hospital bed I lay there beaming, and made friends immediately with the Chinese girl who was physician in charge. Late at night it stopped a little, and they gave me a pill and I slept. It would be all over by the next night, I thought. But it wasn't.

One does forget. I can remember the facts, but not the feeling. It was pretty much the same every day, and it went on every day for five days, until Friday, and I couldn't get rid of that baby. I walked so long that I had a blister from the bedroom slippers. My ankle hurt, but I didn't pay any attention to details like that. Between attacks I began to be frightened. Everyone was very bright and hopeful, but I began to imagine they were holding out on me. And then, too, I felt silly. People would call on me and ask what the trouble was, and go home, and then I would try again. It wasn't any use.

Thursday night Gordon King said, "Do you remember a suggestion someone once made about you?"

"Caesarean, you mean?"

He nodded. He wasn't dead-pan any more; he looked kind. "In America they would have operated already," he said, "but though I'm a surgeon I hate to operate unnecessarily. Now I think it's necessary. Well?"

"Why," I said, "of course."

We had to get Charles's consent first. When he had gone I lay back and thought about the doctor. A few days before he had suddenly amazed me by saying, "How much of this do you want to feel, before we help you?"

I stared at him and said, "Did you think I was doing all this to write a book about it?"

"Why, yes," he said. "Isn't that the idea?" And tonight he had said as he was going out, "Now you will know all about both methods."

People are really very odd. He looked as pleased as if he were making me an invaluable gift, and I suppose from the scientific point of view he was.

I thoroughly enjoyed the operation. It was my ideal of an experience: something happening to you that you can watch without feeling it. They gave me a spinal whatever-it-is, and I watched the surgeon's hands at work, in the reflecting metal on the light overhead. Just once something made me sick, and they gave me morphine and I slept for a minute or two. But for the rest of the time there I was, a living head and brain, and no communication with anything below the neck. I was elated and excited and yet calm.

All of a sudden there was an outraged, indignant little yowl like that of a Siamese cat, only several times, and Gordon and Tony together said, "It's a girl!"

Everybody turned to me, lying strapped and paralyzed, and said again, "It's a girl!"

I said, "Oh?" politely, because they seemed so excited about it, but I was wondering if I quite liked that. Then I asked the other one of the two inevitable questions: "Is she all right?"

"All right. All right."

The Siamese yelping went on and one of the nurses said, "Nothing wrong with her lungs, anyway."

Anyway? Anyway? Immediately I was suspicious again. They weren't telling me everything. There must be something wrong. Why wasn't it all finished? I could see that the gloved hands were still working. Was he doing something that would fix it so I couldn't have any more children? It wouldn't be any use asking him; he wouldn't tell. The clock hands went round and round; the baby had been taken out of the room. What was the matter?

"Fibroma," said Gordon King. "Fairly big one, too. I thought that lump, the last few days, couldn't be twins. Well, you're a lucky girl. We'd have had to have that out within a month anyway, and the child couldn't have survived a normal birth."

"All right, now?"

"Oh yes. Want to see it?"

They were moving my body, so oddly not mine, so heavy and lifeless, to the trolley. I was thinking about something else.

"I'll have a boy next time," I announced, comforting myself, and the nurse in charge rolled up her eyes and closed them.

I wasn't used to new babies, but she did look awfully small to me. The human eye can't be smaller than a certain size, evidently, so her eyes were enormous in her face, stretching out on each side to the temple. She looked like Charles, but not very bright. Then I had a chill and she disappeared.

He came in late that afternoon; I thought it was the same time of day, but it wasn't. He'd been busy with the general, but Tony found him and let him know.

Vera was with him, waiting outside, and driving home he was quiet for a long time, in deep thought. At last with a sigh of relief he said to her, "Anyway, she can never be a Methodist minister." That remote possibility of his son's fate had evidently been bothering him a lot.

"What does the new baby look like, Uncle Charles?" demanded Vera's daughter Bridget.

"Exactly like a poached egg," said Charles.

I had baskets and baskets of flowers, but I didn't care. I lay there howling with the bellyache. I'd never had an operation before, and I felt exceedingly aggrieved. It should have been over, I felt; this was something extra, and it wasn't fair. "I don't think I'll ever get well," I gasped to Gordon King.

"Nonsense," he said, and left the room. Next door to me was the third-class delivery ward, and coolie women were being brought in and out all day. It contributed to my inferiority complex that they did their jobs with such admirable dispatch—a couple of moans, a Siamese cat, and then the nurse saying, "Hand me a safety pin, somebody."

Besides, Carola was so small, so awfully small. She weighed five pounds and a half, and she dropped off to four pounds ten ounces. They didn't tell me, and the nurses were indignant with King because he wouldn't allow supplementary feeding; he was trying to bring me up to the mark by force of practice. Little by little she climbed up again in weight, and my bellyache subsided, and the days dragged on. I had earphones plugged in the wall and the hospital radio gave out the news. There was a lot of excitement about Japan, and then somebody named Kurusu was sent to Washington and all the nurses felt happier. They still crowded in to ask Charles what he thought about things, though, when he came in the evening.

Between Carola's visits every three hours I slept a little, and then I had dreams. I dreamed about air raids in Chungking, and sinking ships, and Carola's face in the sky, all over the sky and all eyes. The rest of the face shrank smaller and smaller, and the eyes got bigger and bigger, and knew she was starving to death.

I would wake up and ring frantically for the nurse, and ask for a pillow or something.

The days dragged on. I thought I would not get home in time.

Chapter 37

THERE WERE days of wrangling between me and Gordon King. wanted to get home. I wasn't rational about it; I just felt that I wa entitled to a few days with Charles before they took him away from m for the war, but I didn't like to say that to Gordon. Nobody talked tha way. It would have been like asking for it in advance. We all skirted th subject, except for one redheaded nurse who was frankly nervous and who pestered the life out of Charles whenever he came in, asking him if he thought it would really happen.

Gordon and I argued about my discharge from hospital for days, th battle growing really intense at the end when I said flatly that he couldn' keep me there legally, and that I was going on Saturday or else. H begged for Monday, but I was firm, and I won. So I had three weeks a home before Pearl Harbor.

As I remember now, those three weeks were nice but confused. I wa awfully frightened of the baby, and though I had taken a couple of les sons in hospital on bathing her, I felt quite unable to grapple with such a big problem alone. Vera had found me a regular English-trained amah a dithering old lady named Ah Cheung. Certain things about her approved of, as an improvement on the Chinese-style amahs I had known in Shanghai at Sinmay's house, but she seemed lamentably old to me and needed a lot of watching. Also, she was entitled to days off, one afternoon a week and one whole day every month. The afternoons were all right I could manage Carola for an afternoon, any time. But as that whole day off approached I was as nervous as I'd been about having the baby. Ove and over I talked to Vera Armstrong about giving her her bath alone

"She gets so slippery. What if she slips out of my hands completely and falls into the water? What about that awful business of cleaning her nose. What if——"

"For God's sake," said Vera, "I'll come over and do it."

"Missy no worry. Ah Cheung stay home until tiffin," said the amah.

"No," I said firmly. "Carola and I must see this through together. It's too silly. Why, Mother had eight of us. . . ."

The Japanese intervened. Ah Cheung never did get her day off, but I learned how to bathe a baby by myself, ultimately.

In the attenuated social atmosphere of Hong Kong the arrival of a Canadian regiment made us all feel a little better. They were given welcome parties all over the place.

We were all in a state of flux. The Governor, Sir Geoffrey Northcote, retired to East Africa with Lady Northcote, because his health wasn't good. I was sorry to see them leave because I liked them enormously from the one or two times I had talked with them, and Hilda reported that the new Governor, Sir Mark Young, wasn't her type. She didn't think she would ever be on the same comfortable terms with him that she had been with the Northcotes.

General Grassett, commander of the forces, had been exchanged. The new general was an unknown quantity and I couldn't make Charles give me any opinion on him at all. I wasn't interested, anyway, in anything but Carola. Gordon had at last let me supplement her diet with ordinary milk, and she was putting on weight fast on a half-and-half basis. I was preoccupied with all that, arranging my day so that I could nurse her at the right times. When she reached eight pounds we stopped the three-hour business, and that was a great relief. The household revolved busily around the nursery, and out in his cage my last black gibbon gnashed his teeth in impotent jealousy. When the coolie wheeled the pram past the cage the gibbon would throw himself at the bars and shake them, and howl bitterly. One day he got loose, but he didn't attack the baby. He just kept circling around us at a distance, looking her over.

"So that's fairly safe," I said to Charles. "Still, until she's older I won't get any more gibbons, if then."

"Much better not. And as for that cat," he said, looking with mistrust at Jocasta, the incestuous Siamese cat that Cooper had given me: "I wish you'd dispose of it. Cats smother babies, don't they? They want to get warm, and they climb into bed with them and smother them."

"Oh, I don't think so."

"Yes, they do. Vera says so. You'd better dispose of it." He added, "I read in the paper Sunday that it's not good for a child to be the only one in the family. We owe it to Carola to have another one, don't we?"

"Yes indeed," I said. "Do you mean to say you really got that idea out of the Sunday paper?"

"Why, yes. Sometimes there's a good deal of sense in those syndicated articles."

The public watched Charles narrowly when Carola was born, hoping to catch him out in some outrageous behavior, but they were disappointed.

"He was buying drinks for his friends and looking happy," one lady reported disapprovingly to Vera, "just like an ordinary father."

"Well, for heaven's sake, he *is* an ordinary father!" snapped Vera.

Hilda came to dinner one evening, and we talked about the war. Everyone in town was supposed to have signed up for some "essential service," and I had missed out in the rush, having been in hospital.

"What can I do?" I asked. "I don't drive a car very well, but I can do that in a pinch. I can typewrite, and manage a switchboard badly, and——"

"You can be a dispenser," said Hilda. "I did that course myself, and all you have to do is telephone the A.N.S. leader, Nina Valentine, to sign up as an A.N.S. (Auxiliary Nursing Service.) In the meantime, while you're untrained, consider yourself a dispenser. You know something about drugs and medicine, don't you?"

"Yes, a little, from Africa."

"Then that's all right. And listen, Charles: if it happens, I think Mickey would be better off with us on the Peak. That's settled; the minute it strikes, I'll come down and pick her up with the baby."

Charles was relieved and grateful. I had better explain before we dive into the war that the whole Colony had already been warned for some months that we would in case of emergency go in for "billeting." The authorities were suitably vague as to why they would want a lot of housing space in such a case, but they were definite in saying that they wanted it, and this is the way they proposed getting it: all of us were to move at the first sign of war. Those of us who lived on mid-level, as I did, would be given addresses on the Peak. We were to lock our best things up but leave all our rooms but one free for the billetees, and our bedding and cooking implements were to be left for their use.

People living at sea level would be moved uphill too. People in Kowloon were to be brought over to the island. Nobody said what was going to happen to Kowloon.

Afterward we pieced it out. The "defense plan" stipulated that the troops were to hold the enemy off as long as possible, probably three weeks. When at last they retreated the civilian population of Kowloon was to have been safely transported to the island, and there we were supposed to hold out against the besiegers for three months. It was all planned down to the last ridiculous detail, and there wasn't anything wrong with it except that it didn't work. We couldn't hold the enemy off at all as it happened.

What with everything going as it did, the letter from Ursula didn't cause nearly the excitement it would have done before the baby's birth. It arrived just two days after Carola. In restrained and ladylike tone Ursula announced that she was applying for divorce, not only for various other reasons but because Charles had said he wouldn't live with her any more in any case. She wanted Vera, in another letter, to send her some decent clothes from Hong Kong, as Vera had such good taste. Ursula was beginning to love Singapore, she said. She would be willing to stay indefinitely.

Vera studied the letter suspiciously.

"It's a great improvement," I said, "over the last letter she wrote Charles."

"So she will get a divorce, and then there'll be six months, and then—— Well, what do you think?" asked Vera.

I said, "Honestly, I don't know. I suppose we'll marry. It doesn't seem to matter any more."

On Saturday, the sixth, a large Japanese armada was sighted steaming south, off the coast of Indo-China. The Volunteers were mobilized in Hong Kong. The paper said that Roosevelt had sent a cable to Hirohito, direct, pleading with him to avert this disaster, and the Japanese in Tokyo must have laughed grimly when it arrived. I don't believe that Hirohito ever answered that cable.

On Saturday afternoon Maya Rodeivitch was taking photographs of Carola and me, and, under his protest, of Charles, who dropped in for lunch in uniform. He was rather sleepy, for the night before he had been at a big Japanese dinner party given by his old friend the general, out on the border of the New Territories. He was worried, too. Me, I had spent the evening Friday with Colin MacDonald of the London *Times,* and an amusing Australian newspaperwoman named Dorothy Jenner. Colin had met her in Chungking, and he took us out to dinner at the Parisian Grill. I invited them both for cocktails at Charles's house on Sunday evening.

They came, and so did Charlotte, looking handsome in dark green. Our good friends, Barbara Petro and her husband, were there. A few others came, too, including Hoffman from our consulate. He told me a story about one of the consulate girls. It seems that she had hurried into his office one morning, twisting her handkerchief, and blurted out in frightened tones, "Emily Hahn has had a baby."

"I know it," said Walter Hoffman. "In fact I've seen the baby. It's a nice baby. Well?"

"Well," gasped the girl, "she'll have to register it here, won't she? I mean, that's my job."

"Yes," said Hoffman. "She's coming in next week; we've already arranged that. What's the trouble? I'll be here; she's going to telephone before she comes."

"Don't you leave me alone with her!" cried the typist.

"I suppose," added Walter, "she thinks it's catching."

Charles had a better story. In Hong Kong when a child is born the parents are supposed to register it in the city registry in person. Although I hadn't known it, the nurses in hospital had been thrown into a regular jitter when it came to signing a required preliminary paper, after the baby's birth. They didn't know what to put in under the heading, "Father's Name," and they milled around in utter confusion until the almoner, Margaret Watson, a friend of Hilda's, reminded them acidly that they had only to ask Miss Hahn. Charles had signed it, naturally, and then gone home, supposing he would be informed when it was time for us to go downtown to the registry office and do the job properly. One morning he received a mysterious telephone message from the registrar. Would Major Boxer come in to see him at his earliest convenience?

Wondering, and a little apprehensive, Charles went. He was taken hurriedly into an inner office, and then into the innerest office of all, and there was the registrar himself, looking very nervous and pink. "Major Boxer," he said, waving toward the hospital slip which we had signed, "you don't have to do this, you know. There's no law that forces you to recognize the child. . . ."

Charles had been angry.

The cocktail party went on to a buffet supper, but none of us was really merry. Charles's uniform, and the fact that he sat at the radio most of the evening, had a dampening effect on our spirits. People went home about midnight. I stayed. We listened to a broadcast from Tokyo at four in the morning, but there wasn't anything special in that, and at five o'clock I had to go home. Carola was to be fed at six. I climbed the hill, holding my long skirt up out of the dew and watching the cracked stairs carefully in the dawning light, for my ankle was still weak. It was a lovely fresh morning, just turning cool. Hong Kong nights are often stuffy, but the dawns are better. It had been raining.

I was feeding Carola when the phone rang at six.

"Mickey?" said Charles. "The balloon's gone up. It's come. War."

Chapter 38

ALL OVER the world, how many people are telling a story like mine? Thousands; millions. It seems to me now that I felt the weight of the world's numbers at that minute, and then I thought of Carola, and then I thought of how to behave, all in a split second. But I was stupid for a little.

"Where?" I asked.

"All over. Pearl Harbor and Malaya and everywhere else."

"How do you know?"

"I can't tell that," said Charles impatiently. "Well, can you manage? I'm going down to headquarters. You had better phone Hilda."

"Yes, I'll do that. You call me back if you have time."

This was two hours before the general alarm was given, but Ah King and the rest must have been waiting, just as I had been waiting, for the news. He was in the hall fully dressed when I hung up, and he looked at me, silently inquiring, and I nodded. "I must pack," I said. "Call Ah Choy and tell her. We'll take all the baby's clothes and my winter things. Two suitcases."

Hilda hadn't heard officially, but when I told her she was calm and everyday in her manner. "So that was it: Selwyn's gone downtown already. Very well, my dear, I'll come and pick you up on one of my trips. Could you be ready this afternoon? I'll be going up- and downhill all day."

We talked about supplies, and distribution of people, and a lot of things I don't remember. "I do hate to pack," I told myself crossly. Then I think I must have gone in and sat down by the cot. I crouched over the sleeping baby for an hour. I don't remember anything about how I felt. Being a nursing mother rather dulls your brain, and very likely I wasn't feeling anything.

Charles called again at eight, to find out if I was arranged for.

"I could probably get away long enough to take you up there," he began doubtfully, and even then I felt glad that he was willing to go back on his Spartan word that much. But it wasn't necessary, I said. "Hilda's all fixed; she's coming for us. You have their phone number? Charles, you'll be all right?"

"Me? Nobody's going to get *me*. They protect staff officers," he said, laughing. "I'll be locked up underground, honeybunch. . . . Listen. Hear it? There they are now."

Through my free ear I heard the siren. Through my telephone ear I heard it too, just a second later. It was a weird effect. Then the bombs, those familiar bombs that I had been hearing since 1937, off and on. . . . The year's dream was broken. I woke up.

Charles was talking through the hooting of the siren. "Well, Mickey, I'm sorry about all this."

"Darling, you didn't do it!"

"Anyway, Carola's too young to care; that's a good thing. . . . All the best."

Click.

I went out on the stone terrace and looked across the bay, and there at Kai Tak was smoke bubbling up. Inside his veranda, my neighbor across the way was sucking his pipe and staring at it. We had never spoken before.

"Good morning," I said. "Here it is."

"Yes." He shook his head. "Japan's committed suicide."

I went indoors and crouched over the baby again.

"Come and eat breakfast," said Ah King.

Ah Choy, the wash amah, folding up clothes in the bedroom, turned to me as I came in. "You scared, missy?" she asked.

"Nooooo. You're not scared, are you, Ah Choy?"

"Yes," said Ah Choy, and began to cry.

I went back and sat over Carola.

Hilda Selwyn-Clarke is an admirable woman, and I wonder now why my fortnight's association with her is marked by so much irritation. It must have seared my soul. Perhaps like a lot of other people I blow off steam by getting angry with the nearest object, instead of letting go and being frankly terrified. Also, I've never liked feeling like a guest too long at a time; I like to be boss in the house.

We were crowded in the Selwyn-Clarke house, big as it was; we had a Chinese doctor and his wife and son, and Constance Lam, a girl who adored the doctor and who was now acting as housekeeper for the mess, and Miriam, a Chinese nurse who was Mary's governess, and the Valentines—Douglas Valentine was Selwyn's assistant, and Nina, his wife, was head of the A.N.S.—and a lot of other odd bits and pieces, doctors and such. On the third day the Armstrongs arrived. They had been warned out of their house next to the Peak tram, because the Japs had begun shelling the face of the mountain with obvious intent to put that tramway out of order. Oh, we were crowded, and the wonder is that we didn't all blow up, but we didn't. We behaved almost admirably. If we slipped now and then, if somebody talked loudly for a moment, we hushed it up straight away. If Hilda seemed shockingly self-centered to me, and obsessed with the welfare of her own people, I know that my seeming oblivion to Carola got on her nerves terribly. I don't deny that I avoided that baby. I made sure that Ah Cheung was standing by, and that she had her food, and I turned up for her feedings when it was time, but for the rest I stayed out of her way. It just hurt too much, looking at her.

"I can't understand that woman," Hilda said angrily to Vera. "Why, when Mary was that age, if she cried I cried too."

"Which must have been a great help," said Vera.

You are to understand that we were under constant fire. I'm not going to write much about that part of it because it is impossible to give you the feeling of it. If you've been in a war you know. If you haven't you can't know. The first day was child's play, but the second day we had more than air raids; we had shelling from the approaching Jap forces across the bay, and from a few of their ships that had stolen up close to the island. It is probably an idiosyncrasy of mine, but I prefer bombs to shells. I'm more used to them. You can see the plane they are coming from, and you can hear the bomb coming down, and you know where you are. To be sure, in Hong Kong you are out in the open, or crouching inside some ridiculous stucco doorway, because there is nowhere else to go: Hong Kong had not prepared many dugouts, you remember. But anyway, once a bomb has popped, it has popped, and the plane can't stay in one place pegging away at you. Shells are different. Shells keep coming and hitting at the same spot. Shells are the devil. Especially were they unpleasant up there on the crest of the mountain, on the tipmost top of the proud Peak.

In those early days none of us admitted that things weren't going to be quite all right. We waited patiently at first, and then impatiently, for planes to come up from Singapore and drive away these impertinent little pests. No planes came. Instead we listened to the radio and discovered that the Japs were having quite surprising luck down in Malaya. But the radio didn't tell the truth either. They kept talking about troops from China attacking the Jap forces in the rear. They talked about us: gallant little Hong Kong, the fortress. People sent encouraging messages, very important people, even the King of England. It all went according to plan, because the authorities really knew, remember, that Hong Kong couldn't be held. We were supposed to delay the enemy, that was all; the enemy was to be delayed from going south for three months.

Hilda and I went downtown on Monday afternoon, and on Tuesday, and on Wednesday. I saw Charles in town on Wednesday, and he looked grim, and he was quiet. I wasn't. I was jittery, worrying about him. Hilda kept me fairly well stirred up. Hilda has a strong histrionic sense, and she must have found some compensation in letting it rip. She talked dramatically and made wide, sweeping gestures like a woman on a lecture platform. She gasped a good deal, and said, "Oh, my God." She stuck pins into me about Charles and Carola. Her idea of comforting talk for a nursing mother was not mine: she would stand, streaming with tears, watching me as I glumly nursed the baby, and she would say: "You'll never keep her alive. Never. Why, I won't keep Mary alive, and she's almost six."

Other people will tell the story of the battle of Hong Kong better than I can. I watched it, and traced what was happening pretty well, but the chess games of military strategy don't interest me, even when I've been a pawn. The Japs came into Kowloon on Wednesday, almost three weeks ahead of schedule. The Royal Scots were supposed to have held the front line, but the Royal Scots didn't.

In our house, preoccupied with medical service, this withdrawal from Kowloon was marked by Nina's indignation over her girls, the A.N.S. There were many of these auxiliary nurses stationed in Kowloon, in hospitals and at first-aid posts, and Selwyn had left them there. Nina was being besieged by outraged husbands and mothers and fathers, demanding to know why their womenfolk had been thrown to the Japs. Strictly speaking, I suppose Selwyn was right; I suppose there isn't a question of it. Nurses must be left to take care of the wounded, and in the old days when war was more civilized, the days in which Selwyn was mentally living, doctors and nurses were treated with respect by the enemy. Maybe. I have my doubts. I think people have always misbehaved in wartime, and they always will.

Looked on as a plain problem in ethics, Selwyn was justified. But this wasn't a bloodless problem. These girls were our girls. Nina knew them all. Nina felt responsible for them. She was a harassed and ghost-ridden woman during those days, and she hated Selwyn bitterly for a while.

Florence Ho-tung, whose husband was a doctor in the medical service, felt very much the same way. She herself was an A.N.S., but she had three small children to look after, and her old father, Sir Robert, had collapsed and the family always depended on Florence more than on anyone else. Her older sister Irene had a baby almost as young as Carola; they were with her too. And now K. C. Yeo, her husband, was trapped over in Kowloon, remaining behind with the others. Florence telephoned to apologize to Dr. Selwyn-Clarke, but she really could not go on nursing for the time being. She was needed at home. It was all too much.

"You must invite her to lunch, my dear," said Selwyn to Hilda.

I found Nina a comforting person during those first days. She was good-looking, and dignified and gracious in her uniform. She maintained a strong, sturdy sense of humor in managing Hilda. She didn't seem to be afraid. Most of all, she didn't go to pieces over her two little boys, who were at school up in Tsingtao, and from whom, of course, she was now completely cut off since the Japanese had occupied North China without opposition. Without Nina I might have misbehaved somehow. I was becoming irritably aware of my own shortcomings. I was no longer the tough baby who had sat it out in Chungking, and galloped around the streets of Nantao under bombardment. I was a craven, trembling female: a nursing mother. I knew it and I couldn't help it, though I tried. Anybody would have tried, under the chilly gaze of Dr. Selwyn-Clarke. He kept me going, and so did Nina, in spite of Hilda.

After Wednesday, when I saw Charles in town, until Sunday I had only one phone call from him. During that time I spent most of the day in the War Memorial Hospital, listing the inadequate medical supplies and rushing home at intervals to nurse Carola. I tried to space those visits home between air raids, but after a few days most of our daylight time was taken up by planes. They came over informally, one by one, and they kept wandering about until the air-raid siren meant nothing at all. It was always too late anyway. Usually the plane had come and gone before it gave its warning. We turned gray trying to keep the children indoors. Little John Armstrong was particularly insistent on getting himself bombed; his father could manage him, but his father came home only at night. During the day he was working downtown, ladling out rice to the Chinese coolies.

The housekeeping slipped into chaos. At last we imported Ah King to the house, for Hilda's servants all ran away. I felt better after that, though we had little time to talk to each other. Sunday afternoon Charles came marching in, his helmet cocked on one side of his head. Alf Bennett was with him, and Max Oxford. They were maddeningly efficient and warlike: they had come up on business, not pleasure. "Who lives over there?" demanded Charles, first off, as they came to a halt before the cellar where we were hiding with the children. He nodded toward a neighboring villa.

"Nobody at the moment, but some tommies are using it," I said. And off they clanked, march, march, march, to play at soldiers. I stood outside the cellar, watching them go, and my heart was full of anger. Pretty soon, though, they came back. They were going to allow themselves a little time to visit, after all.

"Ah," said Max, surveying Carola with his nose wrinkled in fastidious distaste, "growing some hair at last, is it?"

"Why do you frowst in this cellar?" demanded Charles.

Hilda and I looked at each other. The guns which flanked us were silent just then, but we knew they would soon speak. "We like it," said Hilda. "However, if you'd like to sit upstairs . . ."

We arranged ourselves stiffly in the drawing room, and Ah King brought drinks. If I had hoped for a quiet cuddle with Charles I was disappointed. Hilda concentrated on him. She wanted to know what was happening. She had a lot to say and to ask. Charles held my hand and tried to say things in between.

"Why are you shaking?" he asked.

"I'm worried about you."

"Don't be silly, Mickey. Anyway, I've fixed it. You and Carola are going to be all right if anything happens to me. I sent the will to your brother-in-law."

"Don't *talk* like that."

"Don't be silly, Mickey." But he looked pleased, though dirty. Then Hilda butted in again, her voice quivering with hysteria, and we couldn't talk any more.

All of a sudden the shelling began, and the guns replied. Charles looked startled. "Is it often like this?" he demanded.

"Oh yes," I said airily. "All day."

"Well, really . . ." The house shook. The air shook. The heavens shook. We took the boys outside so that they could have a really good look. "This," I said gently, "is why we frowst in the cellar."

Charles stood there looking from right to left, and Alf looked at him, and so did Max. "You've got to get out of this," said Charles.

"Where to?" I asked.

"Well, anywhere else. I didn't realize . . . You're between two batteries here, you see."

"Are you," said Hilda, "telling us?"

"You ought to go to the Canavals' house," said Charles, "in Pokfulam. They wouldn't mind. Or Repulse Bay."

"And what about food?"

He looked miserable, and I said quickly, "It's really not that bad. It just sounds bad. They haven't come near us yet, and anywhere else will be the same."

"You're between two batteries," said Charles.

Alf broke in, his voice rough with disapproval. "You can say the same for every house in the Colony, old boy," he said.

It was time for them to go. Charles and I walked up the driveway arm in arm, and we were laughing. "I can't help it," he said, "when I think of all these fat Chinese bankers. They've been running away from this for years. And now, at last, right in the heart of the British Colony—caught!"

"Yes," I said, giggling, "it's damn funny."

Alf and Max turned their backs while we kissed each other good-by, and I came back to the house feeling fine.

"It just occurred to me, my dear," said Hilda, "that you might have wanted to see Charles alone. Next time, why don't you take him upstairs?"

But there was no next time.

It was an open secret that the Japs were landing on the island. We could see it happening, from a certain point on the Peak. Not that we took much time to go out walking, but sometimes we had to go over to the distributing center for our milk and supplies, which were rather spasmodically given out. One day we had dozens of loaves of bread and nothing else, and another time we had pounds of spoiling beef, and nothing else again. That, by the way, was a large factor of our defeat: the failure of transportation. It was sabotage, mostly. The Chinese chauffeurs had dozens of little ways to do it; they swiped the carburetor, for instance, or just drained the gas tank, or wrecked the truck, or took it, load and all, to a prearranged place to wait for the Japs and never came back. Selwyn was doing his damnedest, making armed escorts go along with the trucks whenever he could find somebody to go. But we were running short of drivers. They tried to persuade me to join up, but Charles objected on the grounds of Carola's milk supply. A girl we knew, Gwen Priestwood, was borrowed from the A.N.S. to drive a lorry and she was doing very well.

We still had the radio, and a semblance of peace after dark when the planes stopped coming over. We heard about the sinking of the *Prince of Wales* and the *Repulse,* down at Singapore; we were all struck speechless except Hilda, who gasped loudly and said, "Oh, my God." After that we stopped talking about help coming from the south. We knew. We saw less and less of Selwyn, but whenever he did turn up he brought fresh strength somehow. I never knew anyone who could radiate it the way he did. And yet I can't say, honestly, that I liked him. Constance adored him and wanted only to die for him. Hilda presumably loved him, or she wouldn't have married him and had his baby. There I was, rather disliking him if anything, critical of his technique, still swayed by his personality until I, too, would have died if he had suggested it. Very odd.

"You know," said Nina once in her offhand way, "Selwyn thinks he's God." That struck me; it rang with truth. Later I was to realize it sharply. It was more than the ordinary careless remark; it summed up the situation.

The radio from London told us blithely that we were putting up a splendid and winning fight. The Japanese were being cleared off the island, said the radio. That evening they had moved into the Repulse Bay Hotel, incidentally, but I'm not going to waste much time talking about that. At the present date I can think of five books people have written about the Repulse Bay Hotel and the Japanese; why should I add to it? I wasn't there. I was shivering on the Peak, listening to the radio. Dr. Harry Talbot had come in from the hospital to try to cheer us up; we sat in the cellar and he sang to the children. He has a nice voice. Afterward we stood out under the stars and he talked blisteringly about the war.

I saw a certain amount of corruption in high places, but it doesn't seem terribly important now. There was a man who wandered drunkenly about the Peak, alternating between d.t.'s and sudden forays into the war. Sometimes he thought he was doing Red Cross work, and then he was a nuisance in the hospital. Sometimes he thought he was back in the last war, and then he lay on his large belly in a trench he had caused to be dug in his front garden. Sometimes he distributed Food Control supplies. He sent Hilda two sacks of rice from the Food Control stores, and several bottles of booze. Hilda owned up to the booze when Selwyn came home and he gave them to me and told me, curtly, to take them back, which I did.

Until our wartime home was broken up, though, I didn't get a real look at the disorder that generally prevailed. In Selwyn's house, until the last, we may have been distressed but we held the fort and maintained a semblance of principle and order. I smile now when I realize how innocent I was, until that day that Selwyn told us to move into the War Memorial. The Japs were landing in such numbers that he had decided we had better shift. He had always held this plan in mind, a sort of ideal picture of hospitals and their use for the civilian population during battle. "The women and children," he had said, "will retire to the hospitals for safety." Blueprint stuff.

I was on duty in the War Memorial, and the whole thing was sprung on me. Suddenly I saw Bridget and John Armstrong walking single file,

with Mary behind them, through the hospital corridor. After them came
a coolie with a couple of suitcases. After them, Ah Cheung carrying
Carola. I hurried over to ask what it was.

"We're moving," said John shrilly. "The Japs are coming."

I went back into the dispensary and sat down. Then after a minute I
realized that Mrs. Murdock, the woman in charge, was feeding me aspirin
and handing me a handkerchief, quite urgently. Dr. Kirk stood behind
her, looking kind. I must have been crying.

"I'm sorry," I said.

"Never you mind," said Mrs. Murdock. "You should have seen me the
first day when my husband left."

"There, there," said Dr. Kirk, patting my shoulder.

"What do they do to officers?" I asked.

"There, there," said Dr. Kirk.

Chapter 39

I WASN'T FATED to stay long in the War Memorial Hospital, but my
impressions of that short interval are vivid. It would be difficult to convince the American public of the strange state of affairs that obtained
in Hong Kong with regard to the nurses. We call them nurses; the English call them all, regardless of church, sisters. Nurses are lower creatures,
according to the English; the little cuties that we know as probationers
are nurses, over there. That isn't particularly strange. What is strange
is that the sisters, wherever I encountered them and almost without exception, suffered from hallucinations. They thought they were crosses between police matrons and queens. I had not noticed this from my eminence as a citizen in good standing with a bank account, though during
my confinement I did resent being bullied, as one always does in an old-
fashioned hospital. Now, as a refugee, it was different.

The War Memorial, owing to its location on the Peak, never did play
much of a part in the hostilities. Now and then some soldiers were
brought in, if they had been wounded near by, but there never was much
fighting near the top of the mountain and the bombing casualties were
picked up downtown or out in the suburbs; it was simpler and nearer
to take them to St. Paul's in Happy Valley or to the Queen Mary around
the island, in Pokfulam. This was just as well, I suppose, for the War
Memorial, though it was the swankiest place among hospitals in the

town, had been more of a nursing home than a real hospital, and it wasn't well equipped with medicines or anything else. None of the hospitals were well equipped as far as drugs and dressings were concerned. For some years the government had held them down to pennies; when I had Carola, for example, they hadn't been able to give my ankle a fresh bandage until I myself telephoned the chemist in town and had a bandage sent out, C.O.D. The same went for all extra medicaments. Such supplies as they had on hand were held against the great day, but when the day came the supplies were still inadequate. The government hospital, the Queen Mary, had a splendid X-ray and electrical therapy outfit, but it was short on surgical beds. I recall vividly that the War Memorial had only three splints in the whole building, which was awkward when the soldiers began to come in with broken limbs.

Although they weren't loaded down with patients, the sisters were frightened and harassed, and bitterly resented us, the refugees. Not only the Selwyn-Clarke household, but the whole Food Control Committee moved in on them that day, for they had been bombed out two or three times and they thought the hospital at least would be left standing. If we hadn't been the family of Dr. Selwyn-Clarke, the director, we would have been turned away. In spite of Selwyn's orders, most refugees were. The sisters gathered in their own rooms and talked about the horrors of war, or galloped about being unpleasant to everyone. They still felt a bit safer than the rest of us, however; they were unconsciously sure that they had the immunity of the sacrosanct. Doctors and nurses are always left alone, they told themselves. It gave them a certain smugness.

The worst factor of the War Memorial was an American gentleman whose name, fortunately, I cannot remember. He sat in an office on the ground floor and snarled at people. When he was tired of saying no upstairs he went down to the kitchen and said no there. The kitchen was overburdened: not only were meals being cooked there, but instruments had to be boiled, and the more refugees who gathered the more people were milling about in the kitchen, trying to prepare food and boil water to drink. The American got to the stage where he stood at the kitchen door and wouldn't let anybody come in at all. He must have thought he was being efficient and organizing things. He wouldn't let the sisters in to boil instruments. He wouldn't let any of us in to get water. He wouldn't let anybody do anything, until at last we ignored him and went ahead anyway. It was an interesting study. People often tend to go dictator under stress. They start ordering other people about and threatening them with dire penalties.

In the course of the day we all started being hungry. It was the beginning of a long period of hunger for us, but we didn't know that. At first we were hungry because we couldn't get in to cook our food, but next day it became evident that we didn't have enough food to go around, cooked or uncooked. I then saw how things worked out in wartime. The Food Control people had plenty of food, naturally, and they had the first sitting in the little room next to the kitchen, when the American manager had at last been removed. They had potted meat and bread and all sorts of things. We watched with bright-eyed interest until it was time for our turn, and then we didn't have anything to eat at all but a dollop of rice or cereal. It hurt our feelings. It made me furious. It startled Hilda, who was accustomed to being the wife of Dr. Selwyn-Clarke, in spite of all her broad-minded political tendencies. Hilda was looking very thoughtful. The War Memorial wasn't really Selwyn's own stamping ground; it was a private concern. Selwyn's hospitals were the government ones, the Queen Mary on the island and the Kowloon Hospital on the mainland. Hilda began to wonder.

I was in a worse position; I was Hilda's poor relation without even the standing of a relation. I envied Vera Armstrong, who had taken her family back to their own house, saying that she preferred the shells to the hospitality of the War Memorial. We had been given a room, and cots were dug out somehow. I don't really blame the sisters for resenting us, knowing that they were worried about their equipment and that they still expected a flood of wounded to come in later. They probably resented Hilda on general principles anyway. I don't exactly blame them; I can understand them. But I don't love them much.

We slept that night, about eleven of us (including Selwyn, who hated sharing his room with anybody), in a hospital room. I was out on the porch, nearest the tall glass windows, and at midnight something smashed the window and showered me with bits of glass. I wasn't cut, because it was cold and I had rolled up like a caterpillar in my blanket. The next day we all had to crowd inside the room and it was pretty dismal. The shelling was getting much, much worse, and for two days I hadn't heard at all from Charles, and he didn't know we had moved.

Also the milk situation was beginning to get me down. I had started the war with what I always considered a spare case of powdered milk, twelve two-and-a-half-pound tins of Cow and Gate. Until the war we had used cow's milk with lactic acid for supplementary feeding, but now that was impossible and we had to break into the Cow and Gate. Carola's appetite was increasing, and each tin was good at the most for eleven days, on our half-and-half schedule. I began counting up the time that the whole case would last. Then I wondered how I could go on, in the face of all these removals, carrying the big clumsy cans with me. I had a dream of myself trying to catch a train or a plane or something—you know those dreams—and I had the cans and the baby to carry, and I kept dropping one or the other. Then I realized that when the looting started they would probably take my cans of milk away anyway. J asked Selwyn what he thought, and he said:

"Bury the tins in the garden, by night." But now we had moved away from the garden: that wouldn't do. I would just have to step up my own milk, I decided. It had never increased as much as it should, but if Carola helped, and if we kept working at it, perhaps . . . I had read a book about that, by Trubee King.

But Carola wouldn't co-operate. She preferred the Cow and Gate. She just took my milk as a sort of polite gesture, and she wasn't going to take any more than she was used to. I thought about it, and thought, and thought. There wasn't enough work to keep my mind off it. There wasn't enough food to keep me going anyway.

Hilda and I didn't discuss the general situation any more; she was a plain scared woman, wandering about the halls of the hospital in her A.N.S. uniform. I was sorry for her, and glad that I was of a more bovine disposition. We did talk, but it was of peaceful things: gossip, and our pasts, and poetry. I still had my Untermeyer anthology. Reading poetry—any poetry as long as it had rhythm and was fairly long—had a hypnotic effect on me. I felt warm and safe when I had read for a while, and I began to understand people who read the Bible under stress. I thought it might help Hilda, but it seems to have been a private peculiarity that I couldn't share. Nina obviously thought me dotty, and regarded the book like a balky horse. Now that we had moved, we lost Nina. She went downtown and lived with her husband at the office. I was alone with Hilda and Constance and the servants and children.

Ah King had been brought over across the street, too, to do the cooking for the hospital after their own cooks ran away. He seemed to be enjoying himself, though they bullied him and he was overworked. He wore a tall chef's cap and looked most impressive, and he tried without success to smuggle us a little extra in the way of rations. It was all scrappy and pretty grim, but I didn't stay there long.

It was the morning of the twentieth that Hilda came and told me about Charles. He had been wounded while leading an attack on the Repulse Bay Road, in the foray known later as the Battle of Shouson Hill. Tony dressed his wound, and they sent him on to the Queen Mary. He had been shot between the chest and the left shoulder. A rifle bullet traveled close to the lung and came out near the middle of his back, just

off center. He had lain in the paddy field all night, losing blood, and was
delirious when they brought him in. He kept saying to Tony, "I had
a hundred and twelve dollars; be careful of it. Telephone Mickey, somebody. I had some money in my wallet. Notify Mickey." After a night
in the resuscitation ward, with frequent transfusions and plenty of salt
water put into his veins, they decided he would live. At the time I didn't
know any details. Hilda just told me, gently and with admirable and
uncharacteristic restraint, that Charles was wounded in the chest but was
now safe.

I am inclined to gloss over it and say I felt nothing but a very strong impulse to get to Charles, but that wouldn't be true. I remember feeling like
a volcano, and then I was mixed up in a ridiculous quarrel, after all those
days of self-control, with Hilda. She didn't think I should go to the
Queen Mary. She was willing to fight like a lioness to keep me with her.
She thought she was acting in my best interests and from principle, but
Hilda isn't very good at self-analysis; it was obvious that she just couldn't
bear being left alone.

"Your Duty Is to Your Child," she said.

"Now where can I get a lift?" I said to myself.

"Are You Taking Carola?" she asked dangerously.

"Huh? No—don't be silly. It's impossible. I'll have to hitchhike. I won't
take anything."

"I," said Hilda, "cannot be responsible for Carola. Your Duty Is to——"

"Nonsense," I said. "Vera will do it." I rushed upstairs and phoned her.
The Armstrongs had funked going back to May Road, after all, and were
hiding out in the Edmonstons' cellar, on the Peak. Edmonston, I now
learned, was vice-president of the Hong Kong and Shanghai Bank.
You must remember his name; I didn't, just then. I hadn't ever met him.
I wasn't aware of his existence.

Vera was warmly sympathetic and promised to come over that morning and take Carola with Ah Cheung to their cellar. After Hilda's
fireworks it was a comforting note to hear her light voice. She sent her
love to Charles, and the world lost a good deal of its nightmare quality for me. After all, people were going on, eating and sleeping and
getting well from wounds. After all, I had friends. There were other
places besides hospitals.

Down in the basement I found a knot of men making plans for the
day. There was a "dead wagon" starting out soon for Pokfulam, with
some bodies which couldn't be buried up there in the rocky ground.
(Phillips, a man from the bank, had to bury his own wife that week, and
his difficulties were tremendous. The soil was too shallow up there for

graves. It was an outstanding problem for us.) The men were willing for
me to go along, though they kept making deprecatory noises at the idea
of a lady taking such means of transportation. But they couldn't promise
to reach the Queen Mary that day. It sounded hopeless. I decided to walk.
It could be done; there are short cuts down the back of the mountain, but
I wasn't sure I knew the way, and they didn't like the idea of my going
alone. At last a young man turned up and said, "I'm going downtown.
I'm aiming for a post near Happy Valley, which is just the opposite direction from yours, but we can go together till we reach the bank." (The
Hong Kong and Shanghai Bank Building was the focal point of the
main streets, and in that building were the medical headquarters and
other important institutions.) "You will no doubt get a lift there," he
said.

Without taking time to tell Ah King, I shouted to Ah Cheung that
she and Carola would be called for later by Mrs. Armstrong, and we
started out.

I got to the Queen Mary by this and that method at three in the afternoon. Mostly I owe it to Gordon King. After having had to run for our
lives two or three times on the way down, when planes flew over and
bombed us, my first helper said good-by and left me near the bank. Another raid had just been announced, and I raced for the nearest door
into the building. I had a tin helmet, but I still didn't feel immune.
This door was doing duty as the main entrance, from Queen's Road: the
real main entrance faced the harbor and Kowloon and the Japanese guns,
and was now miles deep in sandbags. As I reached the revolving door
and the safety of steel-enforced concrete, I was stopped by a fierce-looking
gent in another tin helmet.

"What do you want?" he demanded. "Where do you want to go?"

Somewhat surprised, I stared at him. I couldn't have known that this
was Edmonston, vice-president of that august bank. All I saw was a funny
man with a mustache, a bit of a pot, and a scared frown.

"Medical headquarters," I said mildly, considering that I was standing
out of doors in a raid, and he was keeping me out there. "I want to get
in to see Selwyn-Clarke."

I don't know what would have happened then. He still stood there,
hesitating, and then Gordon King came swinging along, coming out. I
forgot the little mustache and ran toward him. "Gordon! Are you going
out to the Queen Mary? Charles is there; he's been wounded."

We walked off together, and Edmonston stared after us, shaking after
his encounter with a Scarlet Woman. I didn't know that he was even

then preventing Vera from taking Carola into his house. If I had, things would have been different during that interview at the door of the Hong Kong and Shanghai Bank.

Gordon wasn't going to the Queen Mary, but he was aiming in that direction. I went with him to the market and we bought masses of food, supplies for the university, where he was running an emergency hospital. Two medical students, a Chinese and an Indian, helped us. I saw a few people I knew in the street, and I talked with a couple of tommies who wished me and my husband good luck. They didn't quite know what was happening on the island. They had been fighting in Happy Valley and were now in the middle of town, but they didn't know why.

I lunched at the university with a Chinese doctor and his wife, and got another lift afterward in an ambulance. It was all too long for me; I was dying with impatience. As soon as I reached the university it all seemed quieter. On that side of the island we didn't have any shells except a stray one that came hurtling now and then across the Peak. Planes were bombing Mount Davis near by, but they left us pretty well alone, and near the Queen Mary things were even quieter. I looked down Sassoon Road toward Mme. Kung's house and remembered that she and Mme. Sun had escaped on Tuesday night, in the second to the last plane that managed to come in and get out to Kweilin. Thirteen trips were made, I think, ferrying back and forth, and after that it had to stop because the Japs moved in on Kai Tak airdrome.

The elevators weren't running at the Queen Mary, and I ran up and down the big marble steps, trying to find Charles. First they sent me to one ward, and then another. It was nice there, though, and sane and quiet. The sisters hadn't gone to pieces as yet. They and the doctors were still being held up by that serene conviction that they, above all others, were immune. The quiet of the neighborhood added to this illusion. The Japanese planes really behaved well in regard to the Queen Mary and didn't bomb anywhere near it. I felt that the rest of the island must have been a mistake, and that I had come back to reality.

At last I found Charles, though at first I didn't recognize him, he looked so white. He was packed up on an army cot, in a small but pleasant room. On the other cot was a young ruddy blond fellow with one leg amputated, but not recently. His remaining leg was bandaged, and he rolled fretfully and cursed at intervals, paying no attention to us.

I had been in fluttering fragments all day, but now that I had got to Charles I was all right. "Hi there," I said.

"Mickey." He stopped and wet his lips. "I didn't mean for you to come. I just wanted them to notify you."

"Well," I said, "I wanted to come." I took off my helmet and sat down. "What the hell have you been doing to yourself anyway? I thought staff officers never fought?"

"The men were retreating as I came by. They didn't have an officer. You can't expect them not to retreat if there's nobody to lead them. So I led them, and some bugger got me just as I was climbing out of a nullah. I never even saw him."

"Idiot."

"I thought I was dying," said Charles with a spark of interest. "I lay there wishing I would hurry up and die, because it was cold out there. I knew my blood was running away, and there was damn all to do. Then the stretcher-bearers must have found me. How did you get here, and what are you going to do now?"

"I hitchhiked. I can find somewhere to sleep."

"You can't sleep here," he said irritably. "This is a hospital, not a hotel. Where's Carola?"

"With Vera Armstrong. I'll go down now and see where I can stay. Maybe with Margaret Watson."

"It was sweet of you to come," he admitted grudgingly. "But that isn't what I meant. . . . Can you give this bed a push up?"

"It's a cot, old boy," said the crippled officer.

"Oh. I'm supposed to have one of those gadgets on the bed. Probably later on."

"When I come back," I said, "I'll wash you and comb your hair."

Margaret Watson, the almoner, was a close friend of Hilda's and, like Hilda, had red hair and a sympathy with the leftist element in politics. I had always found her intelligent and sharply pleasant, but today she wasn't.

"My flat," she said, referring to her living quarters next door to the hospital, "is already jammed. There's nowhere for you to stay. You shouldn't have come. Go back up the Peak."

"Have you talked to Hilda?" I demanded. Margaret walked off, her starched skirt swishing. I was pretty mad. It is surprising how angry one can get in times like these. Both Margaret and I must have been shaking with rage, and after all, why? She probably thought I had deserted Hilda. Or perhaps her anger was an exhaust. I heard her later on, simply laying out anyone with whom she had dealings, especially one Indian gentleman with a dark red fez. When, after the surrender, he joined the Japanese with a glad cry I remembered Margaret's savage rudeness to him and I thought I understood. Yet when the sound and the fury had died, she was charming again and couldn't remember having been bitchy. When we talked it over she couldn't recall a word of it. Very odd.

Well, there I stood in the almoner's office, wondering if I couldn't break into the Canaval house and stay there. It wasn't far away as distances go in Hong Kong. My luck held, though. Susie Potts had overheard our conversation, and she suddenly stood there, unfamiliar in her A.N.S. uniform, but looking like heaven all the same.

"We live near here," she said. "You come on home with me, Mickey."

Chapter 40

SUSIE came of an international family. Her mother, Mrs. Weill, was born in Stambul. I don't quite know how that works out with the fact that she met the French Mr. Weill in Shanghai or Harbin or Hong Kong, but it does, and they married and had four children and settled down in Hong Kong with a jewelry shop, after wandering about the Far East long enough for Mother Weill to have learned to speak Japanese, Cantonese, and goodness knows what else on top of her French and German and other non-exotic tongues. Daddy Weill, by the time the Asiatic war overtook his family, was dead and in his grave, but Mamma still ran the whole lot of them. She owned a plot of ground out near the Queen Mary, in the lovely countryside, and on this ground she built two large houses, one just above the other on a steep slope. Susie, the baby, married Alec Potts, a Yorkshireman. Susie and Alec were old friends of mine from those long-ago days when I followed the horses. Alec was very horsy and had been "starter" for the races for as long as I could remember. At this time he was fighting in the Volunteers.

The rest of the Weills were new to me.

I was tired and didn't ask questions. At about five-thirty, when it began to grow dark, Susie took me downstairs to the entrance of the hospital and said, "We meet Mother here every night. You remember Mother?"

She was a short, thickset lady with Susie's snapping black eyes, and she accepted the introduction and the addition to her household with a placid lack of surprise that was very comforting.

A remarkably pretty slender blonde A.N.S. then appeared. "This is my sister-in-law, Vera," said Susie, "and you will live in her house. Vera lives in the other house, all alone."

"I'll be glad to have you," said the blonde, "and my name is *Veronica*."

They glared at each other. Even in my egotistical weariness I could see that. A moment later a plump, darkish man with a mustache showed up and was introduced as a relative. Then we all filed out to a small car that was parked in the driveway, and drove about half a mile down the road, and climbed a hill past potted flowers, and came to a halt before a white house. Mother Weill drove the car, with that calm ruthlessness which characterizes elderly ladies at the wheel. On the way we passed among rows and rows of trucks under the trees, and a lot of dirty-faced soldiers who waved at us and saluted.

"These are Canadians," explained Vera-Veronica. "Such nice boys. They drop in sometimes for coffee."

I was staggered by the amount of room Veronica seemed to have in her house near Mamma's. Shades were down and everything looked deserted, but still it was nice.

"Do you like it?" she asked, pleased. "Of course when my husband is home, and the two children, it isn't so empty. I know you, but you don't know me. My husband is Leo Weill. He's fighting with the Volunteers out near Stanley; he talked to me on the phone last night. And the children . . . Oh dear. The children are at school in Tsingtao."

"With Nina Valentine's?"

"Yes."

"My baby's on the Peak," I said, "being looked after by Vera Armstrong. I wish——"

"You must get her down here," said Veronica Weill. "We'd love to have her. Do bring her down."

"How can I bring her down?"

"My mother's at the War Memorial, on Food Control. We'll call her tonight. There must be some way. I remember your gibbons: my baby loved them. I thought if you didn't mind we could sleep on mattresses downstairs in the drawing room. It seems a little further away from the sky. We'll have something to eat and then drop down to the other house. Wait until I've changed my shoes. I'm so tired. We had a lot of casualties today."

At the other house we found a bewildering lot of people. Evidently the Weills just sat there, quietly letting people come and live with them. I met there Lena Glover, one of the two glamorous Russian sisters who had been a thorn in the flesh of the British spinsters of the Colony for years and years. Lena, the younger of the two, had recently capped her irritatingly successful career by marrying a most eligible young Briton. Being rather a lone wolf myself, I had always liked the Glovers and we knew each other well.

"Where's Mitzi?" I asked Lena. "All right?"

"Oh yes, I guess so. She's nursing at St. Stephen's School near the university," said Lena. "We can't seem to find Desmond, my husband, but he'll turn up."

Behind her, Mother Weill gave me a slumbrous, meaning look and I felt uneasy about Desmond. Everyone looked uncomfortable. But it was all a little bewildering, because I kept meeting people I knew. Ritchie Raymond, a handsome lady whose husband had once been an associate of Sassoon's, was there in navy slacks and a bandanna. "We've lost Albert," she said. Albert was her husband. "The last I heard of him he was at Repulse Bay, and now we are cut off from the hotel. Our house is gone, finished. . . ."

"Now, Ritchie," said Mother Weill, "we'll find him."

I also met an incredibly old lady whose name was Auntie. "I'm a very old lady," she said. "And I've seen trouble before."

"Now, Auntie," said Mother Weill. "Oh dear." She sighed. There were many other people around, but I couldn't get them straight. Susie told me gleefully that her big sister Sophie would be home tomorrow, having resigned from A.N.S. duty across town because her husband was now lying in the Queen Mary with a bullet wound in his foot. Sophie, said Susie, was neurotic and the doctor had agreed that she must come home. I was beginning to sort the Weills out, at least. Susie's only son Peter was at school in Tsingtao. Sophie's son David was in Tsingtao too. That was the chief reason why Mother Weill's face was so long. The older son of Sophie, Albert, was in Hong Kong on some duty or other—he was seventeen—and he was accounted for. The eldest son of all, Jackie, was safe in Free China. My head was spinning when Veronica and I again climbed the hill to our quiet house, and I remembered with some surprise that I, even I, had a child. A very little one, but still a real child. It was time to try for news of her, up there on the chilly Peak.

Veronica put a call through and got her mother on the phone, and asked for news of Carola. She looked worried when she reported to me. "There's no evidence that Mrs. Armstrong ever called and got your baby," she said. "At noon Mother was playing with Carola herself, and she says that old amah was getting nervous because they'd been packed and waiting for hours to be called for. Hadn't you better phone Mrs. Armstrong?"

Telephoning at that date wasn't easy, but I did get Vera, and heard her explanation. She hadn't been able to get through the bombardment, she explained; she had been forced to turn back. But she assured me that Carola would be safe at the War Memorial. "She's got Ah Cheung, and a hospital, after all. . . . I'll try again tomorrow, my dear. How's Charles? We had a shell today on the edge of the roof. A spiky one."

It's a story that has been in the newspaper and in several other places, how I lost Carola and how Bill Hunt, the American shipping man and dashing buccaneer, brought her back when I was just about ready to tear my hair out by the roots. I hadn't dared tell Charles about losing her. I was following a pattern by that time, laid down by the Weills' domestic arrangements: every morning we all drove over in one of the family cars to hospital and dispersed to our various jobs. The Weills, augmented now by Sophie, all did A.N.S. work.

I sat with Charles and made little pads for his paralyzed arm to rest on, or wandered downstairs to help make bandages. His roommate, Captain Wiseman, was a jolly young sprig when his leg stopped hurting, and things were getting comparatively gay in our ward, as Charles felt better. Now and then I would go into the other wards to see what I could do. The hospital was badly understaffed and sometimes nobody came in all day to dress Charles's wound. The paralysis was due to the bullet's shaving too close to the nerve of the left arm, and Digby, the surgeon, was hopeful that after the first shock voluntary movement might come back. In the meantime he waited for the slight infection that had developed in the wound near the spine to subside. He based his hopes on Tony's report that during the first-aid dressing Charles's hand had kept opening and closing spasmodically. But Digby and the nurses were too busy to spend much time on the case.

In the next-door ward Major Neave, who had been wounded with Charles in the same engagement, lay battling for his life against the odds of countless shrapnel wounds all up and down his left side. Whenever I brought Charles anything extra to eat he sent the best part of it to Major Neave, and for a while it looked as if Neave would win the battle for life. He smiled and talked sensibly when I went in, and he kept an enormous photograph of his wife and child where he could look at it, and I never had the feeling there, as I did in some of the other wards, that his spirit was flagging. He lost the battle, though.

Mrs. Martin, the American wife of the British consul to Chungking, was another tough nut. Her husband lay dying of stomach ulcer, complicated, I think, by cancer. Mrs. Martin kept him eating the things he should have in defiance of the hospital's growing miserliness with regard to food. She stormed the kitchen, she insisted, she raised hell. She kept her husband alive for a long time in spite of everything. That battle was lost too, in the end.

There was a ward down the hall with two Volunteer men in it, one big cockney fellow who felt miserable but who did finally recover, and a poor little chap who had been shot through the groin and was delirious. Every time I came in he asked me for chocolate. I managed to get some and give it to him, day after day, time after time. He could never remember having had any before. The other man just wanted tobacco, and I got some for him too, but sometimes he didn't even want that.

Through all of this, for three days, I didn't know where my baby was. I should have trusted Ah King, but one doesn't think of that. Vera Armstrong couldn't insist on bringing the baby into the Edmonston house against her host's refusal, and she couldn't very well tell me that, either. She believed sincerely that Carola was all right at the hospital, and of course she was, but I had no way of knowing. Actually, Ah King kept Ah Cheung at her job. When the poor old amah tried to run away, to find her own twelve-year-old daughter in the town, Ah King threatened and stormed and scared her into remaining. Whenever he could, he brought food down to the pair, concealed as they were in a room on the cellar floor. All the other Chinese servants had long since deserted, and the hospital had reason to be grateful to Ah King for remaining at his post—until the morning that Carola was taken away. Then without a qualm he deserted.

Bill Hunt did it. I had reached him on the phone when I was insane with worry, what with lying every day to Charles and then trying to get some news of Carola after I got home. Bill first suggested taking her into his own hotel suite in the Grips, but he was hastily dissuaded by Judge Allman, who with six other refugees was sharing the rooms. There was no water in the hotel, Allman reminded him, and anyway, if Bill was going to the trouble of bringing a baby all the way from the Peak, why not just give her back to her mamma, where she belonged? Bill saw the force of that argument, and so on the morning of the twenty-fourth, after wrecking one car in the attempt, he brought a howling Carola, a quaking Ah Cheung, and a grinning Ah King out to Veronica's house, to me.

He did more than that. He stamped into the house, talking loudly and cheerfully, and he brought me a lot of supplies: tinned stuff of all sorts, a whole caseful of chocolate, biscuits, and fruit, and coffee. I needed it all too. I sat there with my face all tear-streaked, beaming, clutching the baby to me while she made up for lost time at nursing, and asked him about the war.

"Well," said Bill, "the little buggers are being pretty busy. They're all over the place. They're making headway in the Philippines, and they're swarming down the Malay Peninsula, and they're heading for Burma.

. . . Christ, they're all over the bloody place! How's Charles? I'll try to come out and see him later on. Say, that's some cook boy of yours. I told him he couldn't come in this car, because we were overloaded. And between you and me, it's Selwyn's own private car; I didn't have any right to use it. But when we started to unload here he popped up. . . . You should have been halfway up the Peak when that shell missed us by an inch. I thought the old lady would shed her skin."

He left, and I mopped up and showed the Chinese where to sleep, and then I went out to see Charles, with a clear conscience at last. He talked a lot about Carola.

Somehow or other everyone I knew seemed to be working with Selwyn now. Bill had been picked up in the Gloucester lobby. He was caught between planes in this trap, this Hong Kong where he didn't belong. Selwyn, who didn't know him, had come across him on the second or third morning, sitting disconsolate on a staircase with his unshaved chin propped on his hands.

"Would you like to help move an orphanage in from the New Territories?" asked Selwyn, on a venture. He was always in need of men, always looking. Bill stood up, stretched, and said:

"Where do I get the bus?"

Joe Alsop was another. He had phoned me the second day; he said he was sitting in Hal Sweet's bungalow in Kowloon, rapidly giving up hope that he could ever get out to his duty on a plane. I asked him if he would work for Selwyn in the meantime and he was enthusiastic. The last time I saw him he was carrying stretchers of human fragments at the Queen Mary, clad in a blood-soaked waterproof coat and looking grim. He did good work.

Charlotte too. I told her where to find Selwyn because she wanted to volunteer, and God knows what she didn't do before the war was over. She started rearranging an old school building for a hospital, one of her early duties. "There was a telephone in every room," she told me later, "and Selwyn told me to take them out. The sheer joy of pulling telephones up cannot be expressed. Wait until you try it for yourself." Losing Charlotte during the war—we were not to meet again for two years—distressed me almost more than anything.

So there Carola and I were, reunited and among friends. It was wonderful. Susie taught the amah how to give the baby a sun bath out on the lawn. In Pokfulam that sort of activity was still possible; only an occasional plane flew over our house. Little by little I began to sort out all the people who were living there. We ate carefully but adequately. Bill Hunt's load of supplies was a great help. I would eat breakfast, go to the hospital, and when lunchtime came around either I nibbled a piece of Bill's chocolate or went without. Charles couldn't eat most of his lunch—a heap of rice and a spoonful of stew—and sometimes I fell on it and cleaned it up after him, but as young Bill Wiseman got better he became ravenous and even Charles's ration wasn't enough for him. Ah King, now that he had no more cooking to do, took to walking in to town and foraging around. He used his own money. He bought grapes for Charles, and they came in handy for Wiseman and Neave, if not for Charles himself. He bought chocolate and whatever cans he could find. One day I brought a parcel to the hospital; there were cigarettes for Wiseman and a tin of sausages (the little Vienna kind) and another tin of Brussels sprouts for Charles, and I was pretty proud of myself. But Charles looked at the sausages and the sprouts doubtfully.

"You shouldn't do this," he said. "You should keep these things for the baby."

My subsequent lecture was all too successful. For the rest of the time we were in Hong Kong, Charles was convinced that Carola ate nothing but milk and sugar. He was still worrying about sugar and milk for her when we left Hong Kong two years later.

All over hospital the patients were trying to eke out their diet with sweets. There was a certain kind of Australian jam, IXL brand, that flooded the market, fortunately. The men loved it. Charles could take a small tin of apricot jam and devour it in one day. Healthier men could eat much more jam than that. Instinctively they were trying to make up for the lack of fats and sugars that already was bothering them in their diet.

We knew the hospital basement was full of supplies: cases and cases of sardines in oil and fruit and everything else. But the authorities were trying to save it all for the lean months ahead, never admitting to themselves that the Japanese would not be likely to let them reap the benefits of their caution. And upstairs the young men grew hungrier and hungrier.

It made me laugh, withal bitterly, when Hilda and Mary trailed into the Queen Mary the day after my epic hitchhike. Hilda was airy about it. "*Quite* impossible, my dear. We had seven hits on the roof of the hospital the day you left. Constance is supposed to have packed your things and they are mixed in with mine. I'll sort them out in time. My dear, it's heaven at Margaret's. I have her bedroom."

"Oh, she did make room then?"

"Why, yes. I believe there were some people there, but Margaret asked them to move. Why?"

"Nothing. . . . Did you bring my hairbrush?"

"Probably," said Hilda. "Of course I shall never understand why you dashed off as you did, without even packing a bag."

We were on chilly terms for some days. I know it was petty of me but I couldn't help it. Hilda was the director's wife and now at last, in Selwyn's own hospital, she reaped the benefit of her position. She did as she liked there, and acted like the hostess of the place. She gained in stature hourly, only collapsing when her husband came home of an evening. I began to picture to myself those long cozy sessions she had with Margaret in the flat, over a bottle of whisky; they had tried me in the balance and found me wanting. "Rushing off like that, like a madwoman, my dear, abandoning her child. . . . Incredible!"

The British hospital system, and the whole Western-world idea of social relief, develops petty tyrants to a dangerous degree. I was to discover that very shortly. On the day Carola was given back to me I met Margaret, the almoner, in the corridor of the hospital and she hailed me. Her brown eyes were looking hard.

"How long do you intend to hang on with the Weills?" she demanded. "What are you going to do when they are put out of their house?"

Instead of retorting, "It's none of your business," I asked, "Huh?"

She spoke crisply but breathlessly. I suppose she was scared, but it didn't show. "All the houses in the neighborhood are to be dispossessed," she said. "They are to be filled with soldiers who are going to protect us from snipers. So the Weills will be forced to move, and where will you go then?"

"Canavals' house, I suppose."

Margaret took a deep breath. "You had better go away completely," she said. "They will want the Canaval house too, very likely. *They are going to protect us from snipers.*" She spoke passionately. "You are hampering the war effort by remaining," she said. "And another thing: you shouldn't come here every day. This hospital, by virtue of the fact that we are taking in soldiers, is no longer a civilian hospital. It's military. Now in a military hospital visitors aren't permitted except once a week, often not at all. You come here in the morning, outside of visiting hours, and sit with Charles all day. You aren't a relative of his, you know. I've heard a lot of talk about it and action will be taken soon. I'm sorry," she said, "but there it is."

Fortunately I didn't try to answer: I recognize panic when I see it. I walked off and left her, but I went to see Hilda and raised hell.

"You've been working Margaret up. I won't have it. If necessary I'll appeal to Selwyn. Nobody takes care of Charles all day but me; they're shorthanded and they know it. Now——"

Whatever tension had strung Hilda up to this amazing pitch broke down. "Oh, my dear, you're hysterical. I haven't told Margaret to say anything. . . . I'm sorry."

We set to work together making swabs, and when Margaret came back things were near sanity again. The two women now concentrated on another problem. How was Hilda to be smuggled out before the Japanese swooped down and took her prisoner, and tortured her, and murdered her? They seemed to take it for granted that Hilda of all people was in the gravest danger. She had helped Chungking; she was known as a leftist.

"You must dye your hair black and be entered here on the books as Rose Smith," decided Margaret. "Later we'll smuggle you out. Your friends can be trusted."

"Oh, the Chinese won't give me away. But Mary? Selwyn would never consent to my breaking for freedom and taking Mary with me."

"Then let's do this. . . ."

They talked on, and on, and on. Hilda's voice trembled, as though she were wallowing pleasantly in danger. I didn't think that she was in that much peril. Japan, it seemed to me, was now more seriously at war with Western nations than she had been with China or China's champions. I thought for an uneasy moment of my own record—*The Soong Sisters,* and *Candid Comment,* and a lot of other things—and then with genuine relief I decided that I wasn't important enough for the Japs to worry their heads about. I have always been an optimistic ostrich, but it gives me satisfaction now to reflect that this time I was right. I held my tongue, though. Hilda was in the saddle, not Emily Hahn and her Carola. I made swabs.

Chapter 41

GWEN PRIESTWOOD and her government lorry dropped by every day. The war may have shown up a lot of people in a shocking way, so that I still blush for them when I think of it, but it brought out the most surprising heroism in others. It proved to me that I had been wrong in my opinions of practically everybody from the beginning.

It was Christmas morning when Gwen came in. The Governor had already made his rounds the afternoon before. Charles was still too ill to be told the truth, they decided, so the Governor told him a lot of pretty lies about how magnificently we were doing, though when Alf Bennett dropped by later he savagely contradicted all of it.

"They're running a regular ferry service over to North Point in broad daylight," he grumbled, "and God knows what's happened to Repulse Bay. We need you, old boy; why did you go and get wounded? My Japanese is inadequate, to say the least."

Gwen, though, was cheerful and full of fight, and fresh from having driven her lorry through very hot territory.

"Helen and Gustl Canaval," she reported, "have given me permission to raid their house. I want to get clothes for you, Charles——"

"But I'm all right," said Charles. "You've brought most of my kit already."

"Also," continued Gwen, "the Canavals have a cellar of sorts, and since looting seems inevitable, it might as well be me."

"I'll go with you," I said.

I had always thought the Canaval house (next door to Mme. Kung's) very near to the hospital. Today, though, what with a Jap plane sailing about overhead and exhibiting an awkward interest in our khaki-colored van, it didn't seem so near after all. As we reached the Canaval driveway, notorious for its awkward steepness, Gwen peered up at the plane and said doubtfully, "I don't think they'd waste a whole bomb on us, do you?"

"N-n-n-o," I said mendaciously. We drove down the hill and knocked on the door. The plane hovered about, still curious. A frightened servant answered our hail, overjoyed at seeing us, and he made no difficulties at all when we raided the house. Woolies, pajamas, books, and two dozen small bottles of rye whisky rewarded our search, and we felt very cheery as we started back, even though we stalled on the hill just as the plane swooped down to take a good look. Gwen was right; they didn't waste a bomb. We brought the whisky back safe to the Queen Mary and distributed it in the privates' wards, all but one pint bottle.

Nothing marred our simple enjoyment of the day until three in the afternoon, when Hilda ran in. Her hair was mussed up and there were tears running down her cheeks, and a break in her voice.

"Do you know the news, Charles?" she blurted. "We've surrendered. The firing is stopped. There's a white flag on the police station across the road. Selwyn just phoned me."

I suppose Charles was the only really surprised staff officer in town. You see, they hadn't been telling him the truth. He didn't say anything but "Yes, Hilda?" but he looked very grim and set his jaw. Hilda sank down on a chair and talked, and talked, and talked. Neither of us listened. Charles said once, "They didn't tell me," and that was all. After a long time I realized Hilda was still talking, and I didn't want to hear her. I thought it was the end of everything. I thought they would take Charles away immediately. There wasn't any time. "Hilda," I said, "I want to speak to Charles alone."

"Why, certainly, my dear." She was surprised but amiable.

She hurried out to spread the news. Wiseman had gone out already in a wheel chair, and we were really alone, for the first and last time. I don't know what I said. I cried on his good shoulder, I remember that, and asked him what would happen to him. Charles said that they would treat him all right, and that we must just try to see the war through.

"In the end they can't win," he said. "I don't see how they can, do you? Against America and England and Holland and China? We must try to survive, that's all. I'm only sorry you're caught."

"They'll take you away from me," I said.

We heard three loud explosions; that was the big guns they were blowing up, he said. Wiseman rushed in to ask us if we thought it was the truth. Other boys came in then, old friends of ours, walking wounded with their arms in casts, or their heads bandaged, or their teeth missing. I sat there and tried to be normal. I wanted to go back to Carola but I didn't want to leave Charles. I suppose I've never been quite as unhappy and frightened in my life. It is no use trying to write about these things.

Veronica came in to tell me it was time to go home, and she was fighting mad at the Army for surrendering, and then tearful, and then mad again. She walked over with a swing of her fine figure and stared out at the countryside beneath the veranda. "There they are," she said suddenly. "Japs. Little beasts. Swarming all over."

I went and stood next to her and looked. It was true. They were on the roads outside the hospital and inside the grounds; little misshapen gnomes they looked like, dirty and shabby and grinning and busy. They were carrying things into the flat buildings, the doctors' and nurses' quarters. The roads were choked with Jap trucks. The lovely country was covered with Japs. It had happened at last. After running away from their bombs in Nanking and Nantao in 1937, after running the gantlet dozens of times in Shanghai, after escaping them for a year by ducking into Chungking ground, I had been caught. Now. With Carola, and Charles wounded in hospital.

I had seen Japanese armies before. I saw the Victory March in Shanghai. My stomach felt queasy, and I knew we would have to face it now or I would begin to be really afraid. I picked up my bag.

"Come on," I said to Veronica. "Let's go."

Charles, watching me out of the door, smiled a little. He must have been afraid too.

That morning, though we were busy with Christmas junketing, I had seen a truck drive up with a lot of white girls in it, mostly in A.N.S. uniform. I didn't see them close up, but I remembered later having wondered where they came from. Three of them had climbed down out of the back of the lorry in a weary, hopeless way, and they had linked arms and walked into the hospital clinging to each other. Now at the door when I met Susie and Sophie and the others I heard about it.

"We're walking," they explained to me. "Mother doesn't dare bring the car because the Japs will snaffle it. They're taking cars wherever they see them. Those girls who were brought back today are in a bad way. They were caught in Happy Valley in a first-aid post."

"Why?" I asked stupidly. "What happened?"

Susie stared at me and said, "Rape."

I said to myself, "Nonsense. It doesn't really happen." I also said, "Rape is impossible. Unless, of course, you use a sandbag or a bayonet." I said to myself, "I won't be taken in by horror stories. No, no, no; I'll hold on to myself." I said, "If I am raped I won't care. It won't be my fault. It will mean nothing; it is like being wounded. Charles would agree with me."

Just then, as we left the hospital grounds a few yards from the gate, two Japanese came along. One was a private and the other, since he was carrying a sword, must have been an officer. The private hailed us "Oy!" We pretended first not to hear; he yelled louder, angrily. We stopped. My eyes met Susie's. She sat down suddenly on a rock.

The officer grinned and walked off so he couldn't see us. The private approached us at a run and motioned that he wanted to look at our arms. It was our wrist watches he wanted, not our virtue. The relief of it made me shaky in the knees. What's more, he missed my watch; I wear it on the right wrist and he didn't look for it there, under my leather jacket. As he took the watches from the others Susie found the nerve to say, "You have one already." She touched it lightly. "Shame!" said Susie banteringly.

The private grinned awkwardly. He hung his head and grinned like a naughty schoolboy, showing his great teeth like battered tombstones. But he took the watches. Then he let us go on. He stank; I was aware of that.

We found Japanese all over the house. They had taken complete possession of the upper house, and three officers had elected to live in

Mother Weill's living room. Mother Weill was everywhere all at once, talking Japanese in a broken way that was still effective, arguing, giving orders to her servants, working away like a machine. We had no time to repine. She rushed at us like a whirlwind and shoved us indoors, out of sight of the licentious soldiery, up the back stairs to the bedrooms. The officers seemed to be all right, she whispered. We were to stay out of sight. Yes, Carola was safe.

"They're to stay a few days," Mrs. Weill explained. "It's a good thing I can talk to them; they're not too bad. One of them took Chrissie Angus' wrist watch, but he gave her a tin of peas in exchange."

Mrs. Angus, a venerable lady of sixty-five, sent us into hysterical giggles by reporting that one of the soldiers had made advances to her. It was the truth. He had pointed to a couch and then made an unmistakable gesture. Mrs. Angus was the only female in all our crowd who had been approached disrespectfully. "It's my figure gets 'em," she said.

We screamed with laughter, until Mrs. Weill made us desist. We must whisper, she said, and not attract attention until they were gone away.

One of the most awkward features about this irruption of the Army into our house was that Alec had just come home the day before. With his regiment, he had been ambushed in a house on the Ridge near Repulse Bay. He and a friend had broken for freedom, swum the bay, walked several miles along a gravel road in their bare feet, and finally got home. Alec was obviously of military age and the family went to great pains to keep him under cover. As long as the Japs had only women to deal with, as long as they kept sober, they were not likely to get very ugly. We kept Alec wrapped in cotton wool. And through it all Mrs. Weill, her face alight with the effort of battle, striding about the house like a little lioness, kept talking. We owe our safety in those days to her.

You don't know what you think about rape until you are caught in a war, and in those days following Christmas I made up my mind what I would always say to people, forever after. I know what the public thinks. I saw them after the last war when they listened to stories about it. When you talk about "atrocities" that is the first thing you think of. There is a horror about it, and there is also a fascination; people get a kick out of the subject, of course. Their eyes glisten when they hear of rape, and it's always the first question I am asked, now that I'm back in America: "Did you have any—uh—Trouble?" It's a double attraction to the human mind; sex is always fascinating, and sex by violence is doubly so. The second attraction is linked up with the first. We seem to have a sort of race jealousy that is manifested in our lynchings and in the special interest people always show in the sex behavior of other races. For example, when young Belgians go down to the Congo on contract they talk about nothing on the way down on the ship but the black girls they are going to sleep with. It's the first thing they do when they arrive at the first port: they dash for a brothel. That behavior isn't limited to the Belgians, either: look at our own tourists when they land in Shanghai, if you doubt me. "Is it true about Chinese girls?"

I'm no psychiatrist and I won't try to explain this phenomenon. There it is, a very strong force in human behavior. Well, that is why you are always so interested in stories of rape by the Japanese. That is why the Nanking atrocities seemed so special. It's all tangled up in your mind; you get a kick out of it while you are being righteously horrified. Until the war, you stimulated yourself with fantastic stories about the sex behavior of the other races. I remember being amused because I heard such big tales about Negroes and their sexual powers when I went to Africa, and then when I got to China I heard the same tales exactly, only this time it was about the Chinese. I was even more amused when Chinese I knew well began to tell me the same old bogy stories, this time about the whites. You would be surprised if you knew what tremendous things the Chinese think you white men capable of.

All this preamble is just an attempt to understand Japanese behavior, an attempt which always floors me sooner or later. I don't understand the Japanese very well. But I think that they too are prey to this wishful thinking, and so when they run amuck in China those things happen. And there is another element in this calculated mass rape that they go in for: they know that it is the quickest, surest way to humiliate a community. I think that they rape almost as a religious duty, a sacrifice to the God of Victory, a symbol of their triumphant power.

My suggestions to alleviate the misery caused by war rape are not very practical. They would take too long to put into effect. I want us to lift the guilt burden from the minds of the victims. To do this we would have to uproot centuries of diametrically opposed ideas. We would have to bring up our daughters not to fear rape with the superstitious terror with which we have always instilled them. We would have to teach them that rape is simply a physical hazard, one of the penalties of war which might possibly happen to anyone. Do you think it could be done? If so, a lot of miserable little girls would be much happier, and I have never seen why they should have been made miserable in the first place, aside from the misery that naturally accompanies rape on a virgin. I realize that I am trying to go against nature. We don't scare the girls deliberately; we are scared ourselves, and we just pass it on. But my idea ought to be tried out. Really, it ought. I saw the women in Hong Kong and I know. I was infuriated by the unnecessary suffering we cause ourselves.

Once and for all, no, I wasn't. Mother Weill took care of us well during the most dangerous period, while the Japanese were jubilant and reckless and drunk. It is an old Army custom in Japan that when the troops enter a city they are given three days in which they can do whatever they like. That's when the worst things happen. In Nanking it was such a tremendous affair that the men got out of hand and wouldn't calm down after three days, but in Hong Kong they were comparatively well-behaved. I'm not saying they all behaved like perfect gentlemen, because they didn't, but they were nothing like the Nanking troops. I dare say they were better-behaved, number for number, than our troops are going to be when they walk into Tokyo. There were isolated cases; I know of one family where the Japs butchered every man in the house, although nobody offered any resistance to their entry. I know that many Chinese women were raped. Most of the British women escaped this indignity. Either the men were being held in—the Japs certainly did have in mind an idea of showing those snooty British that they could be gentlemen too—or they just preferred Chinese women to British, a preference most people could understand, I should think. Anyway, the Chinese suffered a lot more than we did. I am deliberately not giving any details about rape on white women. A report would not be nice for the women. But at any rate none of them died, and I think they're all all right now.

After the first three days the Japs did settle down to some extent, though the streets of the Colony couldn't yet have been any picnic to walk in. Charles warned me about New Year's Day. "They get pretty drunk, and they take another three days off," he explained. "Yes, they use our date for it." We were still following our schedule, though now we walked to hospital and back again, in groups of at least three. I never made any attempt to leave that beaten path. The quiet Pokfulam roads were full of squatty, duck-bottomed soldiers, carrying furniture back and forth between houses that they had commandeered for their officers. There were great heaps of tins and cases of food lying here and there, British supplies looted from government warehouses, probably. We saw an incredible amount of waste going on. Soldiers would open tins of bully beef with their bayonets, take a bite or two, and throw the rest into the mud. They chopped down trees for firewood, or furniture, or anything handy. They took every house they could find except the hospital itself; our officers saved Mother Weill's lower house from being commandeered. Veronica and I finally got our things out of her house by getting atabrine for one of the soldiers who lived there and whom we found quaking with a malarial chill, lying in his boots on Veronica's satin quilt and wearing my green jersey pajamas over his filthy uniform. They had tethered a lot of horses in the garden. The troops urinated everywhere, in the house mostly, on the floor. That was probably symbolic too.

The doctors and nursing staff of the Queen Mary at last lost their smug feeling of immunity. You could see this loss in their eyes as they pattered about the corridors on their errands; they looked enraged and yet stunned with indignant surprise. They? They, pushed out of their comfortable flats which they had always felt were their own exclusive property? They, angels and such of mercy, treated just like ordinary people? They, crowded now on cots in dormitories like refugees? What was the world coming to? Wasn't there an international law?

Margaret Watson was definitely chastened. She had gone back to her flat at last, after the troops were moved on, and a grinning little ape of a guard showed her around the rooms. In the living room they had selected her best doilies of Swatow linen and placed them about the fireplace in a semicircle, and then had gone to the trouble of defecating on each linen square. The soldier was careful to point this out to her.

"He smiled," said Margaret, her brown eyes limpidly puzzled. "I just can't understand that mentality."

"Can't you?" I replied.

Chapter 42

THE BRITISH TROOPS that weren't killed or wounded were being rounded up and put into temporary camp while the Jap authorities made up their minds what to do with this victory. We waited in hushed fear to see what would happen to the hospitals; for the time being they were leaving the Hong Kong institutions alone. I believe they had already taken over the mainland companion piece to the Queen Mary, the Kowloon Hospital, for themselves, but I'm not sure about that.

Over in my apartment, though I didn't know it, a girl named Irene Fincher was struggling under an enormous weight of catastrophe. She, with her baby Frances, aged about ten months, and her sister Phyllis and *her* baby Bryan, aged a year and a bit, and her old mother and father, the Gittinses, had been hurried from their homes in Kowloon on the day the Japanese marched in. It was her husband, Ernie Fincher, who took them to the ferry in their own car; he was in a hurry to get back into the war and the whole thing was a tremendous rush. At the ferry he saw his family out of the car and then on the spot turned it over to a wrecking crew to be smashed before the Japs could get it. "Close your eyes," he advised his wife. Irene closed her eyes and heard a smash, and then she boarded the boat. She never saw Ernie again.

Phyllis' husband was lost too. The girls had been brought up in the typical Hong Kong manner, spoiled and petted all their lives, in more luxury than our upper classes ever knew, a luxury that is based on human labor and cannot be substituted by any kind of American labor-saving gadget. Suddenly they were dumped into my flat with a lot of other refugees, and they had to shift for themselves. One thing that saved them some grief was that Gordon King, who had delivered Irene's baby and was a friend of her family's, came to see them and brought with him all the powdered milk and baby food that he was able to buy at the last minute, anywhere in town, and any brand. He carried this variegated lot of tins into the Gittins family, looking around at my flat with a queer grin.

"It's Miss Hahn's place," said Irene nervously.

"I know," he said.

"Will she mind?"

"No," said Gordon King. "You'll be all right here. Even if anyone tries to turn you out, just sit tight. She won't, though."

Having done what he considered his duty by his patients, he left them and went back to his hospital at the university.

Ah King went in one day to get some clothes, and brought me back a note from Irene, but I couldn't read her signature. I could only make out that a lot of people were there, and Ah King rather thought they were Portuguese because they spoke such good Chinese. If that puzzles you, I had better explain that there were something like ten thousand people from Macau living in Hong Kong then. Macau is an infinitesimal Portuguese possession four hours by boat from the Crown Colony. It used to be a famous place for fantan, adultery, and easily procured passports from Lisbon. The Hong Kong Portuguese are really "Maccanese"—a mixture of Chinese, ancient Latin, and Japanese or Malay. The Gittinses weren't Maccanese; they were straight British and Danish mixed with Chinese, but Ah King, like the British authorities, didn't make much distinction. The Gittinses did, though.

I have gone to such lengths on the subject at this point because Macau plays an important part in the Hong Kong war: as neutral ground it was to be very useful, even though the Japs did hem it in and watch it like hawks.

Japanese officers began paying calls on Charles. They were exquisitely polite to him and held long conversations in Japanese while I stood in the corner, now and then stepping up to light their cigarettes. I don't know why I behaved that way, except that Charles seemed to expect it of me. He knows Japanese custom. They always talked for five minutes at least before they asked him who I was, and his manner was just the right shade of deprecating carelessness when he replied. I recognized it from my experience with Japs; it amused me. We both seemed to have put on masks for the duration, quite by instinct. Bill Wiseman in his cot was duly introduced as the officer who had lost one leg and been wounded in the other, and the Jap officers, respecting such bravery, would stand up and bow deeply. It was all according to Bushido and not a bit like what was going on outside the hospital walls, in the streets.

Charles didn't realize what was going on in the streets and I didn't like to tell him. Still, I was surprised the day he had a hurried note from Dr. Helen Canaval, asking him to see that some of her clothes were packed up, if possible, and sent to her wherever she was stationed at the time.

"You can run over and get them this afternoon, Mickey," he said.

I said, "Not much I can."

Charles looked surprised. "Why? There's no barrier up in the road, is there?"

"It isn't exactly safe to go running around just now," I explained.

Still he insisted: "Take Ah King with you if you're afraid. Helen needs those clothes."

I looked at him with exasperation, but decided not to reply. It wouldn't have made sense to him if I had told him that the roads were crowded with looters who carried arms, that our hospital workers were always finding dead bodies of civilians who had encountered these people off the main highway, that the Canaval house was undoubtedly gutted already, as were all the other houses in the neighborhood, and Ah King or no Ah King, I would be picked up by the Japs. The only safe road was that between our house and the hospital, and that was because we stepped almost straightway from the Weill grounds to the hospital territory. I was sorry Helen needed clothes, but so did I. I wouldn't have gone to her house just then for anything but Carola. The body of a pretty European girl had been picked up near the Queen Mary and was now in the hospital icebox awaiting identification. I don't know why I got it into my head that this girl was my friend Maria da Roza, a Portuguese masseuse who had given me a course of massage after Carola, but I did. I was sure it was Maria. I made up my mind to go down and take a look, but that very morning Maria herself walked in, well and in uniform, on duty and detailed to massage Charles's arm.

Little by little I was learning my way around the hospital, through the bewildering mass of old friends who were patients. On the last day of the fighting Barbara Petro came in with her husband, who had been wounded in the leg. He had joined up the day before and there wasn't even time to give him a uniform. Petro held a French passport, though in the early days he was a White Russian. Now that he was wounded, we were worried about his status. If the Japs got hold of a Free Frenchman they would be ugly, perhaps, and Petro had a stormy record on behalf of De Gaulle. Barbara was working in the American consulate and she was still on duty. After the surrender she was held with the others incommunicado in the American Club, up on top of the Hong Kong and Shanghai Bank Building. When Petro heard that he got up, grabbed a mop as a crutch, left all his spare change with me and, still in gray tweed, hobbled out of hospital. He got to Barbara somehow, I heard later.

I found Dorothy Jenner too—the Australian newspaperwoman who had dined with Colin and me before Pearl Harbor. She was down with dysentery, after having served with the police during hostilities. She was profane in her criticism of the way the war had been run, and now she watched the campaign in Malaya with agonized interest. She was a jolly soul, and one afternoon when she came up to see Charles we had a brisk argument. Jenner as an Australian began to chip Charles as an Englishman for the way his country was mismanaging everything. I spoke up in her behalf, but suddenly she turned on me, the American, and said, "And what about all that help Roosevelt was going to send?"

It stopped me. You would have to have been in Hong Kong during that period to realize how irritating Mr. Roosevelt's glowing speeches can be, given certain conditions. I sat there looking rueful, and so did Charles, and so did Jenner. There we were, the three of us, quite definitely in the soup.

Charles began to chuckle. Then I did. Then Jenner did. It was the first time he had laughed since the surrender, but it was a good one when it came. We all sat there laughing, wordless and ignoble but still alive. After that, things were never quite so nightmarish again.

Conditions outside were getting so lawless and dangerous that we women at the Weill house put in a request to be allowed to sleep in the Queen Mary. The Rev. Mr. Short, a scared-looking bloke Selwyn had left in charge of the hospital, said we couldn't. He said there was no room. In vain I reminded him of Selwyn's early promise that the hospitals were to be refuges for women and children when the time came; he was paralyzed with fear that the Japanese would kick him, and of course the rest of the personnel, out into the street. He seemed to think that they would be angry if he took in any refugees, and he was definite in his refusal. The sisters backed him up heartily. They wanted to stay in their hospital as long as possible, and they wanted to eat too; they were awfully worried for fear we would encroach on the food supply.

In the meantime they weren't doing too badly, though the patients were starving. I shall never, I suppose, stop being bitter about that period. There were masses of supplies in the basement, and the staff must have thought the Japs were going to let them go on living in the hospital forever—the best hospital in town, mind you—eating their own food. And so naturally they didn't want to waste that food. They were eating pretty well in their own mess; they weren't that parsimonious. It was only in regard to the patients that they were so careful. Once when I was complaining about Charles's rations Hilda said:

"Why, I think we manage admirably. Today Mary and I had our choice of two kinds of soup, and we each had a cup of each, didn't we, Mary? Then there was a salad, and a bit of cold meat——"

"No doubt," I said, "in the staff room. Charles didn't have that."

Hilda looked over my head. "That's appalling," she said. "I do think the staff ought to take what the patients get. . . ." She drifted away then, and avoided me for several days. She had taken over a cabinet in the hospital, with a lock on the door, and I entrusted my cans of Cow and Gate to her, just in time to save them. One had already disappeared, and the can I was using currently seemed to sink in level more quickly than was normal. I was frantic. I tried my best to do better on the milk question myself, but it was no good. The short rations couldn't have helped very much, of course.

Ah King came and told me he had no more money, and I gave him fifty dollars and said that he had better go away. "I have only two hundred left," I said, "in hundred-dollar notes. I can't pay you any more."

"That's all right," he said cheerfully. "I can wait."

The first thing the Japanese had done was to close the banks, and all of us were caught short, save for a few farsighted individuals who had taken the time in the early days to go into their banks and load up on currency. We were pretty sore at the government for waiting with their surrender and then popping it on us as a surprise. "But they wanted to avoid runs and riots," Charles explained.

"But what do we do now?"

There wasn't anything to do but sit tight. It was lucky for me that I was with the Weills, the Weills with their clever, resourceful mother and their inexhaustible cellar. Everything in the world came out of that cellar just when you needed it most. Even Mother Weill didn't have powdered milk, though. Somewhere somebody must have put in a good word for me with the fates. One day the proprietor of the Grips dropped in to hospital. He was a man I scarcely knew. And what do you think he sent up to me? A twelve-pound tin of milk powder!

I slept better that night.

Tony Dawson-Grove was in hospital. He was a patient, but he pretended that nothing was the matter with him. As if it were an obscene secret he concealed the fact that he had got a splinter of shrapnel in the chest, while he was on duty at Aberdeen. Tony is a Quaker and was glad that he was a Navy doctor and so noncombatant. Now, however, he was recovering from the first shock, and he was laboring under a strong sense of rage. I understood him thoroughly; I was too. I was angry with everyone those days, with a deep dangerous anger that burned for several months. Tony must have been feeling the same. He sat with Charles and me on the little veranda of the ward one afternoon, and he suddenly burst out—we had been talking it all over, the ineptitude of the authorities, the stupidity with which they had defended and then surrendered.

"What now?" he demanded. "It doesn't make sense. Look at Charles. Look at you. Mickey, what's going to happen to you?"

Charles looked shocked and didn't say anything. I wasn't shocked; I knew how Tony was feeling. I shrugged, and I didn't say anything either. There was nothing to say.

One of the results of the surrender was that there was a rush on the part of the leftists, Hilda's friends, to save their skins. I suppose I had better not use names. Except for Jim Bertram, who simply enlisted with the Volunteers and fought, and was captured, and in general behaved well, and Max Bickerton, who did his job too and made no attempt to get away, the leftists behaved in a way that made me slightly sick. One after another they came up to hospital with plans for getting into disguise, usually as nurses or doctors (still believing in that immunity of the magic Red Cross, you see), and shaking with terror. Each one seemed to feel that the Japanese had waged this war with the sole intention of getting hold of *him*. After one of them had been in the room and pleaded with me to do something for him that I couldn't, Charles spoke his mind. He felt let down and disappointed in the boys and girls.

"Not much gallantry in defeat there, is there?" he said. "I'm somewhat surprised, I must say. Why should they be so worried? You have as much reason to be afraid, Mickey."

"Well," I said, "I'm not. I don't think the Japs care about any of us. Anyway, Charles, the Chinese aren't acting like this. I saw Chi-cheng yesterday; she's living here on the grounds, and she was okay. Perfectly calm. Maybe you have to be hysterical, rather, to be a leftist on someone else's soil to begin with. I mean—oh, I don't know, but it *is* sort of disgusting."

I almost forgave Margaret Watson all her rudeness when we talked it over. "So far there have been absolutely no inquiries about Hilda," she admitted. "We made fools of ourselves. I think it must be a sort of conceit, don't you?"

And Hilda was funny too. "I've always pictured myself as being able to take it," she said. "I've always imagined I would die gloriously, in a splendid blaze or something. I never in all my wildest imaginings thought of being a prisoner, just like anybody else."

She had come around to normal pretty well. Selwyn, during all these days, was the busiest man in town. He was co-operating with the Japs insofar as he went on doing his job, the normal duties of the director of medical services. His mind had started immediately working on the problem of how to keep the town from the horrors of epidemics and other aftereffects of war, and the Japs seemed to respect this impulse of his. They gave him an arm band, their method of showing authority, which stated that the doctor was "adviser" to their Health Department. It was during those days that I remembered what they had called Selwyn in Africa when he worked there: "the man with the smile of the tiger." He looked ghastly; haggard and bodiless. He worked without stopping to eat or sleep. He worked like a saint and a devil. He talked endlessly with stubborn or threatening or suspicious Japanese officers. Little by little he got someplace.

"My duty," he told me once, "is to the population of this town—the Chinese and Indians and Eurasians as well as the whites. I shall continue to do my duty, if it is permitted, to keep them as healthy as possible. We took on that responsibility when we made Hong Kong a colony. I love Hong Kong."

I looked at him now with awe. If ever I had learned to talk to him during the early days of the war, it was impossible now to communicate with him as human to human. Selwyn was going through the ordeal of canonization. You couldn't get to him, and you didn't want to. But we all leaned on him with all our weight, and he carried us.

It had been a week since the surrender. After all, nothing much had happened at the hospital. In the rest of town there had been tragedies and crimes and conflagrations, but we didn't know about them except by rumor. The telephones were cut off and there were no trams or buses. News went on foot, in the mouths of coolies.

Mrs. Weill decided that we should celebrate New Year's Day, more, I suppose, because she didn't want to default on her duties than because she felt at all joyful. Everyone tried to help with some contribution, and the table at eight o'clock looked lovely. We had no electricity, but there were candles. We had shuttered the windows, of course, and locked the front door, and closed everything up. Men were scarce; there were only Alec and the young Albert, Sophie's son. The rest of us were women of all ages and shapes, from young Lena, who had just discovered she was pregnant, to old Auntie.

Mother Weill had killed her last two chickens. We were going to eat them with the inevitable rice, and the cooking smelled wonderful. Alec poured out a few drops of whisky for each of us; Veronica brought her ukulele, which she played very well. It was quite festive considering everything. Like the other girls, I was wearing my pajamas, ready to go to bed as soon as we had dined. I should mention here that our Japanese guests were gone, having pulled out that morning, and we felt pretty good about that too. The upper house was still too filthy for us to think of moving back, but still, we thought, it was nice to have our houses to ourselves again. We were wrong.

Carola was asleep in the hallway upstairs, in a deep Morris chair which did duty as a cot, and which kept the draft off. The servants were all in the kitchen helping the cook. Veronica swung into "Rule, Britannia" and we sang with her:

"Britons never, never, never shall be slaves."

At that moment a lot of men marched in through the kitchen, shut out the servants, and tied us up.

Chapter 43

IT IS ALWAYS difficult to describe melodramatic happenings like that one. Anyway, it is for me. I don't like using exclamation points, and yet they do seem to be indicated when one is talking about this sort of thing. We thought, of course, that the men were Japanese soldiers; it was only reasonable to suppose so, as the first few of them were wearing Japanese uniform. The others, I noticed, were not. They were just Chinese rabble. When Mrs. Weill spoke to them in Japanese they didn't understand her. The leader, a small fellow with a very dashing way of doing things, was only able to reply to her when she spoke Cantonese. Later we agreed that they were camp followers, or perhaps Formosans, who had swiped the clothes and the weapons.

They had weapons, all right. Two of them were carrying rifles and the leader had a revolver which he pointed at all of us in turn as he declaimed. The purpose of the visit seemed to be the acquisition of a large sum of money which he was convinced Mother Weill had hidden somewhere on the premises. In vain did she deny it. He didn't believe her (and neither did I).

I am trying to be detached as I tell this story, but even as I write it down, thousands of miles away from the scene and two years later, I remember how sick I was with terror. I remember how we all looked, too. Terror seems to make people very, very sad. We were indistinct in the candlelight, but I could see the faces pretty well and everyone was hangdog, and kept his eyes fixed on the table. Actors registering fear in the movies don't do it right. I know that now. Alec had been tied painfully tightly and his face was twisted with the effort not to yelp. They didn't tie me up at all, nor the luscious Lena, nor Veronica, nor Susie, and that was terrifying too. In spite of all the airy things I had been saying about rape, now that I thought my time had come I was so afraid of it that I turned to jelly. Then Carola started to cry, upstairs, and I began to get up to go to her, and they roared at me to sit down. Then I fainted.

A nice, useful thing to do, you probably are saying scornfully. All I know is that I couldn't help it, and that probably I wouldn't again under similar circumstances. There was a noise like rushing water, and then I felt the silver on the table against my forehead and I heard a groaning, gasping, sobbing sort of noise, and soon I realized it was me. Nothing had happened. It hadn't been very long. The leader was still yelling at Mrs. Weill and she was still saying she didn't have any money in the house.

They untied her then and took her and Sophie and Veronica, with their keys, upstairs to open some safe that one of them had found. We were left with about six men to guard us. We heard them stamping around, and we heard their voices. We heard somebody being slapped—that was Mother Weill. Then we heard Sophie crying loudly, begging them not to slap her mother again. Then Veronica came down with Carola, and though the guards for some reason wouldn't let me take her, but forced Veronica to sit down with her, I naturally felt much better. I sat up and felt quite brisk. It began to look as if nobody would be raped, after all. Veronica told me afterward that as she came down the stairs with Carola her guard tried to hug her, and did bruise her pretty badly. But she said gently, "You'll hurt the baby," and she got down without further mishap.

At last they brought the Weills back, tied them up again, and went foraging through the house on their own. They were at that for a long, long time. Altogether they were in the house two hours. Strangely enough, it didn't seem that long. They stamped back into the dining room and screamed at Mrs. Weill, and threatened to flog her, but at last they went away. They made a speech about how we mustn't move for ten minutes, but of course we were at work untying each other as soon as their footsteps stopped sounding in the darkness.

"Wasn't that leader an *impairtinent* little fellow?" said Mrs. Angus, as her daughter Chrissie wept and rubbed her arms back into circulation.

Susie's jewels and money had been taken. Everybody had been frisked, too, and lost things. Everyone had lost clothes, even my old amah, whose coat was gone. Only I came out even. My purse, in full sight of the public, had been left alone; my fur coat had somehow been missed in the rush. My jewels were still knocking around in their old cardboard box which nobody had bothered to open. They had missed my wrist watch again.

The menfolk went back and ate the chicken and rice, but I went to bed. I wanted very much to report the occurrence to somebody, but it was difficult to figure out how to do it. Besides, nobody would have been interested. In a few hours I decided it was better not to try to realize what had happened. We all seemed to come to the same conclusion. We joked about it. As for Ah King and the other servants, they really did laugh, uproariously.

Next day on our way back from hospital we found an iron box of papers and deeds and things that belonged to Mother Weill, none of them worth anything to anyone but her. The box had been left in good condition aside from the broken lock, and it was prominently displayed on the path where we couldn't miss it.

It was New Year's Day, so I brought the servants with me to greet Charles, and Carola, all dressed up. "*Kung hay fat choy,*" said Charles politely to them as they came in. "Well, well!" He hadn't seen Carola since Pearl Harbor. He submitted with good grace to having her plumped down on his whole arm, though Bill Wiseman looked on sardonically and made remarks.

"By the way," I said, "we had rather an experience last night." I told him about it briefly, while he said at intervals, "How unpleasant." He was, naturally, quite upset, and we wondered if the Rev. Mr. Short wouldn't reconsider his refusal to allow us to live in the hospital. I actually went down and routed out the Reverend, and put it to him, as man to man. But he smiled in sickly fashion and said he couldn't see his way clear. I was getting awfully peeved at the Rev. Mr. Short. I then told Hilda the story, and asked her to relay it to Selwyn, hoping vaguely that he could persuade the authorities to do something or other. My arguing point was that the Japanese probably wouldn't want Formosans and coolies impersonating them. It is very difficult to realize, even when you know it, that you are living in a world from which law and order have disappeared. Perhaps it's just as well that one doesn't realize it at the time.

A few days later I found pandemonium at the Queen Mary. Word had reached the hospital that the Japanese had put up signs in town ordering all Dutch, American, Belgian, and British nationals to report immediately at Murray Parade Ground, the big open space in the middle of town, near the Supreme Court Building and just outside of the Murray barracks. The Japs didn't give any explanation of this order, and I think very few people realized what it meant, though they were also told to bring with them a blanket and a few clothes. At that time none of us had heard of mass internment. It hadn't been done, that we knew of, in Occupied France or Norway. Concentration camps, we assumed, were different; they were maintained for special classes, such as Jews, or for criminals. We were rather expecting an internment of Jews and Chungking patriots and such. The Weills and I were worried about that. But internment of all the Europeans? Impossible! There would be too many of them, for one thing.

Nobody could find out *facts*. That whole day the Rev. Mr. Short went around looking even more weary than usual. An important Jap medical officer called on Charles and Short came in too, and hung about hoping Charles could ask the officer what was up. But when he started to talk the Jap cut him off crisply and then rudely ignored him, and went on discussing the weather with Charles until the Reverend wandered out of the room. Neither Charles nor the Jap spoke of the order. I too was feeling an anguished interest, but I understood how Charles couldn't broach the subject.

We found out in the afternoon what was going on. A great crowd of people had reported at the parade ground, and it staggered the Japs that their sign had been taken literally. "British *nationals*," they had said. Well, everyone born in Hong Kong was a British national. Any child born there, no matter what his race or color, was entitled to British citizenship and a passport. That was something the Japanese didn't know. They had assumed that only the haughty whites were British, and they had prepared to intern only whites. Naturally this crowd was far too big to handle, and besides, they didn't feel prepared to decide at just a moment's notice who was "Asiatic" and who wasn't. All day long they interned all comers, sending them off in batches to dingy Chinese hotels down along the water front, and all day long the people kept coming, and coming, and coming, until at last the Japs gave up. They sent the rest of the enemy nationals away, to await their future decision.

So it happened that a scratch lot of people were interned, and most of the whites were not—yet. Among the unfortunates were the Armstrongs, and Billie Lee with her baby, and Mavis Ming, and Alec Potts, and hosts of others. These early-goers had a hell of a time. For about twenty-four hours they were given nothing to eat or drink. Alec got letters out to Susie and we knew what was going on in his hotel, at any rate. Finally they were given raw rice and no means to cook it. They were crowded terribly in these filthy little brothels. You can read about it at firsthand in half a dozen books. Opinion is now divided as to just why the Japanese behaved so badly. Some people think it was revenge for the alleged treatment the British authorities had given the Japanese internees. But according to Charles, the Jap consul, Yano, said they were pretty well treated and he had no complaints to make. I think the Japs just are that way. Their prisons are nearly always unspeakable. They treat people like cattle at a stockyards, that's all; they always do.

Think of it. I don't know if you can, as vividly as I do, because you don't know Hong Kong and the way people had always lived there. But you can take my word for it that they had done themselves pretty well. They had lived as well as possible for years. Hong Kong was full of government servants who behaved like kings, sitting as they did on that heap of coolie labor. Remember that. And then, all of a sudden, this! This indignity, this swoop back through the generations to a level of existence which none of them could imagine. Why, for most of those people just going home to England called for a terrific readjustment. Yet now within the space of a few hours they had been shoved into the life of an oriental jail. They were being treated like coolie malefactors. I am amazed at the number of people who survived it. I am proud of human toughness.

After the first few days Selwyn began coming in with patients from these hotels, or Duggie Valentine did the escorting. Both doctors were grim and silent. It had been a battle to persuade the Japs to let the patients out. A woman with a miscarriage coming was put into our ward and we helped her all night for several nights, because the doctor was too busy to bother. She survived, but only just. One morning I heard that a friend of mine, Addie Zimmern, had been brought in. Addie's husband was missing. I went to find her; she was lying on a cot in a crowded ward with her four-year-old child Michael in bed with her.

"What is it, Addie?" I asked.

She smiled—she's a pretty girl—and said, "Miscarriage, I think. I was four months along. It's just as well."

I said, "Has it happened yet?" and Addie said, like a child:

"I don't know. It was too dark at the hotel to see."

She lay there trying to act normal and jolly. She has always been an outdoors type, winning cups at athletics.

I said: "They've found some of your brothers-in-law. Two of them are in camp and they're all right."

"Good," said Addie, and closed her eyes.

"I have to go back tomorrow," said a gray-haired woman, "as soon as this tooth has been pulled. I do the cooking at the hotel."

"I want to go back with you," cried Addie.

The saving spirit, the team spirit or whatever you call it, had started up already in those communities, under those horrible conditions.

Charles was dazed, and refused to believe in the mess for a long time, though he didn't say so. I was in a tremor over Carola. I didn't know what to do. It was out of the question to walk right into it, to take my baby and go into town and throw ourselves in jail. I don't think my legs would have carried me.

"Wait," said Charles, looking harassed and miserable. "Something is bound to turn up."

But I couldn't wait. I knew that all the houses in town were already registered with their inhabitants numbered and I remembered how quickly the Japanese had appeared after the surrender. They did things suddenly, I knew. I ran to Margaret Watson and Hilda and I made a scene.

"The hospitals are still being left out of it," I reminded them. "You two are still safe and snug. I insist that you let me in on this. I will *not* take Carola into one of those hotels until I know more about it. You let me into the hospital, somehow, or I'll——"

Margaret for once didn't answer back. She telephoned the Rev. Mr. Short and talked to him pithily, and when she hung up the receiver I was accepted as a patient at the Queen Mary, suffering from aftereffect of

Caesarean section, with my female offspring. I ran home to the Weills, told them what I had done, left breathless orders for Ah King and Ah Cheung to pack up our stuff, and ran back all the way, carrying the baby. The Weills approved. They weren't worrying about themselves because they had French passports, and French weren't being interned.

I came into Charles's ward triumphantly, and sat down to catch my breath. "I don't see why you should be in such a sweat," he said disapprovingly. "There's no such mad hurry as that."

But there was. Next day there were guards on the hospital, and we were interned within the grounds of the Queen Mary.

I was assigned to a ward of four, but there were two empty beds when I arrived. We dug out a hospital cot for Carola; it was just a little bit small for a baby three months old, but Carola was small too. The cot stood at the foot of my bed, and now I had the baby's care on my own hands, for although Ah Cheung went to live with Margaret's amah, the nurses didn't want her hanging about too much. For a time my neighbor was Susie, whose neuritis was giving her hell; she decided to take advantage of the hospital while she still could, and give herself a rest now that her husband was locked up. The other Weills managed to get into the hospital every day, just the same as always; they brought extra food to Susie, and her letters from Alec. Those letters were lifesavers. We kept up very well with current events, through Alec. I suppose smuggling was easy then. You just gave your letter to a Chinese servant through the bars of the gate. Things tightened up later.

Those were the days when most of the escapes were made. The historical escape, the famous one, was that of Admiral Chan Chak, for whom it was vitally necessary to avoid the Japanese. With him went Max Oxford and a whole lot of other British officials. They got away in a boat. One boat was sunk under them and Chan Chak, who has only one leg, almost drowned. But they pulled him out and got another boat and they reached Chungking, ultimately. That was a coup for the British.

The troops were first confined at North Point, at the edge of the harbor, and for as long as they were there it was possible to get away quietly by junk, if you had money. A few men made it. More than a few, perhaps.

One day Alf Bennett came in with a Japanese guard. He was being very useful at North Point because of his Japanese, but he was profane when he talked about the conditions under which the men were living. They had permitted him to come in that day with a truck, to forage for food. He glared at me with real resentment.

"You're so well off here, it's unbelievable," he said. "I wish you could see that camp. It's just—it's just *silly*. Yes, old boy, you're well off here."

Charles turned white. I decided, slowly but with decision, that I didn't like Alf.

"Got a drink?" Alf continued. He had been eating our chocolate hungrily, and now I was angry that I had given him any. Charles could have used it. I was in a most uncivilized state, as you may gather.

"No," I said truthfully, "we have no liquor."

He didn't believe it. He started to go at last, on his way to call on a girl friend, but he pleaded to the end, between insults, for a drink.

"We haven't any," repeated Charles.

"This is your last chance. I really mean it, you know," said Alf at the door.

"You," I said, "are a pig. Better go now; Charles is tired."

He suddenly became normal for a disarming moment. "I'm not really a pig, you know," he said. "Bye-bye."

Nobody said anything after he left. "Wonder how long we're here for?" said Charles at last. "This can't go in indefinitely."

"No," I said uneasily. I walked out on the veranda and looked around. It was quiet enough. Most of our friends were waiting on the Peak while their spokesman haggled with the Japs about a suitable internment camp, while the prisoners in the hotels, like Addie, made the best of it.

"Oy!" someone shouted. A sentry gestured at me violently to go back indoors. They wouldn't have anyone looking down on them from a height. I retired precipitately.

Chapter 44

THE MATRON of Charles's floor was a nervous, jumpy soul, but even she continued for a long time to believe in Santa Claus. One morning while she was there in Charles's ward a large party of uniformed Japanese, wearing the medical insignia, came by under the twittering escort of the Rev. Mr. Short and a British doctor or two. They asked a lot of questions about the hospital equipment, and then they went away. Matron stepped out on the veranda to peek at their official car.

"I don't like it," she said. "I don't like it at all." She looked at Charles imploringly, silently begging him to offer her a little hope, but he said nothing and she left the room.

"I don't know how Selwyn-Clarke can figure on keeping this place," said Charles irritably. "It's the best building in the Colony. Of course they'll take it over."

"Then why don't we use the food while it's still in our hands?" I demanded. Wiseman, who constantly suffered from a gnawing appetite, added, "Amen."

"Don't know. . . . Perhaps they hope to get their supplies smuggled out to Stanley," Charles said. He was right. We all knew now that Stanley, the peninsula on the other side of the island, was the place chosen and being prepared for the civilian internment camp. Sir Atholl MacGregor, Chief Justice, as spokesman for the British, had begged without avail for the Peak as a camp. The Japs hemmed and hawed long enough to give him hope. It has been uncharitably suggested that Sir Atholl's real reason for his request was that his own house was on the Peak, and if the Japs had given in he would be able to see the war through in comfort, at home. Most of the richer Peak-dwelling British were naturally on his side in that; the others, who were refugees already, were fairly apathetic on the subject. Maybe the Japs really did consider this preposterous suggestion. They have never used the Peak very much themselves for residential purposes. But there must have been military reasons for refusing it; the Peak has been fortified and fixed up with lookouts since we were driven off it. Another thing that made it impossible for the camp was that the Japs, fully aware of the social implications of Hong Kong's geography, wanted to humiliate the whites as much as they could, and bringing them down from those costly heights to sea level was an obvious and necessary move in the campaign. The third and strongest reason for refusing Sir Atholl's non-altruistic request was that old Japanese idiosyncrasy of not wanting anybody looking *down* on them. They actually did make a law, later on, which made it punishable for any enemy white left outside of camp to live on the hillside. They had to revoke the law, though. Hong Kong is a bumpy place altogether and it was impossible to insist that everyone classed as an enemy be put on sea level. There just isn't that much sea level. After the first few months the Japanese gendarmes had to relax on that point at least, and the Peak was garnished with a Japanese summer pavilion at the top of the funicular, and everybody left loose was permitted to make expeditions up there and drink tea in the pavilion, even white people. Of course there were guards everywhere.

In the meantime, Stanley didn't sound too bad, from the Japanese viewpoint. There were school buildings with dormitories, a nice view, and a lot of bungalows and cottages that had belonged to wealthy Chinese—they were just taken away from the Chinese, that's all—and there were also buildings attached to the Colony jail, Stanley Fort, which was still being used by the Japs as a prison. Its grounds adjoined the camp's. The Army put up a barbed-wire boundary, selected the best buildings for the Japanese guard, and sent a lot of the younger enemy civilian men ahead, out of the hotels, to clear up the place in preparation for a general emigration of prisoners.

Here again I will let other books speak for me. I don't know what really happened out there when the advance guard was finished. I heard rumors, but I heard them from Japanese. They said that the American men who went in advance of the party did a good job of cleaning up, and that their allotted space was in splendid condition when their older people and the women and children arrived. Bill Hunt, Carola's old pal, was in charge of the American section and the Japanese spoke well of him. I know that a lot of the British were bitterly resentful of him and said that he snaffled all the best places, that he must have bribed the Japanese, and so forth. Feeling ran high between the British and the Americans at Stanley. Probably it would have anyway—it always does in Hong Kong—but I'm sure the Japs kept things stirred up. In those days it seemed to me that they were trying to placate the Americans. Not that Japanese are ever really placatory, but I could see, myself, from the way they treated me when they knew I was American, that a prejudice did exist in our favor. I think they felt that they would be able to make a deal with the United States later on. But their feeling toward the British was one of ruthless, revengeful hate. Why should the Japanese have hated the British and rather liked us? In the recent history of world politics England was much more inclined than was the United States to play ball with Japan. I think it was all dictated by Tokyo as a matter of policy, and I think, too, that the British were unjust in resenting Bill Hunt. He has a talent for organization. Undoubtedly it would have gone much worse with everyone if it hadn't been for those two much-criticized men, Selwyn and Bill.

I must get back to Stanley Camp. The unpleasant part of the story dealt with the British. It was whispered in town that the British young men, mostly police—for police were counted as noncombatant because they weren't armed during the war, and they were able-bodied and husky—didn't behave well. They were duly sent ahead to get the place ready and they did, but only for themselves. When the great mass of the British civilian population arrived, the lame and the halt and the blind, the old and the babies, these young men refused to give up their comfortable places to the newcomers.

Extenuating circumstances, I should think, are these: everybody was hungry. Young men suffer much more from hunger than do other people. Also the British had a bigger task than the Americans or the Dutch or the Belgians: their community was huge in comparison with the others. A larger proportion of Britons were very old or very young, which put a heavy burden on the in-betweens. The Americans weren't responsible for many women because of the order, earlier that year, from the American banks and oil companies which had sent most of the wives home. Nevertheless they did send me a few kind messages, telling me that they would be glad to have me and Carola when the time came. They could easily take care of us, they said. Gibson, an oil man, was left free in town to be their representative. The diplomatic squad, however, including Barbara Petro and Walter Hoffman, were cut off from the rest of the Americans and held in a special house outside the boundaries of the camp.

Waiting in the Queen Mary for the end of that phase, I thought that I had made up my mind to be interned like a good girl. I was miserable at the prospect but I didn't see any way out. It was just a matter of time, I thought, before this pretense of being ill would fall down. I tried to be in bed whenever the Japs made a tour of inspection, but it was pretty obvious that none of us could go on like that much longer. Some of the Chinese patients were being removed. It was cold and dark and sad in the hospital and we were all really very hungry. Our food, already insufficient, was being stolen, little by little, as it came up from the kitchen to our wards. Sometimes none of it was left when it arrived. The amahs and the cleaning boys ran away, one by one, stealing blankets as they went. I had acquired two blankets of my own, by special gift of one of the officers who had himself taken those blankets from a dead comrade. They disappeared, and I insisted on taking two of the hospital's blankets to make the loss good. We all began to think hard about blankets and clothing and such, in preparation for the end. The sisters thought so hard about it that many of them neglected their duties with increasing abandon. I'm not naming names, though I should like to. Toward the end many of them acted like dissatisfied guests in a hotel that wasn't being run properly, and they were utterly callous about the patients. All they talked about was their own affairs, and they speculated all day about how much of their property they would be allowed to take with them to Stanley.

Still the cases of food in the cellar were jealously guarded, and upstairs we pulled in our belts and wailed unavailingly. Somebody was stealing Carola's powdered milk at a great rate. Somebody even stole her last orange out of the icebox.

I think it was the twentieth or the twenty-first of January when the

blow fell. Even with all the preliminary omens, Selwyn expressed himself
as amazed and horrified that the Japanese wanted us to get out of the
hospital that day. He acted quite as if it were an atrocity. I suppose it
was, and yet, on the other hand, he should have expected it. The Japanese
have their own code, and it is well known that they consider everything
in a conquered village as their own. Nothing belongs to the inhabitants,
literally nothing, not even the clothes they wear, not even themselves. The
Japanese have always behaved according to this rule and Selwyn need
not have been surprised that they took his prize hospital. And, damn it,
he need not have left that food for them, either. I hate to harp on that,
but I was hungry, and Charles was hungry, and we all were hungry, all
but the staff. At least I will admit one thing: Selwyn was hungry too.
Selwyn never took the better of anything.

I am bitter. I know it. Just about then I realized that I would have to
wean Carola soon; my milk was no good. It was the worst time in my
life to date. I am bitter. I don't blame Selwyn for the war but I can't
forget all the carefully hoarded food that the Japanese took over.

Hilda, during the first days when we knew about Stanley, was wild
with worry. "I'm making Selwyn ask the Japanese for a special camp for
mothers and children," she told me. "Some place like the Maryknoll
Convent grounds, for example. Perhaps they would allow us to have better
rations: they seem fond of children and we can make an appeal on those
grounds."

A few days later when I met her she was looking more cheerful. "It
seems fairly certain," she said, "that Selwyn and the Medical Department
will be permitted to remain out of internment, as long as they are working for the community like this. Colonel Nguchi (Selwyn's new chief)
said that Mary and I can stay out with him. We're looking now for a
building that will house all of the medical officers; the Japanese stipulate
that we must all be under one roof."

"What about the special camp for mothers and children, Hilda?"

She looked at me blankly. She had forgotten all about it. "Oh, that," she
said vaguely. "Well, that seems to have fallen through."

The hospital was suddenly in a terrible rush. The Japanese had evidently been arguing a long time with Selwyn and they lost their tempers.
They often did, arguing with Selwyn. They probably were bulldozed by
him for a certain amount of time and then suddenly they caught themselves up and said, "What the hell are we arguing with this damned
Englishman for? Aren't we boss? Clear the decks, there!" First thing we
knew, patients were being carried out by the dozen, loaded into trucks.

and carried away to other hospitals. When Selwyn said he didn't have stretcher-bearers the Japs promptly supplied their own men for the work. They didn't want to lose any more time moving in. Our doctors stood in a row, their hands upraised in horror, their feet frozen to the ground. Old Digby, the surgeon, made an impassioned speech of protest when the authorities asked him if he were willing, like many of the other doctors, to stay outside of camp and work for the health of the community. No, he said, he would not co-operate with such vandals as the Japs, such barbarians, such—people, in short, who were capable of evacuating a hospital in such a heartless manner. The Japanese officer who heard this outburst said, in a remarkably good-natured way, considering: "You are lucky it's me you are talking to, Doctor," and sent him to Stanley forthwith. The Japanese medical officers invariably seemed better than the other military men.

I want to tell the truth, in so far as I know. I have heard since this all happened that the Japanese stretcher-bearers were brutal in their work that day, slamming sick men around regardless and pulling splints off of broken limbs, et cetera, et cetera. I saw nothing like that. The stretcher-bearers I watched were gentle and considerate. I don't suppose you like to read that. I admit I don't much like writing it. It isn't artistic; it doesn't fit in with the rest of the picture, and it isn't fashionable. It would be easier just to report atrocities. Please bear with me, though: I do want to tell the truth. It seems to me that the truth doesn't hurt anyone in the end.

We should be able to take the smooth with the rough, even in wartime.

We, the hospitalized enemy mothers, were not to be sent to other hospitals unless our own doctors thought us sick enough to go into the old Tweed Bay Hospital that was now open in Stanley. All the enemy patients, except for very special cases, were being sent to Stanley. Almost everyone I knew at Pokfulam was going, except for the Weill family. They had already been to the Japanese Foreign Affairs office in town and got new "passes," pieces of stamped paper that stated they were French neutrals. Veronica was French by virtue of her husband's nationality, but Sophie, whose husband was Russian, managed to retain her French pass anyway. The Japanese were easygoing in such matters. Lena, for example, was given her choice between her own Russian nationality, which she had held until she married, and her husband's British citizenship. Since she would have been popped into Stanley immediately if she had claimed to be British, she called herself Russian. But there was one peculiarity in the Jap reasoning which it took months of experience to figure out. According to them, you were a citizen of that country where you had been born, regardless of any other consideration. Thus my friend the Frenchwoman, Michelle Marty, who happened to have been born in Hong Kong, had a tremendous row with the man who filled out her pass. He said that if she had been born in Hong Kong she must be Chinese. In the end he settled it by writing down, "Place of birth: Paris," and he wouldn't argue with her any more. Lots of people had trouble over that quirk in Japanese law, especially the White Russians who were born on the China Coast.

Anybody with oriental blood was called "Asiatic" and not liable to be interned.

It was Sophie who made me try to stay out of Stanley. It might not have occurred to me, in my then gentle, yielding frame of mind. I thought I simply had to go to Stanley, and on the day everyone was moving I stood out on the veranda and cried. I cried softly because it wouldn't do me any good to yell. I cried because Hilda had rushed in and taken the key of my flat, saying happily that she and Selwyn had to find a place to live immediately, and would I mind? I cried because I thought Charles would be taken away from me for good, this time. I cried because I was afraid Carola would die of starvation. I cried because I was tired; Carola had given me a bad night.

Susie was packing all her things to go home. She came out on the veranda and put her arm around me and said, "Mother says, try to stay out. She's fond of you. She says she'll look after you and Carola. Can't you work it? Can't Charles say something to the Japanese? I'm sure they would do it for him."

I said, "I don't think he would, but I'll ask." I wiped my eyes, powdered my nose, and went up to Charles. I was afraid to ask him. I knew he would be angry. He was.

"Once and for all, Mickey," he said coldly, "I will *not* try to use my influence, if I have any, to get special treatment for my family. Don't be ridiculous."

"I know. Listen, suppose I myself managed to stay out; that wouldn't step on your toes, would it? I mean, if I did it on my own?"

Ah King chimed in: "Don't go Stanley, missy. We can do. Fish is cheap."

Charles studied me warily. "I don't know what you mean. I can't make up your mind for you. . . . Why don't you want to go to Stanley, anyway? Everybody else is going. How can you manage if you don't?"

"I won't be able to see you any more if I'm interned."

"You probably won't anyway. I'll be put into clink myself."

"Not yet. You're too weak. If I take Carola out there she'll die, Charles."
He didn't answer.

"There's no bedding, no food, nothing."

"They're bound to make special arrangements," he said, "for women with children."

"They're bound to nothing of the sort. I don't want to bother you, but gosh . . . Can't you see, I'll die myself in prison? I can't bear it, I can't bear it." I realized with some surprise that I meant it, too.

"Just how do you intend to go about this, Mickey?" he asked, suddenly mild.

"I don't know yet, but never mind. I'll leave you out of it, you and your military honor." I went downstairs again and reported to the Weills. Sophie, the stubbornest one of all, bit her lip and thought hard.

"Can you claim to be something else than American? I mean, German or something? They're accepting that sort of thing. I know several Americans who——"

"Not German, Sophie. What do you think I am?"

"No, I can see that. . . . Isn't there *something*?"

All of a sudden it broke with a blinding flash of light. "I *did* have a Chinese husband once. . . ."

Sophie took no time to be surprised. She grabbed my hand and led me at a run down the steps, out into the green courtyard of the front garden, and over to a small medical officer, a Japanese, who stood there talking to some non-commissioned men.

Sophie made a little speech to this man, who had helped her with her passport the day before. Her friend, she said, was married to a Chinese and hadn't realized until this minute that such a fact could keep her free from internment. Her friend was a patient in hospital and had not been able to get to town during the period when people were taking out their passes. If the officer would give her friend permission to go into town, a written pass so that no soldier would arrest her friend, she could adjust this matter with the Foreign Affairs Department.

The little officer looked at me with interest. "Chinese husband, eh?"
I lowered my eyes and said, "Yes."

He studied me. His eyes warmed. He was pleased that an American girl should have married an Oriental. It made him more friendly to both of us. "Sit down," he said, and sat down himself, plop, right on the grass.

"How many children?" asked the officer.

I smirked demurely. It really would have been impossible to explain, so I just said, "One."

"*So des.*" He smiled at me. He took out a card. He wrote something

on it, and stamped it with his seal, and gave it to me. I was a free woman
for two days more, anyway, until I had consulted the Foreign Affair
office. Sophie and I ran back into the hospital and I staggered as I ran
My head was spinning. I still felt guilty and breathless. I ran slam-bang
into Matron.

"I've got a chance to stay out of internment; should I take it?" I de
manded. I would have asked anybody and taken the advice of anybody
just then.

"Certainly," she said promptly. "Why be locked up if you can help it
Good luck. Wish I could do that."

I went back to Charles and handed him the card; he could read it
even if I couldn't.

Charles lay on his pillow and looked at me, and looked at me.

"God," he said at last. "Do you think you'll get away with that?"

"If I do," I said, "it'll be the best thing Sinmay ever did for me."

There was a long silence. He had a strange expression on his face.
would almost have said he was afraid of me. Or maybe he was beginning
to be afraid of all women.

"You ought to stay with your own people, you know," he said at last

"The British are not my own people. I feel more at home," I said, "with
the Chinese. I'll be all right. But of course it's for you to decide."

With his good hand Charles rubbed his brow. There was a suspicious
quirk at the corners of his mouth. "Oh yes," he said. "Well, Mickey, it's
up to you." Then he said again, thoughtfully, "God."

Chapter 45

EVERYBODY had been shipped out of the place now but a skeleton
staff, my ward of assorted maternity—or anyway, gynecological—cases,
Charles, and the Selwyn-Clarke household. Hilda had found that my flat
was full of refugees, a fact I had already reminded her of, but until she
saw them in the flesh she had been under the impression that she could
easily kick them out. Close up, Irene Fincher and Co. were evidently
uncompromising. Irene was still seething with rage later, when I
got back to the house; some idiot Chinese doctor had said, appalled by
her refusal to step out promptly into the street with her aged parents
when she was asked: "But it's *Dr. Selwyn-Clarke* and family!" However,
Hilda had found a better flat next door, after all, one which belonged to

man in the American consulate. She managed to get a letter from him, or what it was worth, saying that they could live there. The Jap health officer, Colonel Nguchi, was rapidly becoming their guardian angel, and he said that the Selwyn-Clarkes could live in Tregunter Mansions if they liked, and they trustingly planned to move in. We had yet to learn how easily Japanese officers give permission, and how easily other officers take it away again.

So now Hilda was faced with the problem of moving from the Queen Mary with all those stores and things, and with no transportation. I had a similar problem except that I didn't need to move anything but a couple of suitcases and the baby. Old Ah Cheung ran away the day the Japs started moving people out, and I hadn't given any thought to finding another domestic, naturally. I still believed I would be sent to Stanley sooner or later. And I was managing Carola fine by myself, bathing her like a veteran. Oddly enough, in that deserted place there was still one Chinese woman, and she wanted a job—Margaret Watson's amah May, who had been left among the furniture of the Watson flat and who was still hanging on. She came up and begged me to let her come with us, to look after Carola. I didn't know her, but as she had been Margaret's amah I thought she must be all right, and I said, "Sure, only I'll probably go to jail myself pretty soon."

May was willing to take the chance. Her eyes were bright with hope. She had seen Ah Cheung when the old girl left, and she was impressed by the fact that I gave her in farewell, in lieu of wages, a ring of chip diamonds and bits of jade that Sinmay's wife had once made for me. I suppose May thought I always paid off in jewels, or perhaps, like the other British-trained Chinese, she was simply panicky at the idea of being on her own. As it turned out, it was a bad day's work, taking her on, but at the time it seemed a sensible thing to do.

Hilda, when she found out I might be staying out in the world like herself, grabbed at me feverishly. Gone was all that War Memorial resentment and the somewhat gang-headquarters aspect of the Watson household. "Now we're all alone," she said, "and I'm going to be so damn lonely. I won't have Margaret any more. I'm going to live next door to you. Couldn't we mess together as we used to? I have rice. You have Ah King. I'll give your household rice if Ah King will cook for all of us. Other expenses, if one can ever buy anything again, we'll have to share."

"If I ever have any money," I said gloomily. So we struck the bargain with a good grace, since fate seemed determined to keep us together, and we began to take counsel as to how the devil we were to get over to May Road. In the meantime it seemed more tactful to leave the hospital, be-

cause it was filling up more and more with sentries and plain soldiers
carrying fixed bayonets, which they pointed at us at intervals. Once more
—this time, as I thought, for good—I went up and said good-by to Charles.
I had been doing that at intervals for twenty-four hours and we were both
getting used to it by this time. At last Charles was helped up and dressed
by an orderly and taken downstairs and out of doors, where the last remaining nurses and patients were waiting. Hilda and I, with our children
and our luggage, crossed the compound and went straight into Margaret's deserted flat, from where we could watch that forlorn group.

Not so forlorn, at that, as others had been. At least these hospital people
were allowed to take as much luggage as they wanted, and mattresses and
books and things. Most of the unlucky people who had been grabbed up
in that insane business at Murray Parade Ground never did manage to
collect their belongings. By this time their houses had been looted. Looting was going on at a tremendous rate, openly and everywhere. The Japs
didn't care; some of them encouraged it. At the tramways, Japanese had
chopped open the safe and then called the watchman and workers and
said, "Take whatever you want," so full of loot were they already. Money
spilled out on the floor and the coolies fell on it hungrily, as you can
imagine. At that moment, among the poorer element of the town, the
stock of Japan was higher than it ever was again. During those days the
foundations were laid for many new fortunes. In after months, when these
newly rich coolies brought their families into the unfamiliar splendor of
the Hongkong Hotel for lunch, the Japanese were amazed at their appearance. They would come into the hotel wearing cotton pajamas or anything they liked, and the place was so full of bedbugs after a while that
the management stopped trying to do anything about it. Fastidious Japanese were annoyed. Me, I was amused. But just at this moment it wasn't
funny. It was terrifying. These people had found arms. Sometimes on a
quiet night the rifle firing sounded as if the war were still going on,
though the noise was probably only due to one or two battles between
the military and looters, out in the streets. The military did shoot at
thieves on occasion, when they had nothing better to do.

We saw two trucks brought up by Japanese from a big pool of them
down in the road below the hospital, and the people for Stanley were
loaded on and driven away, waving gallantly. Then a special Japanese
Army car came for Charles and he was taken off, presumably, I thought,
to Bowen Road Hospital, the British military haven which was still being
used for our wounded soldiers. Anyway, all the others had been taken
there. The special car must have been a sort of courtesy. I refused to
agonize over it. I had said good-by once too often: it seemed silly.

Something about the possibility of freedom and the general excitement of the situation had done magic for me. At last I felt normal. Not normal, however, according to the past year in Hong Kong. That dreamy, almost respectable phase was over forever. I felt like the person I had been in the Congo and in Shanghai in earlier days: alert and worried and alive and a little bit unhappy but not too much so. I wouldn't have fainted now even if a whole regiment of Formosans threatened me. Maybe it was the sight of Charles being carried off, and the knowledge that I was up against it, alone again. My adrenals probably started to work.

Carola was asleep on the dusty, deserted Watson couch, kicking occasionally. May was hanging out diapers. Little Mary was wandering about, staring wonderingly at the empty rooms and the gaping bookcases. Hilda was on the veranda watching for an ambulance which Selwyn had said would call for her sooner or later.

A sentry came in and bothered us a bit, though I think in the light of later experience that he didn't mean to. He was just curious, and interested in the children. Besides, some officer probably wanted to move into that flat and couldn't make out why we were still there and not on the way to Stanley. It was a dangerous period. The ordinary soldiers had all been told that their wicked enemies were to be carted off to internment, and in their zeal they were rounding up all kinds of innocent neutrals and packing them off too. Lots of mistakes were made that day. We weren't exactly innocent neutrals, and we were nervous. But Hilda had in her own defense an arm band which said that she was a British woman, aged forty-two, wife of the British adviser to the Imperial Japanese Health Department and so on; Mary wore an arm band saying she was a British female child, daughter of the adviser, et cetera, and I had my little card, which was getting rather smudged. We were well equipped. All we didn't have was the ambulance.

It arrived at last, but a Japanese officer saw it first, and he waved imperiously and took it over for himself. That really did tear things, and Hilda and I began to be seriously worried. It was getting late in the afternoon, quite late. Selwyn would expect to find his household on May Road. And my pass was only good for two days. I couldn't afford to waste time.

Finally Hilda had a brilliant idea. She walked back to the hospital building and asked for an officer who could speak English. She showed him her arm band and boldly requested the loan of a truck to take us to May Road. The amazing thing is that she got it, too. You might remember that the first few days after an occupation, while the Army still feels good and reckless, is the best time to ask favors of the conquerors.

A burly little Jap drove the lorry over to our house and helped us load

it, catching things as Ah King threw them. He took a fancy to Carol
He made Hilda and Mary sit in back, on top of the load with May an
Ah King and Hilda's coolie, but he took Carola and me into the drivir
van with him. He drove to May Road at a terrific speed, now and the
almost running us into a ditch when he kissed Carola. I didn't much li
his kissing Carola, but that was no time to say so.

We drove through town, and I peered around eagerly to see wh
changes had been made. Everything was deserted and dismal. The Ch
nese must have been huddling indoors wherever they could go, now th
dark was falling. Windows were still boarded or plastered up with sha
terproof paper. The streets were littered and very dirty. No corpses we
left along the main road, but as we drove uphill a smell indicated th
there was still a lot of work to do in the underbrush. We went sailir
swiftly past sentries everywhere, which was fortunate because the pla
was full of sentries and Hilda and I could never have run the gantl
alone. Strangely, the sight of the town, which I wasn't aware of havir
loved, hurt me as if I had seen a friend lying stricken. I suddenly realize
that I was feeling all those emotions that people do in books; famili
land marks that reminded me of Charles really did twist my heart. Al
at sight of the smashed places I began to feel hateful toward the Japanes
Until then I had only been afraid and stunned.

The little one who kissed Carola, however, was still amiable and didr
seem to be aware that he was our enemy and we were his. He helped
unload our things at the foot of the staircase leading to Tregunter Ma
sions. He begged a can of bully beef from Hilda, and got two with h
grateful thanks. We all waved to him as he drove off. Then—well, the
it was time for me to go home.

Carrying the baby, I ran up the steps, cracked now and littered wi
torn paper. I hesitated for a moment, looking at Charles's building ov
across the nullah. A shell had hit the place just below his veranda an
left a great black spot. There were signs of life in some of the windov
but not in his. Over on my side of the ditch the two buildings that we
called Tregunter Mansions looked solid and whole, though there was n
a window left in the front breadth of the lower house. Mine was in tl
upper, at the back, a safe place to be when shells came from Kowloo
I appreciated that, and wondered why we had ever gone to the Peak.
kept thinking of these things as I puffed up the last steps with Caro
in my arms, because I was trying not to wonder what I would find ther
Would these people let me in?

They saw me coming up the hill, and the door opened as soon as I ran
It was dark in my hall and at first, standing there on the threshold, I ha

a confused impression of crowds of people staring out at me. Then I made out that the front figure was that of a pretty, slender girl in a dressing gown, with her hair down her back. Her eyes were big and frightened. Behind her were two old people, and another girl, and a few Chinese servants, and a couple of babies. . . .

"It's Miss Hahn," said the slender girl over her shoulder. "She's come back."

That was Irene Fincher. She seemed to know me, though I couldn't remember her. I said, "Is there room for us too?" or something silly like that, because I realized that they were more afraid than I was. "I want to sleep here tonight, if I can," I added hastily.

"Well . . . it's *your* house," said Irene, a little out of breath. We trooped into the living room and sat down. I felt my silly smile getting somewhat frozen.

The old lady, the mother of the girls, was wringing her hands and weeping a little already. She had been through a lot and was apt to weep at almost anything these days, Irene explained. We talked with animation, and very soon things grew less tense. Irene told me that a lot of people were coming back to their flats around May Road: Danes and Swiss and such. They had been kicking the refugees out quite brutally, without warning. What flats were left, those belonging to enemy nationals who were now in Stanley, were full to bursting with these homeless billetees. The Gittinses had naturally supposed I would try to kick them out too.

"Well," I said, "it's a little different with me. In the first place I'm not a proud colonial any more; I'm a representative of a vanquished race. Whereas you are liberated."

Irene grinned a little. Phyllis, her sister, looked shocked.

"And I may be interned at any moment," I added. "I'll know for sure tomorrow. So there isn't much point in disturbing you until we know. Even then, if I'm left free, I wish you'd stay. I'm afraid to live alone. Please stay. What are your plans, if any?"

They didn't have any. Their houses were probably gone beyond redemption, over in Kowloon. Irene's husband was missing. Phyllis' husband was missing. They were dazed. For days they had walked miles from camp to camp, trying to find their men, and at last some friends among the soldiers told them the truth. They had been living on short rations, frantic with worry and despair. They inspected Carola and I inspected Frances and Bryan. Mrs. Gittins thought Carola looked peaked. They all seemed to know May already. In a little while we were pretty comfortably settled in, chatting hard.

We put Carola and May into the empty dining room—the table was already in the living room—and the rest of us were distributed between the "master bedroom" and the living room itself. Carola slept in her pram, since I had left her cot on the Peak. The amahs and Phyllis and the babies slept on the floor, on blankets. Japanese soldiers had acquired whatever my house offered in the way of mattresses, so most of the beds weren't much use any more.

Ah King, shaking his head over the state of the kitchen, warmed me up some rice and stuff. We all went to bed, ultimately, and by that time Irene, Phyllis, and I were old friends who understood each other quite well. Nothing is so efficacious as a baby pool to bring women together.

"—*if* I get my pass," I ended some sentence for the tenth time.

"Oh, you'll get it. Don't worry. We'll make out," said Irene.

Carola had an excellent night. I didn't.

Chapter 46

WE HAD TO PLAN my trip downtown like a campaign in enemy country, which, after all, it was. The streets were not safe for a woman alone, or even for two women. Irene said:

"It's quite simple; we'll go down and ask Nemazee to help us. He has a houseful of men, and some of them go downtown every day."

"Who's Nemazee?" I asked, and Reeny stared at me as if I were an Object.

"He's practically your next-door neighbor. Haven't you ever heard of *Nemazee?* Everybody knows Nemazee."

"Well, I don't."

Nemazee's house was across May Road from the archway that led to Tregunter, but a good deal lower on the steep hillside. I knew the garden well, because it was easy to see from the road and quite noteworthy. It was full of statues, Greek mostly, and there were fountains, and a big marble lion, and many flowers. I had often wondered who lived there, and it seemed fitting that it should turn out to be the house of a Persian. Nemazee is the second generation of his family to live in Hong Kong; he is a big shipper. We found his dining room full of people eating breakfast. As Nemazee had a huge dining room with two tables, and as both tables were full, one of grown people and the other of blond children, it was all overwhelming at first. After the introductions I figured it out. The people were all from a Norwegian shipping office, Wallem's, which was managed by one Johanssen. Johanssen, his family, and a lot of other families were taking refuge in Nemazee's house since the Johanssen house, on the Peak, had been destroyed. The Norwegian community was in a nervous state because they hadn't been assured as yet by the Japanese that they were neutrals. They maintained that since the French were left free they should enjoy the same privilege. The Japanese, however, were waiting on word from Tokyo, before deciding on Norway's status. They held that the French were free on account of Vichy, whereas they hadn't yet heard much good of Quisling. The local Japs were not really eager to intern the Norwegians because they were pressed for room, and already the Stanley camp was so disgracefully crowded that even they must have begun to feel guilty. On the other hand, if Tokyo felt that Norwegians were inimical to the New Order in East Asia, the local government would have no choice. Everyone Norwegian was waiting anxiously for a decision.

In the meantime they lived in Nemazee's house, dealing as well as they could with the food situation. Nemazee, like many of us, had been caught short and didn't have any cash, and nobody had much credit in those days. Still, he had some supplies of rice and flour, and already he was managing to get more from the Jap Food Control office on behalf of the crews of the ships. He was a clever, stubborn man, and he had lived through other times of stress. There was a period when he was in Russia, he told us, when everyone was broke and could afford only one meal a day. He and his friends would put off this meal for as long as possible and then go to the best hotel and eat everything in sight against the next twenty-four hours' famine.

Reeny had been Johanssen's private secretary, and it gave her a feeling of security, ill founded but comforting nevertheless, to have her former boss, the Great Man, so near at hand and so accessible. Jo was as broke as Reeny was and far less gallant about it; he was crushed by his misfortunes and was apt to get emotional and choked up whenever he thought about them. Nemazee said, gently, that Norwegians are often like that. They act, he said, the way Russians are supposed to in books. But Jo was volatile too, and he had a way of cheering up and bouncing about that was nothing short of alarming, since he was a large man. His wife, a beautiful Englishwoman, remained serene through it all, and took care of the children. Nemazee was serene too. He was an immense comfort. He had a few bottles of arak, a Persian potion that made me homesick for the corn licker of New Mexico, and in his house, sitting on Persian rugs, standing on Persian rugs or looking at the Persian draperies on the wall, you could forget the stark facts of life out of doors.

This morning a few Norwegian captains, Nemazee himself, and Mehdi a poor relation of his, all went downtown with us. We walked the short steep road that took us under the bridge of Conduit Road and passed through the wooded bit of the city near St. Joseph's Cathedral, coming out in Wyndham Street and dipping straight into the middle of town This way, they explained, was preferable to the others because there were fewer sentries standing about and challenging people. At each stop we came to, the sentry held out his hand for our passes. Everyone but myself had a proper one already issued by the Office of Foreign Affairs. My little smudged card made them worried and suspicious. "Nationality?" they always asked.

Not knowing exactly what it said on the card, I didn't know. But I mumbled, "Chinese-American," which seemed to work all right. Anyway nobody arrested me, and the whole party breathed easier when we passed through the last barrier before I got to the office, my destination. This was stationed, temporarily, in the large, august chambers of the Hong Kong and Shanghai Bank itself. The cashiers' desks had all been denuded of their chicken wire and practically the entire civic government was being carried on at one counter or another. Long queues of people were waiting to make claims or registration. I found a disappointment there though; it was too late in the season to acquire my pass in the ordinary way. The dates for my registration were closed, and I was directed to the Japanese consul, Mr. Kimura. His offices were somewhere else.

Strictly speaking, Hong Kong didn't need a Japanese consul any more because it was now Japanese territory. Unlike Shanghai and the other occupied places of China, the Crown Colony was being claimed as an actual possession of Japan, not a part of "liberated China," not subject to the government of puppets: it was always called "the captured territory of Hong Kong." It had nothing to do, politically, with Nanking. The Japs were very proud of their acquisition and didn't feel like handing it over to Wang Ching-wei, however nominal his powers in actuality. It was a matter of face. There was no nonsense in the Japanese ideology about returning Hong Kong to her rightful Chinese owners.

Later the Chinese were periodically disturbed by rumors that Wang was going to take us over. It worried us, because Wang's gang had a bad reputation and each of us, me included, could remember plenty of enemies in the group, people who would like to take revenge on us for our former criticism of their policy. That blow never fell, though. I dare say there was a lot of argument in Tokyo about it, between Wang's champions and the many Japanese who didn't even pretend to have China's interests at heart. It was lucky for me they didn't decide to give Hong

Kong back. Too many of the Nanking crowd knew my *Candid Comment* record.

Though Japan didn't need a consul any more, trained diplomats like Mr. Kimura were immediately given plenty of new work to do. Kimura was one of the Japanese I had known before Pearl Harbor. He had dined once with Charles and Cooper and me, at the Tokyo Hotel, and after dinner, happy with scotch, he had danced a solo Black Bottom, barefooted on the *tatami*. He and I had sung old American college songs. I wondered just how he would greet me now.

Kimura was embarrassed and anxious to show good will, but scared. He fluttered around me and studied the card with perplexity. "Who gave this to you?" he demanded. Then, lowering his voice, although we were all alone in the office, he said, "Is Boxer all right? I heard——"

I was as casual as possible, and no more polite than I had ever been. How could I bow and scrape to a man like Kimura, a man who used American slang and who had been drunk with me? I couldn't.

"Boxer's better," I said. "I think he's been taken to Bowen Road. Would you be allowed to visit him, do you think?"

"Perhaps, later. The Army . . . very difficult, you know. Sorry. Sorry Boxer was wounded. Now this pass. It says you have a Chinese husband. I did not know that, Miss Hahn. It shows . . . interesting possibilities."

"He's in Shanghai," I said.

"You have never been divorced?"

"No. Will I be interned?"

"No," said Mr. Kimura with commendable promptness. "No, you will not be interned. I ought to know; I drew up this new law myself." Wondering, we stared at each other with a wild surmise. "It is very strange, ha-ha-ha," said Mr. Kimura.

A belated squeamishness overtook me and I made one good try to save my political honor. "Mr. Kimura, you know me."

Mr. Kimura bowed his head.

"You know I'm an American. Everyone knows that. I have an American passport; you know that too."

"I know."

"According to American law this Chinese marriage does not make me Chinese."

"According to Japanese law," he said, "it does."

"And you know that's Boxer's baby, don't you?"

"Of course. Your—uh—private life does not alter the law. You will not be interned, Miss Hahn. Indeed, you cannot be interned. We are ejecting all Chinese subjects from the internment camp."

Staggering a little, I left his office. I now had another bigger card, much cleaner and with lots more red seals, to take over to the Foreign Affairs Department.

A French national, Mr. Walsh from the jewelry store, walked with me through the streets, which were much more crowded now than they had been in the evening of the day before. They were so crowded that we had to take to the middle of the street to make any time at all. The Chinese were all looking shabby, pinched, and frightened. I saw my tailor walking with his wife and children, his face covered with sticking plaster. I wondered if he would speak to me. According to Alec's letters, many of his old Chinese friends had refused to hail him when they saw him at the window of the internment hotel. They were afraid of the Japanese, said Alec. I had argued this out with myself and decided that they could not be blamed, but of course my heart was a little sore anyway. It needn't have been. My tailor waved to me and smiled, and stuck his chin up. A moment later I bumped into Harold Lee, wearing a battered long gown and looking like any poor white-collar worker. He kissed me, right there in the street. Then I was surrounded by old friends, and we all shook hands over and over, and wiped our eyes, and talked fast. Hubert Chen, whose family had been so offended when Charles and I turned up late and merry at their Christmas Eve party, stood there for a long time, saying:

"If you see Bob Ward" (one of the American consuls) "tell him I'm so sorry that I can't do anything for him. The Japanese watch us all the time. It's very dangerous. If I meet Bob on the street I won't dare talk to him. I hope he understands. We don't dare talk to Americans."

"But you're talking to me. . . ."

"Oh well." I've never figured that one out, but I think he meant that women didn't count. It was quite true. For some reason the Japanese never did suspect women as readily as they did men, and I suppose I do know the reason really: they look down on us, on our intelligence as well as our general value, and so they don't pay us the compliment of being afraid of us in any way at all. It was convenient just at that time, however, and I'm not complaining of their attitude.

Walsh and I resumed our journey. "Have you your marriage certificate?" he demanded. He knew the man I was going to interview, and had volunteered to help.

I said, "No, I haven't any papers at all. They're in Shanghai."

"But how can you expect to prove this marriage? I don't think they will accept your word."

"Well, I don't know. We might write to Sinmay. . . ."

Walsh wrinkled his brow. "Write?" He shrugged. "That takes months under these conditions. I doubt that the letter would get through at all. Have you nothing, no word of witnesses, or——"

"Maybe I can find somebody," I said. I turned around and studied the crowd as it shoved and pushed and shambled past us, in front of the American Express office. What followed sounds incredible. That is the trouble with real life: you can't write it down as fiction because it is so impossible. I've known that happen a dozen times. You will have to believe me because this is the truth. I reached into that thick-pressed crowd and plucked out by the arm one Freddie Kwai, a student from Shanghai and a nephew of Sinmay's.

"Hello, Freddie. Will you come with me to the Foreign Affairs Office and bear me out when I tell them that I'm your auntie? I'm getting a Chinese pass as Sinmay's wife."

"Sure thing," said Freddie with a cheerful grin, "if you don't tell 'em I was a Volunteer."

It all went smooth as butter. Freddie signed a statement, and I gave the official the two photos of myself I knew they wanted—Japanese occupation calls for an enormous number of passport photographs; they put photographs on everything—and I received in return a beautiful big receipt telling me to come back tomorrow and get my new passport.

Then Freddie shook hands with me and went away. When I next heard of him he had got out into Free China.

I went home and put my American passport into a clean envelope in the bottom drawer of the desk. Then I started out for Bowen Road Hospital, wondering if I would find Charles.

Emergency conditions can do wonders with the human frame. I had been running down the hill and up again, not stopping to count the number of trips I made in one day, but my shoes were beginning to wear out. Of course I was much thinner now, and that must have made it easier for me. I was feeling fairly cocky. Still, I wasn't cocky enough to think I could get to the hospital alone. The road that led to it was winding and deserted and heavily wooded. Nemazee volunteered to accompany me; he had a friend in hospital, he said, and he wanted to visit this man anyway. Oh yes, he said, visitors were still being allowed. There was no sentry at the gate as yet, or anyway, there hadn't been the day before. Nemazee's house was a clearing ground for prison-camp news.

The few houses on Bowen Road were gutted and gloomy. A dead man lay near the road; a pitifully skinny man he was, with a few rags on his body and a black beard. We saw no wound, and decided he had died of hunger.

The hospital was an old, rambling red brick house, with wide verandas on all three floors. One reached it by walking up a long, winding ramp, and the walking wounded crowded around to watch us as we came up. I saw a lot of people I knew, and I asked Wiseman, who was walking about on his artificial leg, "Is Charles here?"

"Certainly he's here. What the hell are *you* doing, wandering around loose?"

"It's a long story. Where's Charles?"

I found him on the ground floor in a tiny cubicle. He was lying in bed, and he opened his eyes wide and grinned when I came in.

"Don't tell me you got by with that disgraceful notion!"

Triumphantly I handed him my receipt. He studied it with grim interest. "Mmmmm . . . yes," he said at last. "You may have chosen wisely, after all. I hear that conditions in Stanley are bad. But, Mickey, how will you manage? What about money? What about gas, and electricity, and shoes for Carola?"

"I thought I could get a job."

He looked doubtful.

"Charles, in circumstances like this, what sort of job would it be all right for me to have? You see, there aren't any jobs just now except with Japanese. If I could teach English, would that be all right? Or write for a paper, if it's not political? Not that I see any signs of a chance, but later on it may be possible. I hear that a Swede has already got a job like that with some paper. They're carrying on with that English sheet of theirs."

"Well, Mickey, I'm not sure. It seems to me that a population like this has got to make out somehow. We've let them down, and now that we've surrendered, I suppose they are to be excused for trying to make their livings. After all, civilians must manage regardless. I think you can teach or write, if you keep away from controversial subjects. Anyway, that's my interpretation of the code. Of course a fellow like this beggar Kotewall, who couldn't wait to yell, 'Banzai,' at the conquerors—well, that's different. What have you got in that box?"

I put a cardboard case down on his table. "It's my jewels, all but a ring and a pin I gave away instead of money. I think for the next few days they'll be safer here, Charles. Do you mind?"

"No, but they're not particularly safe here either. People steal things around here too, though I believe it's more in the line of food and tobacco that they're interested. If you want to take the risk . . . Look. I still have my money. You'd better take it."

We divided it and I carried sixty dollars home with me. Petro had thrown some money at me, the day he ran out of the hospital, which had helped us all out. I still had some of that. I had continued to hoard my two hundred-dollar notes, watching the fluctuating market value of big notes like a hawk. I was beginning to feel quite wealthy. I was also feeling grave about the war situation, but not at all hopeless. Bataan was still holding out, and that helped our morale a lot.

Charles had said:

"The Nips had better get along to Australia and finish that job, if they know what's good for them. That's what I would do in their place; forget all this nonsense about India and go for Australia. Whoever holds Australia will win the Pacific war in the end. I don't see how they can hope to hold out otherwise. But it's going to be a long pull."

I had a pretty good picture of the setup at hospital. The officers in charge lived in the private houses surrounding the building, and a regular garrison group had been moved into a sort of barracks just down the hill, on a bluff overlooking the harbor. The hospital itself was very lightly guarded, but no attempts had been made to escape. Most of the patients were too ill to have such ambitious ideas, and the Japanese probably banked on that. Charles scoffed at me when I asked him if he were hungry.

"We have plenty here," he said, "a rough puh-lenty. But if you have any chocolate at home that you don't need, I wouldn't say no."

I met Tony on my way out, and we had a talk. "Charles isn't doing well," he said bluntly. "Not at all well. He isn't picking up as he should; he doesn't eat. No sick man could eat this muck."

"He said he didn't want anything but chocolate."

"He's trying to compensate for protein. *He* doesn't know. . . . Look here, you can probably find brains in the market, calves' brains. The Chinese don't eat them as a rule, and you may be able to get some. Cook those up and bring them in. Or soup, beef broth or something like that. Something with strength in it. I don't suppose you can buy Bovril?"

Probably the humble milk bottle of soup that I brought next day was the very beginning of the great parcel-day organization which was to spring up later, all through the camps, all over the Colony.

"You know, Reeny," I said that night, "it isn't too horrible, is it? I mean, I'm glad I didn't kill myself, after all. It may hurt a lot, but it's interesting. You've got to admit that, it's interesting."

"Oh well, if my man were alive, over at Bowen Road, I'd feel that way myself," said Irene. "No. I didn't mean it. I do feel that way too. I get awfully impatient with Mother for crying all the time. I'm damned if I'll cry. It would give those little beasts too much satisfaction. We'll pull through, Mickey, I've made up my mind. But—oh dear, just once I would like to go to bed feeling that my stomach is full."

"And that's no lie." We sat there brooding. "The stomach shrinks in time," I suggested hopefully. "I think you people get more to eat than I do, over at Hilda's. She's a very careful housekeeper, and she doesn't eat much herself. She doesn't understand. We had lettuce for lunch, just lettuce."

"No bread?"

"No, we ate our bread for breakfast."

"We have plenty of bread. I baked it myself. We have some flour."

"Um."

Irene brought out a cupcake affair, made without sugar, and insisted that I eat it. May, the amah, looking on, made a grimace intended for a smile. "Miss Hahn very lucky," she said. "Eats over at Mrs. Selwyn-Clarke's house, then comes home and eats here. Very lucky."

I glowered at the woman, who must have had a tapeworm considering the way she devoured food. She left the room and went in to Carola.

"If she weren't so good with the baby," I said, "I'd——"

"Oh, *May*. She's pretty bad. Well, Mickey, do you think it's all right now about your pass?"

I said cautiously, "For a while. But someday somebody's going to catch up with me, I think. Let's not be too confident."

That day came very soon.

Chapter 47

THE OLD PEOPLE, Father and Mother, suddenly decided that they shouldn't impose on me any more. They went back to Kowloon to live with another daughter, Daisy, where room was made by shoving more people together in a now familiar fashion, and putting up cots. Irene and Phyllis stayed on with me. It was more fun and they felt they had better chances to find work if they remained in Hong Kong.

Getting from the island to Kowloon was not now as hazardous as it had been at first. The ferry was running, and if you didn't mind being thoroughly and lasciviously searched by Indian guards at the ticket booth you could get through. We did mind, though; none of us three went over to the mainland until we couldn't help ourselves. There was plenty of searching to undergo anyway; often the Japanese threw a cordon around some downtown district and searched everyone who was caught inside the barrier. (One of them liked Irene so much he went over her twice.) A house-to-house search for enemies and arms was also under way, but it would take a long time for the search party to reach May Road, and we had no enemies or arms, so we tried not to worry. There were disquieting stories, though, that the search party had a way of picking up whatever items they liked the look of, as they went through the houses.

It is hopeless to attempt to give a detailed picture of conditions. Every five minutes brought a new alarm and at least once a day the alarm turned out to be genuine. We lived in a state of suspended terror, and we learned to dread any knock on the door. Matters that seem small when I look back were grave threats then to our lives. Small things—the fact that the Japanese were going to collect money for water, for example, and would cut it off if payment didn't come promptly—made us thoroughly miserable. We saw our children dying of typhoid or cholera. We didn't have our war legs yet. We hadn't learned to put off our worries until the moment came to grapple with them; it saves a lot of energy to do that.

By nature and training I was less subject to panic than were the refugees in the two buildings that made up our community. All the others, crowded in as they were, sleeping on the floor in rows, in naked, looted flats, upstairs and down, all of them were dramatic, emotional, whipped, scared people. They were Eurasians, Indians, Chinese, even a few European refugees from Czechoslovakia and Denmark. They had quantities of children. They lived on whatever money they had brought with them, but they hated to use it, and they fell eagerly on an extremely meager allowance of food which Selwyn had begun to supply from the hospital leftovers; on alternate days it was possible to get a slice of bread for each person in our two houses, and a half-pint of milk for each child less than five years old. Mixed in with these really needy "volunteer dependents" were a few people who had money but who wanted to save it.

One of these, of mixed blood, part Annamite, I think, learned quickly how to fawn on the Japanese. Pretty soon she was getting more confidence in herself, and she began to cheer up considerably. She was in charge of the rations, the bread and milk; other women started reporting their suspicions of her to Selwyn, alleging that she was stealing the supplies or holding back on her enemies in order to feed her friends. Everyone was quick to accuse everyone else of this sort of thing. Selwyn was livid with rage when he found this out, though her friends had been innocent of any intention to graft in accepting them. There were incredible instances of petty theft and meanness. A British doctor who had been kept out of internment as a member of the Health Department was living with his Eurasian mistress about a mile away. We noticed that he always turned up on distributing days, for half a loaf of bread and a bottle of milk. Since he wasn't exactly a volunteer dependent, Duggie Valentine looked into the matter and discovered that this man actually made rounds every day, to three centers like this one, and in each station took a tax of bread and milk. None of the British could do anything about it because he was getting on well with the Japanese.

It was a nasty period altogether. On the part of the public there was an eager rush to make friends with the conquerors. I discovered that many women have a sort of Sabine complex; they can't wait to get into bed with the triumphant Romans, even when the Romans happen to be duck-bottomed, odorous Japanese. In a way it was understandable. "After all," they must have felt, "we are desperate; there is security only with the Japanese. Never mind what they look like; they whipped the proud British in record time. The British may have been better-looking and bigger, but the Japanese are the bosses, just now. If I can capture a Japanese protector my family will eat." Maybe the original Sabines felt the same way. I can well understand it, though I don't like it.

The first local Chinese whose name appeared in the paper as definitely working for the Japanese was Peter Sin. Peter was an acquaintance of mine, a lawyer who had been very successful in his work. When I spoke to him about his actions a few months after this he was worried and defensive.

"They tell me I'm in bad with Chungking," he said, fidgeting with the pencils on his desk. He was thin and pale. "I can't see that, frankly. Somebody had to offer to take charge, or the people would have starved even worse than they do. Sure, I said I'd take charge of the rice control; why not? Someone had to do it—someone who knows the ropes of this town. But it's no sinecure. Anybody else who wants my job can have it."

We all joined in execrating Sir Robert Kotewall. Sir Robert before Pearl Harbor had been just about the most British-loving Asiatic you could find. A mixed-blood himself, Parsee and Chinese and English, he went in for being violently Chinese, and often published translations allegedly done by himself of Chinese poetry into English. Whether he did them or didn't, they were pretty bad. He was prominent in all civic politics, and an indefatigable and fluent speechmaker. I heard him once at a Sino-British Cultural Association banquet, and he went on for hours and hours.

I think he started out as a clerk in the government, and worked his way up, speech by speech, to his knighthood and a glorious position among the British-tamed cats on the municipal council, before the war. The Hong Kong government were proud of Kotewall and did him honor. It was quite a nice textbook example of how not to run a colony, judging by the results. Sir Robert Kotewall was the very first of the great men to welcome the Japanese. It was Sir Robert Kotewall who made speeches at Jap-inspired mass meetings. It was Sir Robert Kotewall who led the meeting when the new Governor of Hong Kong was welcomed into office; he shouted, "Banzai," three times, and urged the crowd to do likewise, at the end of his speech. By that time, however, he wasn't Sir Robert Kotewall any more. The Japs made him give up his British knighthood. They didn't let anybody keep British titles, even Britons at home in England; they wouldn't call people "Lord This" or "Sir That" in the public prints. They were all, severely, Mr. This and Mr. That. And poor Sir Robert Kotewall became Mr. Lo Kuk-wo. Sir Shouson Chow was Mr. Chow Shouson. It wasn't his fault, I'm sure; Sir Shouson was eighty years old and probably couldn't help himself. He didn't throw himself into the New Order, at any rate, with the glad passion of Mr. Lo Kuk-wo. No one else did.

I don't particularly blame Kotewall, because I don't quite believe he exists. I mean, I've seen him in the flesh often enough, and heard his voice droning away, but I'm not convinced that there was ever anything to Sir Robert Kotewall but sawdust. The British manufactured him and deliberately used cheap material, so they shouldn't be surprised or hurt because he has gone on fulfilling his destiny as a genuine talking doll, now that the Japanese instead of the British are winding him up. How should he know the difference? The Japs let him make speeches too, don't they?

We read about these things in the morning newspaper, and we read the news about the war, as written up by jubilant Jap journalists whose English was faulty, but whose facts, in general, were dishearteningly correct. It looked very much like a long war. We had to face that. But we couldn't and wouldn't face just how long it would be. The North African situation looked awful too. Everything looked awful. Charles seemed to think Britain was about finished. "We'll have to get over laughing at the Italians," he said to Tony. "It isn't seemly. They're a third-rate power, but so are we."

One day I brought Charles his soup and a small carton of cottage cheese, which is about the only thing I can prepare by myself. We used our milk eagerly, that fresh milk Selwyn gave the babies, but we made cheese of it when there was anything sour left over. Emile, proprietor of the Parisian Grill, had opened his restaurant again, and presented me with a dozen cans of some sort of patent chocolate baby food which had milk in it. He said he had bought the stuff for nine cents a tin, to feed his chickens with, before Pearl Harbor, and he insisted on making me a present of it. The kids loved it and we gave it to them once a day. It was a bright spot in my life.

I bounced into hospital feeling cheerful, but Charles looked rather low. "The gendarmes are after you, Mickey," he said. "Some little squirt calling himself Cheng has been here this morning, asking questions about you. He tried to Draw Me Out on politics too. He said, 'Just between you and me, Major Boxer, all this stuff Domei publishes in the paper is probably lies, don't you think?' And I said, 'Probably, but so are the Allied news reports.' That seemed to silence him."

"You think he's from the gendarmes?"

"Must be," said Charles, shifting on his pillow. "He wouldn't have dared come from anyone else. That's their way."

"Well, if they question me, they question me. I haven't broken any laws."

Charles didn't reply. We both knew that had nothing to do with the case.

Next morning I went over to Hilda's, according to schedule, for breakfast—a cup of tea and a piece of bread.

Somebody rang the doorbell, and when Ah King opened the door somebody asked for me. A slim Chinese youth, in gray flannels with a brightly striped necktie, came into the room. Hilda took Mary and went out.

"Miss Hahn? So. I am Mr. Cheng. May I ask—why aren't you interned?"

"Sit down, Mr. Cheng," I said. He sat opposite me at the breakfast table and smiled, his spectacles magnifying his eyes. "You want to see my papers?" I asked.

"Please." He studied them in silence.

"May I see *your* papers?" I asked as sweetly as I could.

"Oh—I have none. But I do have the right to come here," he said, equally politely. "I work for the Japanese."

"I *see*." There was a silence and I looked him over, and he began to be embarrassed.

"I have come," he said, "from the consulate. Mr.—uh—that gentleman you saw before——'"

"Mr. Kimura?"

"Yes, Mr. Kimura. He would like to see you this afternoon, if it is quite convenient. Shall we say three o'clock?"

"That's quite convenient, Mr. Cheng."

"Thank you." He was gone.

Of course, I told myself, it isn't really Kimura. Perhaps they will arrest me just outside the consulate door. I called Hilda back and told her.

"If I don't come back," I said, "please keep an eye on Carola."

"Oh, my dear!"

We embraced and kissed. I went home then to tell Irene.

"I'm coming with you if you want," said Irene.

"Would you? Then at least you'll know. I mean, if I go in anywhere and don't come out again——"

"Don't worry. It's probably just a matter of routine."

But the rest of the morning was pretty difficult to get through. I couldn't go to see Charles in the morning; visiting hours were from two to five. I went next door to see Tui Berg, whose Norwegian husband had been wounded and was in Bowen Road Hospital.

"Tell Charles the consulate has called me to come this afternoon, and I won't be able to come to see him," I said. "It may be the gendarmes behind it. I suppose you'll have to tell him that; he's no fool. Just so he won't wait for me and worry when I don't turn up."

Then I ate something, kissed Carola good-by, called Irene, and off we went. My stomach seemed to want to sink lower than the laws of nature usually permit. My stomach, however, was the only part of me that allowed any thought on the subject. I wouldn't let my mind touch on it. We trotted down the hill at a good pace, chattering about everything in the world but gendarmes.

At the consular offices I caused a lot of confusion. Mr. Kimura's secretary said that I had no appointment with her boss, and I said that she was probably right, but anyway she had better ask him about it. At last, after searching unavailingly through her files for the name of Cheng, she did go in and ask Kimura. This kind of indirect summons is typical of the gendarmerie. Kimura, hearing I was there, hastily sent for me.

"Ah yes, Miss Hahn," he said, looking down at his own hands instead of at me. "It is a very small matter. Colonel Noma, you know, the chief of the gendarmerie—well, yesterday at the club he called me over and made inquiries about your case. He said he would like a little talk with you, just a little talk. There is no cause for alarm. You are to go over now to the gendarmerie—you know, the former Supreme Court Building. Wait; I will give you a card of introduction."

So we trotted further, until we reached the pseudo-classic façade of the

Supreme Court. There I timidly produced my new card and showed it to the sentries stationed at all the doors. Each one beckoned with his bayonet and waved us on to the next, until we reached a sort of arbitrary main entrance, and there we found a lot of sentries lolling about at a kitchen table, out under the veranda roof. That kitchen table is a regular thing among the Japs; they put one up at all important guard posts. Near by, leaning against one of the huge pillars, was a young Chinese, sallow and elegant in navy blue. He approached us and asked us what we wanted.

Irene replied in Chinese that I had been sent for. He stared at her and asked her if she wasn't Irene Gittins, who had formerly worked for a certain engineering firm in Canton. "Yes," admitted Irene, "so what?"

"Don't you remember me, Miss Gittins? I was a clerk there."

After a bit Reeny did recall him. His name was Kung. He said that he could speak Japanese, and so he was now working as interpreter here at the gendarmerie, and he offered to help us out. Reeny chattered with him eagerly, and he led us over to the sentry in charge and explained to this man in fluent Japanese why we had come. After the introduction the soldiers were friendly and offered us chairs while one of their number took my card of introduction inside, disappearing down the corridor. In the meantime Mr. Kung gave us costly gold-tipped Turkish cigarettes and listened sympathetically as Irene told him her troubles. Obviously he was a comparatively big shot here, at the holy of holies.

We waited about an hour on those kitchen chairs, smoking and wondering what was going to happen. I got a bad headache, a sure sign that I am scared. At last something did take place: there was a loud roar from indoors, and all the shambling, dirty little soldiers jumped to attention and saluted. Then there bounced from the doorway a stocky, hairy, thick little fellow, tough as redwood and about the same color. He shouted from a throat that needed clearing:

"What is this? Who you? Who tell you come here?"

We turned pale and jumped to our feet, and once again I made my explanation, as Reeny gestured helplessly toward me: "I didn't come here; I was sent for. A Mr. Cheng came to my house this morning and told me to go to Mr. Kimura."

"Kimura? Don't know him."

"Kimura of the Japanese consulate. And Mr. Kimura said that Mr. Noma wanted to see me."

"Who *you?*" he growled at Irene.

"My friend," I said. "She—uh—she came with me."

"Pass!"

I gave him my passport. He grabbed Reeny's too, and studied them both as if he intended to eat them for breakfast. Then, with a sudden and bewildering moderation of his voice, he said:

"Okay, *you* come. *You* wait."

Together he and I walked into the dread gendarmerie. We marched down the shining corridor, where so lately Charles and I had come to register Carola at the government office. We climbed a stair and came to halt at last outside a closed door. The little lion now talked quite gently.

"You American?"

"Yes, married to a Chinese."

He looked at me piercingly. "You marry Chinese?" Then he chuckled, like thunder, and said warmly, "No! That's not good. Why marry a Chinese?" His voice was unbelievably contemptuous as he said, "Chinese." But he was acting like a human being, and in a rush of relief I answered with assurance.

"Because he's good-looking. He's very nice. See?" I gave him Sinmay's photograph, and he studied it carefully.

"You *like* China?" he demanded.

"Very much," I said firmly.

He looked at me curiously, half pleased, half not. Then a bell buzzed and he straightened up. "Mr. Noma see you now."

He knocked on the door, and, inside, somebody grunted. We went in.

Chapter 48

I FELT exactly as if I had been summoned by the dean for a scolding. Japanese procedure, coupled with the fact that most of the Japanese I dealt with speak broken English, had that effect on me permanently; I became a child with them, and as they treated us all like children anyway it was fortunate that I had made this adjustment. We always got on pretty smoothly in our later official interviews; I would stammer and blush, and they liked that: they were used to it in their own women. At first I would be furious with myself. I wanted to be fearless and defiant with the enemy. But after a while, when I saw fearless and defiant women being slapped around, I didn't regret my weakness. You may shake hands with me if you like; I am the woman who got through the occupation without being slapped. Except once, socially, and that scarcely counts. I'll tell about it later.

Noma, like the late lamented Mussolini, was sitting at a very big desk at the other end of a very long room. He looked like an extra-small goblin in khaki. My escort and I bowed from the waist and then stood there in military posture, our hands at our sides. Noma gabbled some words at the hairy guy—I shall call him by name hereafter; he was Yokayama—and indicated that we were to sit down at a Chinese arrangement of chairs around a table, down at our end of the room. We waited in stiff silence, while I swallowed and swallowed at a lump in my throat. Yet it wasn't so terrible waiting, after all. So much had happened already that all of a sudden I didn't give a damn.

Finally he stalked over to us and sat opposite me. Throughout the whole interview he kept looking at his own clasped hands. He addressed all his words to Yokayama, but in a short time I knew somehow that he could speak English and understand it better than the interpreter did. It was not obvious, but I could tell; it was something in the way he cut in ahead of Yokayama sometimes in the middle of a long speech, and once when he was interested he snapped out another question without waiting for my previous reply to be handed over in Japanese. I found out later that I was right; Noma was educated abroad.

The questions and answers are all between Yokayama and me.

"Why you come here?"

"A Mr. Cheng told me this morning, at Selwyn-Clarke's house, to go to see Mr. Kimura the consul at three o'clock. Mr. Kimura told me," et cetera, et cetera.

"What time you come China?"

"Nineteen thirty-five."

"You marry Chinese husband what year?"

"Nineteen thirty-seven."

"You live Hong Kong?"

"Shanghai. I lived in Shanghai for five years and then went to Chungking." I paused here, but nobody looked surprised, so I continued. "I spent a year in Chungking and then came to Hong Kong."

Yokayama and Noma took me step by step, over and over, down to Hong Kong and then stopped. We went over this data about four or five times, checking and rechecking in a mechanical way. Both men looked bored. Then all of a sudden they shot at me:

"You know *Boxer*?"

This was silly, and I felt annoyed. "Certainly I know Boxer," I said. "I'm his mistress. That's his baby I've got."

Well, anyway, it stopped both of them for a minute; first blood to me. Noma rubbed his chin before he asked the next question.

"You love Boxer?"

"Look here," I said to myself, "this isn't fair. You're supposed to grill me about my political affiliations. You may even, if you like, accuse me of living with Boxer for my own Mata Hari purposes. I expect that sort of thing in a third degree. I even expect a little modified torture, arm twisting and the like. But this? Sirs, this is a personal question. It isn't done. I refuse to answer."

I refused to answer.

"You love Boxer?" asked Yokayama again, grinning. I giggled nervously and hung my head like one of those peasant girls from Central Europe.

"You love Boxer?"

"Uh . . ."

"You love Boxer?"

I was sweating. Why, damn it, Charles himself had never asked me that.

"You love Boxer?"

"*Yes.*"

Well, that was a relief. I sat back, trembling. At the same time I felt much better, as if I had had a glass of brandy. I don't know why. There came to me a miracle. It was as if I had said to myself with conviction, "I can manage these people." That conviction was never to leave me again, all the time I was in Hong Kong, and it never let me down either.

The two men were talking in Japanese, and Yokayama turned to me again. Now his question made more sense. He wanted to know about Charles's movements since I had met him. When did he go where? When was he in Chungking, in Shanghai, in Singapore?

I hope I have made it clear to my public that Charles wasn't the kind of man to talk very much. I knew literally nothing about his work, which was fortunate, because the fact showed convincingly in my replies. Very patiently the men asked me things over and over and over again. I was patient too. I didn't care how long it went on. I was safe. It was good training for the phase I'm going through now with Carola: "Mommy, where's the train going?" "Going to New York, darling." "Mommy, where's the train going? Where's the train going, Mommy?" "To New York." "Mommy, where's the train going?" And so ad infinitum.

Not once did they ask any question about *Candid Comment*. Only once or twice did they ask me about Chungking and my book. I think now that I got in ahead of them on that by talking about it right away. They had read it—I found later that *The Soong Sisters* has been translated into Japanese and is pretty well known there—but they didn't ask much. I said that I liked Mme. Kung best, and they just grunted. As things turned out, I think that they never did get on to my Shanghai record simply because they never asked the Shanghai gendarmes for it. The more I saw of their

methods the better I understood my luck. All Japanese seem to feel inter-
departmental jealousy, and it is uppermost in the minds of the thugs who
run things from the gendarmerie. They won't ever admit they don't already know everything. And then, too, they thought they must know all
about me already, because they knew so much. When you come to think
of it, there's an awful lot to know about me, if you take the trouble.

Also they were very busy people and couldn't think of everything. In
their minds I was a prize only in that I was Charles's mistress, and they
concentrated on that. They were after Papers. Their men were even then
going over Charles's apartment for Papers, ungluing the chairs, taking up
the floors, going page by page through all his precious books. They were
questioning his servant, after taking more than a month to catch him. They
are very proud of the fact that they have a dossier on everybody white in
the Far East, and just then their pride was overweening. It wasn't only
gendarmes, of course, who were proud of their Intelligence Service; every
little man who had anything to do with it was chuckling, rubbing his
hands over Japan's cleverness. So they looked at me brightly, in a good
humor, and so I escaped unpleasantness of a more material sort.

Unaware of what could have taken place, I wasn't panicked. A few
months later I heard of how they questioned other women and I went gray
at the realization of what could have happened to me that day. And yet I
may be doing them an injustice. There is no doubt that they liked Charles
and respected him, and were probably determined to be decent to me if it
remained possible. A long time afterward Yoshida, a gendarme you will
meet in this book, said to me:

"Six months ago I in Canton. I hear Boxer had girl friend—*you*. Everybody say British bad, Boxer okay, girl friend okay. No proud."

Maybe. I don't understand the Japanese, ever, and that afternoon I was
cheerful toward the end, but tired and mystified. Between the questions
that made sense they asked a lot of nonsensical stuff. I can't remember it
all, but it was really silly. They asked all sorts of details about how I was
living now, and what we ate, and what I was paying for milk, and how
long I had nursed Carola at the breast, and what did I bring Charles to
eat at hospital? Those questions certainly did obsess my mind, but why
did the gendarmes care? Of course I realized that in a general way they
were trying to figure out if I was getting money from Chungking, but
that wouldn't account for all of it. Charles guessed, when we talked about
it afterward, that they just fill in time, while they're thinking of important
questions, with anything that pops into their heads. In a few minutes, however, they drew blood.

"Boxer good to you?"

"Why, yes . . ."

"How much rice he give you every month?"

My middle-class training now popped up in the most surprising way. I snapped back at Lieutenant Colonel Noma, chief of the gendarmes of the Captured Territory of Hong Kong. "He didn't give me rice!" I cried indignantly. ("Rice," of course, was their word for payment, money, currency.) "He didn't have to. I earn my own living. I'm very well known. I'm a writer."

"What's that?"

I leaned forward and spoke to Yokayama with kind patience, slowly, as if to a child. "I write. I write stories, poems, books, you understand? I send these to America and the publishers send me money. That way, I earn enough to live on. Nobody here has to give me rice."

They chattered to each other for a long time over that. Then we started all over again. We took it all again, like a rehearsal, until I was groggy. At last even they were groggy, I guess. Yokayama took a deep breath and tried to sum it up.

"Now let's see. You come to Shanghai 1936——"

"No, 1935."

"*So des*. You come to Shanghai and marry Chinese, Mr. Zau. Then you go to Hong Kong."

"Chungking."

"*So des,* Chungking. You stay Chungking from 1938——"

"Nineteen thirty-nine."

"Nineteen thirty-nine to 1940. You come to Hong Kong and go back Shanghai——"

"I didn't go back to Shanghai."

And so on, and so on, and so on. At last he shot his finger at me and cried, for the twentieth time, "*Why,* WHY you marry this Chinese, then come Hong Kong, have baby with Major Boxer? WHY?"

The human frame can stand just so much. Madness took me, and I said, wilting, "Because I'm a bad girl."

A long silence followed. I slumped in my chair. Then I was electrified. Mr. Yokayama, interpreter, had slapped me heartily on the back.

"No!" he roared. "You no bad girl. Good girl. Go home now."

The walk back, down the long corridors and the steps, was very short in reverse order. Mr. Yokayama chattered like a happy schoolboy. "If you need milk or rice, come to us. Don't worry." (They said that to everybody they examined in those days; it was part of the routine.) He also grew gallant in the Japanese fashion, saying that he was not married, and did we have an extra room at my apartment? I said no, we were pretty well crowded in, and it was a shame he wasn't married.

Reeny was still sitting on her kitchen chair, though the sun was low in the sky. Mr. Kung had reassured her, she told me on the way home; he had promised I would come back, and it wasn't too bad waiting. She was amazed, however, to see the change in Yokayama. The roaring lion who entered the Supreme Court had come out, if not exactly lamblike, at least very jolly. She said we were howling with laughter and hitting each other on the back. I think she must be exaggerating a little, but I know I was almost drunk with relief and also with the desire to laugh really loud. I thought the gendarmes had been awfully, awfully funny. But I dare say I was a little hysterical. Anyway, she was puzzled until I got her safely away and halfway up the hill.

We both arrived home in hysterics.

"Do you mean to say that's all they asked you?" demanded Charles in amazement.

"Yep. That's all. Of course you must remember that they asked everything about twenty times over."

"Strange, just the same."

"Your boy says they beat him up," I said, "but he didn't look badly mauled. He must have had pretty much the same experience as mine, Charles, except that they probably slapped him once in a while. They wanted to know where you kept your cables and your code. You know, the Papers."

"They don't give me credit for much intelligence, do they? What Papers, for God's sake?"

"*I* don't know. Anyway, the last time the boy came to see me he said that they had asked him to spy on me. He wanted to know if I'd mind. He said they would give him rice and tobacco if he would, so I said sure, go ahead. . . . But he's not being straight with you, Charles. I'm sure he's run off with all your stuff."

"Probably. If only you could get my fingernail scissors out of the flat I'd be happy."

He had said this every day for a long time, and I was getting sore. "Once and for all, Charles, I will *not* go near your flat. Are you quite mad? Don't you realize they have guards there, waiting? That's the way they got the boy. I don't mind being heroic for something that's worth it, but fingernail scissors—really!"

It was always difficult for him to realize what things were like. Of course when he felt better he saw more clearly, but it was so much like a second-rate movie, around town, that one had to excuse him for not believing in it. I did excuse him after a few minutes, and I was very glad I had a week later, when they closed the hospital gates to us. They said it was because of a cholera epidemic in town, but it wasn't. They refused our parcels for a couple of months and the men nearly starved. Afterward they accepted parcels, twice a week for a while, but we were never to get indoors again. We came to the bottom of the ramp every day until that was forbidden, and then we depended on parcel day to see the men, at a distance. At first, while we knew the guards, they permitted a certain amount of shouting and signaling, but little by little that too was stopped, and when the guards were changed everything was very strict indeed.

Hilda had been staying indoors most of the time. Miriam, Mary's Chinese governess, had married just before the war, and now her husband resolved to take her to Shanghai. Boats were leaving very seldom and they were crowded to capacity, but Miriam's husband managed to get tickets, and at last she left. After that Hilda had Mary to look after, which kept her at home automatically. Sometimes both of them walked over to the hospital with me, but Hilda seldom went downtown. It was safer not to. One of her friends, Max Bickerton, was still at liberty because he was connected with the Colonial Secretary's office, and this whole staff was being kept out until special quarters were ready for them in the camp. Once at least Hilda came downtown to see this man, and he reported to her that she could be easy in her mind about her safety.

"One thing they are definitely *not* interested in at the moment is the leftist crowd," he assured her. My good luck, too, heartened her. She was cheering up generally. We were all pretty busy doing whatever we could for Stanley, because the conditions there were terrible, and it was no secret. Vera Armstrong, by dint of her excellent Japanese, managed to get permission to come into town, to try to sell her watch and buy food for the children. She had been offered a job as interpreter in the early days after the surrender, and the Japs had wanted Jack, too, to help them with their legal problems. The Armstrongs had refused the offer because they felt, as Charles had done about me, that they should stay with their own people. Vera regretted it now, because, womanlike, she was thinking more of her children than she did of principle. She stayed overnight with the Selwyn-Clarkes and talked vividly of what life was like at Stanley. She talked so fast that I stared at her in amazement. She was thin and wind-burned, and very nervous and energetic. Otherwise she was normal, but she had grown into camp life so much that half the time I didn't know what she was talking about. Part of the rest of the time she chattered about her things:

the furniture of the house, which she had managed to salvage, and their linen and silver. It had been so long since any of us had thought of *things*, of anything but food and shelter, that we were bewildered. It was only natural, though. The Stanley people were being starved and herded like cattle, but they had no responsibility, nothing to do except to line up and wait for boiled water and food, after they had cleaned their rooms and picked up their blankets. And so their minds went back to their houses, and they clung to the memory of their lives before the war. They persisted in treating the prewar life as the real one; this camp life, they felt, was only a short interlude, a nightmare, and they ignored it. Camp was still full of social distinctions and petty resentments. They played bridge, they talked of their hunger and their pasts, and of the future, all in terms of possessions.

I don't mean to be snooty about the petty resentments. We had those too. Soon after the old couple left Reeny came to me and asked me very nicely if I minded if she invited Auntie Law to stay with us. Auntie Law, she said, was Father's youngest sister (though she was over sixty) and her husband was imprisoned in Shamsuipo with the other Volunteers, and Auntie Law had taken refuge with Auntie May, but Auntie May's house-mate wouldn't let her stay any more. Auntie Law was pathetic, said Reeny. Did I mind? No, I didn't mind.

So Auntie Law moved in with us. She was a portly white-haired lady with a pretty face, a sweet smile, and a maddeningly simple mind. I liked her, but she did talk quite a lot, and it was always about the things she had lost. She and her husband had owned a little farm outside Kowloon, to which they would repair of a week end. They had had a man in charge there, and chickens and ducks and turkeys. I could go into a lot more detail about the farm, because I heard about it with all its appointments day after day after day. You can't do anything about old people, but in the end I was driven to try. It was all the more irritating because Irene and Phyllis, too, often indulged in lamentations over their losses, and for some reason I got tired of it. I suppose partly I was angered because Irene seemed to hold it against me that my things, save for what I had taken with me, were still there. . . . "Why couldn't you have been looted instead of me?" she would say. "You don't care for things, and I did. I had *lovely* things. You know, all of this would be gone if I hadn't been here to save it."

"Well, for Pete's sake, Reeny, you can have it. Take it. Take it all," I would say. Already I had installed her at the teapot in the place of honor when we had our meals. It meant a lot to her and nothing to me.

"This stuff? I don't want it," said Irene, turning up her nose. "I wouldn't have it. I only meant it seems such a pity——"

So when Auntie added her lamentations to the pool I finally turned. "You know, Auntie, things aren't the most important question. You're still alive, and so is your husband. Can't you see that after a war like this, with people dying or being broken to pieces, things don't matter?"

"Mickey forgets," added Irene with a touch of malice in her voice, "that she didn't lose anything, whereas we did."

"No, I don't, Reeny. You never let me forget it," I said.

It was the nearest we ever came to a row.

Chapter 49

THE SUDDEN withdrawal of Charles from my daily routine left me staggered for a while, and much more inclined to fret. For a month, however, it wasn't as bad as it was going to be later. We were still allowed to bring our parcels up the ramp and into the building, under guard, and our men lined up and watched us pass by. Though we weren't supposed to talk to them, sometimes we managed to whisper and even to slip notes back and forth, though my upright Charles frowned on that sort of thing as likely to endanger the few privileges we had left. So many things were happening to us outside that I was overjoyed to have those few hurried words once a fortnight or so; there was always plenty to tell him. One of the lower-ranking officers of the guard was friendly too, and when I asked permission to bring Carola to see her father he made elaborate arrangements, unofficially.

This is what happened: I carried the baby with my parcel into the office, where we were always told to sit down and our things were taken in turn, politely and properly. This sergeant scrutinized the things, turning back home-cooked food and things he considered "luxuries"—an undue amount of chocolate, for example, though the men needed it badly. Everything we brought was supposed to be in sealed tins or bottles, to obviate the danger of smuggled messages. This was a double hardship; sealed tins were expensive and scarce, and you couldn't get good food value in most of them. But anyway, those were palmy days, because the officers were nice and because we were treated with courtesy. Partly this was because at that time there were very few of us; about twelve at the most. The kindest-hearted officer is apt to grow callous when he is overworked, but these men weren't being overworked.

So there I sat with the baby, wondering what the sergeant had cooked up. Pretty soon he had trouble deciphering an English word on the list. Then he told one of his men to call an interpreter—i.e., Boxer. Charles came in, did not look at me, sat down at the sergeant's command, and started to work. Presently Carola began to cry. What the sergeant would have done if Carola hadn't cried is a question, but she did her stuff. She kept crying and crying until the sergeant said:

"Take her into the next office and give her some milk." I caught on, and instead of telling him she was weaned and it wasn't dinnertime, I went. A moment later Charles came in, alone.

We had almost an hour, though all the time other prisoners were bouncing in, saying, "Oops—sorry," and bouncing out again. Carola finally passed out and slept, her face upside down on my arm. We had a good long talk, for the last time. There was a lot to talk about. Carola was getting very clever, and showing signs of an admiring passion for Bryan, who could crawl about the floor like a veteran and even said "Mamma" and "Ta." Carola could only gurgle and sit still, but she thought Bryan pretty hot stuff, and brightened up whenever he came near her. When these important matters had been thoroughly discussed we talked about Stanley, and what Selwyn-Clarke was doing: we wondered what would be the best sort of food for hospital, if it was allowed and if we could get it; we told each other again that the war would have to end someday and in our favor. It was nice of that sergeant, wasn't it? I brought him extra chocolate after that, whenever I could, until he was transferred.

After the excitement of my gendarme questioning died down we took stock of our resources, and the general report made us very gloomy. We were using up everything and nothing was coming in. I had brought my jewels back from hospital, fortunately, before the gates were closed, but as yet nobody was buying jewels. Everyone was hanging on to his money until he knew what would happen. The Japanese had made us afraid of our Hong Kong money by devaluating it in relation to the yen; still the public shied off the yen. The Japs ranted and raved, and made it compulsory to pay water and electricity rates in yen. At last the public, though still they were convinced that the British would come back soon, began to buy a little Japanese currency; they had to. At once things loosened up to some extent for moneyed people, though a lot more people on the bottom of the heap died of starvation. And we were very nearly at the bottom of the heap, it seemed. I knew we weren't really. I was still held up by that conviction, always held by members of the middle class, that it couldn't happen to *me*. Hungry and worried, I still had that faith. I don't know why. I had learned that I couldn't and shouldn't expect to

lepend on friends. We were all in the same boat and with a few excep-
ions we weren't even friends any more. Whenever I saw someone I knew
coming toward me I was saying to myself, "Can you help us? Is there
anything you can do to help?" and he was thinking the same thing. All
the while we talked to each other, saying hearty, ordinary things, we
were wondering how we could use each other.

Reeny and I found that Needa's office was a good place to visit.
Needa had come safely through the war by virtue of the fact that he
spoke a little Japanese, remembered from the first years of his life when
his Japanese mother took him to Japan. Also, he reminded me that before
he married his English wife, who had left him later and taken the baby
home to Daddy and Mother in Shanghai, he had spent time every year
in his home town, Tsingtao, where Japanese was spoken. Needa was now
in a state of trembling hope and even occasional exaltation. He was as
poor as the rest of us, but he felt that he had a chance to make something
of his brokerage firm. Remember, between winning the races that had
made him famous and popular among racegoers, he had been a commodity
broker, like many of the other "gentleman jockeys." He had preferred his
business to his avocation of riding, all along. Now, though the Japanese
were trying to carry on with the races and were offering inducements to
the jockeys to come back, Needa resolved to be a broker instead. He hated
his reputation as a jockey. He had an idea firmly fixed in his head that
it was rather shameful to be a jockey, but socially very respectable and
solid to be a broker—well, no, not a broker, but a *merchant*. Needa, he
would have us know, was a *merchant*. We didn't laugh at him. There
was something convincing about him, in spite of his well-known genial
manners and his sudden loud laugh. The only drawback to Needa's
company, heartening as it was and in spite of his generosity, was that he
adored the Japanese.

He raved about them. So far he had met only private soldiers with
whom he had dealt at Repulse Bay, during those ticklish hours when all
the civilians had been arrested and marched off to Kowloon. Needa had
been a blessing then, saving the civilians from worse indignities because
of his knowledge of Japanese speech. Some of the soldiers looked him up
again and gave him presents of looted food, tinned stuff and such, and
then he began finding watches for them to buy, and little by little the
Army and Navy knew him and liked him. They were bound to like him,
he liked them so much. Suddenly, you see, that Japanese blood of his
which had meant so much misery, which had kept him feeling sore and
inferior all his life, which had lost him his beloved wife and baby—suddenly it was a damned good thing to have after all. Suddenly his Japanese

brothers were conquerors, on top of the world, courted and triumphant
What an awakening for a Eurasian! Needa was drunk with joy and
gratitude. He had been liberated.

Still, he was the Needa we had always known, and it was confusing and
painful for us to hear him on that subject. At first he tried to control himself in deference to our feelings, but after a while he rationalized it and
then he was comfortable again. Reeny had lost her husband? It was a
rotten shame, but it was the fault of those terrible British and Ernie's own
wrongheaded loyalty to them. Why had Ernie, an Asiatic, taken up arms
against brother Asiatics on behalf of those cheating Britons? (And the
British had taken his wife away too, hadn't they? She, a Briton, had
scorned him, hadn't she? *Now* he'd show 'em all.)

As for me, that was different too. Needa had always had a fondness
for me. He now decided that it was all for my good; Charles had betrayed
me, he thought. Not that he knew the fellow, but what sort of guy would
get a girl into a fix like that? Given time, he would have run out on her
anyway, said Needa to himself. Mickey really loved Asia; Mickey could
now adopt the new Asia, and Asia would adopt her, because she had been
betrayed and abandoned by her own people. She would have a special
place in the new Asia; he, Needa, would help. Everybody in the end
would be happy, all the happier without those British. (And yet some of
them were decent fellows, and Needa shamefacedly sent them food when
he had it, and when nobody was looking.)

So Reeny and I called in at Needa's office every day, and if he had food
he would share it with us, with loud denials of our protests. Sometimes
if we fell into the old discussion of ways and means he would look at our
drawn faces, and he would frown, not liking the wrinkles in our fore-
heads.

"Oh, don't *worry*," he would say, impatiently standing up and moving
about at unnecessary tasks. He slammed drawers open and shut, snatching out samples of this and that, things he was trying to sell, things he
was succeeding in selling, in larger and larger quantity. "Look, are the
kids getting the bellyache? I got a patent medicine here that will fix that.
Sure, go on, take the bottle; I got six dozen more." When Japanese came
in we ran out.

It was not Needa who introduced us to the first Japanese we met socially. The introduction looked accidental in a way, but it wasn't. Kung,
the interpreter who had spoken to Reeny at the gendarmerie, dropped
in on us one evening, just when things looked at their worst. We were all
in the living room, sitting about with the babies. The furniture was full

of drying baby napkins, because it was raining and we couldn't hang them outside. Kung stood in the middle of all this, looking around with slightly wrinkled nose. A man who has lived among the amenities of civilization for a few months would naturally view our poverty with pitying distaste, and he was a model of fashion himself, even to the slight bulge under the right arm where he wore his revolver.

Mr. Kung wanted to know if Irene and I would consider teaching English to a couple of very gentlemanly, scholarly, serious gendarmes. He was emphatic about those adjectives. There would be no funny stuff, he assured Reeny. We said that we would indeed. He addressed all his remarks to Irene and often it looked as if he meant that she alone was to take the job, but always at the end I found myself carelessly but definitely included. So the next day we went to the place he had indicated, a club over a barbershop. We had polished our shoes and done our faces, and Reeny had brushed my hair, and we felt very nervous.

The club was something like Chinese clubs I have seen before, with a big room full of tables and chairs, a little bar, an attempt at decoration in the stained-glass style, and a ceiling fan. There were other rooms in the back, of course, and the inevitable giggling tarts, in black dresses, peeking in at us from the doorway. We saw no signs of dilapidation, no broken glass or shell holes, and it was a queer feeling. Almost every interior in Hong Kong carried some sign of the war these days, but not this one. Mr. Kung ordered sliced pineapple and beer for us, and after a little while his first friend arrived.

"This is Mr. Nakazawa," said Kung.

I almost said, "But he's no Jap!" Then I remembered Matsumoto and other Chinese-looking Japanese I had seen, and held my peace. Nakazawa was a slim, reasonably tall man in business clothes, with a fine thin face and a little mustache. He looked cruel and clever and not very healthy. He spoke perfectly good English, quickly, and all the time he talked he was sizing us up, and suddenly I saw the light. This, I knew, was more investigation, following on my interview with Noma. Mr. Nakazawa was making arrangements briskly with Reeny, talking about his friend Yoshida, who really couldn't speak English; they two would come next day for a lesson at our house. They would pay us—no, he didn't use the word "pay": now that we had met him, he indicated, we need worry no more about *anything*. He and Yoshida would give us whatever we wanted. He brought out a notebook and asked Reeny what, to begin with, they should send up. . . .

It was quite a moment, but Reeny didn't seem at all at a loss. She was prompt with her replies. We wanted sugar, flour, rice, fruit, meat, everything. Nakazawa gravely nodded and wrote it all down. Then he sent us home in a car.

We discussed him agitatedly all the way home, in low tones so the driver wouldn't hear us. Irene's point of view, naturally, was not quite mine. She was not so suspicious to begin with; she thought that Nakazawa might be just what Kung said he was, a wealthy young man with a tender heart and a love for languages. But even she couldn't believe that he would be able to give us the food he had promised. Neither of us even talked about the propriety of accepting food from an enemy. I have discovered since I came home that people raise their eyebrows at such an attitude, but I am pretty sure that nobody in occupied territory would. In fact I just choke up and get mad if you talk about it, and wish that you could have a month of Japanese Hong Kong for the good of your soul, and also for your information.

Well, the food arrived. So did Nakazawa, in uniform and sword, and so did his pal Yoshida. They had a lot of coolies to carry it up, and it was an incredible sight. The whole neighborhood crowded to look. We gained tremendous face under these unnatural circumstances; that afternoon when I met one of the Eurasian boys who was acting as guard for the Japanese he was positively respectful to me, obviously under the impression that I was now being Kept by a gendarme lover. I will put your mind at rest at the risk of disappointing you; during the month that we saw Nakazawa every day and got food from him, and afterward, when he was satisfied with his investigation and didn't give us any more food or come around very often, neither he nor Yoshida made passes at any of us.

Ah King was told to cook up some of the food for the gendarmes, who invited themselves for dinner. (Reeny always grudged giving them any of the food back. She said that in the end there wasn't much left over for us, but she exaggerated. For a while we had plenty of food.) That first meal was definitely uncomfortable, though Nakazawa—Chick, as we called him—kept chattering to avoid pauses. He talked smoothly, like any well-bred conqueror, and I admired his method of attack. He kept at the girls, rubbing it in that they owed their sufferings to England, and artfully playing up any latent pride they had in their Chinese blood. That took a bit of doing, after the lives they had led as despised Eurasians, but Chick did it, and well. If all the Japanese had been as clever as Chick the population would be in love with the New Order today, but I never met another one like him, not anywhere even among the diplomats, who should have been able to beat a mere gendarme at that game.

In the end, though, he overtalked himself. He was human too. The fact that he was the cynosure of so many pairs of feminine eyes acted like wine on him, and he began to boast.

"I have killed, alone, fourteen men," he said. "I, though I was not a professional soldier. All Japanese can kill men. Look at me, playboy, who before the war owned forty cabarets in Tokyo, yet I have campaigned in China like a veteran. That is why I have been given this good job here. In Canton I have a shop for selling gramophone records and cameras, and all the girls in the shop are Chinese girls of good family. I think we must start a business here. I will open a teashop for you. You girls can manage it and be hostesses."

All of a sudden it must have slapped the girls in the face, despite all his siren song at the beginning. He was boasting about having killed men. Their husbands were dead, killed by Japanese, and here sat a Japanese, boasting of it. And on top of that he wanted them to be hostesses in a teashop. And on top of that he had said admiringly of Phyllis that she looked exactly like a Japanese girl. . . . Irene ran from the table and went to bed in the back room, pleading that she felt very ill.

The next month was the queerest, surely, that we will ever spend in our three lives. I remember floods of talk; optimistic, propagandist chatter from Chick, foolish, distracted words from Auntie, hysterical outbursts mingled with reasonable advice from Reeny. Chick had in his mind not one but many little policies and projects. He was a mercurial bloke, brimming over with ambition and ideals for his country. He wanted to keep an eye on me. He wanted to spread Japanese propaganda among the Eurasians. He wanted to see what sort of foreign company we were keeping; he wanted, indeed, to know what we did every minute of the day, and he succeeded. He gave two or three big sukiyaki parties in our flat, cooking the stuff deftly on the floor of the living room, and he commanded us, in the politest terms, to invite all our white friends. Those were mostly Norwegians, and Nemazee; they came eagerly because sukiyaki meant meat—beef, pork, chicken. He watched these Norwegians, and talked with them, and asked us all question after question. As for me . . .

As soon as I had a chance, following my resolved policy, I brought out all my photographs and showed them to the two gendarmes, just as if it were an ordinary polite gesture. Most of the photos were groups in Chungking. They pondered them long and silently. Yoshida studied a picture of the Generalissimo for about five minutes before he said in disappointed tones, "But isn't he very ill, almost dead?"

"Not at all," I said. "He's very well."

Yoshida looked again at the picture and then turned to one of Mme. Sun and asked more questions like that. I had never realized before that they did believe their own propaganda. Yet after all, don't we all?

I'm tempted to write a whole book just about Chick and Yoshida, but of course I can't. It wouldn't interest you as much as it did me, anyway. I had very little else to think about, and under the circumstances everything about them was of agonizing interest to me. Here at last, I told myself, was the essence of the enemy, the driving force, the cause of all the catastrophe. If only I have the wisdom to read this riddle! What a satisfaction it would be to *know* what crushes me, even though I am hopelessly crushed in the end!

Perhaps I wasn't completely wrong in thinking that, but I was too hopeful of finding a simple solution to Japan's problem. Japan is not to be summed up in one man, or two, or twenty, even though they do run so much to type. Japan, indeed, can't even be summed up in one government. Chick left me no wiser than he found me. My attitude toward the Japanese was rapidly becoming one of wary, wondering curiosity, and there it remains until this day. I must admit that I also feel maternal toward some of them, perhaps because I have mothered so many anthropoids with just the same quick changes of temper, the same emotional instability. I have not said that for a joke. I don't think apes particularly funny, you know; they're very like us, that's all. But the Japanese often aren't, and I tried not to forget it.

Chick would telephone each morning and tell us how many people were coming to lunch or dinner. Then we would get our orders of the day. Maybe he and Yoshida were going to take us to a newsreel, showing how strong Japan was and how weak were the other nations of the world. Or perhaps we were to hurry straight downtown to his flat (presided over by one of his many mistresses, a sultry-looking Eurasian girl with a bosom) and be introduced to "an important newspaperman." Or we were to lunch with him in the Parisian Grill, with some other Chinese wards of his. Chick's interests were wide and varied. Chief of these was his ambition to make lots and lots of money in business, quick. He wanted to open a shop, two shops, three; he wanted to own a newspaper and put me at the head of it; he wanted to start a night club. He also did a lot of gentle squeezing, extorting from anybody with money whom he happened to encounter.

Chick was a mixture, as you can see. He was passionately sincere in his belief in Japan. He must have been nurtured in that belief since he lay in his cradle. He spoke fluent German and was well up in all the Gestapo methods. I am sure he was pretty good at torture and questioning. But that patriotic passion didn't prevent him from indulging in petty graft, or even in the pleasures of generosity now and then; he had a delicate way of giving us things, or helping us out of fixes, that nobody in the civilized world could have surpassed. It was damned useful, having a gendarme around, though it certainly had its disadvantages. He was in the house with Yoshida the day that long-dreaded search party finally arrived; and he sent them off without ceremony.

I wish he had been about when May left us. May had taken to stealing on a really unpleasant scale, and at last we got rid of her. She had a way of going crazy now and then, which was one reason I put off this operation until the last moment, and she went crazy when the blow fell. She screamed, and tried to loot the house more thoroughly than she had already done, and then she called in the local gendarmerie and turned us in for looting! That was in the period before Chick had turned up and it could have been nasty; the local police, mostly Chinese, just went through the house, however, and took whatever they wanted, calling it "enemy property." There wasn't much left to take. Ah King soon found me another amah, a pretty young woman named Ah Yuk.

Chick could have prevented all this, though I suppose he would have thrown May into prison, and I wouldn't have liked that. He did relieve me of another lot of incumbents, a group of petty gendarme spies, Millie Chun and her three young men, who had been hanging around me like rats ever since I came home. The minute Chick turned up they melted away like summer snow and they never bothered us again. From that time, even after Chick himself melted away, I was not bothered often by such people. I'll explain more about them while I'm on the subject. Millie and Agnes and Gloria and Margaret and so on were all Chinese girls who had been favorites of young Englishmen and Americans before Pearl Harbor. Many of the British cadets, studying Cantonese for the required three years of training, fell in love with these girls as a kind of ritual. It meant that they could practice their language under pleasant conditions, and it also gave them the comfortable feeling that they were really Mixing with the Natives, Understanding the Chinese. . . . Well, of course most of these girls have been drawing pay from the Japanese on the side, probably for years and years. After the surrender they came out of hiding all bright and cheery, and all with cushy jobs in the gendarmeries (the smaller military police stations) around town. Some of them succeeded in capturing quite important Japanese protectors, and a few, like Millie, promptly settled down and started having Japanese babies.

Naturally I didn't like them very much. And they were suspicious of me and treated me as a favorite subject for aspiring young spies who

wanted to get along in the world. After Chick appeared they all let up
Millie did try to push in on the party, because she thought it was just an
ordinary *affaire* and that I had caught a prize, but Chick soon called her
off.

That was one good turn he did me, and there were others. I am grateful
to the gendarmerie for assigning me to Chick. I might have drawn an
ordinary policeman, and that would have been bad. I'm sure it was
Charles's reputation that helped me. When the authorities finally decided
to take over Tregunter Mansions for their own uses it was Yoshida and
Chick who moved us to another house down in Kennedy Road. Moving
was a tremendous affair, and we couldn't possibly have paid the hire of
coolies, let alone trucks. Yoshida paid them, in rice, and provided a lorry
—and then after we moved in, all innocent and thinking it was all right,
the Army came along and told us to move right out again. That was an
awful business; an angry man in boots stamped in at ten in the evening
and told us to get right out. Well, we yelled for Chick, and Chick phoned
Noma, and Noma fixed it, though he did say sourly that if I had been in
Stanley this need never have happened.

Unfortunately, after a month Chick decided that I was really harmless
and even rather a nice girl, and so he dropped me, and we got no more
food from the gendarme kitchen. Soon after that he was edged out of
Hong Kong altogether. The expulsion was due to some matter of his selling government oil for his own purposes; Chick said Yoshida had con-
nived at his downfall, and Yoshida had been triumphant. Yoshida, he
said, had always been jealous of his, Chick's, influence with Noma.

When I next heard of Chick he was in Canton, trying to get a monopoly on the city's cabaret business, and also he owned two department
stores. He was a smoothie all right, and not the sort of man I would like
to see my daughter too chummy with, but for a gendarme, you must
admit, he was not so bad. I should like, someday, to be able to give *him*
food, when he's starving in prison. I told him so.

Chapter 50

Concurrently with this gendarme-geisha existence, we were becoming acquainted with a few civilians. After the hospital doors were
closed to me I put into action an idea I had been holding for some time
and I went downtown to call on the chief of the Domei office. (Domei

you may remember, is the official Jap news agency, and my friend Matsumoto in Shanghai had been the chief there.) Nowadays it was getting safe to walk alone, though accidents still happened sometimes. Hilda had been held up and searched by a young hoodlum one day, near our house, but she wasn't carrying any money.

"Of all the impertinence," she said when she told me about it. I can't help loving the British.

So I went to see Mr. Ogura alone. I found a small curly-headed man who laughed nervously in lieu of words when he couldn't think of the correct English, but who, when he did talk, usually said something worth hearing. He was a civilized chap. He had a sense of humor and a sense of shame; he didn't like the war, though he never said so. We discovered a bond between us immediately. Before Pearl Harbor he and his wife had often gone to see my gibbons in their cage and had fed them. (My last gibbon, by the way, died during the hostilities, of starvation. The coolie ran away and left him locked up in his own room.) Now Ogura's wife was home in Japan; she had had a girl baby the day before Carola was born, and Ogura had never seen his child. So he liked Carola. Also Ogura knew Charles by reputation and admired his books. He tried hard to help me. He said that he would cable Matsumoto and ask if there was any way in which I could do some non-political work.

He lied. It was the first time I knew a Japanese to tell a tactful and well-meaning lie. He told me he had cabled Shigei Matsumoto, but he hadn't really. He told me next day that he had received a reply and that he would do his best to find me a job, and in the meantime did I need anything? He put his hand in his pocket tentatively.

No, I said, I didn't need anything, thanks. Except—it's the first and only time I did beg from a Japanese—could he give me some sugar or tell me where to get some? I had none for Carola's milk, and there was none to be had in the market. Reeny, Phyllis, and I pooled all our resources, but I didn't tell him that. He might have boggled at the idea of feeding three babies. Ogura immediately gave me the office tea-hour supply of sugar, a pound box which still had about half a pound in it.

He did get me a job, teaching English to another newspaperman. It didn't pay much, but it helped. Anything helped.

We come now to another crisis. Before Pearl Harbor the Japanese I knew best through Charles (he had dined with us three times) was the young consul, Oda. Like most men in the consular service he had been to America as a student for at least a year, spoke English fluently, and looked less uncouth to us than did most of his compatriots. Oda had been transferred from the Hong Kong office long before the war. Now, we read in the paper, he was back in a new capacity; he was chief of the Foreign Affairs Department.

It was just after the Nakazawa period that Ogura told me Mr. Oda wanted to see me. I was startled and dismayed, and resolved to do nothing about it until I had to. Maybe, I reasoned, he would forget about me. I was afraid of more investigations.

One day, however, he telephoned me. (We had not yet moved.) "Miss Hahn? I think you will remember me. I met you with Boxer. This is Oda."

"Oh yes. How are you?"

"Oh, fine."

"I heard you were back in town," I said idiotically, trying to stave off whatever was coming.

"I heard you were too," he said dryly. "Miss Hahn, what is your nationality?"

There it was. Still, if I had passed muster with the all-powerful gendarmes . . .

"Chinese—now," I said.

"What do you mean by Chinese *now?*" he inquired sternly.

I said in desperation, "Well, Mr. Oda, you know what I mean. I'm American, but after the war I—well, there was that marriage, and——"

"Never mind then. I am calling you because there is on foot a plan to repatriate some of the Americans," said Oda.

"Oh?"

"Yes. People to be included in this exchange are diplomats, members of the consular department, and newspapermen. Your name has been included. I did not know you were a newspaperwoman."

"Oh yes, I am."

"Well, you are to be repatriated, Miss Hahn: congratulations. But if you have not been in Stanley first, like the other Americans, there is likely to be a question raised as to your nationality. So I suggest you enter Stanley now, and in a few weeks you will be on your way to America." He sounded pleased.

"You mean I must go to Stanley?"

"If you wish to be repatriated, yes."

"But if I don't wish to be repatriated I can stay out of Stanley?"

"Why—uh—yes, I suppose so." Mr. Oda sounded surprised.

"Then I don't want to be repatriated," I said flatly.

"What?"

"Mr. Oda, do you know what Stanley is like? Can you promise me there will ever be a repatriation, honestly? I might be caught out there for life. Unless you insist. I'll never do it, never. I have a baby."

There was a long silence. At last he said, "Don't make up your mind yet."

"But——"

"Come and talk it over," said Oda. "Our offices are in the Peninsula Hotel—the Toa, as it is called now. Are you afraid to come to Kowloon?"

"Oh no. I'll bring my girl friend."

"Then I'll see you tomorrow. Think it over."

I wouldn't think it over. My mind had made itself up on the second. I was trembling as I hung up the receiver.

The faithful Irene came along, though she hated going to Kowloon. Everything she saw there reminded her of her lost home. Even the people she met made the experience painful—the Indian at whose shop they had always bought cloth, and the barber who always cut the Gittins hair. Today we didn't have to go far, however; the Toa Hotel (Peninsula to you) is near the ferry station. When we came in to the lobby we found that it had been fitted up like a fortress rather than a hotel. There were guards everywhere with bayonets, and we were questioned a lot before being given little tags of green cloth to pin on our chests. Decked with these tags, we were allowed upstairs, to the sacred office of the Foreign Affairs Department.

Oda, at the end of a long emergency desk full of busy workers, was looking plump but older, dressed in khaki uniform. He stood up and shook hands quite as if I were still somebody respectable instead of being just a woman. Most officials did not, because this was Japanese territory now.

We went over the same ground we had covered on the phone. Oda seemed to feel that it made no difference to his side whether I departed or not. It didn't even matter if I went to Stanley or not. He wasn't at all *au courant* with what had happened to me; he knew only what Kimura must have written down in his records about my legal standing as a Chinese. When I told him again that I didn't want to take my baby into camp he sat up.

"A baby? You said so, but I——"

"Why, yes. Didn't you know? Boxer's baby."

Oda sat back in his chair and opened his eyes wide. He looked frightened. When he spoke his voice was hushed yet stern.

"Do the gendarmes know about this?" he demanded.

I giggled. I couldn't help it. Irene and I eagerly told him about Chick, and the interview with Noma, and all the rest of it. Gradually Mr. Oda caught his breath again. If the dreaded gendarmes already had me under observation his responsibility was much lightened. He would inquire on his own, naturally, to make sure, but the whole thing was easier now, and he didn't care so much; he could relax.

At last he sighed and said, "Well, if that's what you think about it there is no more to say."

"After all," I said, "you can't promise that this repatriation is going to take place definitely, anyway."

"No, I can't," he admitted. "By the way, Miss Hahn, do you know why you are on the list?"

"Well, no. I suppose, though, that if all newspaper people——"

He shook his head. "No. You were put on the list later, specially, by cable." He seemed impressed. "They have cabled from Tokyo. Do you know anybody important in Tokyo?"

"Only Matsumoto."

"It could not be Matsumoto. Think hard. Don't you know someone else in Tokyo?"

"No."

Again he shook his head. It was the first hint I had of what was going on in the world outside on my behalf, but I didn't read it correctly. He misled me. Because he thought this urgent demand to send me away came from his own government I thought so too. I couldn't imagine why it was so. Actually the cabled order must have been the first faint echo of the hell my sister Helen was raising over here with the State Department, but I had no way of knowing that. I was beginning to think I had never had a sister Helen, or any other family. I had been cut off for four months now; it was the end of March. They had been quite full four months, too. Naturally I wasn't taking much stock in my family's power to help me, by this time.

"Well . . . ," Oda said. We stood up and shook hands all around. "My office is moving to the other side next week," he said. "I shall be living in Robinson Road. I will come to call on you when I have time. And how"—he dropped his voice in a way which I was beginning to recognize—"how is Boxer?"

I told him as much as I knew.

"I have tried to get permission to see him," Oda said. "I think I shall be able to see him shortly. Do you wish me to inform him of this decision you have made?"

"Yes, please."

He remained standing until we had left the office.

We have no telephone in the new house, and no prospect of ever getting one. It was wiser, we discovered, not to have one even if we had been able to pay for it, because all telephone wires were tapped. Ogura therefore sent a message to me through my new pupil, a news agency man: "Matsumoto will be in town tomorrow. Come to the office if you wish to see him, at three-thirty. He arrives by boat from Canton."

I was there. I was intensely curious to see Shigei after all this time; I had last encountered him by accident in Hong Kong during the month of early spring that I had come down from Chungking, and our interview then, in the hotel lobby with everyone glaring at us, had been uncomfortable and full of awkward silences.

When he did come in, big and important, surrounded by little Japs like tugs, he was so surprised at seeing me that he stopped short at the door. Then he asked me to go upstairs to Ogura's private offices, and soon he came in, smooth and silent and impassive, wondering, very likely, what the hell he was to say to this embarrassing reminder of his past. For Shigei was a great man now, and full of triumph in his own right, not only as the cousin of Konoye. If he had ever been sincere in his pacifism and in all the criticism of the militarists that he had expressed in Shanghai, it was forgotten now. Perhaps not quite forgotten, or he would not have looked a little foolish, as he did now, when I spoke.

"Well, Shigei," I said. "Here we are. Fancy meeting you here!"

"I could not believe it," he said solemnly. "When I last saw you, in the spring of '40, I thought I would never see you again. I knew what was going to happen. All this time I assumed you were still in Chungking. I could not believe it, seeing you. What . . . why . . . ?"

"You remember Sinmay." Yes, Shigei did. I told him what I had done. He was slow to grasp it, and very, very much surprised when I was finished. Then I waited for him to say something about the war, but still he talked about mutual acquaintances, and Charles, and other subjects. At last I said: "Well, Shigei?" again, and he capitulated.

"Mickey," he said, smiling, his whole face suddenly pink, "we are living, just now, in the most interesting period of history. Think of it, Mickey, the most interesting period in the world's history."

"What happens in the end, Shigei?"

He didn't answer. He sat there smiling, seeing visions. . . .

"Do you remember," I said, "a conversation we had once in Shanghai, after Nanking, about the *fait accompli*? It seems more relevant now than it did then."

No, Shigei had forgotten. I looked at my watch. It was getting late and he was busy. He was a very important man in the New Order.

"But what is this I hear about your child?" he asked.

"Yes. I have a baby."

"I inquired for Major Boxer as I got off the boat. I am sorry he was wounded. If I had the time . . . How does it happen that you have had this child? You did not know Boxer in Shanghai, did you?"

"No. The child? I wanted it and he wanted it, so we had it."

"You are a nicer girl now than before," said Shigei. "Tell me, can I do anything for you?"

I looked at him curiously, saying, "I'm all right, thanks."

"Because," he said, "as it happens, the new Governor is a very old and good friend of mine."

"Just ask Ogura to keep a protective eye on me, then, if you would. If ever I am in danger of being interned, perhaps he would appeal to you."

"I think you will be all right if, as you say, the gendarmes don't mind. . . . But look, Mickey; I shall be in charge of all my offices from now on. I will travel constantly between Tokyo and Singapore; I shall be able to see you. . . ."

"Traveling will be interesting for you," I said. "I must go home. It's dangerous for me to stay downtown after dark."

He insisted on sending me up the hill in his car, but when we were out of sight of his office I stopped the car and walked home. I didn't know why myself.

In 1943 Ogura told me that Shigei was dying in Tokyo of some mysterious complaint, that his wife would not permit anyone in to see him, and that the end couldn't be far off. Whatever he died of, it was not the pangs of conscience.

Chapter 51

ALMOST the entire Health Department was still outside of Stanley, in actuality working away under Selwyn's direction, though the Japanese managed to satisfy their own pride by calling the British "advisers" and keeping a few of their own men in the office for show. Colonel Nguchi, the medical officer who had befriended Selwyn, turned out to be a wonderfully lucky accident for us. It seems that he had been one of a party sent by Tokyo, a few years before the war, to Hong Kong on a polite tour of inspection of British methods of hygiene. At that time he had been so much impressed by Selwyn's elaborately formal politeness, in comparison with the usual British offhand manners that he as an Oriental had already encountered, that he made a vow to himself. "Here for once is an Englishman of true courtesy," he said. All his inferiority complex contributed to the pleasure he felt in Selwyn's attitude. "If ever I have the chance," he thought, "I will repay him for his politeness."

It was on his urgent representation to the higher military authorities that Selwyn still retained his position, but that position was always precarious. Selwyn was up against the swollen suspicions of the entire Japanese crowd, the hatred they felt for Englishmen, and the resentment of the gendarmes, who were always jealously watchful of their powers and who felt that Nguchi, a mere medical military man, was trying to put something over on them. The gendarmes were for the most part totally uneducated thugs, whose only aim in life was to get as much for themselves as possible, in the quickest time they could. Nguchi was no Sunday-school teacher, but he did have a vague desire to keep the city healthy. The gendarmes didn't give a damn about the city's health. They hated the city, they hated the Chinese, they hated the British, and they were not fond of the Army and the Navy; they were jealous of their power though they themselves were in the saddle. The Army and Navy, they felt, were a constant threat to their authority. Everything was a threat to their authority.

The only way Nguchi could keep a hand in on this matter of health was to appeal to their common sense on behalf of the Japanese servicemen stationed in town and the Japanese residents of Hong Kong. Cholera among the despised Chinese would mean cholera among the Japs, he reminded them. Grumbling, they admitted this, and Selwyn was suddenly informed that he could now do something which the British Government had never in all his years of pleading permitted—he could inoculate the entire population, by *law*. Not that he was particularly pleased with this power, for he was not convinced that inoculation against cholera did any good. But the Japanese were superstitiously faithful to Western science, which they love; they love needles and medicine. We were all grabbed and jabbed, sooner or later; in the streets, on the ferry wharves, anywhere. People who could not show little pink cards in proof that they were inoculated were done then and there, even if they had been inoculated a dozen times in the past week. Other treatments followed: vaccination by law, typhoid inoculations by law, and anything else they thought of. Chinese who didn't like it managed to buy fake tickets, of course; one man died as a result of nineteen needle jabs in one day, but he had collected a nice sum of money for his inoculation cards before he died. I myself cheerfully bought a whole set of cards for Carola. She had been done thoroughly by my own doctor, and I was damned if I'd put her through it again in a dirty government medical post. It was noteworthy that the Japanese weren't prepared for this sort of graft. Japanese ev-

idently don't behave like that in Japan. Our liberators were horrified and
flummoxed, as they so often were in their dealings with Chinese. They
never could catch up. Certain things were outside their experience and
beyond their comprehension.

The Medical Department was busy but running as smoothly as one
could reasonably expect, considering the difficulties, when disaster fell on
them. One of the British doctors jumped his parole and escaped from
Hong Kong. I am not going to pass judgment on him now. It was our
private belief that he just couldn't bear the prospect of working through
the war under Selwyn-Clarke. Many of the doctors hated Selwyn bitterly,
and this unprecedented wave of Selwyn-worship which was sweeping
the community, foreigners and Asiatics alike, must have been gall and
wormwood to people who felt they really knew the man. The medical
group that practiced in Hong Kong before the war had always seemed
to my innocent opinion to be particularly virulent, one against the other,
even for a medical faculty. And if you know anything about them you
know how little brotherly love does prevail among rival doctors in most
communities. I had been shocked sometimes at the unethical mutual
criticism that seemed to furnish an everyday topic of conversation among
Hong Kong doctors. So perhaps this man felt that he would go mad if he
stayed longer, or maybe he felt that his higher duty called him to escape.
Knowing him, I'm sure he felt morally justified in his action. Anyway, he
beat it. That was the end of the British Health Department's freedom.
Nguchi could not fight the gendarmes any more on behalf of everyone.
He did manage to keep some people out, even so; Selwyn still retained
his comparative liberty, though Duggie and Nina Valentine had to go to
Stanley. A handful of English doctors, chosen by the Japanese, not by
Selwyn (including the ration stealer), were still left outside. The rest,
and all the enemy-national Red Cross workers who were driving trucks
to Stanley, and a lot of other whites who had been associated one way or
another with the department, were popped into camp on very short notice.
Regulations all over were tightened up too. The gendarmes had one of
their field days.

Hilda and Selwyn were ordered to move, henceforth to live in St. Paul's
Hospital, usually called the French Hospital, in Happy Valley.

When the gendarmes had satisfied their passion for vengeance, and I
had said good-by tearfully to Nina, they let up a little. (Nina, going into
camp, had a nasty experience. A gendarme with a chip on his shoulder
confiscated all her stores when she was about to go through the last gate
at the camp, and he slapped her. Nina is a beautiful, dignified woman,
gray-haired and sweet. I still flush with rage when I think of it.) It was

permitted that Selwyn bring out from Stanley one patient at a time for X ray at the French Hospital. This person was allowed to stay overnight, or for a longer time if the doctors (Japanese and British) pronounced it necessary, and he was permitted to bring a certain amount of supplies back into camp when he returned. So it turned out that Hilda became a shopper for Stanley Camp's three thousand plus. It was a job requiring a lot of manual labor and more time than existed in one day. The patient would come in to hospital in the evening, duly escorted by Selwyn and guards, give Hilda his list, and go to bed. (Selwyn was angry in his chilly way if Hilda failed to keep fresh flowers in the patient's room.) The Selwyn-Clarkes tried hard to provide him or her with decent food and plenty of it, as long as he was free, but this was difficult.

Next morning Hilda went downtown with two big baskets, and she shopped. Shopping was our chief interest and it was becoming less and less fruitful, more and more of an ordeal. Although Selwyn was mysteriously producing funds for this work, he didn't have much money, and Hilda had to go wearily all along the little side streets which were full of outside street-corner shops and were supposed to be comparatively cheap, haggling and searching and figuring, staying within the limits of the Japanese law on what could be taken in to Stanley and what couldn't, carrying backbreaking loads back to Happy Valley on the tram. After a week or so she asked us, her foreign friends, to help. Then she got the housework coolie to do some of it, for it was much too big a job for one woman. Then we hired an Indian besides.

In time the shopping routine became one of the group's biggest jobs. In camp there was a strong feeling of hysterical gratitude for Hilda, replacing the earlier outburst of jealous resentment. She grew thin, but she told me she felt much better for the work. This sort of thing was what she was used to; she had done it on a larger and easier scale in the old days, when she was working on relief for China. Selwyn permitted himself to express a few words of approval now and then, when he came home late at night.

I still saw Hilda almost every day. When we weren't doing something about Stanley we were shopping for the three military camps, Bowen Road, Shamsuipo (where the enlisted men were), and Argyle Street, the officers' camp. Each camp had one day a week when women were permitted to bring parcels. Bowen Road, as a hospital, still allowed us two days. That meant four mornings a week. Besides, Oda's department now permitted parcels for Stanley once a week; we brought these parcels, carefully wrapped according to specification, to the bank building and listed them there, and turned them in. We had to guess as to what our friends needed, because letters had not yet been permitted from any of the prisoners. But we were sure they needed everything, and we went accordingly, within the limits of the law. Certain things only were accepted, and the rules were chopped and changed every week.

Where, you will ask, was the International Red Cross all this time? Well, there wasn't any. It took almost a year to get one set up. The Japanese even then maintained that they had not recognized it officially; the Red Cross was permitted to keep an office in town, and the Swiss in charge was permitted to make representations to the camp commandants, but nobody promised ever to listen to him or to take action on his suggestions. Officially, the Japanese said, they did not hold themselves bound by any rules laid down at Geneva as to international law in regard to prisoners of war. *They* made all decisions. *They* were the judges of what was humane and what unnecessary. *They* kept control of everything, and usually forgot all about it. "We do not recognize Geneva" was a common saying. I don't know how many times Oda said it to me. Yet in his cynical way he did try to help, because Oda was a confirmed capitalist and he had been severely shocked at the sight of many Hong Kong millionaires he had known, brought low at Stanley. Even enemy rich men are still rich men, and Oda felt sympathetic toward them. His orderly instincts were horrified at sight of Bagram, a local taipan, wearing an apron at Stanley and peeling onions. Oda's eyes were full of tears when he told me about it. I don't think he was sorry for ordinary Chinese coolies, but British bank directors were different. Oda obviously felt that his country was going too far.

A subtle change had taken place in the population. Most Chinese, even when they are very hungry, try to keep some wealth hidden away, and as the months went by a few brave greedy souls began to dig their money out and speculate with it, and put out feelers to see if business could be resumed. There was an odd little boom in brokerage. People sold medicine and tinned food at huge prices. People juggled with currency, betting on the Japanese treatment of the Hong Kong dollar against the yen. (Japanese did that too, and usually made a lot of money out of it.) We were rationed on rice, oil, and sugar. Each person, baby or full-grown man or whatever, was entitled to 6.4 teels of rice a day—roughly, a third of a catty, the Chinese pound. That is not nearly enough rice for a Cantoness to live on, because the average coolie, who can't afford much *soong,* the other food he puts with his rice, makes up for the deficiency by eating more of the rice itself, and he needs at least a catty a day if he wants to do any work on it. So they bought rice in the black market, and venal Japs smuggled rice from the stores and sold it to the Chinese. The ration rice, besides, was seldom edible. It was dust for the most part, or a kind of broken grain that Chinese had always used for pigs. Broken rice had almost no nutritional value at all. We had to depend on the black market for food. As for oil and sugar, the crowd waiting for the ration was always so big that you had to stand in line for three or four days before you could get your supply, and then it was completely insufficient and usually adulterated. Rationing in general was a huge bad joke. Soon we lived on the black market completely. Once in a while the Food Control authorities would "investigate" the situation and a few Japanese and Chinese heads would be cut off, and in the end we, the public, suffered more deprivation than ever. As for fuel for cooking—but I can't even begin to talk about that racket. There is no time.

How were we managing? Well, as speculation increased, so did our chances of getting money. The first thing I did, as soon as I could, was to grab the chance offered me by Selwyn to buy two twenty-eight-pound tins of powdered milk. It was an Australian brand made on Trubee King's formula, called "Trufood." I paid a hundred and ten dollars for the two tins, and gave six pounds of milk back to the man who sold it, as a bribe. That about cleaned out the Hahn purse, but I never stopped blessing the day I bought that milk, for it saw Carola through the whole show. Later powdered-milk prices reached an incredible height.

So now I was broke and needed money. But money was looser in town, and I had jewels. Reeny did too. I sold my diamond ring, and that kept us going a long time. Then gold began to go up in value; we agonized as to what would be the best time to sell our gold jewels, and usually we guessed wrong. But with the help of Reeny's family, who knew all about pawnshops, I turned my gold chain into money, and then my bracelet, and then some watches from a collection of French watches I had once made. I kept a jump ahead of destitution. The time was coming when any commodity would be worth more than money, and I had lots of stuff in the house. I sold a fur coat, and some books, and all sorts of things. I know now what to take with me the next time I'm going to be caught in an occupation. I will sell whatever I have in advance and buy gold instead, just lump gold, and in that gold I will put diamonds, like currents in a bun. When people get afraid of paper money they rush for gold and diamonds, and now I do too. It may look like gold and diamonds to you, but it means powdered milk to me, milk and baby shoes. I developed an obsession for powdered milk and shoes. I couldn't see baby shoes anywhere in town without haggling for them and buying them; I was buying bigger and bigger ones, shoes that Carola couldn't have worn until she was five years old, against the time when there would be none to buy. Carola was trying to walk, but she hadn't succeeded as yet. Reeny's Auntie May made shoes for her out of our old felt hats, and those were good enough at first.

The new old house was big and rambling, and full of leaks and shell holes. We welcomed the discovery of every shell hole, because we hoped that the house was ramshackle and ancient enough not to tempt the Japanese. It was a vain hope, because the Japs were suddenly taken with a passion for grabbing all the houses they saw, even ancient ones. First the Army, then the Navy, then the government employees tried to kick us out. All over town this was happening, and the air resounded with shrill cries of civilian protest, usually unavailing, as households were booted out with four hours' warning, or at the best a week's notice. Theoretically only "enemy property" was liable to confiscation, but if a Japanese had enough power he didn't worry about such little refinements. And if a *gendarme* wanted anything you just didn't quote the law at all if you knew what was good for you. The rent situation was a mess. Nobody could pay rent, but the house owners naturally kept after everybody for rent until the government made some kind of law giving them retroactive powers of collection. On the other hand, the government said cautiously, if the tenant couldn't pay—well, he couldn't pay, and the landlord ought to be nice. The pronouncement changed nothing.

Following on this, that same government told me to pay my rent or else. Until then I had managed to get rid of all comers by rushing straight downtown to Oda whenever somebody ordered us to move out. Oda would then telephone a Major Nakano, who arranged it. There came an awkward time when Major Nakano himself wanted the house . . . but Oda fixed that. As for the rent, it wasn't due until September and I put the worry off. I was learning how to think properly under occupation conditions, and how to wait for trouble until it arrived.

In many ways our new house wasn't so good. It was surrounded, for one thing, by Japanese tenants; ours was one of a row of houses and every other one had Japs living there. It was across the street from St. Joan's Court, a modern apartment building which had been taken over by one Japanese admiral, not as a residence but as a kind of week-end cottage. At the time, when there was a severe housing shortage due partly to the Japanese passion for commandeering buildings and partly to the fact that a lot of houses had been bombed, the public felt indignant at this lavish use of St. Joan's Court. It was a big place with twelve apartments, and we were irritated when we saw two little Chinese tarts lolling about, now on one veranda and now on another. Nobody else ever came there but the admiral and a few select pals. Our house was also next door to a big building, formerly the property of the Ho family but now the swankiest geisha house in town. At night you could hear sounds of revelry in the Japanese tradition.

Worst of all, there was a tree on the slope above us which the soldiers often used for their own amusements. They tied Chinese malefactors to this tree and flogged them. They took turns at this, because they enjoyed themselves at it and each one wanted his share of the fun. And when the soldiers weren't indulging in this pastime Indian watchmen were. The tarts leaned out from their apartment house, from the window nearest the flogging tree, and called shrill encouragement to the executioners or scolded the Chinese victim, until one day Ah King could bear it no longer. In his choicest Cantonese dialect he talked to the ladies, reminding them of the day of judgment in the future. After that they stayed indoors quietly when people were being flogged.

I've seen a soldier leading a peasant woman on a string, like a dog. She must have been caught stealing dry leaves or branches for fuel; it was a common misdemeanor, punishable by death if the Japanese gendarme happened to feel that way. The woman was yelling and then at intervals getting down on her knees, bumping her head on the ground. The soldier was highly amused. I think he was in such a good temper that he may possibly have let the woman go, but if so I didn't see that part of it. I wish I had.

When she was six months old Carola sat up, and two weeks later her first tooth appeared. I asked the sentry at the hospital to tell Charles about the tooth. Charles had disappeared from the veranda. For months I didn't see him when I brought the parcels, and I couldn't find out why. The officer in charge, an amiable little fellow named Sieno, just opened his eyes at me when I asked, and said, smiling:

"Oh, Boxer very well."

I heard afterward why it was. The imprisoned officers had all been told to sign paroles, promising they would not try to escape. Such a promise should have been merely an academic matter to Charles, because his arm was helpless and he wouldn't have had the strength to make such an attempt anyway, but he maintained that as a regular officer he must not sign a parole. The duty of an officer, he insisted, was to escape if he possibly could, and he would not sign.

Tony Dawson-Grove wouldn't either. So Tony and Charles were put into a ward in back of the building and weren't allowed to walk on our side of the hospital on parcel day. It was planned as a punishment for

Charles; he couldn't look at me or the baby until he signed. We got around that, afterward; I walked along another lower road at the back of the hospital at a certain time on a certain day each week, and though there was a tremendous distance between Charles's beat and mine, I could still make him out, with his white sling, and he could still see me with the baby. When Carola learned to walk, at ten months, I took her along that road and then she walked with me, hand in hand, up and down. I heard Charles laugh. Then an Indian watchman came and chased us away.

I have come to a ticklish part of the book. It is so ticklish that I am not going to write anything about it. I have been thinking it over and this is the safest way. The war isn't over yet.

I will say this much: I never did any spy work during my stay in Hong Kong, and to the best of my knowledge Selwyn never did either. If we were dealing with any enemy but the Japanese my secret would not be a secret at all. We did nothing wrong even from their point of view, but they wouldn't believe that. As it is, I am still full of a guilty feeling, and I don't dare write about our activities. Anyway, I can say that they were entirely to do with relief work. Selwyn was getting money from friendly natives in town, and we used this money in certain ways, to provide food and medicine and clothes for people who needed it. We took risks. Some of us were caught. The work was the whole meaning and aim of our existence, for months. I will not say any more. You can't go through months of discretion without feeling the effect of it.

I have spent hours in bed, there in Hong Kong, thinking of ways and means to manage different things. Charles used to call me the original sucker, but I learned then how to be disingenuous. I planned my day as an actress plans her part. I tried over to myself this inflection, that phrase; I thought of some man I was to interview, and decided hours in advance on the best thing to say to him, considering his character. It got so that I was on guard no matter who was talking with me; without thinking of it, I learned how to act with this type of person and that. I didn't sleep very much, but I did learn many lessons.

Chapter 52

WE HAD all forgotten that repatriation rumor, out and about town. In Stanley they hadn't, but then in Stanley they had little to live on but hope, and they kept the wildest rumors going, rather than settle down to despair. I thought of the exchange as just that: a rumor. Then all of a sudden in May it materialized, swiftly, like a blow. This time, however, it wasn't just a selected group who were to go; diplomats, newspapermen, *and* common ordinary mortals were included, as long as they were American. The banks downtown, where our bank boys were still coming to work every day under guard, marched from their brothel by the bay, were full of happiness and excitement. I was not happy but I was excited, because I had already heard about it direct.

Oda sent me a rush message, by hand, to come down to the office that very minute, no matter how late it was when I received the summons. This happened the day before the news broke. I turned pale, as I always did when I had any kind of official order, and I howled for Reeny, equally as usual. Together we jog-trotted down the hill, wondering what the hell it could be this time. In the office were Oda and Gibson, the American representative at large in town.

"Repatriation, Mickey," said Gibby. "Want to go home?"

I looked at Oda, and he nodded gravely. "Do I have to go to Stanley first?" I asked in what must have sounded strangely like a bargaining tone.

"No," said Oda hastily. He had learned a lesson. "No, never mind Stanley. It is not necessary this time."

"We have had a discussion about your case," said Gibby. "Mr. Southard (our consul general) has been in the office today, brought in from Stanley to go over the list, and Mr. Oda has kindly made it possible to include you in the exchange. Anyway, you're included already." He added that swiftly, as Oda got up and left us to talk alone. "He asked Southard if the American Government was still willing to claim you as a citizen, and Southard duly said yes, and there you are. So!"

"Gibby, is it really true this time?"

"It really is, Mickey. I've seen the cables myself. Everyone's wild out at camp."

"Only Americans?"

"Unfortunately, only Americans. We'll hope the British and the others can follow along later. Maybe if this works out satisfactorily——"

"When will it be?"

"No telling, but probably the beginning of June. You'll have to decide now, this minute. . . . You're coming, of course?"

I looked at Reeny, and Reeny looked at me. I couldn't talk.

"If it's Charles you're thinking of," said Gibby, "isn't he pretty well off? After all, he speaks the language."

"Yes, but he isn't pretty well off."

There was another long, long, long silence.

"It's a difficult decision to make, all right," said Gibby.

"Gibby," I said at last, "if it was your wife, and you were locked up like that, what would you do? How would you feel?"

He thought about it briefly and gave his pronouncement. "If I could decide for her, arbitrarily, and for my baby," he said, "of course I'd send them away. But if I were helpless, and my wife had to decide for herself, and if she stayed in spite of a chance to get away—well, I would be sorry in a way, but I'd be mighty glad. I'd be mighty proud."

"Oh, thank you, Gibby. It was like a fence I couldn't get over. Will they understand at home?"

"They will when I've talked to 'em. Now can you manage?"

"If I had money. I think the other difficulties aren't so bad."

"That's how it seems to me. You certainly seem to have them under control." He took a furtive look at Oda, way off on the other side of the room. *"He,* for example, seems to feel friendly toward your setup. He seems to think you may decide to stay."

"Does he care if I stay or not?"

"Doesn't seem to. It's a matter of indifference, according to him, to the Jap Government whether or not you accept this chance. Well, the Red Cross is being organized now, and I think they'll fix it so you women can get money out from the officers. The officers are being paid now, you know."

"I know. Charles managed to slip me quite a wad, last time I ever saw him. Almost two hundred yen. It was back pay, he said, for two months; he gets a hundred sixty a month."

"Yes. Well, that is going to be made legal, according to Oda. In time Charles can send it to you through proper channels."

We shook hands, and then I called Mr. Oda and told him I wasn't going. He raised his eyebrows a little, but I think he had expected it. Then we went home again, hastily because it was getting quite dark.

Irene was bitter about the American bankers and me. She felt that they should have tried to help me out more than they did. I argued that they, like everyone else, had their own troubles, but she retorted that they had fewer troubles than most people. "Their house is provided; their rice is provided; they get some kind of salary," she said.

"Hardly anything, Reeny."

"They ought to take up a collection for you or something," she insisted. "They're going away now and won't need any money, and you can't tell me that some of them didn't manage to keep supplies after the surrender. They're helping other girls."

"Reeny, that's just it; they're helping their own girl friends. They haven't anything left over for renegades like me. Remember, I chose a limey, of my own free will and volition; let me stew in my own juice."

"It's your bank, besides. They know you have money at home. They ought to try and arrange something. They can. Bankers always can."

"So they can. But they didn't, and I'm damned if I ask any more."

Before they left, however, one young bank boy did make a helpful suggestion. "John Stenerson is still here," he said. Stenerson was the Norwegian manager of the American Express. "He may be able to find you some cash when you're hard up. Ask him," said young Lindabury. "He said he'd keep an eye on you."

"Well, gosh, that's a relief," I said, frankly for the first time. "I've been feeling pretty low."

The young man at that moment expressed the entire state of mind of the bankers, and of anyone who is involved in his own problems. It was a staggering thing he said, and yet it expressed the innocence of the whole community.

"Why!" cried Lindabury. "Have you been worrying about money?"

I haven't any idea of how the Stanley Camp, the British and Belgians and Dutch, felt about the American exodus. I know how the bankers who had been left behind felt, though. Of course there was a certain selfish relief in the knowledge that they would now have more room in the Sun Hwa Hotel, which was the name of their water-front brothel, but the mothers who were cooped up there with their children must have felt an agonizing jealousy. One of them told me after the departure that she had almost killed an American. They were walking on the roof, discussing the repatriation, which was scheduled to take place in a day or two. The American, Dorothy said, must have forgotten that he was talking to a woman with no hope of freedom for herself, her husband, or her two small children, or he could not have been so tactless.

"Well," she alleges that he said, in satisfied, judicial tones, "on the whole, it's been a vurry *interesting* experience."

She nearly shoved him off the roof.

On the day they were to go all the white people I knew were stirred to wild excitement. We would have no opportunity to see the main crowd going away, but we could at least watch the departure of the bankers from town. They were to go by bus out to Stanley, where the whole crowd would embark together on the Japanese boat that was to take them to

Lourenço Marques to meet the *Gripsholm*. Other people were going too: a Dutch girl who had been interned until now in the Bowen Road Hospital as one of the V.A.D. nurses, a Frenchman who was leaving his Japanese wife behind in Hong Kong to watch the house, and other bits and pieces like that. I stood by the bus as everyone said good-by, talking to the Dutch girl. She told me that Charles was well, and she explained about the parole and why I hadn't seen him.

There was a flurry at the doorway of the bus; people were kissing each other good-by and weeping. I crossed the road to be out of it. Nobody especially dear to me was going, but I had a stone on my chest. In the crowd on my side of the street was Yoshida, looking on with an impassive face. Billy Poy, an Australian-born Chinese who had been friendly with Yoshida and Nakazawa, was going on the boat as a special favor of the American Government, because he had worked for the Canadian Trade Commission for years. Yoshida was seeing him off, but he didn't want to compromise him too much by any obvious friendship, so here he stood across the street, and I stood next to him, myself being compromised in *his* company by the minute.

The Foreign Affairs officials finished checking over their human exchanges. There was a shout, and a fresh burst of sobs and waves, and the buses started up. I stood there with my gendarme pal, waving. I was still wondering if I had signed Carola's death warrant by my decision.

"She would want to stick by her father if she could think," I argued. But I didn't feel very well.

Charlotte had sent word out to me that she would be glad to take Carola home to the States if I would send her. So had Joe Alsop. But even if I had decided to do this Charles's own attitude was uncompromising. In the early days of the surrender a woman going to Macau had begged me to give her the baby and let her smuggle it out to neutral territory. I was so wild that I was ready to do it. Macau seemed a safe place then. For an adult it was possible; Petro had got away through Macau, and now his wife Barbara was on the repatriation steamer and would be able to join him in the States. But a small baby couldn't do that on her own. Also Charles was violently disturbed by the suggestion.

"No, Mickey, no. A child must stay with its mother. No! You must never do that." I had never before seen him so emphatic. Remembering this made it easier to follow my own selfish desire, and I never again tried to send Carola away from me, even for her own good. When you are not sure if you are right or wrong you must take someone else's decision. I was glad to have Charles to guide me, even in retrospect.

The departure of the Americans hadn't taken place as early as Gibby had expected. Nothing takes place when you expect it in the Orient, and the Japanese are longer in making up their minds than even the Chinese. It was the end of June when I waved good-by to the bank boys. Our children were shooting up. Bryan and Frances were chasing each other around the house, fighting over toys and demanding more than milk to eat. Carola tried valiantly to bridge the tremendous gap of four months between herself and Frances. When the older babies ran after each other I would sometimes hold her up and run after them, bending low so that her wildly kicking feet just cleared the ground and she thought she was running too. I was doing that the day she first laughed, a low, delighted chuckle.

"Was that my baby?" I demanded of Irene.

"Yes," said Reeny.

I wanted terribly to tell somebody about it, or to write home—Carola had laughed. But there was nobody to tell or to write to, except Ah King, so I went down and told him. He made a satisfactory fuss about it, however; he called his wife and daughter and told them, and then they went out and told the neighbor's servants. I felt better.

The newspapers printed little in the way of news. Through neutrals and daring Asiatics we still got the general outline of the world's doings, but that summer there was a long and dreary time when nothing really did seem to happen; nothing, that is, to cheer us up. Our local paper only yammered over and over about how well Hong Kong was getting along under the Japanese, and how much happier everyone was. But Hong Kong was not getting along well. The military control which overshadowed the civilian government was a deadly influence. In the ordinary way the Chinese can't be kept down. They *will* trade, they *will* flourish, in spite of all. But these Japanese measures with slow, stupid, stubborn weight managed to crush all human endeavor sooner or later. Even Japanese tradesmen were complaining. Red tape strangled any attempt at starting business, no matter who made the attempt, friend or enemy. Corruption ate away at the trade that did exist. Yoshida and his kind flourished, but it was better not to ask how. Yoshida suddenly appeared in business clothes and told me he was thinking of quitting the gendarmerie; he spent at least two hundred yen a night, according to Ah King's cousin, who managed a Chinese restaurant that the Japanese patronized. Finally his behavior couldn't be ignored, even though he was a gendarme, and he was suddenly sent back to Japan, or to Formosa or somewhere. Ogura was discreet about it, but I gathered that Yoshida's record of graft had attracted the attention of his chief, even in that milieu of universal graft. We heard constantly of other petty scandals and wrangles. The collaborationists settled down to enjoy the fruit of their labors, and that summer must have been the happiest one they were ever to have. The shoe hadn't begun to pinch yet, and they still hoped for a lifetime of easy money and rewards. Everyone was living on the hump of prewar supplies that were still extant in Hong Kong. There was little normal give and take; all trade was fading away. Farseeing Chinese began to make their plans; one by one they disappeared, sailing down to Kwangchowan and walking in to Free China across the border. We heard all about that avenue of escape. Reeny began to look thoughtful.

It was in August 1942, wasn't it, that America attacked the Solomons? The news came as a shot in the arm to us. We were living on such things; between the secret news bulletins we did nothing but worry about the rapidly mounting inflation, so our hunger for encouragement was becoming ravenous. It is a mistake to think that the Japanese put out only lies and contradictions in their news. The men in charge of propaganda were not well co-ordinated, and by their contradictions we could tell more from the news columns in the paper than they ever guessed. They didn't suppress outstanding news items, either; perhaps they knew it was no use. They announced the attack on the Solomons, for example. They admitted the loss of the Aleutians too, though that admission was delayed for several days and was then produced as a triumph. "A magnificent psychological victory over our enemies," they called it, "who had never expected that Japanese would die to the last man, rather than give in. Now they know how hopeless this war must be for them!"

I had a private joke about that. When Attu and Kiska were first taken by the Japanese they promptly rechristened them and gave them Japanese names which I can't now remember. Sometimes you would see a long, stirring account of how life was going for the brave Japanese garrison on these islands. A few days before they announced the loss of those spots on the map I noticed that they were calling them "Attu" and "Kiska" again. Aha, said I to myself, something has happened in the Aleutians! And I was right.

Oda kept his promise and called on us. We invited him to dinner, along with a Mr. Imamura of his office, a man who had been introduced to us by Nakazawa a few months before. We made a great effort and produced a good dinner, considering; Oda watched us all and was very cautious and discreet, but he asked a lot of questions.

"Mr. Imamura," said Reeny pleasantly, though it was always an effort for her to be pleasant with Japanese, "Mr. Imamura is practically a Chinese, Mr. Oda."

"Yes, he has lived in Hong Kong and Canton for many years," said Oda.

"He speaks excellent Cantonese," said Phyllis. Imamura smiled and bowed.

"Do you know, he was our neighbor in Kowloon," continued Reeny. "He lived next door to my father's house for seventeen years, and I never knew him."

"I suppose," said Oda in a surprising flash, "you never looked at that little yellow man!"

We were all quiet for a minute. Reeny had had a cocktail, and her natural feelings were rapidly getting the better of her. I sat next to her and watched her anxiously; you never knew, with Reeny. The conversation drifted around inevitably to ways and means, the black market, the inflation. Reeny excitedly asked Oda what the government meant to do about her kind of person, the Eurasian who was left homeless, workless, husbandless by the war.

"You've got to do *something,*" she insisted. "That's what a government is for, to govern the civilians!"

"A military government?" I saw the weariness behind that speech. "When," asked Oda, "did an army party ever care about civilians?"

I saw the weariness; Reeny didn't. Reeny saw a jeering enemy, one of the people who had killed her husband and who were now menacing her parents and her baby and herself.

"You want us to starve," she shot at him.

"*They,*" said Oda, "don't care if you starve or not. There is a slight difference."

"You want us to starve," repeated Reeny, "so we won't bother you any more. Well, I won't starve! I won't starve! I won't!"

"It is getting late," said Oda. He looked at her with amused admiration, and bowed good night. Imamura shook hands hastily and trotted out after his chief.

Chapter 53

THE RED CROSS had been set up at last, and a Mr. Zindel was put in charge. Mr. Zindel, who had lived in Hong Kong for years, was an anxiously honest gentleman, very conscientious, but with something of that trustful quality which made Chamberlain such an easy mark for

Hitler. Aware that he had no official position with the Japanese, he behaved like a man with no official position. When he had collected a store of medicine, for example, to present to Bowen Road Hospital, and when he went up to hand it over to the authorities, they chased him away with the curt remark that they didn't need British medicine for their prisoners: they had plenty of medicine of their own. This was not true and Mr Zindel knew it was not true, but he went away without demur. With the Japanese you have to demur, but it took him a long time to find it out. He was not permitted to visit any of the military camps. He wrung his hands and sat in his office, and hired more people (Swiss) to do the paper work that mounted and mounted.

The camp for enlisted men, Shamsuipo, was being punished for something or other, and for months no parcels were allowed. This hit them hard, for nearly all the Volunteers, being local men, depended on their families for food to help out their starvation diet. Although we weren't supposed to know about it, we did: so many men were suffering from beriberi and other symptoms of malnutrition, burning feet and blindness, that at one time fifty per cent of them could not stand up. The Japs had begun to call on them for labor and some of the women in town learned that at certain times of the day these workers would be marched through the streets to the airport of Kai Tak, where they were set to enlarging the field. The women stood on the street corners to see them go by. Always at the end of the day some of them had to be carried back on stretchers.

The Red Cross supplies that came with the first exchange ship helped out a lot. We knew how welcome they were at Stanley, and we could imagine what they meant to the camps. The specially packed parcels which were distributed at Christmas were made up of lovingly wrapped but infinitesimal tins.

None of the hardships were the fault of our local Red Cross, nor of Mr. Zindel. He did the best he could, and he learned to do better, but the task was probably beyond the powers of any Swiss. In the first heat of criticism I wanted him to resign. I thought that a quiet protest like that would do some good by calling attention of Red Cross headquarters in Tokyo to the situation. But all his compatriots when I said this looked very much startled.

"Such an action, I am sure, has never occurred to him. He is a good man, and at least he can try to do something. If he were to resign there would be nothing."

The Swiss man in charge of all the Far East Red Cross was one Egle, of Shanghai. He came down to Hong Kong to inspect the office when it

vas under way, and Oda invited me out to dinner to meet him. The din-
ier was to be at the Grips, and on that evening we were visited by a
oouring summer thunderstorm, so I paddled down the hill in wooden
logs, like any amah, and carried my shoes. I was drenched when I ar-
ived; the color of my dress had run; I had been shabby when I started
out and now I was a mess. It didn't improve my spirits when I got there
o see that there was another girl on the party, though I was fond of her.
t was Mitzi Glover, the Shanghai Russian who had been one of the most
oeautiful girls in the prewar Grips of a Saturday night. Mitzi had landed
a job as sort of hostess-manager for the Japanese who was now trying to
make a go of the hotel. She lived there, had her meals there, and ultimately married Gatti, the Swiss hotel chef, thus in one master stroke
acquiring a man she loved, a neutral passport, and a fair certainty of eat-
ng until the end of the war. I hand it to Mitzi. . . . But that evening I
could find it in my heart to wish she hadn't chosen to put on a stunning
red chiffon evening dress.

The rest of the guests were men, subordinates of Oda in the Foreign
Affairs office. I knew them all as an old lag knows the police in the station
where he goes to report every week. There was also Egle, the great man,
head of the Red Cross.

Oda is one of those unusual Japanese who can drink. He gave me two
martinis immediately so that I could catch up with the rest of the party.
Egle talked a lot. He said many pretty things about Japan, and he raved
about the way the Japanese were governing in both Shanghai and Hong
Kong. He also spoke appreciatively of the German community in Shanghai. Now and then, perhaps to reassure me of his heart of gold beneath
all this diplomacy, he would wink at me. I hated his guts.

I hated his guts and I drank quickly to forget him. I hadn't had anything to drink in quantity since before Pearl Harbor, and I had lost the
knack. Also I had been undernourished for a long time. We had a lot
of wine with dinner; Oda knew how to give a foreign dinner and he
spread himself. It was on government funds anyway.

Maybe, too, my nerves were near breaking point. Just that week the
gendarmes had scared me again by suggesting I go away. They were in
the middle of a drive to "repatriate" the Chinese, i.e., to get them out of
town and out of sight, where it would not be necessary to bring in food
to feed them. These drives came along at short intervals and while they
lasted nobody was secure. Trucks rolled around the streets and their
drivers stopped now and then to wait while gendarmes rounded up beggars and anyone else who didn't look wealthy enough to make trouble;
these people were then carted down to the water front, loaded on junks,

and "repatriated." Sometimes they were dumped out in the country, and sometimes—well, we didn't know.

Naturally the gendarmes couldn't send me out of town like that, but still I was one more mouth to supply and in the routine course of events it was their duty to ship me off to be someone else's headache. "Why not go back to Shanghai, your native place?" asked Mr. Yokayama. "Why not go back to your husband?" The Shanghai authorities would have to ship in rice for one more person in that case, of course, but that would be up to the Shanghai authorities.

"Mr. Yokayama," I said, "I have Boxer's baby."

"Yes?" said Yokayama. "Yes, I know."

"Well," I said, "if you were me, and if you had a Chinese husband, and if you had Boxer's baby, would you go back to your Chinese husband carrying Boxer's baby?"

Mr. Yokayama scratched his head and admitted that I had something there. But still, he had scared me. Life, I felt, was bloody. The full-course dinner did not cheer me up. And I drank more wine, and more wine, and talked about life with Mr. Kawaminami, on my left. I didn't talk to a man on my right: that was Egle.

I woke in the morning with a terrible sense of guilt. I usually do when I've had too much to drink. But this time it was overpowering. Somehow I felt that I must call up Oda right away, *right away*. Something awful had happened. I knew that, but I didn't know what.

Dragging my feet, dressed in whatever I had first picked up, I climbed the hill to the house of the neutrals, where I was permitted to use the phone if I didn't say anything incriminating. I called Oda.

"Oh, good morning," he said. He sounded icy.

"I believe I forgot to thank you for the party," I said in as sprightly a tone as I could manage.

"Did you? Yes, you did," said Oda. Then there was one of those pauses. I was scared stiff. For God's sake, what had happened? Didn't I know any better than to go out and get that drunk with Japanese? Anything could have happened; my imagination began to boggle right away.

"Mr. Oda," I said desperately, "how did I get home? I mean, when I woke up this morning I was at home. That's something to go on, isn't it? I mean——"

"Home? I brought you home," said Mr. Oda. "With Mr. Mayajima and Mr. Kawaminami. In my car." He stopped, coiled for the spring. "You slapped me," said Mr. Oda.

"WHAT?"

"You—slapped—me."

"No!"

"Yes." Was that a chuckle? I shall never know. It may have been, but on the other hand it may not have been. You never knew with Oda.

"Why did I slap you?" I asked, capitulating. I was curious.

"I don't really know," he said crisply. "But I think it was probably that you had a subconscious desire to slap a Japanese."

I got down the hill all right, but I was talking to myself. "Out of the whole lot of them, you would pick the chief of Foreign Affairs, Mickey Hahn. You couldn't have done better. Well, yes, there might have been an improvement. It could have been a gendarme." I stopped on the last landing before I reached the house, gripping the rail for support. "Oh no," I decided, reaching the climax of my monologue. "No. Not even I would ever get that drunk."

Chapter 54

THE CHINESE had reinstated a sort of Underground. They were in practice for it, because there had been an active trade in smuggling people across the border into Hong Kong long before Pearl Harbor, when the British authorities were trying to stop immigration from occupied Canton. It was an open secret that Hong Kong's official census fell almost half a million below the actual number of inhabitants in 1940. Now the smuggling had begun again, but it worked both ways. People crept into town without the required permits to enter, they lived there without the necessary permit to stay, and they crept out again without getting permission to do so. The Japanese tried to stop it by means of searching and surprise raids, but as fast as they put it down in one spot it would pop up again at another.

In this way people often received messages from the interior, by word of mouth and even by letter. Letters, of course, were very dangerous. I knew people who corresponded with Free China in that way, but I never did it myself, and nobody sent me letters from outside either. I hoped they wouldn't. I sweated for fear they would, because when such a letter was found by the gendarmes they had a way of reading it, copying it, letting it go through and then, when they had collected enough evidence, pouncing on all the parties concerned.

Just the same, I picked up news through other people who were more daring than I, and so did Reeny. One day she came home in wild excitement because she had encountered an old woman, a friend of her mother's, who had just come in from Free China. She told Reeny enough about conditions in the interior to hearten her and to give her the audacious idea of herself escaping to friendly territory.

If she found work inside the old people could follow. That woman said it would be feasible even for the old people. But Irene would have to go first. She would have to get a permit to go to Kwangchowwan, the French colony; from Kwangchowwan one rode by sedan chair, or walked, to Kweilin in China.

"I'll have to take Frances, of course. This woman says there's plenty of milk inside. Think of it—plenty of milk! And so many of our friends that you would think Kweilin was a part of Hong Kong. They say more than four hundred of our boys got away after the surrender and marched into China. They say there's a British major from here, at a post quite near by. Perhaps I could get more definite news of Ernie, even. Oh, I don't suppose Ernie could be alive; if he were he'd have got in touch with me, but still . . ."

For days and nights we talked it over and planned this way and that way. Then there came a piece of news that simplified matters. Maya Rodeivitch, the Polish girl from Chungking, was still in town, disconsolate now that the Americans were all gone. I sent her with a card to Ogura, that champion of all white ladies in distress; he found her a Japanese pupil to whom she taught German. Maya had made another friend, De Roux, manager of the Banque d'Indo-Chine. She told me that he was well worth knowing, and one day when we had spent some hours in the street where looted books were sold by weight we dragged our baskets into the bank and had a talk with him. De Roux was so shy that I had never seen him around at parties before the war. He was very nice, however, when you got to know him. Forced to abandon his Peak house, he had fixed up a flat on top of the bank building, and later he introduced me there to Sir Vandeleur Grayburn of the Hong Kong Bank and Lady Grayburn, who sometimes dropped in on De Roux to take baths and to forget the Sun Hwa Hotel for a few minutes.

De Roux often said of himself that he was a born uncle. Certainly Carola thought so. He was one of the kindest people I have ever known, and all of us have lots to thank him for. At that time he was busy advising Maya as to her future actions; he urged her to get out of town while it was still possible. Maya got her permit reasonably quickly. It took only two months, almost record time for the Hong Kong gendarmes, who were so busy urging people to get out of town that they had no time to make it possible to leave.

As a Eurasian, Irene was able to get a similar permit. Only enemy nationals had to stay in Hong Kong under surveillance. Paul de Roux even thought that I would be able to put it over, by virtue of my Chinese passport, but I knew I wouldn't. One slight attempt to get away to Free China and I would land in jail: I knew it. Besides, though I couldn't convince him of this, I still felt that I should stay. "I could have gone in the *Gripsholm* if I wanted," I said. "But who else would send food to Charles?"

"Why, anybody."

"But who? There was no money to leave for that. Things were still awfully tight. Oh, I know it's easier now, but that was four months ago; it would have been impossible to make arrangements."

"I see. Yes, that is different. Yes, naturally you would want to remain even now. But these two girls can go without hesitation."

Maya and Irene decided to join forces. At Kwangchowwan they would have to join a larger party anyway; that was the method by which most of the refugees got through without being molested by bandits en route. For some weeks Irene collected things to take in, until I was moved to secret laughter. Irene had vowed ever since I met her that never again would she collect things. She had seen her house and everything in it lost. She wanted to travel light for the rest of her life. She was cured of the desire, inherited from her Chinese ancestors, to own things and more things. She said this often.

But now, as every day brought her nearer to the great adventure, she forgot her pious resolutions. She had never gone into rural China and she thought of it as a desert to which she must bring all the amenities of civilization. She didn't have much, but with the earnest help of her mother and sisters she managed to collect a truly awe-inspiring heap of clothes and tins and things. "With a baby you have to take a lot," she explained at intervals.

"But, Reeny, have you thought what a lot of trouble and expense you'll have, carrying all this stuff through no man's land?"

"I won't be able to get a thing inside," she argued. "Not a thing. And look what happened to us before. I didn't regret anything I brought over from Kowloon, not anything; I was only sorry I hadn't brought more."

She picked up another giant duffel bag and started to pack it.

Everyone knew that the last hurdle, and the highest of all, was the dock of embarkation. It was there that the authorities, the ubiquitous gendarmes, scanned your papers for the last time and picked up your rice ticket, that document which meant so much to the inhabitants of Hong Kong. It was there that your luggage and perhaps you yourself were searched thoroughly for articles that must not be taken out of town, and for papers of any sort. We had heard from many sources that the searching was terrible, because it was left to the far from tender mercies of the coolies who carried your bags. The thing to do, said our advisers, was to slip the chief coolie a good tip as you walked onto the dock; then it would be all right.

I was there, and so was Paul de Roux in Maya's honor, and so were about a dozen Gittins relatives.

Irene, wearing slacks and a broad-brimmed straw coolie hat, carried the heavy baby slung on her back. She looked very small and young to be going off into the blue with such a responsibility. The searching, in spite of a large wad of yen duly slipped to the chief coolie, was really an outrage. With loud cries to each other, coolies fell on the luggage and tore it to pieces, pouring everything out on the filthy boards of the dock. There was no pretense at searching; it was sheer malicious vandalism. When they had turned everything out and had picked up odd bits that they liked the looks of, they abandoned the whole matter and left Reeny to pack up again as best she could. It was a hopeless job, for the giant knapsacks had been impossible to pack properly to begin with. Odd shoes of the baby's and clean underwear, dress hangers and cooking pots, tinned milk and wadded gowns lay spread out where passers-by stepped on them. We gathered it together as well as we could, and Reeny, prey to the tearing claws of nostalgia, rage, shame, and fear, put it all away doggedly, tears dropping into the bags before she tied them up again. During the entire proceedings an elegant gendarme, his white-gloved hands resting on his knees, questioned an Indian peddler a few feet away from us, not deigning to drop a word to the coolies.

"But really, it is a shame, you know. A shame," muttered Paul.

A little fellow named Eddie Elias, who had helped Maya get ready, hung about waiting to wave good-by to her. Eddie had a strong sense of drama. After the girls had walked on board where we could not follow them, and had gone into the saloon, so that the door smothered even Frances' howls, Eddie walked up close to the boat, closer than we dared go, and stared into the saloon porthole fixedly. He seemed to be watching something that alarmed him. The rest of us were in a mood to be alarmed, for it was always a tense moment, that embarkation. Now was the time the gendarmes often swooped down on a suspect and put him into jail. Many of their arrests were made at that moment, just when a malefactor thought he was safe at last and on his way to freedom. Paul and I stared at each other when we saw Eddie's face. Then, as he turned and hurried back to us, we were more alarmed than ever.

"Something's wrong," gasped Eddie. "A party of gendarmes just went on board. One of them spoke to Maya. They're looking at papers of some sort. They've taken the girls into another cabin. . . ."

"Oh, God," I said. "I wonder if I could reach Yoshida on the phone."

"Wait, I'll see what else is going on." Eddie hurried back to his lookout point and stood there again, craning his neck. Just then, in time to cut short his hysterics, the gendarme party walked down the gangplank without any prisoners, looking calm and peaceful. A moment later the little ship sailed. We saw Maya on deck, waving to us; Reeny was probably below, mingling her tears with Frances'. The whole story had been a characteristic fable of Eddie's; he loved to stir people up.

"So!" sighed Paul as we walked back to the bank. "They are well out of it. My poor Mickey, you are not cheerful. I too, I will miss Maya. But that was a moment, *hein?* That Eddie!"

I went home. Auntie and Phyllis, much subdued, were rearranging the bedroom furniture. There was a lot more room now in the house, but we took no comfort in that.

"She said she'd send for you if it was all right," I reminded Phyllis.

"But what about me?" said Auntie. "I don't want to leave Hong Kong."

"You don't have to, Auntie. That kind of trip is only for young people. You're like me; your husband's still here in camp. That makes it different. Cheer up; things look much better in North Africa. The Allies have taken a lot of prisoners."

"Oh dear," wailed Auntie Law. "Now we'll have to feed them all!"

As if they had at last decided to throw us a grain of comfort, the Americans suddenly bestowed upon us the first sign of life we had seen since the beginning of the occupation. I was playing with Carola on the floor when the air-raid siren began to sound. Ah Yuk scampered in, calling me.

"Tai-tai! Planes are coming!"

"Nope," I said, putting one brick on top of another brick. "It's false, Ah Yuk, it's a practice alarm."

"Boom, boom," sounded the horizon; "karump, karump."

"Rat-tat-tat," went the ack-ack guns.

"Practice?" scoffed Ah Yuk. She grabbed Carola and raced for the stairs. "This is real. Come on, Tai-tai."

The first air raid from our own planes! Somewhere inside of me a flower burst open. It was amazing, the happiness of it. Only a child is capable of that pure ecstasy, in the ordinary way, but this was no ordinary occasion. Those of us who were home—the servants and Carola and I—gathered in the basement, from the front door of which we could see through trees to the Kowloon side. We saw a few puffs of smoke, we heard more explosions, and that was all.

Viewed as more than a token raid, it was disappointing. The raiders actually accomplished nothing, except to light up our lives again and to blow the cinders of hope to roaring flames. That was enough for the time being, but there were two bad aftereffects. The first one to come to our attention was the boastful reports that came through immediately from Allied broadcasting stations. Chinese and American pilots claimed to have destroyed the Hong Kong power station and to have left the military parts of the city in flames. This wasn't true. Whatever the planes did accomplish, we didn't see any signs of it. And so these broadcasts were bad for us in the end, because they devaluated all the other reports we had been getting of Allied victories elsewhere in the world. We heard the Japanese laugh at the Allies for their lies, and we knew the laughter was justified, and we were ashamed. Until then we had thought that only Axis people lied and boasted.

In my mind I held long indignant conversations with the people who had spread these false reports, back in Chungking. It is seldom vouchsafed a mortal to carry out his dreams in practice, but this time I made that record. Twenty months later I did have such a conversation, safe and snug in my New York apartment, with Teddy White.

"How did it look from the ground, Mickey?" he asked. "I was in one of those bombers, you know. I waved to you; did you see me?"

"It looked lousy," I said emphatically. "You didn't hit a damn thing except some civilians. I can't tell you how awful it was, listening to those crazy reports afterward."

Jack Belden, still limping from a wound he got at Salerno, leaned back and roared with laughter at Teddy's face. "But honest, Mickey," Teddy pleaded, "it looked as if we hit everything in the world. It looked fine, it looked swell!"

"Well, it wasn't," I growled. "I was safe as houses. Phooey! Now the raids that came next year—oh, those *were* something."

The other bad result was manifested up at Bowen Road. When the siren went off all the wounded and sick who could walk rushed to the veranda on the east side of the hospital. This veranda was just outside a ward full of diphtheria patients who were all seriously ill, and some were dying. The able men crowded there at the railing and cheered. I can't tell

ou how I know this story, but I do. Next day arrived one Lieutenant
Saito, in a passion of rage, to "investigate this incident." His investigation
did not take long. The men were guilty of a grave crime in having made
such a demonstration, he decided, and those directly responsible were
Charles Boxer, highest-ranking officer among the patients, and Colonel
Bowie, surgeon in charge. Saito made all the walking sick stand in line
and he paraded Bowie and Charles, whose arm still hung helpless at his
side, up and down in front of them. Then he slapped Charles and Bowie.
Then he stormed into the diphtheria ward and slapped all the men in
bed there, the sick and the dying.

For a few days it was better not to go out if you could manage to stay
at home. The Japanese were sullen and all too alert. We had had two
more raids within thirty-six hours, one at midnight. For several nights
we were blacked out, but then the Japs decided, very sensibly, that blackouts would do no good, and they relaxed their rules. As it turned out, we
were not to have another visit from the Americans, anyway, for nine or
ten months.

I have forgotten to mention one of the cruelest of the occupation nuisances, which now increased to a point almost unbearable. This was the
institution of the "curfew," as we called it for some strange reason. Anyone who has lived in Japan during the few years preceding Pearl Harbor
knows what it is anyway. I don't know what you call it in Japanese; it
has nothing to do with nighttime. What happens is this: for their own
reasons the Japanese will suddenly call a halt to all traffic in a certain
part of the city. You run into a policeman who tells you to stop in your
tracks, and you do. There you stand until he tells you to move again.
Or perhaps, if it is that kind of a day, you don't stand: you squat. Or
maybe you have to kneel. At any rate, you stay where you are told to stay,
in whatever position you are ordered to hold, until the order goes around
to release you. Sometimes this state of affairs lasts for two hours, sometimes for eight. In Kowloon, where it happened more often than in Hong
Kong, it was sometimes held for the entire day. There were various reasons. Sometimes the public was held up like that because of troop movements which were to be kept secret; sometimes the Governor was traveling
around town and the Japs wanted to prevent his assassination, or an
illustrious visitor was going on a sight-seeing tour and the Japanese felt
he would be safer without any spectators. There was a violently uncomfortable period when a Prince of the imperial family was in town. Every
time that Prince moved from his hotel Kowloon *and* Hong Kong were
thus frozen into immobility. I happened to be in Kowloon that day,

fortunately without Carola, for she would have had sunstroke under such conditions of heat and glare. I was stopped four times, an hour each time. I didn't get home until six that night, for of course the ferry was stopped too. I was dehydrated and exceedingly anti-Emperor by that time.

After the first American raid the authorities went mad on these stop pages: we had a curfew every day. They also stepped up the rate of searchings in the street. They also put Selwyn into custody—not into prison, not yet. They just kept him under guard at his office and allowed nobody to talk to him on the phone or bring him food or anything. They seemed to hold him directly responsible for the raids, whereas in actuality he was livid with rage against his own side for attempting to destroy the powerhouse.

"Can't they realize what that would do to Stanley?" he demanded of me when he was set free again. "The entire population out there depends on electricity for cooking, heat, and everything else. How would it help the war effort, anyway, to destroy Hong Kong's electric system?"

I couldn't answer because all of this kind of thing is beyond me anyway. It was an interesting side light on the eternal struggle that goes on between the military mind and the civilian point of view.

"Anyway, Selwyn, they didn't. The bomb that fell on the powerhouse was a dud."

"Fortunately," he said in bitter tones.

It's a mixed-up business, is war.

Chapter 55

CAROLA WAS one year old. The sergeant who was in charge of parcels at Bowen Road was an old friend of ours by this time and we took little liberties with him now and then, especially the old-timers who had been coming there from the beginning—Hilda, Sophie Odell, one of the Weill girls, and me. He liked children, especially Hilda's Mary and my Carola, and so when I asked him if I could send in something special to Charles because of the baby's birthday he looked sideways at me and grinned in an encouraging way. Emboldened by this, I brought my offering the next week—a bottle of sparkling Burgundy, contributed by De Roux. Charles got it in spite of the rule against sending liquor, and shared it with his ward: Harry Odell, Tony, and a Canadian Major MacAulay. With Sophie's even more than usually lavish parcel, they had quite a day of it. I think back on that bottle of wine as a major triumph against fascism. All their desires and attention were focused on food. The men in hospital were now permitted to write their orders on special slips which were read to us women and duly filled, as well as our means allowed. The Red Cross had at last prevailed upon the commandant, Colonel Tokunaga, in charge of all the camps, to allow the prisoners to write cards to the outside world once a month. These cards took at least six weeks to get to me, though I lived only a few hundred yards from the hospital; the Japanese interpreters who acted as censors were slow and cautious in passing them.

The Red Cross was at last functioning, though in a limping way, and had succeeded in getting funds to Hong Kong for relief work among the volunteer dependents, whom Selwyn still had hanging around his neck. Zindel was a Roman Catholic and he discovered to his distress that a lot of the women who were applying for relief as soldiers' wives were actually unmarried, though they had children by these men. Catholic Zindel tried earnestly to straighten the matter out by demanding that they show him marriage certificates before they got their money, but too many people had lost their documents in the war to make this fair or feasible. Selwyn was opposed to Zindel's moral attitude, maintaining that common-law wives could be just as hungry and just as needy as the more regular incumbents of the British Army. According to British law they were entitled to help. In my own case I refused indignantly to make a claim for an allowance. "I'm not a dependent of Charles," I argued when Selwyn put it up to me. "I never was. Carola, yes. I'll apply for Carola, but not for me."

"Would you not be willing to sacrifice your pride in order to be a test case?" he urged. "If they give in on your account it would be a great blessing to all these wretched women who can't get help. Think it over."

Very reluctantly I did agree at last and made my claim. Zindel turned me down, though the Japanese were behind me on that. In their simple morality, a man's own woman is his woman, and of course is a dependent, church blessing or no church blessing. They were shocked by Zindel, and I believe that he did ultimately give in, in the other cases, though I never put in another claim. Carola at once got her regulation twenty-five yen a month, and the sum was boosted later to keep pace in its forlorn, lagging way with the rapidly rising cost of living. Nobody pretended that this figure was in any way adequate, being about one fifth of the necessary amount, but it was all the Red Cross could get for the purpose, and that was that.

At the same time funds were sent in from Geneva for Stanley Camp, and for the military prisoners who were not receiving other money. Did you know that according to the Geneva Convention only commissioned officers in military prison camps are paid? Privates go without. That's the truth, and a shocking truth it is. That is one reason why our enlisted men in Stanley were starving. The officers at least had their pay and could pool their resources and buy extra food, but if they had not sent half their monthly money to the men there would have been even more death from malnutrition in the enlisted men's camp. Regarding the pay, the Japs did abide by Geneva rules. It certainly didn't cost them much to do so.

Sometimes thereafter the men got Red Cross money; more often they didn't. There was one unsavory interlude when the Swiss in Tokyo were caught out, juggling with Red Cross funds from Geneva in such a way that they profited heavily on exchange. Infuriated, the Japanese closed down on everything for months. Before the matter was cleared up we had appalling casualties in Hong Kong, from hunger. It should be known as the Swiss Famine, and it went on for more than two months. I doubt if the starvation and suffering in Hong Kong troubled the Tokyo Swiss very much. That year they had something to celebrate, and they celebrated it with enthusiasm: a record of one hundred years of peace in Switzerland.

A fresh blow suddenly fell. Charles was discharged from hospital, though his arm had not recovered. What with epidemics and malnutrition, they needed room at the hospital, and his recovery if it ever did take place would be a long slow process. Except for his arm he was quite strong again, and well enough to take his place in Argyle Camp over in Kowloon with the other officers. Sergeant Sieno told me this apologetically when I turned up at hospital early in November with my parcel. Owing to their nonsensical passion for secrecy, Sieno couldn't tell me what camp Charles had gone to, though there was only one prison camp for commissioned men.

"He's gone to Argyle, of course?" I asked.

Sieno sighed. "I don't know. You must go to Argyle and ask there if they have Boxer. I cannot tell you; it is not permitted. Military secret!"

I was sure and didn't need confirmation. On Monday, parcel day for Argyle, for the first time I joined the other women who rode across the bay to the mainland on the nine o'clock ferry, fought for places on an overcrowded Number 1 bus, and got off about half a mile before they reached headquarters in order to be able to walk past the camp. I discovered to my delight that now I was closer to Charles than I had been at Bowen Road. Our men were waiting at the corner of the barbed-wire enclosure, lounging about carelessly beneath the eyes of the guards who sat in lookout posts high up on stilts, always watching for signals. (Signals of all kinds were forbidden between the prisoners and the public outside.) The men were on only slightly higher ground than we were. At Bowen Road Charles had stood on top of a hill; my view had been foreshortened and unsatisfactory.

Two by two or one by one we walked along, across the street, at a distance of about three hundred meters. We could not stop, or loiter, or look squarely at the camp, nor could we approach closer, for if we did any of these things there would be an enraged shout from the guards, or even an attack. One sentry stood in the road brandishing his bayoneted rifle, waiting eagerly for somebody to break the rules. We walked slowly as we dared, and the men stood there grinning, picking us out as we came by. Charles always walked along step for step with me, up to the other end of the enclosure, and waited there until I had turned the corner into headquarters. His arm slowly grew better; I could see it. At first he carried his helpless left hand behind him, carefully supporting it with the right. As the months went by he became able to swing the injured arm, though the fingers were still immobile. The Japs were supplying massage to him. For this reason too I was glad he had been transferred, although now he was very far away from the house in Kennedy Road. After all, what difference did it make? Only a sentimental one.

I continued to carry parcels to Bowen Road Hospital just the same, because Charles's friends there still depended on me. But at Argyle I had to make a bigger effort for Charles himself. The rules there were less elastic and the Japs spurned homemade food, which meant that I had to spend lots of money on strictly sealed, commercial tinned foods. I planned the weekly parcel with intense care, and after delivering it I went home feeling rather smug, sure that I had sent enough food to keep Charles well for the following week. It was rather a shock, then, to receive his first card from Argyle:

DEAR MICKEY:
   Many thanks for your Monday parcels. They are all the more welcome as I am sharing them with seven other men who get nothing otherwise. . . .

I cursed and worried and forthwith began trying, willy-nilly, to plan parcels eight times as big as those I had been sending hitherto. If De Roux had not helped me on this work I couldn't have done it. He knew all there was to know about local shopping, and he had Chinese friends who helped me with supplies and advice. He sent his houseboy to carry the extra basket for me. Charles, I am pretty sure, didn't go hungry. At least I sincerely hope he didn't. Making sure that he didn't was my whole existence, save for the effort I put in at home to seeing that Carola too was adequately fed. My universe shrank to the dimensions of a digestive tube. There was nothing else to think about, no world outside, nothing. My stream of consciousness went something like this:

"Eight eggs a week for Charles, two for Carola, that ought to be about even considering their respective sizes and weights. . . . If I buy a dozen tins of bean curd that will last him six weeks. Will there be any bean curd left in six weeks' time? Shall I invest more money and buy two dozen? Prices will never go down, only up. . . . I have a dozen slabs of chocolate. Chocolate is one thing Charles assured me in his last card that he doesn't share, so I must go on sending chocolate. I wonder if we can get chocolate until the end of the war? One dozen, twelve Monday mornings, three months. Better not buy more though prices are going up; it won't keep that long. How long will this war go on? Marmite is too expensive. We can try that other stuff, Yeastrel; it costs only half as much and tastes the same. Marmite is vitamins; is Yeastrel equally good? There's no way for Charles to let me know. What can I send for protein? They get no meat or fish. Should I go on hoarding those prunes for Carola? If I open the big tin they'll spoil before she can eat them all, whereas if I send them in to Charles he'll eat them immediately. But it's wicked to give prunes to a man when there's a baby in the family and not many prunes in town. . . . Still, Carola can eat fresh oranges when they're in season, and I don't think the prisoners will be allowed to accept oranges. Must go to Kowloon this afternoon; Sophie says one shop there has Japanese tinned fruit at a reasonable price. Oh damn, there goes my shoe leather. Now what can I wear to walk past the camp? Wooden clogs? Eight eggs a week for Charles, two for Carola; it doesn't sound right somehow. Remind Selwyn to give me more cod-liver oil if he can spare it. Eight eggs . . ."

Then there was soap. Or rather, there wasn't. Charles needed a cake of soap every fortnight. We ran out of soap in Hong Kong, until local factories started making it, and they produced inferior stuff without fatty materials which spoiled and crumbled to dust unless you used it up right away. And jam: the supply was dwindling in the market, yet the men needed it. A prisoner could eat lots of jam.

All of these petty troubles shrank to their true proportions after Christmas had come and gone and January had dragged by. In February 1943 the Reign of Terror opened with a bang. It coincided with Wang Ching-wei's belated declaration of war on the Allies.

By this time I was alone in the Kennedy Road house. Phyllis had gone into Free China with the old Gittins parents; Reeny sent for them via the Underground, even sending money with an enthusiastic account of her new job in Kweilin. They got out just before the route was closed by the Japanese take-over of Kwangchowwan. Auntie, frightened away by the fact that we now had to pay rent to the government for tenancy of the house, had moved over to Robinson Road and was living with another old lady, a crony of hers. Losing Auntie's dither was not hardship exactly, but I didn't like living alone. I had become accustomed to vast crowds in the house, and these empty, echoing rooms scared me.

Maria de Roza, the masseuse, turned up at the right moment and gladly accepted my invitation to share the house. She was living with her mother in Kowloon, but she had other sisters and brothers to take her place, and my house was near town, and if Maria was ever to find work again it would be necessary to live near town. That worked out all right. Maria was a nice girl and we left each other alone in a satisfactory way.

Life was getting complicated for the local young girls. Some of them were already expert little tarts, partly because their schools were closed, they couldn't find jobs, and they were bored. They would haunt the cafés, coming in in pairs or alone. They would sit at tables until parties of soldiers or sailors or gendarmes picked them up, but competition with the regular hostesses was keen, and these restaurant girls resented amateurs. In the end most of them, like the others, took jobs as hostesses; it was simpler and it avoided this professional difficulty. A few of them were cleverer, and if they did practice the oldest trade in the world it was in private. They went only to parties, not public cafés. I have seen girls I knew well slipping into geisha houses where presumably they met their hosts in private rooms. I would sigh and shake my head for all the world like one of my own old aunts, or like any respectable old cat. I *felt* old and respectable.

The Reign of Terror had been in force some months before I was aware of it. Among my best friends was a Chinese dentist well known to all the "foreigners" in Hong Kong long before the war. After I came back to May Road I made the disturbing discovery that my teeth were going bad and my hair falling out. Johnny could do nothing about the hair condition, which was due to my bad diet, but he did work hard on my teeth, and he insisted on putting off the reckoning indefinitely. He was a darling. He did his best for all of us. It was one of the biggest shocks I received during the war when Johnny disappeared. It was horrible. His wife and children, his mother and friends were wild with worry before they found out that the gendarmes had spirited him away, and then the worry was even more intense.

Johnny was held for a month. It was the first time we had run into this manifestation of Japanese justice and we learned a lot from it. The gendarmes never admitted officially that they had taken him prisoner. Inside, they never told *him* why he had been thus kidnaped, either. They starved, beat, and tortured him, and on the day he was released they cautioned him never to tell anybody where he had been, but to announce to the world that he had been ill and in hospital. He still doesn't know why they did it. I heard from him all the details of his torture, from the "water treatment" to the thumb-hanging.

We thought that the arrest might have had something to do with gendarme suspicions of Selwyn and the vast net of espionage which they obviously thought Selwyn was managing. But it was all so vague, and Johnny's family had been so terrified, that we couldn't make it out. Following this arrest, others came on us thick and fast. One by one almost anybody might disappear, Chinese, Indians, Eurasians, and especially Europeans. The gendarmes did not always maintain much secrecy in their methods; in the case of one young Chinese friend of mine they simply marched into his bedroom at four in the morning, robbed the room of all the money and jewels they could find, insulted his wife with foul words, and dragged him out in handcuffs.

There were around town quite a few British and one or two Americans who had been, as we called it, "guaranteed out" of Stanley by neutral friends. At one time Oda had seemed quite eager to get as many people out of camp as possible, and if a Swiss or Portuguese or French citizen would sign a paper promising that his friend would not work against the Japanese and that his expenses would be met, these enemy nationals were permitted to come into town and live comparatively freely, as I did. The Foreign Affairs officials lived to regret this kindness, for the gendarmes found excuses to arrest one after another of the free enemy nationals. Some were released after weeks of bad treatment and questioning; others were not, and are still there, unless they are dead. I was not overly worried for myself. Officially I was Chinese, not an enemy, and though all Chinese didn't escape, I hoped for the best.

It seemed obvious that sooner or later they would get around to arresting Selwyn. He expected it, I am sure. Hilda didn't, quite. Colonel Nguchi still adored his protégé, and Hilda thought that the colonel's protection would continue to serve. However, like all the others of his household, she held herself ready for the crisis. He warned her time after time: "If ever I am taken up, do *not* attempt to do anything for me.

Don't try to communicate with me; don't try to send food. You will only implicate yourself. Just take care of Mary and wait for the end."

After a long period when nobody was allowed to come out of Stanley for X ray or any other purposes (because an enemy-national patient had run away while he was in French Hospital) Selwyn did at last succeed in getting a Stanley man out again for treatment in town. This was Dr. Harry Talbot, the man who had operated on so many Soong sinuses up in Chungking. Harry was brought in for a serious kidney operation. That was when the worst of the trouble began. Nobody put in his way any strictures against seeing callers. He had come out under Selwyn's faithful promise not to carry letters back and forth, and Selwyn saw to it that he kept this promise. But something else happened. The day before he went back Sir Vandeleur Grayburn, Far East manager of the Hong Kong and Shanghai Bank, accompanied by Streatfield, one of his men, called on Harry and gave him the sum of four thousand yen, I think it was, to take back to camp with him.

The stories differ as to what was to be done with this money. I think it was intended for some old rich taipan inside, some man who probably had lots of credit with the bank, though Sir Vandeleur later "confessed" falsely to the Japanese that it was to be distributed evenly among the government nurses. Unfortunately for everybody, Harry was too sick to conceal the money in a safe place. He left it lying loose in one of his bags, an incredible blunder, for of course on returning to camp he was searched thoroughly, the money was found, and he was thrown, sick as he was, into prison while the matter was investigated. He would not give Grayburn away.

A lot of small people were arrested and questioned. Harry had had many Chinese patients and friends; they were all dragged into it. The gendarmes were sure that they had uncovered a plot to aid in some important person's escape, and they were excited and zealous. They dug up somewhere a bit of phony information that the Chinese guerrillas were asking around four thousand yen to rescue people, and it seemed highly significant that Harry was bringing in just that sum to camp. After a few agonizing days of this sort of thing, with a surprise raid on the French Hospital made by a naval party, Sir Vandeleur went down to the Foreign Affairs office and confessed that he had given Harry that money.

Oda was surprised and worried. He duly handed the confession on, however, to the gendarmes, and we all sat back and waited to see what would happen next. Shortly afterward Sir Vandeleur and Streatfield were arrested.

Even Japanese civilians were shocked. Sir Vandeleur was such an important man that they could not believe the gendarmes would treat him just as they did other victims. There must have been a lot of communication with Tokyo on the subject, but it was no use; the gendarmes were supreme. All the other bankers of all nationalities were told to hurry up with their work of cleaning up the banks; sooner or later they too would be put into Stanley, where they could do no more mischief. Lady Grayburn went out at once to Stanley, at her own request. From there she pelted the Foreign Affairs people with letters, her own and the Colonial Secretary's.

At this critical juncture Oda was transferred back to Tokyo. He had long since told me that he was going; he hated his job and was anxious to get into some other work, away from the sad, moribund little town. We were alarmed at the prospect, for we knew Oda and he knew us, and we dreaded a new man who might change all his policies without warning. Lots of people hated Oda, but he was pretty good to me, and I was sure we couldn't have another man in that job who would be as sympathetic and helpful as he was.

"Don't worry, you'll be all right," he said, but he looked worried too. "By the way, how much money have you?"

This question was not asked in any kindly spirit, and I knew it. I had been waiting for it for a long time. Part of the investigation arising from the Grayburn case was applied to the incomes, if any, of all suspicious characters; the gendarmes were combing the town for evidence of funds coming in to us from enemy countries. I had my story ready. I had figured it all out, down to the exact sums that would look reasonable and would still serve, in Japanese minds, to carry me along.

"Gibson left me four thousand yen," I said promptly. This, as we know, was unfortunately not true. Oda looked angry, but he believed me.

"Gibson seems to have given money to everyone," he said. "He gave a lot to Selwyn-Clarke too. Well, how much of that have you left?"

"Two thousand."

"Where do you keep it?"

"On the ledge in my bedroom fireplace chimney." I smiled.

"That isn't safe," said Oda. "Better put it in the bank."

"But what bank?"

"The Yokohama Specie Bank, of course."

"Can I? Will they accept my account?"

"I'll call them myself," said Oda, and grabbed his phone. "The man in charge, Mr. Onuma, knows Boxer; he used to fence with Boxer. He'll open a special account for you." And to show he meant business, he telephoned the bank right away. He talked Japanese for a long time.

Do you understand? If I had a bank account which the gendarmes could watch without undue trouble they would be less suspicious. We counted two hundred yen a month for my expenses, and so they could be sure that I was all right for ten months to come, at that rate. I duly went and opened the account as I had been ordered to do. It was a scramble to collect the money, but I did it. . . . Because of course I had lied to Oda. Gibson had left no money with me, and I didn't want to go into details with Oda as to where I did get my money. I'm not going into details even now in this book, because the war isn't over. I can say only that friends lent me money every now and then.

It wasn't much of a hardship, keeping an account where the gendarmes could watch it. I used much more than two hundred yen a month, but I didn't want them to know that. I just had to be sure that I drew money out at reasonable intervals, in reasonable sums, and everything would be all right—for the time being. That wasn't what scared me.

There was something else to worry about, something much more serious than my bank account, if they were going to examine Sir Vandeleur's papers and of course they would, without the shadow of a doubt. He held my note for two thousand yen, and I knew that this loan was not likely to be approved by the gendarmes. I waited, sure that I would be called in for investigation. Something did come of it, but not exactly what I had expected; somebody tried to blackmail me.

Chapter 56

I can't think that I offered promising material for blackmail, but I dare say the enterprising man who tried it on must have figured that I had secret resources, and since he was a romantic type he decided that these resources were rich and vast. You couldn't tell who was well off and who wasn't, in that sad city. To be sure, I was very shabby, in poor physical condition, with thinning hair and a constantly worried look on my face, but still, there I was, indubitably alive and with my own house, my own servants, and a baby who looked healthy and happy. Other men as clever as he were puzzled by this state of affairs.

I met him first in Needa's office just after the surrender, in those days when Irene and I used Needa's room to sit in, to rest our swollen feet. The office was a central place and attracted other people beside ourselves, and one of them was this plump little Chinese fellow with a pleasant soft voice and fluent English. Needa often joined queer business pacts for this or that project and I think he was in one with Tse. Before the war Tse was known as Howard Tore, or Choa, and had been proprietor of a few dance halls in the red-light district of Hong Kong, "West Point." I paid little or no attention to him at first, except to agree with Needa that he was an amusing liar whose imagination could scale incredible heights.

During the Reign of Terror Needa told me that Tse had been arrested by the gendarmes and decapitated for petty graft. Needa believed the story, and wasted no tears over Tse. We were all surprised when he turned up again, fat and sassy, with a tremendous story of his own importance in Japanese circles. He again spent a lot of time in Needa's office; a new office now, a big set of offices, in fact. Needa had realized his ambition; he was now a flourishing merchant with a lot of men working under him, scouring the town for iron and bronze and aluminum and things like that, all of which the Navy eagerly grabbed and paid for. Needa was a coming man, and he showed more cleverness than I had expected in him by staying out of politics with anxious modesty.

Needa told me impressively that Tse had "pull" with the gendarmes and that he was a good guy to be polite to. "But I don't like him," I protested. Needa squeezed my arm with impatient urgency.

"You don't have to like him; use your head. He's a big fellow now. I don't like him around myself, but am I saying so? Not much. Use your head, old girl. Where's that baby of mine? When you going to give her to me? I love that kid, Jesus, I do."

When Grayburn was arrested I began to think, furiously, as I said before. Here are the details. It had become known among us that Sir Vandeleur was collecting money from friendly natives in town and distributing it for relief work. Naturally he kept quiet about this, knowing that the Japanese would not approve of anyone but themselves picking up any extra cash that was lying around. But as my purse grew thin, and after the girls left me, I cast around for help and I thought of that fund. "Bankers," I said to myself, "always have money even when they are imprisoned. Bankers know the real value of money, which is nil; they can make it and throw it away in this knowledge. I will ask Sir Vandeleur to help me out with a loan. He must be aware that I'll be good for it, after the war."

So I put in my bid for two thousand yen, which seemed a tremendous sum according to Japanese standards. The unofficial relief committee picked up my request and studied it. Sir Vandeleur was in favor of honoring it, in a mechanical way, but his assistant Edmonston, my old adversary of the bank doorway and air raid, the man who had refused to take in Carola—Edmonston was violently opposed to letting me have any money.

"But why?" asked Grayburn, mildly puzzled. "I admit she is not British, but she is certainly an ally of ours; she has worked hard for our men; she is entitled to aid——"

"Because," said Edmonston passionately, "Boxer treated his wife disgracefully, and I for one do not intend to overlook it."

Sir Vandeleur grew more puzzled. "Is that any reason," he asked, "why an American woman and her child should starve now, in the streets of occupied Hong Kong?"

"*Yes,*" snapped Edmonston. Grayburn did not argue. He simply sent me the money on his own private account instead of from the bank, and I made out a receipt to him and signed it duly. . . . So that was the story, and somewhere, I knew, that receipt lay among his papers, ready to be pounced on by the Japanese. What would they do to me? It depended, I knew, on luck. If they found a lot of similar papers, and if they were pressed for time, they might possibly ignore it. But if by bad fortune they noticed it in a special way, my goose was cooked. I would be thrown into prison and "investigated." Ladies were not tortured in gendarme prisons to the extent men were, but it would not be nice to have Carola in there with me; it would not be nice to be flogged and starved and frightened and threatened. I slept badly again, and thought a good deal about the gendarmes.

One day Needa cried out to me jovially, in the presence of Tse, "What do you know? Tse's goin' to arrest you. You're implicated, he says, in the Grayburn case!"

"Ssssh," said Tse crossly, his face growing red. But I knew, as Needa only guessed, that he had helped turn over those papers, and he had come across the receipt. I waited, thinking things over while I talked to him. Tse always acted anxiously polite to me, trying to impress me for some twisted reason of his own. I talked very politely too, and my mind went racing ahead of me. Had Tse approached Needa for protection money on my behalf? I think so. Had Needa paid him something? I think so. I don't know.

As soon as I could get away I ran to my one trusted Japanese friend, Ogura, and told him the whole thing. Ogura looked troubled.

"You used to be an object of suspicion," he admitted, "but for some months all question on the subject has been dropped. I have watched the case anxiously. It would be a pity to start more trouble now. Even though you would be declared innocent in the end—for our gendarmes are very just, though you do not believe it—the period of investigation is unpleasant."

"I know that," I said, and waited. He was always slow.

"Our gendarmes," he said at last, "employ these low characters for good reasons. However, this sort of extortion is inevitable. I myself would like to prove their crimes against these criminal types, just to show the gendarmes how unwise it is to allow them too much freedom, but I can do very little."

"I know that too, Mr. Ogura."

"I have a friend in the gendarmerie where this man claims to have his influence," said Ogura. "I shall make inquiries on the matter. We newspapermen still have a little influence; not much, but a little. Do you think our friend Needa has already given this Tse any money to protect you?"

"I—I think it likely."

"Well . . . Of course he would not admit it. Do not worry. I will find out and tell you, if you are under suspicion. Do not worry. But in the meantime be careful. Have you spoken to Oda about it?"

"No. He's going away so soon, I don't like to bring it up." And also, I thought, it would decide him to intern me.

Months later the kindly Ogura reported that there was no charge against me in the Grayburn case, and no record of the receipt. Tse had probably abstracted it for his own uses. I met Tse again on this matter, but that comes later. Grayburn, tried and found guilty of the trifling charge of smuggling money to Stanley, was given a sentence of three months' hard labor. This was to be served in full, on top of all the months they consumed investigating him. Halfway through the sentence, in midsummer, the gendarmes without warning delivered his dead body to Lady Grayburn, in Stanley Camp. They said with amazing candor that he had died of beriberi. The most powerful financier in the Far East, chief of the biggest bank, had died of starvation.

I don't believe it. First of all, they *said* it was beriberi, so it couldn't have been. Second, Lady Grayburn had been sending her husband food in large quantities every week and we have reason to believe that he got it. Third, the body was very much decomposed when it was handed over to the British and the doctors couldn't make sure of the cause of death. I am inclined to believe what the Chinese said: that he died as an accident after too enthusiastic an "investigation." It could have been the famous water treatment, which has many forms but in Hong Kong is done this way: a gendarme sits on your stomach and places a large wad of cotton wool over your mouth and nose. On this he drips water until in spite of all threshing and fighting you drown. Then they revive you with artificial respiration and do it again. Your struggles with the man sitting on your stomach are supposed to be very amusing. Grayburn was not young and he had been ill for a long time. The water treatment leaves no marks.

Grayburn was brave, stubborn, and dignified. As I had reason to know, he was kindly too, although many people would not admit that before the war. I am grateful, and I grieve for him.

The old nightmare quality had returned to our life. The arrests and investigations and disappearances and rumors sent everyone into a chronic hysteria. The French became convinced that it was the turn of their community next. The Irish felt the same; so did the Portuguese and the Norwegians and the Danes. Chinese told each other not to speak to white people in the street; it was Johnny's friendship for us, they muttered, which brought calamity on him. For all their fear, though, some of the ratty ones began to look on me with admiring favor, thinking that my immunity proved I was a collaborationist.

The next phase was when people began to think they were being followed by spies. Sophie was particularly vulnerable to such suggestions; she was scared stiff. The Weills had been questioned several times as to their source of money supplies, and though they told the truth, which was that they kept selling things, they were afraid the gendarmes didn't believe them.

One by one I heard from every single community that was still at large in Hong Kong. The gendarmes had warned this one; were following that one; had sent word that the next week would bring investigation of a third one's activities in regard to parcels for the prisoners. Many of the wretched local inhabitants didn't dare send food to Stanley any more. "They watch you, and if you send very much they arrest you and ask you why. . . ."

At last I tired of all this hole-and-corner panic. Suspense is the only thing I really can't bear. I did a little investigating on my own and found out interesting facts. The gendarmes had merely instituted a "whispering campaign," calculated to keep us nervous and easy to handle.

"*Who* talked to your sister and told her you had better be careful?" I demanded of Maria, who had been quaking with terror for a week. "It was that little rat—no, he's a mouse—Da Silva, wasn't it? Well, do you think Da Silva would dare betray his bosses the gendarmes by warning you on his own hook? No, no. They told him to spread these warnings around."

"But why, if they don't mean it?"

"To keep you frightened, out of mischief, disinclined to stir up rebellion even if you had had such a notion, which I know you didn't."

"Do you honestly think so?"

"I know it," I said firmly, and turned to the Chinese group.

"Following you? But why? What sort of thing could he find out from following *you* to market?" I asked Constance Lam. "And you—why do you care if that gendarme scowled at you?" I demanded of Sophie. At length I delivered a compilation of my discoveries.

"The gendarmes are trying to scare all of us on purpose," I announced. "It is part of an organized plan to keep us healthily quiet. They do this kind of thing every so often, just as a matter of routine. They pass the word around among their running dogs, the running dogs go out and start whispering, and *voilà!*—everybody's afraid to stir up trouble against the gendarmes. It's cheap and it's easy and it saves police. See?"

At any rate, I convinced myself. Proudly I snorted, alone in my room, "Trying to stampede *me*. Pooh!" But still I winced at every knock on the door.

Like everything in the Japanese administration, Oda's departure took a long time to carry through. His relief, that feared and yet eagerly awaited official, was shy about making an appearance, and Oda went from one farewell party to another, winding up his affairs.

"I have those two trunks of Boxer's personal effects," he told me one day, having summoned me to the office. "Is there anything you can use among them?"

"No, thank you. They would be safer with your successor, I suppose, than with me. But perhaps I'd better look through them."

Oda consented to this and I spent an afternoon in the consular flat going through the pathetic little agglomeration of stuff the gendarmes had scorned. I saved a few worthless books—Charles's real library had been carried away all in one piece, soon after the Japs landed on the island—and I found some family photographs. The rest, scraps of paper with poems written on them, and Japanese prints, and souvenirs of Japan, were better left there, as I had said. My own life was too uncertain for me to take the trunks home. After doing this job I had a drink with the ex-consul and we talked.

When he wasn't enjoying his new-found power Oda was a civilized fellow. He was always civilized with me and we were on honest terms; there was no necessity on my part to conceal my sentiments, which he knew were inimical toward his own people. In the back of his mind was always the conviction that I could be brought round to a sensible philosophy, if only somebody would take the trouble. "She has a grudge against the British," I think he said to himself. "Even Boxer left her in a bad spot." Aloud he said, "Do you regret not going in the exchange ship?"

"Yes and no, Mr. Oda. It was a bad move for the baby."

"Why don't you take back your American nationality? Then you would be able to get money from your government through the Red Cross. As it is, the Swiss Ambassador in Tokyo says you have sacrificed your nationality and he won't permit you to accept help."

"The Swiss Ambassador doesn't know his law. But I wouldn't claim to be American anyway. You have overlooked the fact that I would then be interned, Mr. Oda. Or have you?"

"Mmmmm, yes, that's true. But I have been thinking. I am going away, and life is growing very—uh—strenuous. If it grows more so, wouldn't you be *better off* in Stanley than Somewhere Else?"

My spine turned chillingly cold. "Is it so bad?"

"Not yet," he said, and laughed like a Japanese. "We can wait and see how it goes. . . . Only remember that the hospitality of Stanley is always open to you if you want it. For the time being, perhaps you had better go on pretending to be Chinese."

"Oh, I do," I assured him earnestly. "Nobody knows I'm not but just you and me."

It is difficult to explain how this man, so much hated by many of the prisoners, so dangerously liable to attacks of conceit, still went on being extraordinarily and subtly decent to me. It was Charles again, I suppose, and a sense of honor that most of his compatriots did not possess. There were many differences between him and the other officials. He treated his servants well, and his Indian chauffeur cried when he went away. His successor, the tall, good-looking Hattori, had beautiful British manners and a lot of physical charm, but in his unguarded moments he was a brute to all his servants. It was hard sometimes when I was with Hattori not to show how I felt when he flew off the handle at the amah or the chauffeur. Oda was different; the Ho girls, who worked in his office, were so upset by his departure that they wanted to quit, though other jobs were impossible to get and they depended completely on their salaries. They acted with Oda like handmaidens, in an innocent way, rather than like typists, and the other Japanese looked on sourly at the intimacy Oda achieved with their family group.

Kathleen, the elder of the two, decided to quit after all and to marry her cousin in Kwangchowwan. Yvonne, the younger sister, was a girl of unbelievable beauty and almost incredible innocence, though she considered herself very sophisticated. Both girls went to fortunetellers all the time, chattered like adolescent magpies, and added a good deal to the gaiety of the Foreign Affairs office. Oda decided to celebrate Kathleen's *fiançailles* and his own departure with one of those dinner parties he loved to give. As an adored auntie of the girls, I was invited too. The rest of the people were from the office, just as they had been on the fateful night I slapped the boss.

"Tonight," I said to myself as I dragged out the old faded party dress, "I must really be careful and sensible. Tonight I must not drink too much and I certainly must not talk politics. It wouldn't be fair to those kids: they have to be so careful all the time, what with their jobs and everything."

So firm were my resolutions, so good my control, that at nine o'clock I heard my own voice holding forth like this: "The Axis is finished. The Axis is dead. Look how Germany is retreating everywhere: North Africa and then Russia; obviously it's only a matter of time. You can see that for yourselves, gentlemen."

Oda's spectacled eyes looked calm and reflective. "And what do you think will happen to Japan in that case?" he asked gently. The others on the party were hushed and horrified.

"Japan? Oh, it's hopeless, Oda, hopeless. Germany's let you down and you can't swing this proposition alone. Mind you, I give you your due; you can fight, all right, and if Germany had held up her end you could have got away with it, but fortunately——"

Yvonne giggled nervously. Kathleen's eyes glowed. Oda just went on probing, calmly and politely. "You are wrong," he said flatly. He drew himself up and delivered the next speech with what was almost a burlesque of boasting. "Why, Japan's destiny is assured. She will rule the world, she will conquer everybody. She——"

"Nuts!" That unaccountable voice of mine rang out clear and loud.

Then Oda slapped *me*. "I thought we had better get evened up before I left," he explained.

There were no hard feelings to mar the rest of the going-away party. I could see the justice of that slap. We all laughed heartily.

It is as well that the unhappy days that followed Wang's fantastic declaration of war against the Allies were not made worse for me by knowledge of what was happening to Shanghai. Strange as it seems, all this time I had been unaware of my friends' fate. I had assumed for months that everyone was interned just as our people were, at the same time, but I was wrong. A few leading men were put into clink at that time, but the Japanese stood by the skeleton protocol and left the other whites in their thousands to wander about until Wang joined in the war. Shanghai, one must remember, was not like Hong Kong, a colony formerly under the jurisdiction of Europeans. Shanghai was China, and before 1943 the Nanking clique kept out of the war.

Of course the foreigners were not really free. Some check was kept on them, but even so it was possible for people to slip out into Free China now and then. Lots of my friends did that: I found out all of this when I met my compatriots at last on the exchange ship. And now, what about my Corin?

I should have thought that Corin would have had a bad time of it because she had been working for a propaganda broadcast station. And Jacques, who had deserted Havas in disgust when the Havas people embraced the Vichy principles, was certainly in for trouble because he had been loudly in favor of De Gaulle, I thought. I hoped for the best, though, and went on thinking about my own troubles, like all the rest of us sorry mortals. The true story came out in my hearing on the exchange ship, when a friend told me on the crowded deck, and I was sick with dismay.

Corin and Jacques with a lot of other people attempted to make an escape from Shanghai. The entire party save for Jacques was apprehended in a near-by village. Jacques, fortunately, had gone into town to buy supplies, and they missed him in the roundup. The other members of the party, with Corin, were put into the Shanghai gendarme station known as Bridge House. They were there for some weeks, and everyone said Corin was in fine shape under those conditions, laughing a lot, cheering up her friends, and being very brave indeed.

In the meantime Jacques found refuge in a Parsee's house where he was safely hidden until his second escape attempt was successful, much later on. The Parsee had three handsome daughters. When Corin was released from Bridge House, full of excitement at the news that the exchange was actually going to take place and she would be eligible to sail as correspondent of an American news agency, she was greeted with the rumor that Jacques was engaged to be married to the prettiest of his Parsee hostesses.

Evidently she tried to be very simple and efficient about it all. She told John Alexander, who with his family was confidently awaiting the ship on which the Alexanders would sail as diplomats, that she intended to kill herself. John knew her well and probably thought that he knew what to say.

"If you do it just now you'll make the exchange impossible, perhaps," he said. "The Japanese have closed their lists and they must deliver every one of us safe to the Americans at Lourenço Marques. Think of what it might mean to thousands of people if you are selfish enough to commit suicide now! You know how touchy the Japs are. I am not arguing with your intention, Corin; your life and death are your own affair. But promise me, at any rate, to wait until the ship has sailed."

Corin promised, after an argument. That night she wrote a letter to John saying that she was breaking her promise. He had extracted it, she said, under compulsion, because as he well knew she had been in no posi-tion to take a stand against him. Now she could not wait any longer. Her death was due, overdue by many months of anguish. "I can't bear the torture of living for another five minutes," wrote Corin in a precise hand. Then she drank a bottle of Lysol and died.

But the exchange was not, after all, spoiled by this action.

Chapter 57

THE SELWYN-CLARKES were disturbed by the news that Colonel Nguchi, their patron and protector, was going away. The whole setup in the government was constantly changing like that; Noma of the gen-darmes was the only official who stayed all the way through while I was in Hong Kong, and we should have expected Nguchi's departure. Prob-ably Selwyn did, but hung on as long as he could and hoped for a miracle. Though Selwyn always had a reputation as an alarmist in his own govern-ment, and though I myself had occasion to resent his dramatic presenta-tion of the worst news and his tendency to make gloomy prophecies, he remained tough in his estimation of facts. He was always expecting worse, and so the catastrophe when it arrived usually shocked him less than it did us mere humans. He was no alarmist. He merely foretold calamities which came to pass, and everyone hated him for it.

I saw him working under the new conditions often and often, when I went into the Health Department offices. One day I turned up there with a needy case which did not come exactly under the heading of volunteer dependent. Rather, this lady was a regular dependent, for her husband was a regular soldier, connected with the Royal Army Medical Corps and now interned at Bowen Road. The wife was Chinese and had not been evacuated with the other soldiers' wives because she had been so near her confinement. Now, with the new baby and two older children, she was hard up, because she was a northerner without relatives in this strange southern city. She clung to me because I spoke her dialect and she had very little English. After carrying the responsibility for a very short time indeed I realized I couldn't do it any more and I took it over and dumped it into Selwyn's lap. I have gone into this detail just to show what sort of thing he was up against in his moments of leisure. All of these people, bewildered and lost and scared and hungry, had nowhere to go but to Selwyn. Though he couldn't do anything officially, he did manage somehow to help, and all out of that tremendous saintly conviction that it was the duty of England, through Selwyn-Clarke, not to let down her colonials.

Of course the colonials agreed with him, and I seldom saw signs of gratitude. A handful of women adored him to the point of dying for him; that is true. More than a handful went through torture for him and didn't fall down on the job. But the majority of the women hated him, for cheeseparing, for arguing with them when they made their claims, for not doing more.

Well, there I sat with my regular dependent, waiting to see Selwyn-Clarke. First we waited until he came in; that was one hour. Then when he did arrive, full of the old formality, apologizing just as if my bedraggled Chinese charge and I were people of importance instead of serfs, he was called away by someone in the office. After another hour he was able to talk to us. We had gone through most of the case, with me interpreting, when a uniformed clerk came and told Selwyn that Mr. Kiribayashi wanted to see him.

"Tell Mr. Kiribayashi I will be in as soon as this business is accomplished," said Selwyn, and resumed his conversation with us.

All of a sudden there was a thump, thump, thump outside the office, and a big bully in uniform stamped in, his eyes blazing. He halted opposite the desk and thundered, "Selwyn-Clarke! You come—*now!*"

Selwyn turned slowly toward him and surveyed the uniformed gent over his spectacles, just like a reproving schoolmaster. Then he turned deliberately back to me and said, "I apologize for this outrageous behavior."

Not having his capacity for dignity, I had already jumped to my feet, and my Chinese girl was with me on that. "No, no, Selwyn, you go along. We can finish this another time. Come on, Tai-tai." I hurried out, expecting to hear a slap at any moment, but I didn't. I dare say Selwyn went in and lectured Mr. Kiribayashi on his manners.

Throughout the occupation I had heard a lot about Nguchi but had never met him. According to Hilda he was charming, though she had never been able to talk with him. He had taken over the house on the Peak, the same house where we had cowered so long in the cellar. He had shown the greatest amiability in the world by doing this, for he managed to preserve the Selwyn-Clarke possessions by virtue of his presence. Going even beyond that, he had kept on the housekeeper, Constance Lam, who was in charge during my visit to the Peak and who had never gone away.

Constance was one of the ladies who wanted to die for Selwyn. He had done her a good turn once when she was very ill; she said that he saved her life, and it is probably true. No longer young and not particularly beautiful, she ran no danger, we assumed, from the licentious soldiery or from Nguchi. He found her at the house when he moved in, and he just told her to go on living there if she liked, so Constance sent for her little niece Annette and settled in. Nguchi sent up an occasional sack of rice or flour, and once or twice he came up in person with a party of companions, intending to have a nice old-fashioned Japanese orgy in his house. Constance, according to her own story, told him that it wouldn't do; she would not permit ladies of the town to stay the night in that house. She says he agreed and never did it again. I can't believe that part of the saga. But it is probably true that he didn't come up the Peak very often. Gasoline was scarce even for officers, and so was time. Nguchi had his fun elsewhere and plenty of it.

Constance stayed on in the Peak house, complaining no more. She was very helpful indeed to Selwyn and Hilda, and kept bringing down things she had picked up here and there around the house—and perhaps from other houses in the neighborhood. One of them was a blue dress which she sold to Hilda and which I promptly tore from Hilda's back when I recognized it, for it was my dress, which I had asked Constance for repeatedly and in vain, as she said she couldn't find it.

All this I heard about Nguchi, without having seen him. Then at last I met him, and how!

There was a doctor in town who was very well known. His name was Li Shu-fan. It still is. He is in the States at this moment, but until July of 1943 he was in Hong Kong, managing cleverly to hang onto his hospital, one of the best in town, and getting by with the Japanese, perilously, but still getting by. People wondered at his immunity, because he had been an intimate friend, we all knew, of T. V. Soong. He was seen everywhere, arousing jealous criticism by his jaunty bearing and his good clothes. He went to the races, he ate, he played around exactly as if there had been no war. I was introduced to him by Mitzi, who had married her Swiss chef. I dined in his flat in the hospital, with the Gattis. I invited him to dinner at my house. Next thing I knew he had asked Maria and me to tea. We went down to the hospital at about four o'clock. It was a long way from town and we wanted to get back early.

I was surprised and vexed to see the other guests. Dr Li had said that he expected Nguchi—it was a farewell party for Nguchi—but he hadn't told me that all the Girls would be there, those fifth-columnist ladies who had been anathema to me since the beginning. There they all were, the darlings of the British cadets and the American bank boys, and now of the Japanese gendarmes—Agnes and Rosamunde and Margaret and the others, dressed up to the nines, chattering and giggling and whispering to each other. Maria and I sat a little apart from them, stiffly. The men were doctors, one Chai, a Formosan who had acted as liaison in the Medical Department since the war, and an old Chinese chap, Dr. Ma, familiar to all of us. We waited for the colonel and made polite talk. Nobody could have guessed, watching Li's smooth hospitality, that all his plans for escape were completed and polished and perfected. He got out two months later, but only he knew what was going to be.

All of a sudden, with a loud whoop and a hurrah, Colonel Nguchi arrived. He had two other officers with him and they were all noisy, but he was the noisiest. He was a short, stocky chap, he needed a shave, but his face was pleasant and he had a sense of humor. He started out, as Dr. Li introduced him around the circle, by kissing each of us, the men too. Chai, who had known him for months, objected strenuously. "He put his tongue in my *mouth!*" he protested. By that time Nguchi was over at the bar, pouring himself a whisky, and then he came back and insisted on pouring half of it into my brandy, mixing it up and taking back a half portion of the result, which he downed in a gulp. He must have been pretty drunk when he arrived.

A busy half hour followed. I had been talking against the difficulties of language with one of the officers, a Major Ota, when I happened to look around and saw that the Girls had all disappeared. Things had evidently got too rough for their liking, and they had given each other a high sign and slipped away. I had just time to realize this when Ota clapped me on the back, made an imperious beckoning signal, and said, "We go dinner. Come!"

Then suddenly, in spite of Li's fluttering protests, I was being herded into the elevator and carried away. Maria was left behind. I called out as I departed, "Don't worry, Doctor; I'll be all right," and I really thought I would, because Chai and Ma were still with us. Down on ground level, however, some of my confidence evaporated. There were two cars, a big Army model and a little chummy one. Nguchi now took charge of the party, and he put everybody else into the big Army limousine, then joined me in the back seat of the little car. We all started for town.

I had never before realized how very far town was from Li's hospital, or vice versa. Nguchi was feeling amorous, and though I think I could have managed him all right if we had been able to talk, we weren't able to talk. We just struggled. He was drunk and he must have thought

I was being coy. I said to myself, "Well, we've got to arrive sometime, and then I can explain to Ma and Chai, and Chai will talk him out of it."

But when we reached town I saw through the window that the car ahead of us slowed up, Ma and Chai stepped out and waved good-by, and our car, scarcely slackening speed, went on after the other one. That left me alone with three Japanese officers, all drunk, all strangers. I didn't feel confident at all any more. I went on mechanically shoving Nguchi's hands and feet away, thinking fast. Thought was no help.

When the cars did stop I recognized where we were. It was the Kam Loong Restaurant, that same Golden Dragon where Charles and "the office" had often played host. We got out and joined the other officers on the pavement. There followed a long argument between them. I gathered that Nguchi didn't want any dinner; he wanted to return to his hotel with me. The other officers, not having girl friends, did want their dinner, and they tried to prevail upon him to curb his impatience. Nguchi staggered up and down the pavement between them, talking, and I slipped into the restaurant.

The manager stood behind his little counter, Chinese fashion, and he looked a bit surprised when I rushed in. I was rather pulled about, and though I didn't realize it at the time, he was Ah King's brother and knew me well.

"Get me out of this!" I gasped.

I suppose the restaurant staff had had plenty of experience. They leaped to their posts like veterans. Before I had taken another breath I had been put into a pantry place, and when the officers came in looking for me the manager said, "Missy go upstairs." They resumed their wrangling, telling Nguchi to follow me to one of the private dining rooms, and while their backs were turned I was whooshed out the back door, into a ricksha and away, waved off grinningly by a couple of Chinese waiters. One of the men who helped me by acting as lookout was Nguchi's own chauffeur.

I didn't meet the colonel again before he left.

The gendarmes didn't wait a week after he had gone, before they swooped down and arrested Selwyn. It happened on a Sunday morning, so early that even Selwyn was not yet awake. He was given time to dress and to take some clothes with him, and then they took him away.

The job was done in really good style. They had planned it down to the smallest matter because, after all, they had been at it for a long time, for months and months. The entire hospital was closed off by police and soldiers. It happened that the former consul general, Reynaud, lay dying there, but his doctor was not permitted to go in and see him. The gendarmes meant to find out everything they could about that hotbed of espionage, and no sick people were going to interfere with their work. It is not true, as some hysterical patients averred, that the soldiers came whooping over the wall as if they were attacking a fortress, but their entry must have been sufficiently melodramatic to put the fear of God and the devil into the French sisters and the rest of the staff.

We first heard it from Hilda's cook, who brought a message from her that she would get in touch with me as soon as possible. They were all held prisoner: Hilda, Mary, Helen Ho, who had been working with them and looking after Mary (Helen was a sister of Kathleen and Yvonne), and a number of others. In the course of the day Constance Lam was brought in and set down there, and a few other people showed up, Chinese doctors suspected of working in the espionage game with Selwyn and the like.

The cook stayed outside the hospital and bought supplies for the household, and handed them in through the barred gate which was now kept locked. All over town, in the bankers' hotel as well as in my house, in a hundred hovels and tenement rooms, were people holding their breath, terrified for Selwyn's safety and for their own. The Ho girls wept and went about their work for the Japanese with sullen faces.

I was summoned to the Foreign Affairs office by Hattori, the successor to Oda.

Hattori had made a good impression on everyone by his politeness. It was a pleasant change for everyone, to find a man who didn't feel it necessary to remind us all the time that we were in a bad spot and that he was boss. Oda toward the end of his stay had even committed the unforgivable crime, in the eyes of the Ho girls, of losing his temper with Selwyn and shouting at him, and pounding the desk. Though the Ho girls loved Oda, that they could not forgive, and Yvonne that day sat at her typewriter and wept as she worked. She made excuses for him. He was unhappy about the way things were being run; he was overworked; he drank too much and his nerves were suffering. But he should not have been rude to Dr. Selwyn-Clarke, of all people. Yvonne would try to forgive and forget.

When I first met Hattori I too was charmed. He was so civilized, so smiling (and not in a Japanese way, either), so tall! He asked me to come and see him at home and to bring Carola, and I did so just about a week before Selwyn was arrested. He had provided himself with a toy for Carola, and we had drinks, and we had a talk.

"You have been left to me as a legacy, Mickey—I shall call you Mickey," he began. "Oda was worried about you and this is what has happened. I need not tell you how strenuous life is going to be in the near future. You people in town have seen enough to understand. The gendarmes are in an ugly mood. And Oda had you on his mind, because he is Boxer's old friend and he feels he has a duty to Boxer."

"Yes. He has been very kind indeed."

"Yes, this Hong Kong is not an easy job. That's why I held off so long, before I would consent to take it. That's why Oda had to wait for some months instead of going straight to Tokyo last year, as he wished. But I will tell you why I did come at last. I was in Australia for years, in the consular service. I was interned there after Pearl Harbor."

"Did they treat you well?"

"Oh yes. Diplomatic status, you know . . . though, strictly speaking, consuls are not diplomats. We have been treated well in England too, I know that. So I said to myself, 'Wouldn't it be better for those poor people in Stanley to have a man in charge who bears no animus? I know the British a little. Perhaps I can be of use.'"

I made expected and sincere compliments to his humanity. He liked them.

"And there is another thing," he said, pouring me a huge drink. "I have a sister-in-law in England. Her husband is British."

"Do you think she'll be all right?"

"I hope so." He drank off half his glass. His capacity, I observed, was even better than Oda's. We have underestimated the Japanese in many ways. "Now," he resumed, "as to you."

"Yes."

"Oda told me to watch the barometer. At the first sign of trouble from the gendarmes I am to intern you. Do you see? At least in Stanley you will be my prisoner and not theirs."

"I see. But that would be terrible, Mr. Hattori; I would never forgive myself. I kept my baby here in spite of everything, and now, if I shall have been responsible for putting her into Stanley after all——"

"The time has not come yet," he said soothingly. He stood up, walked to the window, and looked out at Bowen Road Hospital, just opposite us and a mile away. "You love Boxer?" he asked.

It wasn't a bit like the gendarmes: I said yes right away.

"So," said Hattori. "If you need anything you are to come and ask me immediately. You are my responsibility, my legacy."

I thanked him a lot more, and then I took Carola home. I was touched and grateful and reassured, but I was also sorry that I had to feel all those things. I do like to be boss.

Well, now he had sent for me. The time, I felt sure, had come. Carola and I were earmarked for Stanley.

"Well," said Mr. Hattori. His smile was as wide as ever, and I took heart. "There is a sad thing," he said, "about Selwyn-Clarke. But we cannot discuss that here. The little Ho girls are very much upset about their sister, and I have asked in certain places what can be done to hasten her release. . . . Now about you."

"Yes."

"We know," he said, "that you are very, very intimate with the Selwyn-Clarkes. You are under observation. Be careful. Do not correspond with Mrs. Selwyn-Clarke, do you understand?"

"Yes." I thought of the three letters she had already sent me through the cook, telling me to come down to the hospital at five o'clock so that we could call to each other through the iron gate.

"Do not go anywhere near that French Hospital," said Hattori, looking me in the eye.

"No."

"That is all. Don't forget what I told you. If you get into trouble over this I may not be able to keep you out of the gendarmerie. So far you are in the clear. Stay that way. You are my responsibility."

"Yes, Mr. Hattori."

When I got home I found four more notes from Hilda. She was not in her most coherent mood. She seemed to think that I could get Selwyn out of prison. She told me to see Hattori, to see Noma, to see the Governor, and to tell them to let Selwyn go. She also wanted me to cable Nguchi, now supposed to be in Mukden, though nobody knew for certain. And besides that, she wanted me to come straight down to the hospital and demand entrance.

Naturally I did none of these things. I stayed home. Down in the French Hospital, Constance and Hilda ranted and said that I was a false friend and a traitor. The notes kept pouring in. Maria went down to hospital as deputy for me, and there was a little communication between Hilda and her, but a soldier chased her off. After that, though, Hilda was not so sure I was a traitor.

I was sure I was not. I couldn't see Noma or the Governor, I couldn't do more than I was doing with Hattori, and I couldn't do anything at all about Hilda except for certain practical considerations which I did take care of. Helen Ho told me two weeks afterward, when she had been released and Hilda was in Stanley, that for the first few days Hilda was in a bad state, but that she was all right afterward. Fortunately the gendarmes never questioned her at all.

For that week, however, it was embarrassingly evident that the Hilda who was then uppermost in her character was determined to get me sent to Stanley too.

"Good morning," Mr. Hattori would say, having sent for me by note. "Is everything all right? You have not received any communications from Mrs. Selwyn-Clarke?"

"Oh, no indeed, Mr. Hattori, how could I?"

"That is true."

"Is there any news of the doctor?" I asked.

"No, nothing. I trust they're not mistreating him. I saw him only a few times, but he impressed me as being thoroughly *sincere*."

"Oh yes, Mr. Hattori, he's sincere."

I walked home slowly. It seemed to me that everyone I met looked stunned. No one dared stop to speak to me; no one dared stop to speak to anyone. There were no little groups at the street corners. There were only isolated figures, hurrying along.

Chapter 58

AH KING always insisted that Sophie Odell was responsible for making me ill, but I don't think that is the truth. Certainly Sophie had that strong desire you often find in warmhearted people for being the first to bring bad news. When she was in distress herself she couldn't wait to plunge other people into the same bath.

In our little army of parcel-carrying women there was a strong esprit de corps and an equally strong intelligence department. The Japanese officers would have been amazed—in the end, because of me, they were amazed—at the things we managed to find out about the prisoners. It was all done with mirrors, piecing together bits of news that leaked out I don't know how. Some of it was no doubt due to the fact that a lot of the Japs now had Hong Kong girls as mistresses. They had employed the same means themselves, before the war, to get information; yet they too fell into the oldest trap in the history of the world's battles. The commandant of camps, fat Colonel Tokunaga, may have been one of our sources of supply, because he was what the Cantonese call "wet salt," which means "oversexed." He ogled women. I never knew what ogling was until I saw the colonel. His whole fat face lit up when he saw a pretty piece, and he rolled his eyes with a simple, honest lubricity that would have been laughable if he hadn't been commandant of the camps where our men were held prisoner. He had installed himself in a good house near Argyle, with a Chinese woman we all knew as his housekeeper.

But the colonel was decidedly not the only one. I never knew where the news trickled out, or how; I just guessed. A lot of it was false but some of it sometimes was true, and what Sophie brought me that morning sounded genuine.

"The men are being taken away, Mickey, this morning. All of them. In Kowloon they're marching through the streets."

"From Argyle too?"

"From Argyle too." She was crying. "I suppose they'll take Bowen Road next, and my Harry has just started to walk with his crutch."

It was not only the prospect of losing Charles, what very small portion I still had of him, that agitated me so much. Once before a large shipment of prisoners had been sent off by ship, the *Lisbon Maru,* to Japan or Formosa. Wherever it was aiming for, it didn't get there; the *Lisbon Maru* was sunk, and a lot of our men were drowned. They must have been battened down in the hatches, from the percentage of losses; I haven't yet interviewed the few survivors who made their way to Chungking. Hong Kong when the news came to us was a pit of horrible misery, and the Japanese rubbed it in cruelly in the paper. The Americans had sunk their ship, had they? And drowned their own Allies, hadn't they? That would teach the Americans. That would teach the foolish women of Hong Kong, who were still hoping that the United Nations would win the war.

In time the Japanese must have been scolded so heartily from Geneva for breaking a few major international laws that they quieted down. They discovered that they should have announced it to the world whenever they moved prisoners by sea. They found out that they had made other mistakes. But this new development hit us too soon, while the tragedy was still poignant. All I could think was, "Charles's arm is paralyzed; he won't be able to swim."

Five minutes after Sophie left I was violently ill.

I should like to agree with Ah King in his attractive idea that I was merely suffering from a broken heart. It is a pretty notion and romantic. To the best of my scientific knowledge, however, broken hearts don't lead directly to high fever and severe cramps. Ah King spoke his mind to Sophie in an outburst which must have been refreshing to all concerned. *"Don't* tell the mistress these things. Wait. Wait until you're sure. Wait until you don't see the major at Argyle before you scare my mistress like that."

Then he hurried upstairs to soothe me. He had it on direct authoritative evidence, he said, that the major was not being moved. He, Ah King, *knew* that. Then he gave me the Chinese equivalent of a tisane and closed the door and left me to sleep.

And after all, he was right and Sophie was wrong. It had been a shipment of prisoners, but of enlisted men, mostly Canadians. Charles was still there. Nobody had left Argyle. Moreover, the Japanese behaved in a chastened manner this time and broadcast their intentions to the world through Geneva, and arranged for safe passage, and told us via the Red Cross the minute the men arrived safely.

It made me think, though. That week was the first and only time I ever missed a parcel day; I was laid up for six days. All the while I lay there I said to myself, "If he is sent away someday, then what have I done to Carola?"

Hattori had sent for me. "There is going to be another repatriation," he announced. "Two repatriations, one for British and one for Americans!"

"Oh, that's wonderful!"

He fiddled with his pencils. My reply had been a bit perfunctory, because I really didn't believe it. I had heard that story fifty times, usually from Hilda, who always believed it and was always painfully disappointed. Now, with Hilda in Stanley and Selwyn in the gendarmerie, I was free to be skeptical.

"It will really take place, though I don't know when," Hattori insisted. "I called you to ask you in which boat you prefer to go."

"Me?"

"Yes. This time," he said pleasantly, "you will not refuse, will you? As an American you can sail in the American ship, naturally, with your child. As a British child, your Carola can sail in the British ship and you would naturally accompany her as her mother; I think the British would accept you. I don't know the details yet; I don't know how many British civilians they are willing to take, but I think there would be more room, you would be more comfortable, on the American boat. What do you say?"

"But I am still not sure if I want to go at all."

Mr. Hattori drew a deep breath. "Do you think," he asked patiently, "that you should take on yourself the responsibility of——"

"Could you get in to see Charles?" I demanded suddenly.

"Perhaps. Yes, as a friend of the chief of staff I——"

"Would you? Then you could ask Charles himself what he wants. Last time it was all so sudden, and Oda was so busy, that I didn't think of it. But it is his affair too, isn't it?"

"Certainly," said Hattori in approval. "I shall try to do that. It will not be easy. This is purely a civilian affair; the military, unfortunately, never exchange prisoners, so there is no chance that your Charles will come home before the end."

"I know that. Thank you, Mr. Hattori, very much."

I put it out of my mind. The repatriation would never take place, I was sure, and if in the meantime it kept Hattori happy, thinking it would, who was I to argue?

Day-to-day life was incredibly monotonous. The only thing that was alive, growing and constructive, was Carola. She was, of course, the most precocious and brilliant child in the world, and both De Roux and Needa assured me of this whenever my own faith might have wavered. For regard, as De Roux would have said: on Christmas, when Carola was a year and three months old, I took her downtown to look at the feeble display in the shops, and she took a fancy to an enormous baby doll in Lane Crawford's, now called the Matsukaya. I ignored her pleading, because it cost eleven yen. Next day she and I set out on our usual gentle afternoon walk, down the bluff to Kennedy Road, around to another staircase leading up to MacDonnell Road past a sentry (but he liked Carola), and after we had bowed to him we usually made our way home. This afternoon, however, the baby balked as we reached the wide staircase that led down to town. She took my hand and urged me with her eyes to go along with her down the stairs instead of following Kennedy Road. I let her lead me—she was walking well by this time—to see how far she would go. Down and down went Carola to the tramway, past the Peak tram station, past the cathedral, through Battery Path and down to Queen's Road, definitely in the middle of town. Along Queen's Road she got lost and couldn't remember further. She stopped, looked at the bewildering crowd on foot and in ricksha, and began to cry uneasily. I carried her as far as the outside of Lane Crawford's, because I knew by then what it was, and she promptly led me inside and along the corridor to the toy department, back to the object of her desire, the baby doll.

So then, of course, I bought it, eleven yen or no eleven yen. Needa said I was quite right, and gave me the eleven yen back again as his Christmas present to Carola.

We had a regular beat of an afternoon, Ah Yuk and Carola and I. First we went to the French Bank and saw Uncle Paul, and Carola would demand in Chinese to see the lesson books, Paul's Mandarin primers with their highly colored pictures of babies and balls and slates and things. We had a glass of grenadine there. Then we traveled on to Needa's office, now humming with big business, and there Carola asked for candy and got sweet vitamin pills by the handful. Then we strolled through the streets, and then we made our way home, Ah Yuk and I taking turns carrying the baby when she was tired.

Even in the Foreign Affairs office she was spoiled. Hattori gave her all the pencils on his desk.

The chief of staff in town had been changed, and the new man was rumored to be a civilized sort, speaking good English. One evening Hattori took the Ho girls and me up to meet General Suginami. It was all very hush-hush. The Hos seemed to know him of old, but they had refrained from saying so. Suginami was a short, slight, tired man, and his English was so pure that it was Oxonian down to the slight lisp that used to be the fashion there. He told me immediately that he was an old friend of Charles, had known him in England, and had seen him in Argyle Camp.

"How does he look?" I demanded.

"As well as can be expected under those sad circumstances. They are good to him and will continue to be good to him. He gets treatment for the arm in our own hospital."

My visits to the general were limited to the occasions when Yvonne could be persuaded to spend a little time with him. The general was much more keen on those visits than was the lovely Yvonne, who, though she protested she liked him, was still somewhat shy and canny of so much grandeur. I am sure that he could have dispensed with my company too; he adored Yvonne's dramatic beauty, and no doubt he would have adored it more without my chaperonage. But Yvonne would not go to see him without her beloved Mickey, and there you were. He was always a gentleman, as the shopgirls say, just the same. He was most reassuring to us after the American 1943 air raids started, as they did that summer. We were up there to dinner the night before the first raid took place, and the general promised us on his word of honor that there would be no raids for a long time.

"Oh, I'm so glad," breathed Yvonne. "Thank you, General. I *do* get so frightened."

"You need not be, little girl," he said. "I have told them myself, 'Do not bomb Hong Kong, because Yvonne gets frightened.' Seriously, they haven't enough petrol as yet. The Americans have brought in many planes to Chungking; we know that. But they have not brought enough petrol."

Next day we had the first raid and it was a honey. Yvonne came up to see me that afternoon when the All Clear sounded, and her terror was pretty well under control, all things considered. The bombers had improved in their aim so much that you couldn't think of those first raids in the same class. This time they concentrated on the gendarmeries, and they knew exactly where to look and where to let go. They couldn't have done anything better calculated to cheer us up. Only in one place, at the Central Police Station, did they miss: that miss cost three hundred civilian Chinese lives. And later on, when they pounded the dockyards, they killed many of the workers, so that the government had to make a new law prohibiting their employees from quitting their jobs. Also they locked the coolies into the dockyards, so that the wretched people had no choice; they had to be bombed.

"There's no help for it," said Ah Yuk. "We must die by thousands, we *must*. China has too many people anyway."

I stared at her in appalled silence. The air raids had gone to her head; she jumped and clapped and laughed for joy at every alarm, not caring who may have been watching, and equally careless of the possible effect on herself.

"You mustn't cry when the planes come," I heard her telling Carola. "There is nothing now to cry about. They won't hurt *us*. Those are *our* planes."

"I saw Boxer," said Hattori, who had come to see me one evening.

"Oh, really? What did he say?"

Hattori stared at me, his lips compressed. He was laboring under strong emotion. He often was, so I didn't worry about it; he was what the British would call rather unstable emotionally. "He wants you to go, if there is a repatriation," he said.

I wasn't really surprised, but I said, "Oh, does he? Really?"

"Yes. At the moment the repatriation excitement has died down," Hattori admitted, "so I couldn't tell him just when it would take place. He was delighted, however, at the possibility, and I have come now to tell you that I must add your name to the list of possible repatriates immediately, in order to send it off to Tokyo. That is what I will do this evening."

"But I'm still not sure——"

"You said you would abide by Boxer's decision."

"So I did."

"He told me something else," said Hattori. "He told me that he intends to *marry* you."

Then he beamed. The secret was out. That was why he looked so excited and mysterious and moved. He was not prepared for my reaction; neither, I suppose, was I.

"Oh," I said, "does he indeed!"

A very peculiar half hour was the result of that exchange. I don't suppose Hattori and I could have reached any more of an understanding in ten times the period; certainly we were nowhere near an accord when he left my house and slammed my door.

It had been foolish of me, I told myself when I went to bed. I should not have forgotten I was talking to a Japanese, chief of the Foreign Affairs Department and a man of fixed ideas. Centuries of feminism stood between us, but I at least should have realized that and acted accordingly. And I should have realized too that Charles hadn't said it that way. He had said it at all only because he knew they would treat me with more care if they thought of me as his wife and not as a light of love.

Oh dear, I groaned in the weeks that followed, how right he was! He had been far too right. Hattori and I never saw each other nowadays without having a row.

"I have heard," he said icily, "that you were Out to Dinner last night?"

"Yes, I was. Needa gave a dinner party."

"Who is this Needa, anyway?"

I explained. I bore down heavily on the fact that Needa was in the good graces of the Army and the Navy. Also, I said sincerely, he was a good man, a very sweet man, generous and an old friend of mine. . . .

Hattori's face did not relax as I talked. He looked more and more like the dean of women at my old university. "Does Boxer know this man?" he demanded at last.

"Why—uh—no, as a matter of fact he doesn't. You see, Charles was never keen on racing. He just wouldn't go to races. And I met Needa years before I knew Charles, back in '35, in Shanghai——"

I could scarcely have done worse. The result was that Hattori immediately invited Needa to dinner so that he could have a look at him, on behalf of Boxer. So we had dinner, and even Hattori had to admit that there was nothing inimical to the welfare of Boxer's Family in that gentle soul.

"Nevertheless, I do not think you should be seen so often in public," he said grudgingly. "There will be criticism if the gendarmes see you around so much. In fact there *is* criticism. I am always being asked about you. It is dangerous."

"Honestly?" Frankly, I was skeptical. "Really, Mr. Hattori, do you think you ought to worry so much about your responsibility? Mr. Oda couldn't have meant that you should waste so much time on me. He didn't, you know; I scarcely ever saw him. And he trusted me, too, more than you do."

"It is my responsibility to Boxer that now motivates me," he said grimly. "Since I have seen him, and have seen what a fine man he is, and how upright and honorable——"

"Well"—I played my trump card—"*Charles* doesn't care if I go out. He never did. He encouraged me to have my own friends, Mr. Hattori. If that is what you are thinking of——"

"It is different now. He intends to marry you."

I went home cursing under my breath, in a tangle of exasperated gratitude, laughter, and desperation. I do like to be boss. Like Mélisande, I was not happy there.

Helen Ho after her release came to see me, as was natural, and when we had drunk tea together we both started for town. When we came out of my door a young man in a long white gown, who had been loitering up on MacDonnell Road, looking at a brook that ran down by the house, strolled after us. Helen turned white.

"Is he following us?" she demanded. "I saw him, I'm sure, on my way up. He is following me, Mickey."

"Oh, I don't think so."

But he was. Helen was arrested again that night and questioned for two more days before she was again released. It was the first time I felt directly responsible for that kind of thing.

"Oh, good Lord," I groaned, "actually, I wish there would be a repatriation. They're bound to take him away someday, now that the Americans are bombing us; they won't keep any prisoners here to escape back to the Allied lines." There, I had faced it at last. I ran down to the kitchen and talked it over with Ah King. Even Ah King thought that if by any chance a repatriation took place—well . . .

Upstairs I went again, to look at Carola in the nursery.

"You've had ice cream three times in your whole life," I said. "How would you like an ice-cream soda every day—twice a day? And enough eggs, and fresh milk? And a doctor when you're sick? And no bombs? And a grandmother?" Carola, who spoke no English, stared at me, and I chattered on. "Do you think there's still a New York, Carola, with drugstores? Do you think any of my family are still alive?"

"*Tang-kuo*," said Carola, which meant that she wanted a piece of candy.

Chapter 59

EXCEPT for the uncertainty that one would find anybody at all left in the camps, the parcel-bringing had become fairly routine. We brought fresh fruit when fresh fruit was allowed and we wailed when it wasn't, and carried our scorned offerings back home to eat there. We waited in tense hope when it was rumored that we could bring lard or margarine; for many anxious months nothing like that was permitted, as somebody smuggled radio parts into Stanley buried in lard, and the built-up radio was finally discovered, and twenty people were implicated and handed over to the gendarmes.

Any woman who really went in for parcel duty had her day's work cut out for her. Monday was Argyle, Tuesday was Stanley, Thursday was Bowen Road, and Saturday was Shamsuipo. Each parcel day meant that more than half the daylight hours were taken up with the mechanics of getting there and back. The other mornings and the afternoons were insufficient for the necessary marketing, preparing of the parcels, and finding the necessary sacks or boxes to send them in. Transportation grew less and less, we walked everywhere, and the distances in Kowloon are long.

Added to this was the anxious business of getting food into the gendarmerie for Selwyn. A dozen women were eager to help, though it was dangerous to show too much of an interest in the prisoner, and it was Constance who seized the coveted honor of carrying the food to the gendarmes' desk every week. We all took a hand in supplying the food, though we suspected he got very little of it. It was much easier to send things to Hilda and Mary. Hattori did all he could to alleviate Hilda's lot. Although he was strict about forbidding our communication, he did everything else that he could to help.

There were clashes, however, between Hattori and the civilian camp, and I was very much worried for a while. Although the Foreign Affairs chief had come to Hong Kong full of the milk of human kindness, he was in a King Cophetua mood rather than the humble state of mind that one has learned to associate with Christ's sort of charity. He expected the Stanley prisoners to fall on their knees to him in a passion of gratitude. Instead, in truly British fashion they took his favors with offhand thanks and went right on demanding more. They didn't think he was dispensing favors; they thought he was doing his duty, however belatedly, and they were willing to point out to him wherein he was still falling short. That didn't go down well at all with Mr. Hattori. Often he came to see me when he had dined next door at the super-geisha house, and he was usually a little drunk and very much wrought up over the latest "impertinent demand" from that troublesome community at Stanley.

"Letters, letters, letters! Letters every day, and in English! Do they think I have time, your precious Hilda and Lady Grayburn and that ex-Colonial Secretary, to read long English letters every day, and what is more, to answer them? I'll show them. I'll write a long letter in Japanese and send it out tomorrow. I'll quit this job. I'll hand them over to the gendarmes, and then see if they appreciate what I have been trying to do. . . . Those British, I'll——"

"Shhhhh," I said, anxiously fluttering around. "Now listen. *You* know what the British are like. *You* understand them; you're the only man in Japan who really understands the British."

"Yes, and that is why I made the sacrifice and took this dreadful job, but nobody appreciates me, nobody——"

"Shhhhh. Of course people appreciate you. But you know the British. It isn't arrogance, it's just their way. They lack imagination. They——"

"And what is more, they refuse to realize that there is a war, and that Hong Kong has been captured by the Japanese, and that they are no longer the government. Do you know what that ex-Colonial Secretary said today in his long letter? 'In my capacity as the highest official of the Colony,' he said. *His* capacity? They are impossible, those British."

After blowing off steam he usually felt better, and Stanley was safe again from the gendarmes until he got another batch of letters. We allowed the vexatious question of his duty to Boxer to slip into the background, where it remained for as long as I could keep it there. In the meantime I gave him another problem, which kept him busy and unhappy for quite a long time.

My little blackmailing friend Tse Liang had come onto the scene again. His name began cropping up every day. After the Grayburn case was closed and Sir Vandeleur was in prison, Tse was transferred to Kowloon duty with his patron gendarme, Nakajima.

Then Maria's Portuguese friends began talking about Tse a lot. He had begun arresting a few of their men, always backed up by Nakajima. In oriental or Chicago style the families of these men paid heavily and got their prisoners out again, but there were two exceptions, people that Tse had old scores against. They remained in jail, hidden away somewhere, and Tse rambled about their houses, tried to seduce their women, and extorted as much of their money as the traffic would bear.

It's a long story and I can't tell all the details, but I dug some of the business out, turned it over to Hattori, and on the grounds that Portuguese were the responsibility of the Foreign Affairs Department I bludgeoned the poor guy into doing something about it. He didn't like to. It meant stepping on the gendarme toes, and although he always insisted he wasn't afraid of the gendarmes, of course he was. Protesting to the last, and always telling me that he would drop it like a hot nail if my name ever came up, he went to bat for the Portuguese. There was a terrible stink. Everybody got into trouble—everybody, that is to say, but me. Hattori was stanch and courageous and he won his point at last. Tse ran away, Nakajima was demoted and sweated a bit (which is all the punishment you could expect for a gendarme), the chief of the Kowloon gendarmerie lost face, and Tse's little private extortion prison was found and turned out and cleaned up and closed. Hattori probably gained a couple of bitter enemies, but anyway, I can now report that one Japanese in Hong Kong really is capable of honest government. Afterward he said to me, "All right for this time, but never again. Never again, do you hear me? Why did you do it anyway? Why don't you mind your own business?"

"I really don't know," I said, honestly perplexed by my behavior. "I guess it must be the American reformer in me."

"I hope that repatriation steamer comes soon," he said. "British or American, whichever goes first, you are going to be on it."

Sophie came rushing and tumbling into the house with another rumor. It was not quite such a distressing one this time, but it was bad enough. The officers were going to be sent away. Anyway, a lot of them were going. She couldn't tell me how she knew, but she knew. No, it wasn't that she herself knew where the news came from; she didn't. But all the women in town were talking about it.

They were, too. So many of them were talking that I was convinced at last. I didn't get a fever this time, but I did run around like a decapitated chicken, and the final goal of my wanderings was the august house of the honorable chief of staff to the Governor of Hong Kong, the General Suginami. Yvonne, Carola, Ah Yuk, and I waited on him one afternoon on a special mission. The general was indulging in his favorite sport of archery, out on the lawn.

We stood there and watched him shooting bulls'-eyes, and after a while he rolled down his sleeves and took us in for coffee. It was all formal, as usual, and a little bit uncomfortable. He showed us his latest paintings and photographs and fans and things. Finally I came around to the reason for the visit.

"I've heard," I said, "that the British officers, prisoners of war, are being sent away. Naturally that makes me feel worried about Boxer. Is it true?"

I would never have come on such a crackbrained journey if Hattori hadn't encouraged it. Now I understood why; he had wanted the general to hear it for himself. The general, I must say, took it big. I had really startled the chief of staff, he almost dropped his coffee.

"What? Why—uh—no, Miss Hahn, no. You haven't heard it correctly. Officers above the rank of colonel, and including the rank of colonel, are going this time. Not Boxer."

"Oh, that's wonderful. Thank you so much, General."

We finished our coffee. I sent Carola home, now that the softening-up process was completed, and Yvonne and I stayed to dinner. We talked about the war.

"It will not be so long now," he avowed. "I used to think this war would take ten years, but now, what with the German collapse, it will be over quicker than we figured on. About two years, dear ladies, two years."

Neither of us was tactless enough to ask him in whose favor the war would end. Anyway, I knew already from Hattori what the big bugs were counting on: an arranged peace with America. America, the big, rich, lazy country, the nation that was dilettante in her wars because she could so well afford it, would yawn when Germany had been swallowed, would turn over in her hammock and look to the East and say, "What's that making a noise over there in the Pacific? Oh, Japan? Oh hell, let's stop this silly war. . . . Java? Hong Kong? Singapore? Oh, let 'em have it. Why argue?"

Next day I received the usual summons from Hattori. "We do not wish to frighten you," he began gently. "The general especially said that you are not to be frightened. But where on earth did you hear about the departure of those officers? Try to think. You see, Mickey . . ." He paused and cleared his throat apologetically. "That was supposed," he said, "to be a military secret."

"But honestly, Mr. Hattori, I couldn't tell you. We all know. Everybody in town knows. I couldn't possibly trace it. . . . Oh, I think maybe I could guess. It just *might* be Colonel Tokunaga. . . . But if I were you I wouldn't say that to the general."

"No," he agreed, "that wouldn't do. Suppose we simply forget it."

"You dined last night," said Hattori accusingly, "with officers. Army officers. I heard about it at the restaurant."

"Why, yes. It was a nice party." I was pleased about that party for a special reason. "It was Charles's own jailers," I said triumphantly. "The men who are stationed there at headquarters at Argyle Street. One of them has turned out to be a darling; of course he won't carry messages to Charles or anything like that, but he does like him a lot and he tells me Charles is awfully popular among the prisoners. And he's allowed word to go through to Charles, officially, that the divorce is going along smoothly. His friend the captain is nice too. They are both old friends of Needa."

Hattori had slowly turned to ice. "You are *not* to dine with Army men," he said. "Can't you see for yourself what an impression that makes? People will talk. The gendarmes will grow suspicious. I will be questioned. I—how can you be so reckless?"

"But it was all right, I tell you. It was a polite party. I admit I drank too much, but that was only because I used beer for a chaser."

"Do not do this ever again," said Hattori.

I went home feeling less pleased with myself than usual. I had a headache anyway. That evening, strolling down the hill, I met Yvonne on her way up.

"I just missed the last bus," she said, "but I have a message for Mr. Hattori and so I'm walking up with it. Where are you going so late?"

"To dinner in town," I said. "Come along?"

"No, thanks; the family's waiting at home for me."

I went on down the hill, amiably humming. We had dinner in Paul's flat on top of the bank, with his friend Wong who lived with him, and then I went home in the luxury of a sedan chair. Walking through the streets after dark was still asking for trouble.

Next morning Helen Ho came in early to see me. "I have a message," she said, "from Mr. Hattori, through Yvonne. Yvonne is terribly upset. It seems Mr. Hattori is angry with you. He says you are to stop going out at all. You must stay at home. You can only go shopping to buy things for Charles, and over to Argyle to hand your parcels in, and for the rest of the time you must stay home, or he can't be responsible for the consequences. He says if you disobey he will have no alternative but to intern you. Oh, Mickey, please be careful. I couldn't bear it if——"

I fumed and stewed all day. The minute Yvonne came in that evening I seized on her. "Don't say anything," I said. "Is Hattori at home?"

"Yes, I think he is. I——"

"You come with me," I said. "I want to see him."

I ran most of the way, Yvonne at my side talking in disjointed sentences. She hadn't meant any harm. She had naturally mentioned to Hattori that she had met me, and he had said, "Where was Mickey going?"

and she told him, not thinking it would make any trouble. After all, Paul was a neutral, and . . .

I burst into Hattori's living room. He was sitting there peacefully with a large glass of whisky and soda in his hand. He was politely surprised to see us and expressed his pleasure formally at the unexpected visit.

"Yvonne," I said, "would you mind going into the bathroom for a minute?"

She scuttled out. "And just why are you giving orders to my secretary?" asked Hattori.

"Just why did you send me those orders by your secretary?" I retorted.

"I was questioned today," said Hattori, "by the gendarmes. About you. You have disobeyed me; you have gone out again to dinner. You were seen in a public restaurant with this Frenchman. This has gone too far. You would not believe me——"

"I dined," I said, "in the Frenchman's own flat. I was not seen in a public restaurant because I wasn't in a public restaurant. Somebody is lying. It is probably the gendarme, but it could also be you. Well now, listen. I agree that this has gone far enough. I thank you for all your extraordinarily kind protection. I can't accept it any longer; it puts you in too much danger. There are limits to your duty to Boxer. I insist that you intern me, right now."

Mr. Hattori waited a minute. Then he said, "You are very noble."

"I owe you too much," I said firmly.

He waited another minute. Then he stood up and walked around. His face was red and emotional. "No," he said dramatically. "No. I cannot do that to Boxer. I cannot put you into Stanley, for your own sake and his. I would be failing in my duty. I refuse to intern you," said Mr. Hattori. "And since you seem to be so upset about my latest order, I rescind it. You need not stay at home. . . . Would you mind calling my secretary back now?"

The repatriation steamer became an actual, concrete thing. It was coming; it would be leaving Japan on the first of September. This was to be the American boat; an English one would follow, with Hilda and perhaps even Selwyn. (It never did.)

"So you will be leaving us," said Mr. Hattori.

"It really begins to look like it, Mr. Hattori."

"Are you sorry?" he asked.

"No. Charles will go away soon anyway. For the first time in her life I can look Carola in the face. It will be a great relief."

"You're telling me," said Hattori.

Chapter 60

THERE were lots of things to be seen to. I must sell everything and get money to give away, to Ah King and Ah Yuk, and above all to the women who had promised to go on supplying Charles with food. I must persuade the Army to allow Charles to give me documents for Carola, about her legal status. I must argue with the people who didn't think I should go away.

"Craziest thing I ever heard," said Needa bitterly. "Don't you know that America is near collapse? They haven't had any coal in New York for two years, and they're far worse off for food in the States than we are. It's criminal, taking that kid back to a broken-down country like America. Hong Kong is the best place to be; stay in Hong Kong."

"Now I wonder," I said, "how much you really believe of all that?"

"Anyway, it's the best place for you," he insisted. "Why, those Yanks will put you in jail for fraternizing with the enemy. They'll raise hell because you wouldn't come home in the first boat."

"But Charles is being sent away soon, I'm sure. Twenty officers went away this last week. What would I do with myself here?"

"Oh, Charles." Needa had forgotten Charles. "But he hasn't any claim on you, Mickey, not a real claim. You're an Asiatic at heart. Let me be responsible for the kid. She's such a swell kid. I promise that kid won't want for anything. As for the war, it'll be a compromise peace. America's worn out; she won't carry on. We'll be all right; you'll see. These air raids are her dying gasp."

"Needa, you don't really hate America, you know."

"No," he admitted, "I don't. I wish this would all clear itself up."

The general asked me to a farewell dinner with Yvonne. "Tell America," he said, "that there's no reason we should fight. No reason at all."

"Two years more, did you say, General?"

"Perhaps not quite two years," he said.

There were so many things to do that we were glad when the inevitable postponement came along. For one thing, I had not yet persuaded the Japanese to let me say good-by to Charles. It was strictly forbidden, as Hattori explained, and all other women had been turned down when they made similar requests.

"Not always," I insisted. "There were some Russians, going to Shanghai, and they cried on the colonel, and he let them."

"Well," said Hattori, "you can try that. Cry on the colonel and see."

"Thanks, I will."

"Do you know," said Hattori, "that I just turned down a job for you?"

"No, really?"

"Really," he said. "You have been sent for, from Tokyo. It was thought that you could help us a lot in our propaganda work."

"Your propaganda is lousy."

"I know it. That's why somebody thought you could help."

"But I couldn't go to Tokyo! You mean, with Carola and all?"

"Certainly; we wouldn't separate you from your baby. You would have been very happy in Tokyo. But I thought you had better go back to the States."

"Why, Mr. Hattori, I couldn't go to Tokyo. They must have overlooked something. You know perfectly well—I mean, it isn't a thing we could talk about politely very well, but of course I want *us* to win the war. America."

"Oh yes," he said, "I know."

"And there's something else. I don't want to be indelicate, but Tokyo's going to be bombed to hell pretty soon."

"Oh yes. I know. But you can tell Roosevelt," he said, getting rather excited, "that he will have to kill at least half of all the Japanese in the world before we will be beaten. I think he would like that. I think Roosevelt wants to kill every Japanese in the world. Well, anyway, you will be better off with your mother."

"Thank you, Mr. Hattori."

As it turned out, I didn't cry on the colonel. The colonel cried on me.

I took counsel with the officer who had caused my trouble with Hattori, the man who lived at Argyle, and he said the thing to do was to write a letter to Tokunaga, stating my case. I did this. I wish I had a copy of it now. It was dignified but flowery, and very unmilitary. It was also sincere. I said that the circumstances were rather special, that Charles and I might very easily be separated forever, and that he might never see his only child again. I presented the letter in person, and the officer interpreted.

The colonel cried, and then he told me to go and wait in his anteroom while he thought it over. For twenty minutes he wrestled with his conscience, and then he called me back and said that he would break the law (if I was quite sure the chief of staff wouldn't make trouble) a day or two before the boat sailed. I was to tell nobody, *nobody,* except the chief of staff. I didn't. I didn't even tell the chief of staff, but he knew. The only person concerned in the matter who didn't know was Charles.

That morning I dressed Carola in a blue organdy dress and hat that Paul had paid too much for, and with the amah, Boxer's Family turned up at the prison gates at ten o'clock. Charles was having his arm massaged, and they didn't tell him I was waiting, so we bit our fingernails for an hour and a half, and Carola's dress was all crumpled and I was very much upset.

For a year and eight months we hadn't talked to each other nor seen each other up close. I knew he would be changed. I supposed I was changed too. I was prepared for anything but the truth, which was that he hadn't changed at all. He came in at last, standing at attention behind the officer, and when he saw me he grinned and made a face, and everything was all right.

I don't remember what we talked about. It didn't matter, because we couldn't really talk. The officer sat there listening, and though it went on for half an hour we didn't say anything I remember. It wasn't what I had expected; I had thought I would feel frantic, and that I would be sorry afterward for all the things I hadn't said, but it wasn't like that. It was all right. What can you say, anyway, under those circumstances? For half an hour I wasn't boss, but I liked it.

The officer turned his back a minute and we kissed each other briefly, and then it was time for Charles to go. As they walked away I heard the officer say:

"You're allowed to kiss her good-by."

"But I did already," said Charles.

"Did you? I didn't see you."

"Well, I did, I tell you."

They went out through the door arguing about it. Carola, who had been shy of Charles, now looked disconcerted. "Uncle's gone," she said.

"Uncle? That wasn't Uncle, you silly baby," said Ah Yuk. "That was your daddy."

"Oh?" She accepted the correction without argument. "Daddy's gone," she said. She began to whimper.

"Daddy's gone," I said. "So now, Carola, we go to America."

Index